A Dictionary of

Derivatives and Financial Engineering

10,000 + Terms Currently Used in the USA, UK, Canada and Australia

Guy Lynn, PhD, CPA

A Dictionary of Derivatives and Financial Engineering

-- 10,000 + Terms Currently Used in the USA, UK, Canada and Australia

Library of Congress Cataloging-in-Publication Data:

Lynn, Guy 1963 –

A Dictionary of Derivatives and Financial Engineering ----- 10,000 + Terms Currently Used in the USA, UK, Canada & Australia

LCCN: 2004104707

ISBN-13: 978-0-9744-1843-8

ISBN10: 0-9744-1843-9

Printed in the United States of America.

September 2007

Contents

Preface

Financial derivatives have become a much-discussed topic in the investment community. Investors are curious to learn more about them. The language of derivatives has been expanding.

More and more new words are created every day. Do you know the meaning of any of these words: alpha-quantile option, barstrier, boil spread; bondor; bookbuld, cartwheel, delta, gamma, G-hedge, haircut, rho, swaption, theta, vanna, vega, wrangle ...? Each term has its unique meaning. You may not be able to find its definition in an ordinary dictionary.

New meanings are added to the old words. Asprin means Australia stock price riskless index note. Tiger means Treasury investment growth receipts. Spider means Standard & Poor's Depositary Receipt. Cats means certificate of accrual on Treasury securities. Lion means Lehman Investment Opportunity Note.

Financial engineering is a dynamic area with a vocabulary that is constantly changing. It is this dictionary's purpose to present an up-to-date vocabulary. More than 10,000 entries have been drawn from all areas including futures, options, risk management and derivatives. Definitions are precise and right to the point.

This dictionary has a brand new design, and is very easy to use. Almost all terms are defined in one clear and simple sentence right to the point.

The author sincerely hopes that this dictionary will be a handy accessible guide to everyone from the layman to the expert.

Whether you are a student, an investor, a professional trader, a broker or an amateur trying to make your savings grow, you will find this dictionary of immeasurable help.

To this end, this dictionary features:

Inclusive: About 10,000 words and phrases are included. Acronyms are also included.

International: The dictionary covers terms used world-wide, especially in the United States, Canada, Australia and the United Kingdom.

Up-to-date: This dictionary covers all new words such as arrears swap, Asian tail, ask IV, path-dependent option, yield swap, etc.

Strategies: This dictionary contains many money-making strategies (e.g. dividend stripping), risk-managing strategies (e.g. dividend swap), and a complete list of hedging strategies (see Index of Hedging Strategies on page viii).

Full Cross Reference: All related terms are cross referenced by three signals as "***Also***", "***See***" and "***Opp***" in bold and italic type.

How to Use the Dictionary

Abbreviations: Abbreviation of an entry is placed inside a parenthesis "( )". Abbreviation is also treated as a main entry, followed by the words and phrases it represents.

Alphabetization: All entries are alphabetized by letter rather than by word. For example, **account period** follows **accounting statement**, and **for short account** follows **formula method**.

Antonym: Antonymous words are introduced by "***Opp***:".

Bold type: Bold type is used to highlight main entries.

Cross references: Related entries are crossed referenced by "***See***:".

Definitions: Definitions follow the entries. If an entry has more than one definition, each definition will be marked and separated by <1>, <2>, <3> ... .

Foreign words: Foreign words will be marked by "<UK>", "<Canada>", "<Australia>", "<French>", etc. For example:

split spread <UK> a spread over LIBOR that has different figures in different periods of the credit.

Italics: Italic type is used to indicate that italicized words and phrases will have a definition under that entry.

Old terms: Old terms and old names are introduced by "***Formerly called***:".

Parts of speech: All entries without special indications are nouns. All verbs are indicated by "<verb>".

Synonym: Definition of synonymous entries will be placed on the most frequently used entry. All other synonymous entries will be introduced by "***Also***:". No definition will be given under the synonymous entry, but linked to the italicized entry with definition by the mark "=".

Word order: Symbols, such as $, % are listed before numbers, and numbers are listed before alphabets.

Index of Hedging Strategies

% $

% double = *percent-to-double.*

% O/U percent over/undervalued

2-against-1 ratio writing = *half-hedge option.*

2-against-1 writing = *half-hedge option.*

2-factor option pricing model the new option pricing model which uses only two variables: volatility and interest rate.

2-point arbitrage = *arbitrage in space.*

2-sided market <1> = *2-way market.* <2> = *double auction market.*

2-tier bid = *2-tier offer.*

2-tier offer the tender offer under which stockholders who respond quickly can get a better deal. ***Also***: 2-tier bid. ***See***: *any-or-all bid.*

2-way market *Nasdaq* rule that *market makers* must quote both a bid and an asked price in every listed security. ***Also***: 2-sided market.

3-cent de minimis exemption an SEC rule under which market participants can trade through three cents or less without having to follow the *trade-through rule.* ***Also***: de minimis exemption.

3-day fund = *clearing house fund.*

3-Ds = *virtual currency option.*

3-handed deal municipals underwriting where the issue has 3-term maturities.

3-phase DDM a form of *dividend discount model* that applies different expected dividend rate depending on three life-cycle phases: growth, transition or maturity.

3-point arbitrage an arbitrage done in three currencies. ***Also***: triangular arbitrage; trilateral arbitrage. ***See***: *compound arbitrage.*

4-point arbitrage the arbitrage between 4 markets in which there are 2 or more differences in exchange rates.

5B bond = *crossover bond.*

7-day put bond a bond redeemable 7 days after a written notice from its holder.

11 bond index an index that is based on the average yield of 11 municipal bonds that mature in 20 years with AA rating. ***Also***: eleven bond index.

11th District Cost of Funds Index (COFI) an ARM index published by the Federal Home Loan Bank of San Francisco. ***Also***: Cost of Funds Index.

12b-1 fund a mutual fund which takes out up to 1.25% of average daily fund assets each year to cover the marketing costs.

20% margin = *cushion.*

20-bond index an indicator of the level of municipal bond yields, which consists of the yields on 20 US general obligation municipal bonds with 20-year maturities with an average rating of A1.

20-day ATM IV an estimate of the front month at-the-money implied volatility.

20-day period = *cooling period.*

30-day visible supply = *pipeline.*

30-day wash rule = *wash sale rule.*

30-day wash sale = *wash sale.*

30-year Treasury a Treasury debt that has a maturity of 30 years.

60/40 contract = *Section 1256 contract.*

65 Stock Average = *Dow Jones Composite.*

80/20 rule the rule that claims that 80% of the Treasury bills will be bought by 20% of the buyers. ***Also***: Pareto's law.

90-10 strategy a strategy which commits 10% of portfolio assets to the purchase of options and investing the balance of the portfolio in bonds.

144 stock = *restricted stock.*

1244 stock = *Section 1244 stock.*

A a

A <1> a bond rating of the third highest credit. <2> in puts, January. <3> a Nasdaq descriptor meaning class A shares. <4> option strike price for 5.

AA <1> against actuals. <2> = *double A.*

AAA = *triple A.*

AAPP average all pig price

AAU agreement among underwriters

abandoned option an option that was not exercised because the price of the underlying was against the buyer. ***Also***: lapsed option.

abandonment an option holder's choice not to exercise his or her right to buy or sell the underlying. ***Also***: release.

abandonment option an option to close out a position prior to the fulfillment of the original conditions.

abandonment value asset value that can be realized by selling the asset now. ***Also***: liquidation value.

ABC agency backed compounder.

ability to perform financial capacity of a person or organization to perform a contractual obligation.

able buyer a buyer with legal capacity and financial ability. ***Also***: ready, willing and able buyer.

abnormal yield curve = *inverted yield curve.*

above par the issuing price of a security is higher than its face value or stated value. ***Also***: at a premium.

above water current value of an asset is above its book value. **See**: *below water.*

ABS agreement an agreement between the Trans Canada Options, Inc. and a US *broker-dealer* who has a membership in the Options Clearing Corporation, which provides for daily reports by TCO to the broker/dealer.

absolute call privilege the right of an issuer to redeem a bond at any time.

absolute market risk = *market risk.*

absolute par of exchange = *fixed par of exchange.*

absolute priority a rule that senior debts will be satisfied before other classes.

absolute quotation a quotation of explicit interest rate on a swap.

absolute rate the fixed portion of the *interest-rate swap,* usually expressed as a percentage rather than as a premium or a discount to a reference rate. ***Also***: absolute swap yield.

absolute return = *total return.*

absolute return fund the mutual fund that seeks to maximize the *total return* instead of matching the benchmark.

absolute return strategy a strategy that seeks to provide a consistent return rather than fluctuating returns.

absolute risk = *total risk.*

absolute swap yield = *absolute rate.*

absolute value = *intrinsic value.*

absolute volatility <1> = *total volatility.* <2> = *volatility.*

absorbed securities the securities sold to the public, not being held by underwriter. **See:** *fully distributed issue.*

absorption <1> the complete purchase of an issue by the general public. ***Also***: assimilation; pot is clean; sellout. <2> = *merger.*

absorption point the price level at which the market no longer can accept more new securities offering without reducing price.

A/B structure a two-tranche structure consisting of senior and subordinated securitized loans.

academic arbitrage an arbitrage done without risk management. ***Also***: pure arbitrage.

ACARS American corporate accrual receipts

acceptance ratio the rate of bonds sold expressed as a percentage to the bonds being offered.

accordion swap = *rollercoaster swap.*

account = *account period.*

account day the 5th day after the close of *account period* when amounts due are settled, or carried forward, and deliveries are made. ***Also***: day of reckoning; delivery day; pay day; prompt day; settlement day; settling day.

account dealing settling to be made in the next *account period.* ***Also***: dealing for the new time; time bargain. **See**: *dealing within the account*; *for the account.*

account equity = *equity.*

accounting analytic the method for credit quality valuation by using the accounting ratios.

accounting exposure = *translation exposure.*

accounting for derivatives accounting methods and procedures for recording and reporting of derivative transactions and hedging activities. ***Also***: derivatives accounting.

Accounting for Derivative Instruments and Hedging Activities = *FAS 133.*

accounting risk the risk of loss due to an inappropriate indication of accounting.

accounting statement = *financial statement.*

account period a period of 14 days in which the settlement of transactions between the members of an exchange is deferred. ***Also***: account; stock exchange account. **See**: *settlement.*

accredited investor one having a net worth of $1 million or an annual income of $200,000 or putting at least $150,000 into the deal, and the total investment is less than 20% of his net worth. ***Also***: qualified investor. **See**: *nonaccredited investor*; *swap participant.*

accreted value <1> theoretical price a bond would sell at if the market interest rates were to remain unchanged. <2> the current value of a *zero-coupon bond,* including interest that has been accumulated and reinvested. ***Also***: compound accreted value.

accreting notional swap = *accreting swap.*

accreting principal bond (APB) = *accretion-directed bond.*

accreting principal swap (APS) = *accreting swap.*

accreting swap a *swap* the principal of which increases by a fixed amount each period. ***Also***: accreting notional swap; accreting principal swap; accrual swap; accumulation swap; appreciating swap; drawdown swap; escalating swap; staged drawdown swap; step-up swap. **See**: *amortizing swap*; *reverse index principal swap; traditional swap.*

accretion bond = *accretion-directed bond.*

accretion bond index range note = *accrual note.*

accretion-directed bond (AD bond) the *collateralized mortgage obligation* that pays principal and interest from the accretions of *zero-coupon* *bonds*. ***Also***: accreting principal bond; accretion bond.

accretive increasing in the earnings per share of a company by acquisition of a company with higher EPS.

accrual basis the length in years of each payment period in a derivative instrument.

accrual bond = *zero-coupon bond.*

accrual lock-in a credit derivative feature which allows investor to receive the interest accrued if a credit event occurs.

accrual note a *fixed income note* that pays a coupon depending on the number of times a floating rate stays in a range in a period. ***Also***: accretion bond index range note; accrual range floating rate note; boost; boosted coupon note; day count note; enhanced coupon; fairway bond; fairway note; index floater; index range note; LIBOR range note; range accrual note; range accumulation note; range floater; range floater note; range note. **See**: *corridor note.*

accrual option an option that gives the holder the right to receive daily interest when the underlying stock trades within a given range. ***Also***: banking on overall stability; corridor option; EARN option; expected to accrue return on nominal warrant; fairway option; hamster option; hope for a market stabilization in a given range; index range option; range accrual option; range accumulation option.

accrual period the period during which the underlying asset price is monitored to determine the payout of an *accrual option.*

accrual range floating rate note = *accrual note.*

accrual swap <1> the swap in which interest is earned and paid on one side under the circumstances determined by the range of certain index rate. ***Also***: range accrual swap. <2> = *accreting swap.* <3> = *zero-coupon swap.*

accrual tranche = *zero-coupon bond.*

accrued dividend the dividend accrued on preferred stock at a particular time.

accrued interest interest accumulated between the most recent payment and the sale of a bond or other fixed income security. ***Also***: built-up interest; interest accrued.

accrued market discount an increase in the market price of a discounted bond resulting from an approaching maturity.

accumulated amount total of the principal and interest in a given period. ***Also***: amount; both principal and interest; capital and interest; future amount; maturity value; principal and interest; terminal value; termination amount.

accumulated dividend the dividend not paid when due. ***Also***: unpaid dividend. **See**: *dividend in arrears.*

accumulated interest the interest on bonds due or overdue but not yet paid.

accumulation <1> adding income from interest or dividends to the principal. <2> the deliberate assembling of block of stock without necessarily bidding up prices.

accumulation price = *step-up price.*

accumulation swap = *accreting swap.*

AC/DC option = *as-you-like option.*

ACES <1> automatic convertible enhanced security. <3> automatically convertible enhanced security.

acid-test ratio current assets / current liabilities. ***Also***: current assets ratio.

acquired company a company the controlling interest of which has been held by the acquiring company. ***Also***: victim company. **See**: *target company.*

acquiring company a company set up to acquire a *target company*. ***Also***: offeror; predator company; raider; raider company; successor company.

acquisition discount the amount by which the price of a government security is below its redemption value. ***See***: *market discount*; *original issue discount.*

acquisition of assets the acquisition of the assets of a *target company* in order to take over it. ***Also***: exchange of assets.

acquisition of shares acquisition of the shares of another company in order to take over it. ***Also***: stock acquisition.

acquisition target = *target company.*

acquisitive D reorganization company A's transfer of its assets to B, followed by A's distribution to its shareholders what it received from B, then A winds up. ***See***: *divisive D reorganization.*

across the board the price movement which affects almost all stocks.

active arbitrage a foreign exchange arbitrage made by the bank. ***Opp***: *passive arbitrage.*

active bond crowd the NYSE members who are responsible for the heaviest volume of bond . ***Opp***: *cabinet crowd.*

actively managed fund = *managed fund.*

active market <1> a market for popular stocks frequently changing hands. ***Also***: free market. ***See***: *inactive market.* <2> the market in a state of activity with much business being done. ***Also***: broad market. ***See***: *ready market.*

active portfolio strategy a strategy that uses forecasting and other techniques to seek better performance of a portfolio.

active premium the return of a portfolio less the return of a chosen index or benchmark.

active return the return that is relative to a benchmark return, e. g. if a portfolio's return is 7%, and the benchmark's return is 5%, then the active return is 2%. ***See***: *exceptional return.*

active risk the risk accepted by an investment manager when he tries to add value to a portfolio relative to the benchmark. ***Also***: tracking error.

active stock a stock frequently traded in a stock exchange. ***Also***: piece of action; TV stock.

active trading month the month during which trading in a given commodity is initiated, e. g. wheat in March and May.

Act-of-Devil bond = *catastrophe bond.*

Act-of-God bond = *catastrophe bond.*

actual/actual the day count convention that counts the actual number of days.

actual exchange rate = *effective exchange rate.*

actual exposure the credit exposure inherent in a derivative. ***Also***: actual market risk; mark-to-market exposure; mark-to-market value; replacement cost; swap replacement cost.

actual interest rate = *effective interest rate.*

actual market = *cash market.*

actual market risk = *actual exposure.*

actual price (AP) the price at which a stock jobber bought or sold a stock. ***Also***: adequate consideration.

actual rate swap = *zero basis risk swap.*

actuals = *cash commodity.*

actual stock = *underlying stock.*

actual volatility <1> volatility measured from a set period of time to maturity. ***See***: *forecast volatility; historical volatility; implied volatility; relative volatility.* <2> = *historical volatility.*

actual yield = *current yield.*

actuarial rate = *internal rate of return.*

adaptive mesh model a numerical process for valuing derivatives in which the regions of high resolution are embedded in critical regions of a lower resolution.

adding to a position buying when a favorable position has been created.

additional bonds test a test to ensure that bond issuers meet the requirements of debt service.

additional collateral additional asset pledged as collateral for a loan or a debt obligation.

add-on a percentage of the estimated value of a derivative to a firm's capital.

add-on yield (AOY) annualized interest divided by original principal.

add shares to buy more shares.

adequate consideration = *actual price.*

adjustable rate = *floating rate.*

adjustable rate convertible note (ARCN) a note that is issued at a large premium, and is convertible into a fixed number of shares of the issuing company.

adjustable-rate debt = *floating-rate debt.*

adjustable rate instrument = *adjustable rate note.*

adjustable rate mortgage securities (ARMS) the securities representing a proportionate ownership in a package of adjustable rate home mortgages.

adjustable rate note a fixed principal note with a long-term and floating rate interim interest. ***Also***: adjustable rate instrument; floating rate note.

adjustable rate perpetual preferred stock (ARPPS) = *adjustable rate preferred stock.*

adjustable rate preferred stock (ARP) (ARPS) <1> a floating rate preferred stock with a dividend rate that changes with the Treasury rate. ***Also***: adjustable rate perpetual preferred stock; controlled adjustable rate preferred stock; <2> = *auction rate preferred stock.*

adjustable tender security (ATS) an adjustable rate bond with an option to redeem it at par. ***Also***: bond interest term security; tender option put security.

adjusted bond = *income bond.*

adjusted duration = *modified duration.*

adjusted exercise price the strike price adjusted taking into account the bond coupon rates of GNMA mortgages.

adjusted futures price the equivalent of the underlying cash market price that is reflected in the current futures price.

adjusted issue price the issue price of discount bonds plus the daily interest additions of *original issue discount.*

adjusted rate of return = *internal rate of return.*

adjusted strike price the strike price of an option adjusted after a significant change in the stock, e. g. *stock split.*

adjustment the correction of price.

adjustment bond <1> new bond issued in exchange for an outstanding bond after authorization from current holders of a corporation which is facing bankruptcy. ***See***: *reorganization bond.* <2> = *income bond.*

adjustments new price range of stocks and options on *ex dividend date* due to a *stock split* or dividend.

adjustment swap <1> = *coupon swap*; <2> = *off-market coupon swap.*

admitted to dealings = *listed security.*

ADP alternative delivery procedure

ADR <1> American depository receipt. <2> automatic dividend reinvestment.

ADS American depository share

advance commitment a promise to sell a security or derivative in the future at the price set today.

advance contract = *forward contract.*

advanced methodology credit capital allocation methods used by banks to determine credit losses.

advanced swap a swap with complicated term and structure . ***Also***: complex swap.

advance rate the prevailing interest rate for the advance fund.

advance refunding <1> the exchange of maturing government securities prior to their due date for issues with a later maturity date. <2> the sale of new bonds in advance of the first call date of the old bonds. ***Also***: pre-refunding.

advance refunding bond the bond issued to refund an outstanding bond.

adventure syndicate security undertaking.

advisory fund = *discretionary fund.*

AEP aggregate exercise price

aerospace and defense stock a stock issued by companies engaged in the development and manufacturing of equipment for space and military.

α **factor** = *alpha factor.*

affected party one party to a swap that experienced a termination event.

affiliated company <1> the company some or all of the shares of which are controlled by another company. ***Also***: associated company; related company. <2> = *subsidiary.*

affiliated person = *control person.*

affiliated purchaser a separate entity with no officers in common with the *distribution participant*, who bought securities being offered in the ordinary course of business.

affiliated transaction the trade between a firm and a mutual fund that it owns.

affiliate of the issuer one who controls or is controlled by or is under common control with the issuing company.

affinity fraud = *affinity investment scheme.*

affinity investment scheme an illegal operation in which investors with common interest or heritages are the target. ***Also***: affinity fraud.

affirmative covenant = *positive covenant.*

AFOF authorized futures and options fund

after market = *secondary market.*

against actuals (AA) = *exchange of spot.*

against the box a person actually owns the security sold short prefers not to or can not deliver. ***Also***: sale against the box; selling against the box; selling short against the box; short against the box; shorting against the box.

agency-backed compounder (ABC) the trade mark of Kidder Peabody & Co. for its *zero-coupon bond* on Ginnie Mae and Fannie Mae securities sold at deep discount without current interest.

agency incentive arrangement using the index prices in calculating commission of a broker in a program trade.

agency note one or 2-year note offered at a discount by the US government.

agency pass-through the pass-through security the payments of principal and /or interest of which are guaranteed by government agency.

agency security = *government security.*

agency trade a trade done between two broker-dealers.

aggregate exercise price (AEP) the number of shares in an option multiplied by the strike price. ***Also***: aggregate option exercise price.

aggregate market price the sum of the weighted average trading price of a new issue multiplied by the total number of shares issued.

aggregate option exercise price = *aggregate exercise price.*

aggregation <1> a rule under which all positions in the derivatives owned by a trader are combined to determine the reporting status and limit compliance. <2> = *netting.*

aggressive growth fund a mutual fund which seeks maximum growth rather than income by investing in small companies with higher growth potential. ***Also***: capital appreciation fund.

aging comparing the number of days that an outstanding margin call moves from receivable to a liability status.

agio <1> = *agiotage.* <2> = *premium.*

agiotage <1> the speculation in the rise and fall of public debt or funds. <2> fee charged for exchanging currencies. ***Also***: agio; exchange premium; premium. <3> = *speculation in stocks.*

agreement among underwriters (AAU) the agreement among all participating members of the *distributing syndicate.* ***Also***: dealer agreement; purchase group agreement; syndicate contract. **See**: *underwriting agreement.*

agreement value the market value of a swap based on the cost to replace it in the current market condition.

agreement value method a method for determining the damages upon early termination of a swap by using the current market quote for a replacement swap.

agricultural commodity the agricultural based commodity and similar product traded in the futures market.

agricultural trade-option (ATO) OTC commodity option traded by those engaged in the production or selling of the underlying commodity.

ahead of itself of equities, overbought or oversold on a fundamental basis.

AI <1> and interest. <2> = *ARMS index.*

airport revenue bond a bond secured by income from airport facilities, such as landing fee.

AJOJ the abbreviation of four dividend paying months: April, July, October, & January.

albatross a wingspread the inside body options are at least two strikes apart. ***Also:*** seagull. **See**: *pterodactyl.*

alligator spread <1> the combination of puts and calls in which the broker's fee is higher than the client's profits. <2> = *butterfly spread.*

all in of the bond issuer's interest rate, net of commission and related costs.

all-in cost the total cost of a portfolio, explicit and implicit.

all-in premium the option premium expressed as a percentage of the current price of the underlying asset, including cost and all other fees.

All-Ordinaries Index <Australia> an index of 330 public companies traded on the Australian Stock Exchange. ***Also***: Australian All-Ordinaries Stock Index.

All-Ordinaries Share Price Riskless Index note (Asprin) <Australia> the zero-coupon index-linked note issued with a fixed-rate participation in the All-Ordinaries Index and redemption at par. ***Also***: Australian stock price riskless index note.

all-or-none (AON) an offering that gives the issuer the right to cancel the issue if the underwriting is not fully subscribed.

all-or-nothing option = *binary option.*

all saver certificate an one-year CD up to $1,000 of interest income of which was not taxable if deposit was made between September 1981 and the end of 1982.

all square share = *fully paid share.*

all-star fund a mutual fund in which some highly regarded portfolio managers run a portion of the fund.

alpha <1> the measure of selection risk of a portfolio in relation to the market. **See**: *beta.* <2> relationship between a mutual fund's beta value and its actual performance. ***Also***: Jensen index. <3> = *alpha factor.*

alphabet stock <1> the common stock of a company which is associated with a subsidiary resulting from merger and reorganization. <2> = *tracking stock.*

alphabet tranche a term loan which has different final maturities or different seniority of claims on corporate asset. ***Also***: back-end tranche.

alpha equation an equation expressed as: return - Treasury bill = alpha + beta + error.

alpha factor a factor for measuring the volatility of stock, e. g. an alpha of 1.25 is projected to rise in price by 25% in a year. ***Also***: α factor; alpha.

alpha quantile option path-dependent option the barrier of which is based on the α-quantiles of the Brownian motion. ***Also***: quantile option.

alpha risk = *unsystematic risk.*

alpha stock <UK> = *most active list.*

alternative currency option the *foreign currency option* that, if exercised, settles in any one of two foreign currencies at the election of the option holder. **See**: *dual currency option.*

alternative delivery procedure (ADP) a procedure in futures, both buyers and sellers agree to deliver under the terms other than those specified in the contract.

alternative investment the investment in hedge fund or managed futures product.

alternative investment market (AIM) <UK> the market within London Stock Exchange for trading the shares of new small, and growing companies.

alternative mortgage instrument the variation of a mortgage instrument such as *adjustable rate mortgage securities.*

alternative option an option on the best or worst return of two or more securities or indexes in a given period of time. ***Also***: either-or option; multi-factor option; specialty option. **See**: *best-of-two option*; *multi-asset option*; *rainbow option*; *outperformance option*; *worst-of-two option.*

Altman Z-Score an index for predicting whether or not a company is likely to go into bankruptcy.

amalgamation <UK> = *merger.*

amalgamation by absorption = *merger.*

AMBAC American Municipal Bond Assurance Corporation

American binary option = *binary barrier option .*

American cash-or-nothing binary the binary option that is issued out-of-the-money and makes a fixed payment if the underlying value ever reaches the strike. ***See***: *European cash-or-nothing binary.*

American corporate accrual receipts (ACARS) the stripped coupon and principal payments based on corporate bond. ***See***: *separately traded registered interest and principal securities.*

American depository receipt (ADR) the receipt which indicates a claim on certain number of shares in foreign corporations that a depository bank holds on behalf of American investors.

American depository share (ADS) any foreign stock issued in the USA and registered in the *American depository receipt* system.

American fund a European fund that invests in the US securities and US currencies.

American option an option that can be exercised at any time before its maturity. ***Also***: American-style option; normal exercise option. ***See***: *Bermuda option*; *European option*; *Japanese option.*

American Parisian option a Parisian option that can be exercised any time before expiration.

American party the price equivalent in US fund of the US securities traded abroad.

American share certificate a stock certificate on the face of which is given the name of the registered holder and on the back a blank form of transfer.

American Stock Exchange (Amex) the second biggest stock exchange in the United States. ***Also***: Curb; Curb Exchange.

American-style option = *American option.*

American-style swaption a swaption that can be exercised any time.

American terms = *direct quote.*

American warrant the warrant showing evidence of subscription rights to additional *American depository receipts.*

American window the modified form of *American option* with an exercise time interval at the end of the option's life that permits exercise in the *window period.*

Americu's trust = *Humpty Dumpty fund.*

Americus trust unit an instrument that can convert stocks into a five-year warrant and a five-year covered call writer's position at a relatively low cost. ***See***: *buy-write option unitary derivative.*

Amex American Stock Exchange

Amex Major Market Index the weighted average price of 20 blue chip stocks introduced on Apr 29 1983 by *American Stock Exchange*, base value is 200.

Amex Market Value Index (AMVI) the market weighted index of 800 industrial stocks that are traded on the *American Stock Exchange*, the base level is 100 in September 1973. ***Also***: ASE Index.

Amex options switching system the computer system which transmits all incoming orders for options to the proper trading posts in the *American Stock Exchange.*

Amman Financial Market (AFM) the largest exchange in Jordan.

amortizing cap a cap option the principal of which amortizes over time during the life.

amortizing collar the collar which has a provision that covers decreasing notional principal amounts.

amortizing debt a debt the principal of which amortizes (as repayments) over time.

amortizing interest rate swap the swap the principal or the face amount rises (falls) as interest rates rise (fall).

amortizing option an interest rate swap or option with a declining principal.

amortizing principal swap = *amortizing swap.*

amortizing swap a swap the principal of which is reduced by a set amount each period over its lifetime. ***Also***: amortizing principal swap. ***See***: *accreting swap; index principal swap; traditional swap.*

amount = *accumulated amount.*

amount at interest = *principal.*

amount at risk <1> the present value of a replacement swap. <2> 95% or 99% loss limit of an investment for a fixed time period.

AMPS auction market preferred stock

Amsterdam Exchange (AEX) stock exchange founded in 1611 in Amsterdam, now part of *Euronext.*

AMT bond the *municipal bond* the income of which is subject to AMT.

AMVI Amex Market Value Index

analytical valuation method the method for valuing derivatives which relies on the rigorous deviation of a formula.

anchor a frequently quoted bond that is used to price infrequently traded bonds.

and accrued interest = *and interest.*

and interest (AI) of bond prices, indicating that the buyer will receive the accrued interest. ***Also***: and accrued interest; plus accrued interest.

"and interest" price = *market price.*

ANFM the abbreviation of four dividend paying months: August, November, February, and May.

angel = *investment grade bond.*

ankle biter = *small cap stock.*

anniversary day <Canada> the end of a day that is one year after the day of the issuance of an investment contract.

annual effective yield = *annual percentage yield.*

annual general meeting (AGM) <UK> = *annual meeting.*

annual inflation swap a swap involving the exchange of actual inflation with fixed inflation at the end of each year.

annualized gain a monthly gain that is converted into that of 12 months, e.g. the monthly gain is 1.5%, annualized gain will be $[1 \times (1 + 1.5\%)]^{12-1} =$ 19.6%.

annual meeting the annual meeting of stockholders to hear the corporation's operations and elect directors. ***Also***: annual general meeting; general annual meeting; stockholders' meeting.

annual percentage rate (APR) yearly percentage cost of a loan or a credit. ***Also***: true interest rate.

annual percentage yield (APY) the rate earned in 1 year, taking into account the effect of compounding, if monthly yield is 1%, then APY = $[1 \times (1 + 1\%)]^{12-1}$ = 12.68%. ***Also***: annual effective yield.

annual report the annual summary of important information about a public company. ***See***: *Form 10K.*

annual yield = *effective annual yield.*

annuity bond a bond with no maturity, redeemable when the issuing company is bankrupt. ***Also***: irredeemable bond; perpetual bond; undated stock.

annuity certain an annuity the amounts paid and the payment dates of which are preset and guaranteed by an insurance company. ***Also***: term certain annuity.

annuity due an annuity under which each payment is made at the beginning of a period. ***See***: *deferred annuity*; *ordinary annuity*.

annuity in arrears = *deferred annuity*.

annuity swap <1> the *foreign exchange swap* on interest payments only, without exchange of principal. ***Also***: coupon-only swap. <2> an amortizing swap in which an irregular payment stream is exchanged for a regular payment stream of the same present value.

annuity trust a trust the trustee of which is required to pay some money annually to one or more beneficiaries.

anomaly the tendency of small stocks to outperform large stocks, of stock with low price-book ratio to outperform that with a high P/B ratio, and of *discount currency* forward to outperform *premium currency* forward. ***See***: *January effect*.

ante-spot value date the second date that is treated as the *value date*.

anticipated by the market = *discounted by the market*.

anticipated holding period the period an investor expects to hold an asset.

anticipated interest the interest earned on a savings account assuming there is no withdrawal.

anticipated transaction = *forecasted transaction*.

anticipatory hedge a hedge done with a purchase or sale of futures contracts in anticipation of a merchandising contract to be made later.

anti-crash warrant the call-type index warrant with a strike price equal to the lower of the index level at issuance or at a predetermined future date. ***Also***: partial look-back warrant; step-down option; step-down warrant.

anti-dilution clause = *anti-dilutive clause*.

anti-dilutive clause a clause that allows the exercise price of an option or a warrant to be adjusted to account for the stock splits, dividends or rights issues. ***Also***: anti-dilution clause.

anti-dilutive effect the result of a transaction that increases earnings per share by decreasing the number of shares outstanding.

anti-dilutive transaction the transaction that increases *earnings per share*.

anti fishermen's method the method of buying different kinds of shares and then buying only those that rise, and selling those that fall.

anti-greenmail preventing *greenmail* arrangement unless the same repo offer is made to all shareholders.

anti-takeover measure a measure done on a sporadic basis by the management in order to prevent or deter unwanted takeovers. ***See***: *poison pill*.

antithetic variate technique a method used with a numeric method e. g. the *Monte Carlo simulation* to improve an estimate of a *derivative*'s price.

any-interest-date the feature of a municipal bond that establishes the redemption right on any interest coupon payment due date.

any-or-all bid a takeover bid whereby the acquiring company offers to pay a set price for all the outstanding shares of the target company, or any part thereof. ***See***: *2-tier offer*.

AO option exchange code for *American Stock Exchange*. ***Also***: AQ.

AOAP all-or-any-part

AOY add-on yield

APB accreting principal bond

apex trading selling and adjusting far out-of-the-money deferred month put or call options on bond futures.

APO average price option

apocalypse stock a stock which represents equity in a company that can benefit or suffer from a global catastrophic event.

application the *pre-arranged trading* of a security or a derivative in the current bid-asked range.

applied proceeds swap = *bond swap.*

applied science stocks the shares issued by the companies engaged in developing products from research and development in applied science.

appraisal ratio a measure of the skills of a portfolio management, computed as: <a> the portfolio's incremental return relative to a benchmark index, divided by its incremental risk, or <b> alpha divided by the unsystematic risk.

appraisal right a shareholder's ability to demand payment of a fair cash price for his shares, as determined by an independent appraiser.

appreciated financial position a position in which there would be a gain if it is sold. ***See***: *unrealized gain.*

appreciating swap = *accreting swap.*

approved list a list of securities selected by states in which certain banks, institutions, fiduciaries and funds may invest. ***Also***: legal list. ***See***: *non-legals.*

approved person one who is a director of an NYSE member firm, or an owner of 5% or more of the voting shares thereof but who is a member of the NYSE.

APS <1> accreting principal swap. <2> auction preferred stock. <3> average price system.

APT <1> arbitrage pricing theory. <2> automated pit trading.

APY annual percentage yield

AQ = *AO.*

arbi loan = *interest arbitrage.*

arbitrage <1> the simultaneous buying and selling of a commodity, a security, option, foreign exchange, or futures in different markets in order to yield profits. <2> a swap between similar securities denominated in different currencies. <3> = *switching.*

arbitrage activity the process in which traders identify pricing inefficiencies, engage in trading to profit from those inefficiencies causing such inefficiencies to be removed from the market.

arbitrage bond <1> the municipal bond issued to gain from lower interest rate by refunding higher-rate bonds before their expiration. <2> a government bond the proceeds of which are used to invest in higher income securities.

arbitrage free meaning no arbitrage opportunities.

arbitrage-free model = *yield curve option pricing model.*

arbitrage free price = *fair price.*

arbitrage hedge a hedge that emphasizes increasing the expected returns rather than reducing risk exposure. ***See***: *identified hedging.*

arbitrage house a financial institution that engages in arbitrage as a normal business.

arbitrage in space an arbitrage which takes advantage of the price difference between markets in two different places. ***Also***: 2-point arbitrage; geographic arbitrage; inter-market arbitrage; space arbitrage; spatial arbitrage.

arbitrage in time an arbitrage that takes advantage of the difference in prices between two contract months. ***Also***: calendar arbitrage; forward-forward arbitrage; intra-market arbitrage; temporal arbitrage; time arbitrage.

arbitrage portfolio a portfolio of transactions carried out for arbitrage purpose.

arbitrage pricing theory (APT) a theory for estimating security returns based on systematic risk factors and arbitrage free assumption.

arbitrage profit the net profit or gain from arbitrage.

arbitrager = *arbitrageur.*

arbitrage stock the stock purchased and sold in securities arbitrage.

arbitrage swap = *yield curve swap.*

arbitrage table a table which shows the payoffs of two positions involved in arbitrage.

arbitrage trading program (ATP) a plan used to simultaneously place orders for stock index futures and the underlying stocks to exploit price variations. ***Also***: program trading.

arbitrageur a person or firm practicing in *arbitrage*. ***Also***: arbitrager.

arbitration the legal forum for impartial settlement of disputes in the derivative industry.

ARCN adjustable-rate convertible note

arithmetic average annual return = *arithmetic mean return.*

arithmetic mean average = *arithmetic mean return.*

arithmetic mean return an average of *sub-period returns*. ***Also***: arithmetic average annual return; arithmetic mean average.

arithmetic return = *simple return.*

arithmetic step option = *simple step option.*

ARMS adjustable rate mortgage securities

ARMS index the index calculated as: [(the number of advancing issues / the number of declining issues)/(total up volume / total down volume)], a value of less than 1 indicates bullish, greater than 1 will be bearish. ***Also***: AI; MKDS; trading index; TRIN.

arm's length price the price at which a willing buyer and a willing seller would agree to trade.

ARO average rate option

ARP adjustable-rate preferred stock

ARPPS adjustable-rate perpetual preferred stock

ARPS <1> adjustable-rate preferred stock. <2> auction rate preferred stock.

arrangement fee a fee paid to a broker , an agent or other intermediary for its role in initiating or implementing a trade.

arrearage = *dividend in arrears.*

arrear certificate a document given by a company to the holders of bonds when the interest payment is deferred. ***Also***: deferred interest certificate; deferred interest warrant.

arrears rate reset swap = *LIBOR in arrears swap.*

arrears reset swap a swap the floating rate is set and paid at the end of a period.

arrears swap the swap the floating rate is set in arrears, based on the index at the end of the period, applied retroactively to its whole life. ***Also***: back-end set swap; delayed reset swap; in arrears swap; reset swap; swap in arrears.

arrow-debreu security a security with a fixed payout in one state of the United States and no payout in other states. ***Also***: pure security; state contingent claim; supershare option.

ASC all savers certificate

ascending a chart tracing price over a period of time and showing that each peak is higher than the preceding peak.

ascending yield curve = *upward sloping yield curve.*

ASE American Stock Exchange.

ASE Index = *Amex Market Value Index.*

A share <1> a class of mutual fund share characterized by charging a *front-end load.* <2> <UK> a stock classified as A, but with no voting power. ***See***: *class A stock.*

Asian dollar bond a bond issued in non-Asia markets, denominated in Asian dollar.

Asian option = *average price option.*

Asian tail <1> the length of time in an average price option. <2> option feature whereby a reference price is activated at the end should the underlying fall below an average level before expiration.

ASIC Australian Securities and Investment Commission

ask the price the trader is willing to sell. ***Also***: asking price; offer; offered price; offering price; offer price; selling offer. ***Opp***: *bid.* ***See***: *left-hand side.*

asked to bid to ask for a bid from an investment banker before selling a stock.

asked to offer to ask an offer from an investment banker before buying a stock.

asking price = *ask.*

ask IV implied volatility computed from the ask price.

ask size number of shares offered for sale at the asked price. ***See***: *quote size.*

ASO average strike option

as-of trade in futures, a trade which is recorded or booked on a calendar date after the actual execution date.

Asprin <1> All-Ordinaries Share Price Riskless Index note. <2> Australian stock price riskless index note.

aspirin count theory the theory which states that when the aspirin production rises, the stock market will fall, and vice versa.

ASRO average strike rate option

assented stock a listed stock the holder of which has agreed to some changes e. g., paying less dividends, otherwise he gets nothing. ***See***: *non-assented stock.*

assessable stock a stock the holders of which can be assessed for further liability in the event of insolvency. ***Opp***: *non-assessable stock.*

asset <1> a property or a title to it. <2> = *underlying asset.*

asset accretion an improvement in the value of a firm's assets through growth, expansion, or acquisition. ***Also***: resource accretion.

asset allocation the selection of investments to reflect the objectives of the firm. ***Also***: style allocation.

asset allocation fund a mutual fund which invests in a wide variety of domestic and foreign securities, metals, derivatives, fixed-income securities, financial instrument, and real estate.

asset allocation puzzle the observation that investors typically allocate a fraction of wealth to bonds independently of the ratio of bonds in the portfolio.

asset allocation swap a swap which is intended to effect the asset allocation of a project.

asset-and-liability statement = *balance sheet.*

asset-at-expiry option <UK> = *asset-or-nothing binary.*

asset-at-hit option <UK> = *asset-or-nothing binary.*

asset-backed bond a bond secured by the assets of the issuer.

asset-backed commercial paper the commercial paper that is backed by some specific assets of its issuer.

asset-backed security (ABS) the fixed income security that pays its coupon interest and principal from a specified revenue stream and also has a specified asset as collateral.

asset backing = *book value per share.*

asset-based swap an interest rate swap where the fixed-rate payer holds bonds with the coupon rate reflected in the swap terms. ***See***: *asset swap.*

asset cover the extent to which assets as collateral for stockholders. ***Also***: asset coverage; net book value per share of common stock.

asset coverage = *asset cover.*

asset dividend = *property dividend.*

asset/equity ratio the ratio of a firm's assets to its stockholders' equity. ***Also***: total assets to equity ratio. ***See***: *equity multiplier.*

asset-linked trust securities (ALTS) a *collateralized bond obligation* giving access to a diversified portfolio of low rated bonds. ***Also***: secured loan trust.

asset-market theory the theory which holds that exchange rate is determined in the short run by equality of supply and demand for assets denominated in different currencies.

asset-or-nothing binary a binary option that pays the value of the underlying asset at expiration if it expires in the money. ***Also***: asset-at-expiry option; asset-at-hit option.

asset-or-nothing call an option with the full asset value as payoff if the underlying asset price is above the strike, or nothing if it is below. ***See***: *cash-or-nothing call.*

asset-or-nothing put an option with the full asset value as payoff if the underlying asset price is below the strike, or nothing if it is above. ***See***: *cash-or-nothing put.*

asset play an attractive stock since its assets per share are worth far more than its market price.

asset share value the policyholder's share value of the life insurance company.

asset stripping buying up companies with poor results or in financial difficulty, then selling their assets one by one at a gain and closing down the business and terminating the companies. ***See***: *milking.*

asset swap a swap which converts a fixed cash-flow asset into the floating cash flow asset, or vice versa. ***See***: *asset-based swap.*

asset swap package a credit derivative instrument with payoff features and a corresponding financial derivative that exchanges the fixed cash flow of that instrument for a floating rate cash flow stream.

asset swap spread the fixed coupon basis points paid in an asset swap by the participants.

asset turnover the net sales divided by total assets of a company. ***Also***: total asset turnover.

asset value model a model for assessing the credit risk of a company debt. ***Also***: Merton model.

asset value per share = *book value per share.*

asset volatility the historical volatility based on the tick data calculated by obtaining a simulated scalping profit on a long gamma position and comparing the profit to the cost.

assignable contract <1> the contract with a clause which allows the holder to convey his rights to a third party. <2> = *transferable option.*

assignable instrument = *negotiable paper.*

assignment <1> the replacement of the originals in a swap by a new counterpart. <2> the sale of a swap contract. <3> a tenant's transfer of all interests in the leased property to a third party. <4> = *assignment notice.*

assignment notice a notice sent to the *writer* indicating that the holder has exercised an option. ***Also***: assignment; exercise assignment; exercise notice. **See**: *guarantee letter.*

assignment of option the transfer of rights to purchase an asset, usually real estate.

assignment separated from certificate = *bond power.*

assimilation = *absorption.*

associated company <UK> = *affiliated company.*

assumed bond = *guaranteed bond.*

assumed debt the debt obligation of an acquired company which becomes an obligation of the acquirer.

ASX 200 a capitalization-weighted index of the top 200 companies traded on the ASX. ***Also***: S&P ASX 200.

asymmetric information = *inside information.*

asymmetric information approach = *signaling approach.*

asymmetric volatility a situation where option volatility is higher in down markets than in up markets.

as-you-like-it option = *as-you-like option.*

as-you-like option an option with a clause permitting buyer to designate it as either a call or a put for a limited time period after the offering date. ***Also***: AC/DC option; as-you-like-it option; call or put; chooser option; hermaphrodite option; preference option; regular chooser option; you choose option; you choose warrant. **See**: *straddle option.*

as-you-like warrant a warrant with a provision that allows the holder to assign it as either a call or put warrant for a given period of time.

at a discount (AAD) = *below par.*

at a premium = *above par.*

at cost when the selling price equals the cost. ***Also***: no-load; selling flat.

at-expiry option <UK> a binary option which generates a payoff only at expiration that is equal to a fixed asset or cash if the price of the underlying asset breaches the barrier at any time.

at-hit/at-expiration option = *binary barrier option.*

at-hit option <UK> a binary option that generates a payoff immediately as the price of the underlying breaches the barrier. **See:** *one-touch all-or-nothing.*

Atlantic option = *Bermuda option.*

Atlantic spread going long in an *American option* and short in an otherwise identical *European option*, or vice versa.

at limit in a *limit order* placing a specified limit on either the highest price to buy or the lowest price to sell a security.

ATM <1> agricultural trade-option merchant. <2> at-the-market. <3> at-the-money.

at market meaning that transactions are traded at market price.

at-market swap the swap with a coupon reflecting the market rates of interest. ***Also***: par swap. **See**: *off-market coupon swap.*

ATM option = *at-the-money option.*

ATO <1> agricultural trade-option. <2> at the opening.

ATP arbitrage trading program

at par designating a security issued or sold at its face amount.

at risk exposed to the danger of loss.

ATS <1> adjustable tender security. <2> Alternative Trading System. <3> Automated Trade System.

at the figure of a quote, at the nearest whole number, the integer closest to the decimal quote. ***Also***: at the full.

at the full = *at the figure.*

at the market (ATM) a bid or offer that is equal to the market bid or offer.

at the money (ATM) of an option, the strike price is equal to or near the market price of the underlying asset. ***Also***: on the money.

at-the-money forward a forward contract the strike price of which equals the forward price.

at-the-money option a call or put option the strike price of which is equal to the spot price of the underlying asset. ***Also***: ATM option.

attribute bias the tendency of securities selected by the quantitative methods to share some characteristic such as low P/E.

ATX Australian Traded Index

auction <1> weekly offer for the sale of Treasury bills in Dutch auction. ***Also***: public sale; Treasury auction; weekly auction; weekly tender. **See**: *price auction*; *tender offer*; *yield auction.* <2> a public sale of assets to the highest bidder. ***Also***: sale by auction.

auctioneer the person who is hosting an auction.

auction market the system of trading securities through brokers or agents on an exchange such as NYSE. **See**: *call market*; *continuous auction market*

auction market preferred stock (AMPS) = *auction rate preferred stock.*

auction preferred stock (APS) the preferred stock offered by Goldman Sachs through a *Dutch auction.*

auction rate note the *floating-rate note* with an interest rate reset on the bids received at a *Dutch auction* conducted near the end of the reset period. ***Also***: auction-remarketed note.

auction rate preferred stock (ARPS) an *adjustable-rate preferred stock* with dividend adjusted every seven weeks through a *Dutch auction.* ***Also***: adjustable-rate preferred stock; auction market preferred stock; Dutch auction rate transferable security; flexible auction rate preferred stock; market auction preferred stock; money market preferred; money market preferred stock; remarketed preferred stock; short-term auction rate.

auction-remarketed note = *auction rate note.*

auction value = *liquidating value.*

aunt Millie an unsophisticated investor.

Aussie bond a bond issued and sold in the USA by an Australian company.

Australian All-Ordinaries Stock Index = *All-Ordinaries Index.*

Australian stock price riskless index note (Asprin) = *All-Ordinaries Share Price Riskless Index note.*

authority bond the bond issued by and payable from the revenue of a government or a company formed to administer a revenue-producing public enterprise. **See**: *revenue bond.*

authorized capital the highest amount of capital that can be raised according to the articles of incorporation. ***Also***:

free capital; registered capital. ***See***: *contributed capital*; *nominal capital.*

authorized common stock the common stock that is authorized to issue by the corporation's articles of incorporation.

authorized futures and option fund (AFOF) <UK> an investment fund that invests in futures, options and other interest-bearing deposits.

authorized participant (AP) a *specialist*, *market maker*, or an *institutional investor* which has signed an agreement with a distributor with an exchange-traded fund setting terms for the creation and the redemption of ETF's shares.

authorized shares maximum number of shares that a company can issue as set by the articles of incorporation. ***Also***: shares authorized.

authorized unit trust = *unit investment trust.*

auto cap = *auto-flexible cap.*

auto-flexible cap a *flexible cap* which supplies a limited number of *caplets* to reduce interest rates each time the reference rate exceeds the cap until all the caplets are exhausted. ***Also***: auto cap. ***See***: *chooser flexible cap.*

automated bond system (ABS) a system that records bids and offers for inactively traded bonds.

automated clearing house (ACH) a collection of 32 regional electronic inter-bank networks used to process financial transactions electronically.

automatically convertible enhanced security (ACES) the debt security with an embedded short put option and a long call combined with an interest coupon. ***Also***: debt exchangeable for common stock; fixed-income equity-linked debt; protected equity participation. ***See***: *dividend enhanced convertible stock.*

automatic cash-out call = *up-and-out call.*

automatic cash-out option <1> option that enables the holder to sell it at a fixed price in the event of a change in ownership of the issuing company. <2> an option that enables an investor to cash out income at the investor's choice. <3> = *up-and-away option.*

automatic common exchange security a note linked to the price of the issuer's stock. ***See***: *equity-linked note.*

automatic dividend reinvestment plan (ADR) a plan under which stockholders can receive more shares instead of dividends.

automatic exercise an arrangement under which options with strike prices that are more than a prespecified amount above or below the spot price can be automatically exercised. ***See***: *capped-style option.*

automatic investment plan (AIP) = *automatic withdrawal.*

automatic investment program = *automatic withdrawal.*

automatic reinvestment a mutual fund service which gives its shareholders an option to buy additional shares with cash from dividend and capital gain distributions.

automatic stay a provision preventing creditors from liquidating collateral of a counterparty who defaults.

automatic stock picking software the computer software that can generate buy and sell signals for stocks.

automatic withdrawal (AW) the mutual fund plan that entitles shareholders to a fixed payment periodically. ***Also***: automatic investment plan; automatic investment program; withdrawal plan.

auto parts shares of companies in the business of manufacturing automobile parts.

Autoquote <UK> the computer system that calculates theoretical option prices using an option pricing model.

auto-quote system a system generating quotes of exchange-traded or actively traded OTC derivatives based on the input from a market data feed.

autos shares issued by the automobile companies.

available-for-sale securities (AFS) the equity securities not classified as either debt or held-to-maturity or *trading securities.*

available short stock the stock that an investor may borrow from a broker to make delivery on a short sale.

average the average price of an asset in a given period. ***See***: *stock average.*

average annual compound return <UK> the annual return of a stock calculated taking into account the reinvestment of dividends.

average annual return (AAR) the annual return of a mutual fund stated after the expenses and all fees have been tallied.

average cost investment buying the same amount of shares or futures in a declining market each month in order to lower the average cost.

average due date the date on which several coupon payments coming due at differing times, can be paid. ***Also***: average maturity; equated maturity.

average effective maturity weighted average of the maturity of bonds, taking into account mortgage, puts or adjustable coupons. ***See***: *average normal maturity.*

average equity the average daily balance of a client's account calculated by the broker.

average exchange rate = *middle rate.*

average expected risk exposure the credit exposure based on the average maturity of the transaction and the expected market movement of the underlying asset.

average exposure the average mark-to-market exposure arising from some market-driven instruments such as interest rate swap.

average implied volatility <1> weighted average of the implied volatilities in several periods, or weighted average of the implied volatility of a group of assets in one period. <2> = *implied volatility index.*

average maturity <1> the average time to maturity of the securities held by a mutual fund. <2> = *average due date.*

average measure the average price of a large number of trades.

average normal maturity the average maturity of bonds which does not take into account mortgage, put or adjustable-rate coupon. ***See***: *average effective maturity.*

average option = *average price option.*

average portfolio maturity the weighted average maturity of all bonds in a bond portfolio.

average price the option price predicted by an econometric model or any similar technique. ***Also***: normal price.

average price option (APO) the *Asian option* that pays the difference between the *average price* of the underlying asset recorded over a fixed period and a set *strike price.* ***Also***: Asian option; average option; average rate option; average strike Asian option; currency average rate option. ***See***: *average strike option.*

average price system (APS) a service that gives institutional money managers an average price for their positions and transactions.

average rate cap an *interest rate cap* based on the average interest rate over a period of time rather than on a date.

average rate option (ARO) = *average price option.*

average return warrant a stock warrant that pays off at the average price of the holding period.

average shortfall the average of all potential losses due to the tail (extreme value) of probability distribution.

average strike Asian option = *average price option.*

average strike option (ASO) an option that pays the difference between the terminal value of the underlying asset at expiration and its average strike price. ***Also***: average strike rate option; floating strike Asian option; floating strike option. **See**: *average price option.*

average strike rate option (ASRO) = *average strike option.*

average true range the moving average (generally 14 days) of the *true ranges.*

average volume the straight average of the volumes of the last four trading days of a particular stock.

average worst-case credit exposure based on the average risk exposure maturity of the transaction and the worst-case market movement of the underlying.

averaging = *constant dollar plan.*

averaging down a method to lower the average price paid for shares on a declining market, e. g., for 1000 share, one can buy 400 at the current price, and three blocks of 200 each as the price fell.

averaging up buying on a rising market so as to lower the average cost, e. g. buying the equal number of shares at $50, $52, $54, and $58 will make the average cost of $53.50. ***Also***: pyramiding.

avoidable risk = *unsystematic risk.*

award acceptance of a bid.

away from blue of municipal securities offering by the dealer who has not made an advertisement in the *Blue List*. ***Also***: away from the blue.

away from the blue = *away from blue.*

B b

B <1> bond rating, it is speculative, lower than BB. <2> in a put option, meaning February. <3> the Nasdaq descriptor meaning class B. <4> the option strike price code for 10.

B2B stock business to business stock

B2C stock business to consumer stock

Ba = *BB.*

Baa = *BBB.*

baby bond the bond with a par value of less than $1,000. ***Also***: consol.

baccalaureate bond a zero-coupon bond that is issued by some states for assisting certain families in saving funds for college tuition by means of added tax benefits.

back bond a bond obtained through the exercise of an option or a warrant.

back contract currently trading distant expiration futures or option contract.

back-dating <1> a mutual fund feature allowing the holders to use an earlier date on a promise to invest a stated sum over a period of time in exchange for a reduced fee. <2> = *dating ahead.*

back door <1> a corporation which fails to fulfill the SEC listing requirements, makes itself eligible by taking over a shell company and merging itself into the new one. <2> = *US Treasury.*

backed bond <1> = *guaranteed bond.* <2> = *secured bond.*

backed in of an unanticipated event that allows for a purchase at a discount or a sale at a premium.

back-end fee = *back-end load.*

back-end load a charge for withdrawing money from a mutual fund. ***Also***: back-end fee; deferred sales charge; exit cost; exit fee; exit load; redemption charge; redemption fee. ***See***: *front-end load.*

back-end load fund a mutual fund that charges a *back-end load.*

back end right the right given by the target company to its shareholders to exchange one share for cash, preferred share, and/or bonds before the acquirer takes over the company. ***See***: *triple-option preferred stock.*

back end set swap = *arrears swap.*

back-end tranche = *alphabet tranche.*

back fee <1> a fee paid on the extension date of the buyer who wishes to continue the option. <2> premium paid on the 2nd leg of a *compound option.*

back-in poison pill = *poison pill.*

back month = *furthest month.*

back pricing a method used in futures whereby the price of the commodity to be delivered is set by the buyer at some future date after the contract.

backspread <1> a spread that involves the purchase of one call and the sale of two calls with a lower strike. (Unlike *ratio spread*, the spreader buys one call and sells two calls with a higher strike). <2> a strategy the number of options bought is greater than the number of options sold. ***Also***: ratio vertical spread. ***Opp***: *front spread.* <3> a spread that exists when the price for an identical item in two markets is less than the *normal difference.*

back stop to provide last-resort support or security in a securities offering.

backstopped deal = *firm commitment.*

back stub period last payment period on a floating rate note. ***See***: *front stub period.*

back testing the process of designing a trading strategy based on the historical data.

back-to-backing = *principaling.*

back-to-back swap the *swap* which will reverse the cash flow pattern of a simple swap, by modifying the net paying or receiving position of the counterparts, thus canceling the current swap. ***Also***: reverse swap.

back-up <1> the sudden *reversal* of the market trend. <2> the arrangement whereby investor swaps a security to another with a shorter current maturity. <3> of a market condition, in which the prices are declining.

back-up bid = *take out.*

back-up offer the secondary offer for a security accepted if the first offer fails.

backwardation <1> the percentage fee paid by a short seller to the buyer for delaying delivery. ***Opp***: *contango.* <2> a situation in which the forward price of a commodity is below the spot price. ***Also***: inverted market; on basis. ***Opp***: *contango.* <3> <UK> a market condition where the ask price is higher than the offer price.

backward induction = *roll back.*

bad delivery the delivery of security which is found to have some fault, such as unclean title.

badla/seedha badla/contango the process of forward trading, where one who does not wish to settle a trade, carries it forward to the next account period by paying backwardation.

bailout <verb> <1> to rescue a company in financial difficulty by providing it with capital. <2> to provide a company with loans at lower interest or tax concession by the government. <3> to transfer to shareholders payments that are taxable at desirable capital gains rates.

bailout period = *payback period.*

balance certificate the document sent to the shareholder showing the balance of unsold shares.

balanced fund a mutual fund that buys varieties of securities, the income of which consists of interest and deferred capital gains. ***Opp***: *pure stock fund.*

balance receipt = *balance ticket.*

balance sheet (B/S) a financial statement that shows assets, liabilities and capital on a specified date. ***Also***: asset and liability statement; statement of assets and liabilities; statement of the resources and composition of company capital; static statement.

balance sheet static synthetic CDO a synthetic CDO under which the SPV sells a credit default swap to the sponsoring firm on a portfolio of diversified credit obligations.

balance sheet variable synthetic CDO a synthetic CDO under which the SPV sells a credit default swap to a single CDS counterparty on a diversified portfolio of credit obligations.

balance stabilized swap a swap where an investor receives the net interest spread between the fixed rate and a floating rate (e.g. LIBOR) based on the notional balance of the swap.

balance ticket the document given to a broker by a company for the remaining shares unsold after a some of them have been sold. ***Also***: balance receipt.

bale packing = *bundle.*

balloon option an option for which the notional payments increase significantly after a set threshold is broken.

ballpark figure an estimate of a stock's prospectus based on the preliminary information or incomplete data.

band given range of acceptable exchange rates fluctuation between two currencies.

banded swap = *collared swap.*

banging the market sudden offering of large volume of shares without considering the fall in prices.

bank basis = *bank discount basis.*

bank discount basis a basis for quoting US Treasury bills prices in terms of the annualized yield. ***Also***: bank basis.

banker's acceptance swap an interest rate swap with a banker's acceptance rate as the floating rate.

banker's receipt the receipt given by the bankers on behalf of a company, for the payments made on stock application or redemption.

banking on overall stability (BOOST) = *accrual option.*

banking syndicate = *distributing syndicate.*

bank investment contract (BIC) an investment contract the interest payment of which is guaranteed by a bank over a specified period of time.

bankmail a banker's agreement with an acquiring company not to finance any other potential acquirer's bid to take over a *target company.*

bank prime interest rate the interest rate at which bankers lend money to their largest and credit-worthy clients. ***Also***: bank rate; base rate; blue chip rate; concessional rate; fine rate; preferential rate; prime interest rate; prime rate; prime rate of interest.

bank rate = *bank prime interest rate.*

bankruptcy future a futures contract that is based on the CME Quarterly Bankruptcy index.

bankruptcy remote entity a subsidiary or an affiliate company whose asset-liability structure and legal status make its debts secured even in the event of bankruptcy of its parent company or the guarantor of its debts. **See**: *derivatives product company; special purpose vehicle.*

bankruptcy risk = *credit risk.*

bank stock the share issued by a bank.

barbell portfolio a portfolio that consists of short- and long-term bonds only, with less or no intermediate-term bonds.

barbell strategy the strategy that trades only bonds with long and short-term maturities, excluding all medium-term bonds. ***Also***: dumbbell. **Opp**: *butterfly.* **See**: *laddered maturity strategy.*

barefoot pilgrim the unsophisticated investor who lost a fortune trading the futures or stocks.

bare hand an investor who is neither a bull nor a bear and holds no positions.

bargain = *deal.*

bargain counter a stock offered for sale at a price lower than its *intrinsic value.* ***Also***: bargain stock.

bargain element the difference between the strike of an option and the market price of the underlying when exercised, multiplied by the number of shares.

bargain hunter a patient speculator or an investor who waits until the stock becomes *bargain counter.* **See**: *bottom fisher.*

bargain stock = *bargain counter.*

barometer stock the stock the current prices of which are considered the measure of the condition of the market. ***Also***: bellwether.

barrier = *barrier price.*

barrier-European combinations the strategies involving European options that are adapted to use barrier options in one or both legs.

barrier event risk the risk of loss caused by the abnormal price behavior around the barrier price level.

barrier level = *barrier price.*

barrier option <1> the option the value at maturity depends on the market price of the underlying asset and the prices between inception and expiration. ***Also***: barrier warrant; limit option; special expiration price option. <2> an option which creates an underlying European option as the price of the underlying moves through a barrier, such as *down-and-in option, up-and-in option*, etc.

barrier price the price which may activate or deactivate a *barrier option*. ***Also***: barrier; barrier level; excursion level.

barrier warrant <1> a warrant that pays a fixed amount if the barrier price is triggered. <2> = *barrier option*.

barstrier the derivatives with a payout determined or altered by the underlying trading at or through a level.

BAS block automation system

baseball option a *barrier option* that is knocked out after the out-strike price has been touched for the third time. ***See***: *touch option*.

base currency <1> the currency in the currency pair which will go up or down in value when the currency pair is going up or down. <2> = *reporting currency*.

base interest rate = *hurdle rate*.

baseline instrument = *benchmark instrument*.

base market value the average market price of a group of securities at a given time as a basis of comparison in plotting dollar or percentage changes for the purpose of market indexing.

base period the year in which the index value is 100, e. g. NYSE is 1965. ***Also***: fixed base period.

base point = *point*.

base probability of loss the possibility of not achieving expected return or of losing the original investment.

base rate <UK> = *bank prime interest rate*.

base stock = *buffer stock*.

basic earnings per share = *primary earnings per share*.

basic minimum inventory = *buffer stock*.

basic net income per share = *primary earnings per share*.

basic P/E the price/earnings ratio that has been discounted at the market rate of interest.

basic point = *point*.

basic swap = *plain swap*.

basic time the time left before an option expires. ***Also***: time. ***See***: *duration*.

basic yield the yield of an investment with no risk. ***Also***: risk-free return. ***See***: *benchmark return*.

basis <1> = *basis point*. <2> = *buying basis*.

basis book a book of schedules which convert bond quotations into numbers in dollar amount.

basis grade = *contract grade*.

basis of exchange = *conversion ratio*.

basis point the smallest point used in quoting yields on bonds, one basis point is 0.01% of yield. ***Also***: basis. ***See***: *point*.

basis price the price artificially fixed by a stock exchange official at the end of a day's trading for a buyer or seller of an odd lot.

basis quote sale of a cash commodity in terms of the difference above or below the price of a futures contract.

basis rate swap = *basis swap*.

basis risk <1> the risk occurred when the difference between the spot and the futures price narrows or widens from the historical norm. <2> the risk of the price movement of an asset relative to the price of the hedge vehicle.

basis swap a swap under which both parties swap floating rate on different markets. ***Also***: basis rate swap; floating-floating swap; floating-for-floating swap; floating to floating swap. ***See***: *coupon swap.*

basis swing option a swing option based on two locations with variable volume.

basis trade <1> a portfolio in which the price for the position is determined by a spread against the market price of an exchange-traded derivative, such as a futures contract. <2> = *basis trading.*

basis trading buying spot commodity and selling futures if the spot price plus the cost of carry is lower than the forward price, and doing the opposite if the forward price is lower. ***Also***: basis trade; carry arbitrage; cash and carry arbitrage; cash and carry trade; relationship trade; relationship trading; yield trading.

basis trading facility (BTF) <UK> the system that enables the futures leg of a basis trade to be transacted without the execution risk.

B/A size bid/ask size

basket a group of stocks created for simultaneous buying and selling. ***Also***: basket component stocks; basket stocks; market basket; stock basket.

basket component stocks = *basket.*

basket credit default swap a credit swap based on a basket of credit entities. ***Also***: basket default swap; default basket swap.

basket default swap = *basket credit default swap.*

basket deposit receipt (BDR) a deposit receipt issued by the *exchange-traded fund.*

basket hedging using a basket of currencies to offset the risk of the *non-base currencies* in a portfolio.

basket option <1> a naked option or *covered option* on a basket of underlying assets. <2> an average return or average change option on any group of interest rates, exchange rates, or indices.

basket options a package that involves the exchange of more than two currencies against one *base currency* at expiration. ***Also***: currency basket options.

basket stocks = *basket.*

basket swap a credit derivative that involves the exchange of a premium for a compensatory payment if the reference credit entity in a portfolio defaults.

basket swap rate an interest rate that is equal to the weighted average of swap rates with a common term, but denominated in two different currencies.

basket trading assembling a basket of securities, both in terms of the securities chosen and the number of shares, so that the market performance of the shares chosen will track the index. ***Also***: index program; market basket trading; package trade; portfolio trade.

Bayes theorem a theory for estimating the conditional probability of a cause given that a particular event has occurred.

BB <1> S&P's or FIS's bond rating that is speculative, lower than BBB. ***Also***: Ba. <2> baby bond. <3> bearer bond.

BBB bond rating of medium grade, lower than A. ***Also***: Baa.

BDN bearer deposit note

BDR <1> basket deposit receipt. <2> bearer depository receipt.

bean, oil and meal spread = *crush spread.*

bear one who believes that prices will fall, and tries to profit from any further drop in price. ***Opp***: *bull.* **See**: *short.*

bear call ladder a ladder created by selling a lower strike call option and buying a higher strike call option, and another higher strike call option.

bear call spread a bear spread created by selling in-, at- or out-of-the-money call option and buying a further out-of-the-money call option, profiting from the price fall. ***Also***: bear spread using calls; call bear spread; call credit spread.

bear campaign the action to drive the price down by selling so that bears may buy back at a lower price later. ***Also***: bear clique; bear raid; bear tack. **See**: *bull campaign*; *hammering the market.*

bear CD a CD that pays a fraction of the drop in a given market price.

bear clique = *bear campaign.*

bear combination the combination like a bear straddle but with different strike prices. ***Also***: short combination; short combo.

bear cylinder selling a call and buying a put with a higher strike price. **See**: *bull cylinder.*

bearer one in possession of a negotiable instrument payable to the bearer. ***Also***: fictitious payee; non-existing payee.

bearer bond (BB) a bond the interest of which is payable to the bearer. ***Also***: debenture to bearer. **See**: *coupon bond.*

bearer certificate = *participation certificate.*

bearer deposit note (BDN) a short-term discounted deposit note in bearer form.

bearer depository receipt (BDR) the depository receipt in bearer form.

bearer form stock format not registered on the issuer's book, payable to bearer.

bearer instrument a physical evidence of ownership of a bond or stock or other instrument.

bearer note an instrument payable to bearer. ***Also***: note payable to bearer; note to bearer; paper to bearer.

bearer participation certificate = *participation certificate.*

bearer script a scrip issued as evidence of title by a company making a new issue, until such time as all installments are paid in full, this scrip is exchanged for a *bearer bond* or a *registered bond.*

bearer stock a stock the dividends are paid to those who hold the certificate. ***Also***: floater; street certificate.

bear floater a *floating-rate note* which resets at a multiple of the floating reference index rate minus a fixed rate. **See**: *bull floater.*

bear gut a bear strangle created by in-the-money options. ***Also***: short gut.

bear hug a raider's offer in takeover bid that is attractive to draw protest from the shareholders if the firm turns it down.

bearish factor any factor which can put the price down, thus benefiting bears.

bearish spread = *bear spread.*

bear market (BM)(B/M) a market full of bears because the prices are thought to decline soon. ***Also***: declining market. ***Opp***: *bull market.*

bear market fund a fund that engaged in short selling.

bear market warrant a put option, if the underlying exceeds the strike, the strike is reset higher to meet the market price.

bear note an interest rate or equity-linked note that benefits from falling prices or rising interest rates. ***See***: *bull note.*

bear position = *short position.*

bear put ladder a ladder created by selling a lower strike put and buying a higher strike put and another higher strike put.

bear put spread a vertical spread created by selling an at- or out-of-the-money put and buying a further out-of-the-money put, hoping to profit from price drop. ***Also***: bear spread using puts; put bear spread; put debit spread.

bear raid = *bear campaign.*

bear raider a person who tries to sell a stock with the intent of buying it back at a lower price later. ***See***: *short seller.*

BEARS the security the holder of which receives the strike price of the bonds underlying calls that are exercised by the holders of the *CUBS.* ***Also***: Bonds Enabling Annual Retirement Savings.

bear sale = *short sale.*

bear spread the purchase and sale of options simultaneously, profiting from a drop in the price of the underlying asset. ***Also***: bearish spread. ***See***: *bull spread.*

bear spread using calls = *bear call spread.*

bear spread using puts = *bear put spread.*

bear squeeze the central bank's action to bid up the currency until time comes for the bears to deliver what they had sold short, then it can force the bears to sell back at a loss. ***Also***: classic bear squeeze. ***See***: *short squeeze.*

bear straddle a straddle created by selling both a put and a call with the same strike price. ***Also***: short straddle. ***See***: *bull straddle.*

bear straddle writing selling a covered put and uncovered call on the same underlying at the same strike price and on the same *expiration date.* ***See***: *bull straddle writing.*

bear strangle the position created by selling out-of-the-money options in equal amounts with the same expiration, but with different strikes. ***Also***: short strangle. ***See***: *bull strangle.*

bear strategy an investment strategy that is based on the belief that prices will fall.

bear swap <1> an *interest rate swap* that amortizes more rapidly as interest rates rise, allowing the fixed-rate receiver to "reinvest" at higher rates. <2> a basis swap with both streams of payment based on index rates characterized by different credit qualities.

bear tack = *bear campaign.*

bear trap when the stock falls, attracts heavy selling, but suddenly it rises.

bear vertical spread the spread created by buying one option and selling another with a lower strike price. ***Also***: vertical bear spread. ***See***: *bull vertical spread.*

beating the gun (B.T.G.) <1> buying and selling securities on the information before it is known to the public. ***Also***: gun jumping. ***See***: *front running.* <2> soliciting of buy orders by an underwriter before the SEC registration is complete. ***Also***: jumping the gun.

bed and breakfast deal = *bed and breakfasting.*

bed and breakfasting selling securities which have fallen in value at the close of a trading day, recording the loss for tax purpose, and buying them back on the next morning. ***Also***: bed and breakfast deal; swap.

Belgian option a stock option originally struck slightly out of the money, pays off like a standard option if the underlying is in the money at expiration.

Belgium BEL-20 a modified capitalization weighted index of the 20 Belgian stocks traded on BSE.

bell and whistle <1> the unusual or unique feature of a financial instrument designed to appeal to a specific issuer or investor. <2> = *kicker.*

bellwether = *barometer stock.*

bellwether issue = *on-the-run issue.*

belly spread the spread created in pork bellies, e. g. buying an August contract against the February contract of the following year.

below-investment-grade bond = *junk bond.*

below par of the price of a stock, below its nominal or stated value. ***Also***: at a discount.

below the market the bid that is lower than the then highest bid.

below-water of an asset the actual value of which is lower than its book value. ***Also***: subpar. **See**: *above water.*

below zero when the market price of a stock is less than its paid-up value.

benchmark a zero level or neutral point against which risk or performance is measured. ***Also***: normal portfolio.

benchmark bond a bond outstanding in a class that provides the benchmark for evaluating other bonds.

benchmark error an error caused by the use of an inappropriate proxy for the portfolio.

benchmark excess return = *benchmark return.*

benchmark government bond a bond used as a basis for pricing other bonds with similar maturity and quality.

benchmark instrument an instrument serving as the benchmark to which all other instruments are to be compared. ***Also***: baseline instrument.

benchmark interest rate = *hurdle rate.*

benchmark issue = *on-the-run issue.*

benchmark price = *fair price.*

benchmark return the return of a benchmark index, such as the S&P 500. ***Also***: benchmark excess return; benchmark timing return; risk-free return; riskless return. **See**: *basic yield.*

benchmark timing return = *benchmark return.*

beneficial owner an investment firm's customer who is the actual owner of a stock held, even though the stock is registered in the firm's name.

benefit of carry = *negative carry.*

Bermudan exercise the exercise of an option several days before expiration.

Bermudan option = *Bermuda option.*

Bermuda option an option that can only be exercised on certain dates before its original maturity date. ***Also***: Atlantic option; Bermudan option; limited exercise option; mid-Atlantic option; modified American option; multi-European option; quasi-American option; semi-American option. **See**: *American option; European option.*

Bermuda swaption a swaption created with predefined limitation on exercise.

Bernoulli option an option the payoff of which depends on the Bernoulli jump diffusion process.

Bespoke tranche = *single-tranche CDO.*

best ask = *best offer.*

best bid the highest bid in the market.

best bid or offer (BBO) the highest bid or lowest offer price available in a market at a specific time.

best bond to deliver = *cheapest to deliver.*

best buy option the partial or full look-back strike *call option.*

best effort a new issue which is not underwritten or bought as a whole but is sold by securities dealers on a sell-what-can-be-sold basis. ***Also***: placed deal.

best-interest-of-creditors test the test of requirement that a claim holder voting against a plan of reorganization must receive at least as much as if the debtor were liquidated.

best offer the lowest offering price of a bond or stock. ***Also***: best ask.

best-of option = *best-of-two option.*

best-of-two-assets option = *best-of-two option.*

best-of-two option an alternative option the payoff is the maximum of two option payoffs. ***Also***: best-of option; best-of-two-assets option; better-of-two-assets option. ***See***: *alternative option*; *worst-of-two option.*

best-of-two option return the maximum return of two options.

best price option = *lookback option.*

Best's rating the financial rating given to insurance companies by Best's Rating Service. (Top rating is A+).

best strike option = *lookback option.*

beta a measure of the magnitude of an asset's past price fluctuations in relation to the fluctuations in the overall market. ***See***: *alpha.*

beta coefficient <1> a measure of the systematic risk associated with a single stock or a portfolio. <2> sensitivity of the asset returns to market returns. ***Also***: financial elasticity.

beta equation beta = $(\sigma_p \times \sigma_{p,m}) / \sigma_m$, where σ_p is the return volatility of a portfolio, σ_m the return volatility of the market, and $\sigma_{p,m}$ the correlation value.

beta risk = *systematic risk.*

beta stock <UK> the second-tier stock in terms of relative size and volume. ***See***: *most active list.*

bet option = *binary option.*

better-of option a bundle of forwards with the same expiration dates but different underlying assets, only one of them settles at the holder's favor. ***See***: *worse-of option.*

better-of-two-assets option = *best-of-two option.*

BEY bond equivalent yield

biased expectations theory = *pure expectations theory.*

BIC bank investment contract

bid <1> the price at which a buyer is willing to buy. ***Also***: bid price; buying offer. ***Opp***: *ask.* <2> the rate at which a bank is willing to pay for a fixed term deposit, a security, or currency. ***See***: *right-hand side.*

bid and asked <1> a quotation to buy or sell a security, a derivative or other asset. <2> = *unlisted security.*

bid-asked spread = *bid-ask spread.*

bid/ask size (B/A size) the number of shares or contracts being bid divided by the number of shares or contracts being asked at a given time.

bid-ask spread <1> difference between the bid and asked price. ***Also***: bid-asked spread; bid-offer spread; dealer spread; pay-receive spread; spread. <2> gain or loss realized if buying and immediately selling a security.

bid bond a surety bond guaranteeing the performance of a contract when the bid is accepted. ***Also***: refundment bond.

bidder an investor who wants to buy by placing a bid.

bidding block financing new bond issue through the competitive bids from the underwriters.

bidding through the market aggressive willingness to buy at a premium.

bidding up moving the bid price higher. ***Also***: by-bidding.

bid-in-competition institutional investor's soliciting bids from the broker and dealers for a block of bonds he wants to sell.

bid IV implied volatility computed from the bid price.

bid-offer spread = *bid-ask spread.*

bid price <1> the price at which a mutual fund will buy back its shares. ***Also***: book value; net asset value; redemption price. <2> = *bid.*

bid size = *quote size.*

bid-to-cover ratio in Treasury auction, the number of bids received divided by the number of bids accepted.

bifurcation = *stock split.*

big blue = *eye beam.*

Big Board = *New York Stock Exchange.*

big dogs large traders in the futures or options market.

Biger and Hull model = *Garman-Kohlhagen model.*

big figure = *handle.*

big picture the major trading interest highlight due to the size of the trade.

big, swinging duck a huge money maker on Wall Street.

big ugly <1> the stock of a corporation that is a basic manufacturer with big and noisy facility plants. <2> = *wall-flower.*

bilateral arbitrage = *simple arbitrage.*

bilateral exchange the foreign exchange which can not be converted into other currencies without proper permission of the issuing country's central bank. **See**: *free exchange.*

bilateral margining agreement the contract that requires each party to a swap to deposit cash margin with each other or with a third party depending based on the change in margin.

bilateral netting an arrangement made between 2 parties where they exchange only the balance in the obligations to each other in swap trades.

bill option an option on the bill of exchange futures contract.

bill over bond spread (BOB) the yield spread between a specific maturity US Treasury bill and a bond. **See**: *bond over bill spread.*

bill pass the purchase of Treasury bills from dealers who are representing the Federal Reserve.

bill strip a Treasury bill auction in which the Treasury simultaneously offers bills of different maturities at one price.

BIMBO buy-in management buyout

bin <1><UK> a group of stock for which a market maker has the right to make a market in options. <2> = *bucket.*

binary accrual note an accrual note that pays one of the two fixed rates selected by the holder.

binary barrier option an option with payoff at expiration or when the price of the underlying asset touches the barrier. ***Also***: American binary option; at-hit/at-expiration option; one-touch option.

binary double-barrier option a double-barrier option the payoff is made at the first exit time from the corridor.

binary LIBOR note a binary accrual note the reference rate of which is LIBOR.

binary LIBOR swap = *binary swap.*

binary option an option whose holder receives a fixed payoff if the price of an underlying rises above the strike price on the date of expiration. ***Also***: all-or-nothing option; bet option; digital option; lottery option.

binary swap a swap with the floating rate set at a spread over the reference index rate if the reference is within the designated range, and with zero payment if the reference is outside the designated range. ***Also***: binary LIBOR swap.

binomial option pricing model = *Cox-Ross-Rubenstein model.*

BIP basis point

bipolar bond the principal-protected *equity-linked note.*

BISTRO <1> BIS total rip off. <2> Broad Index Secured Trust Offering.

bitrage = *simple arbitrage.*

BITS bond interest term security

black box <1> the pricing formula for a security not explained to users. <2> the assets used to collateralize a trust and provide a revenue stream to the owners of the trust units without collateral.

Black-Derman Toy (BDT) the interest rate option pricing model that uses a binary interest rate tree as the basis for generating price estimates.

blacked-out quiet period = *quiet period.*

black exchange rate the exchange rate used in the black market. ***Also***: black market rate; unauthorized exchange rate.

Black formula a version of the Black-Scholes formula in which the underlying asset is a futures contract, and the dividend yield is replaced with the risk-free rate.

black investing investment in the stock of any companies no matter what they do. ***See***: *green investing.*

black knight a party who makes a hostile tender offer or merger proposal. ***See***: *white knight.*

black market an illegal market in which commodities and foreign currencies are bought and sold.

black market bond the bond that has been traded after the registration with the SEC but before the official date of public issue.

black market rate = *black exchange rate.*

blackout <1> the period in which a firm will only provide answers to straightforward questions from the security analysts or the press because of a pending new securities issuance. <2> the period during which employees are restricted in their purchases or sales of company stocks. ***See***: *restricted stock.*

Black's 76 model = *Black's model.*

Black's approximation the method for calculating the approximate value of a call option on a dividend-paying stock.

Black-Scholes formula the formula developed by Fischer Black and Myron Scholes for the pricing of call options. ***Also***: Black-Scholes option pricing model.

Black-Scholes hedging the hedging against the risk exposure by selling option valued under the Black-Scholes formula.

Black-Scholes Merton model option pricing model using a risk-neutral mean of the probability distribution assuming no risk premium.

Black-Scholes option pricing model = *Black-Scholes formula.*

Black-Scholes value the option premium calculated by using the Black-Scholes formula.

Black's model a model by Fischer Black in 1976 for pricing options on futures. ***Also***: Black's 76 model.

Black Tuesday Oct 18, 1983, Tuesday, the day IBM announced the invention of two new computers, causing extreme drop of the share prices of its competitors.

Black Wednesday <UK> Wednesday, Sep 16, 1992, the day sterling left the Exchange Rate Mechanism.

blank check offering a new security issue by a speculative company.

blank check preferred stock written authorization given to the management to issue preferred stock without the approval of the common stockholders.

blanked out the lack of trading in a stock during a market session.

blanket fidelity bond a brokerage firm's surety bond against fraudulent trading by its employees.

blank stock a stock the terms and rights of which are not set in the articles of incorporation.

blended index a weighted average of two or more indexes.

blended index swap a swap in which at least one leg pays off that is based on the total return on a blended index or reference.

blended interest rate swap the combination of 2 or more interest rate swaps, e. g. a spot with a forward.

blended VAR = *composite VAR.*

blend fund a mutual fund that invests in a combination of both value and growth stocks.

blind brokering the repo in which an institution makes a loan to unnamed dealers, against their securities, usually using an intermediary or a broker to bring them together. ***See***: *conduit-type customer.*

blind pool securities offering by a limited partnership in which management has not disclosed the exact assets.

blitzkrieg tender offer the tender offer so compelling that it is accepted quickly by the target firm. (In German, blitzkrieg means lightning war.)

block a large sum of stock, usually 5,000 shares or more, or $200,000 worth of bonds. ***Also***: lot; parcel.

blocked rand = *financial rand.*

block list a list of derivatives that an investment banker is looking for the counterpart traders.

block offer a special offer by managers of a unit trust to sell units to the public at a fixed price.

block order the order to buy or sell a large volume of securities, 10,000 or more shares of a stock or $200,000 or more worth of a bond.

block positioner a firm which acquires stock in blocks in order to facilitate the handling of customers' orders.

block positioning buying stocks and bonds in large scale.

block purchase the purchase of a block of shares or bond.

block trade a trade in large quantity, usually 10,000 shares or $200,000 worth of bond or more. ***Also***: bought deal.

block trader a dealer who is willing to take a position in block trades.

block valuation factor the impact on the value of a financial instrument of a *block trade.*

block voting the group of shareholders acting together to vote in one block.

bloodletting a period of severe investment losses.

blow off a sharp price rise on large volume after an advance. ***See***: *crash.*

blow-off top a steep and rapid price rise followed by a steep and rapid drop in a short period of time.

blowout quick sell-out of all shares in a new offering. ***Also***: going away; hot issue; out of the window; out the window.

blowout bid the large premium over the previous prices, offered to shareholders of a *target company.*

blue button <UK> a member of London Stock Exchange who wears blue badges in the label of coat. ***See***: *pink button.*

blue chip a stock of the highest class, e. g. IBM. ***Also***: Bo Derek stock; fancy paper; investment quality stock; quality stock. ***See***: *secondary stock.*

blue chip rate = *bank prime interest rate.*

Blue List the daily financial publication listing bonds offered for sale by more than 700 banks and dealers. ***Also***: Blue List of Current Municipal Offerings.

blue list the trade offering sheets used by bond traders and bond dealers to list their offerings.

Blue List of Current Municipal Offerings = *Blue List.*

blue sheet the letter sent from SEC to a market maker requesting information about some transactions.

blue-skying stock = *worthless security.*

blue sky laws the laws enacted by various states to regulate the selling and the issuance of securities. ***See***: *sunshine laws.*

blue-sky securities offering = *direct public offering.*

BO buyer's option

board lot = *round lot.*

BOATs BOAT spread

BOAT spread (BOATs) a *yield spread* between German bonds and *French OATs*. ***Also***: Maginot spread.

BOB <1> bill over bond spread. <2> bond over bill spread.

bobtail pool a group of investors with common goal, but acting independently.

BO Derek = *BO order.*

BO Derek stock = *blue chip.*

body the two middle strike options in a butterfly or condor. ***See***: *wing.*

bogey <1> a *benchmark* return used in evaluating fund managers' performance. <2> a target rate of return an investor is aiming for. ***See***: *expected return*; *hurdle rate*; *maximum return criterion.*

boil spread the *yield spread* between a bond and an oil contract.

BOLO borrower's option-lender's option

BOM <1> bean, oil, and meal. <2> beginning of month.

Bombay Stock Exchange Sensitive Index an index composed of the 30 most active stocks traded on Bombay Stock Exchange. ***Also***: Sensex.

BOM spread = *crush spread.*

bond <1> the acknowledgement of the existence of a debt. ***Also***: certificate of liability; debenture; loan stock; loan stock debenture; tranche. <2> = *corporate bond.*

bond anticipation note (BAN) the note issued by a state or municipality which will be paid off with the receipts of a forth coming bond issue.

bond average daily index of bond price changes published as an average.

bond basis a method of interest calculation using a day count fraction equal to actual days divided by 365.

bond bought flat = *flat bond.*

bond broker the broker who executes bonds trades.

bond buyback a company's purchase of its own bonds at a discount in the open market. ***Also***: buy-back.

Bond Buyer's index a daily index composed of 20 long-term bonds rated A or above.

Bond Buyer's municipal bond index an index published by *The Bond Buyer* tracking US municipal bond prices.

bond certificate = *certificate of bonds.*

bond conversion premium = *conversion premium.*

bond counsel the attorney who handles the legal matters on a municipal bond.

bond coupon a warrant for the payment of interest, which is attached to a bond for payment of interest when matured. ***Also***: certificate of interest; coupon; coupon of bond; coupon sheet; debenture coupon; interest coupon.

bond covenant a contractual provision in a bond indenture, that either requires or forbids some act.

bond crowd the members of a stock exchange who deal with bonds.

bond discount the amount by which the bonds are sold below their face value. ***Also***: debenture discount; debt discount; discount on bonds; discount on creditors. ***Opp***: *bond premium.*

bond equivalent yield (BEY) = *equivalent bond yield.*

bond fund a mutual fund that invests in income-generating bonds. ***Also***: bond mutual fund.

bond future a futures contract the underlying assets of which are the notional bonds with standard features.

bondholder the person holding a bond.

bondholder's percentage the ratio of the principal of the bonds issued to the aggregate principal of the collateral.

bond indenture = *indenture.*

bond index an index of the performance of a large number of bonds.

bond indexing = *indexing.*

bond insurance an insurance covering the payment of principal and interest of bond.

bond interest rate = *coupon rate of interest.*

bond interest term security (BITS) = *adjustable tender security.*

bond issue all bonds issued at a given time by a single bond issuer.

bond ladder a strategy for managing fixed-income bonds by dividing investment evenly among bonds maturing at regular intervals.

bond mutual fund = *bond fund.*

bond of credit <UK> personal guarantee for a bond. ***Also***: cash credit bond.

bond offering new offering of bonds to the general public.

bond option an option that grants the owner the right to buy or sell a bond future before a given date.

bondor = *iron butterfly.*

bond ordinance the authorizing of a bond issue. ***Also***: bond resolution.

bond over bill spread (BOB) difference in yields between a specific bond and a specific maturity US Treasury bill. ***See***: *bill over bond spread.*

bond over stock warrant (BOS) an out-performance option with payoff based on the performance of a bond index less the return on a stock index.

bond point 1% of the face value of a bond, e. g. 80 points meaning the bond is trading at 80% of its par value.

bond power a legal document for the transfer of the registered bonds from one person to another person. ***Also***: assignment separated from certificate.

bond premium the amount by which the bond's sale price is above its face amount. ***Also***: credit spread; premium; premium on bonds. ***Opp***: *bond discount.*

bond quote a quotation of bond prices.

bond rating the valuation of the bond issuer's possibility of default.

bond ratio total liability represented by bonds due after one year divided by the same figure plus stockholder's equity.

bond reconstitution purchasing some zero-coupon bonds

bond redemption retirement of bonds on payment of principal and interest. ***Also***: redemption.

bond resolution = *bond ordinance.*

bond scale a schedule of average yields for each maturity of serial bonds.

Bonds Enabling Annual Retirement Savings = *BEARS.*

bond sinking fund assets accumulated to pay a bond issue at maturity. ***Also***: fund for retirement of bonds.

bond stock ratio the ratio calculated as: face value of bonds divided by issuer's earnings yield.

bond stripping = *coupon stripping.*

bond swap selling one bond and buying another. ***Also***: applied proceeds swap; debt-for-debt swap. ***See***: *refunding.*

bond table a table showing investment and trading information for bonds.

bond trust a *trust* the subject matter of which is the bond with interest income.

bond trustee a trustee for the holders of a bond.

bond value the market value of fixed-income element of a convertible bond.

bond warrant an option that gives the buyer of a bond the right to acquire a second bond with a similar coupon from the same issuer. ***Also***: contingent takedown option; debt warrant. ***See***: *kicker.*

bond washing selling bonds ex-interest before ex-date to exempt taxpayers, after ex-date buying them back at a price representing original price plus interest, thus the interest is not taxable.

bond with attached warrant = *host bond.*

bond with warrant = *host bond.*

bond yield the present income of bonds divided by their current market value.

bond yield warrant an exchange-traded warrant with the payout dependent on a specific *bond yield* or yield index.

bons French Government bonds.

bonus certificate a statement received by the policy holder from the insurance company on the occasion of a division of its earnings to inform him of the amount payable to him.

bonus dividend = *extra dividend.*

bonus issue = *bonus share.*

bonus share a free additional share issued to the existing shareholders as a stock dividend. ***Also***: bonus issue; bonus stock; capitalization issue; dividend stock. **See**: *excess share*; *rights issue*; *stock grant*.

bonus stock = *bonus share*.

book <1> a preliminary indication of the interest on the part of prospective buyers of a new issue. <2> a banker or trader's current position.

bookbuld the way of conducting issue of shares where the price is not fixed, but rather is determined by an auction in which investors bid for the shares.

book cash = *ledger cash*.

book entry security a security not in the form of a certificate, but as an entry in an account at a bank. **See**: *uncertificated share*.

booking a swap recording a swap in the books. ***Also***: positioning a swap.

booking the basis the arrangement between a buyer and a seller whereby either party has the ability to fix the cash price of the forward sales contract.

bookout closing out a position in swap or an OTC derivative before maturity.

bookrunner the managing underwriter who maintains the book of the securities sold for a new issue.

book share = *uncertificated share*.

book to market ratio a ratio of the book value to the market value of all shares outstanding. **See**: *price-book ratio*.

book value <1> the value of asset shown on the books. ***Also***: carrying value. <2> = *bid price*. <3> = *net asset value*.

book value of common stock asset value minus the value of the preferred stock.

book value of preferred stock preferred capital plus preferred dividends paid on the preferred stock.

book value per share the book value of a company divided by the number of shares outstanding. ***Also***: asset backing; asset value per share; net assets per share.

BO order the US Treasury bond with the maturity in May 2010. ***Also***: BO Derek.

BOOST banking on overall stability

boost = *accrual note*.

boosted coupon note = *accrual note*.

boot = *boot dividend*.

boot dividend money or the fair market value of property of a party to the reorganization that is received by the target company or by the shareholders in exchange for their stock. ***Also***: boot.

bootstrap a start-up company with very little capital.

bootstrap acquisition the transaction in which the assets of the acquired entity are used to fund the merger.

bootstrapping creating theoretical spot rate curve using a yield projection as the basis for the yield of next maturity.

bootstrap sale using the cash assets of the acquired company to pay for the cost of the acquisition. **See**: *busted takeover*.

borrowed capital dividend declared and retained by the issuer pursuant to the agreement with the stockholders.

borrowed stock the stock borrowed for the performance of delivery under a short sale. ***Opp***: lending stock.

borrower arbitrage = *spot hedge*.

borrower option a *cap* set on a forward rate agreement that limits the floating rate.

borrower's option-lender's option (B-OLO) an option embedded in a debt instrument that gives the issuer the right to change coupon and holders the right to put (sell) back to the issuer if the new rate is not acceptable.

borrowing arbitrage the arbitrage done by swapping the assets or the liabilities from one interest rate basis in one currency to another.

Borsa Valori Italian Stock Exchange.

BOS bond over stock warrant

Boston option <1> a *deferred premium option* whereby the premium is paid at expiration whether it is exercised or not. <2> = *break forward.* <3> = *deferred payment American option.*

Boston snow indicator a theory stating that a white Christmas in Boston will result in rising stock prices.

both ends of the list the long-term US Treasury bonds and the short-term US Treasury bonds.

both principal and interest = *accumulated amount.*

bottom <1> the price pattern incurred when price falls to a low point, and attracts new buyers, then begins to rise. ***Also***: fulcrum. <2> the lowest price in a trading day, a season, a week, a month or a year.

bottom fisher the investor who likes to buy stocks of bankrupt or near bankrupt companies. ***Also***: grave dancer; vulture capitalist. ***See***: *bargain hunter.*

bottom line the last line of the income statement that shows the net profit or loss. ***Also***: operating results.

bottom of the harbor the practice under which corporate founders strip the assets, fail to pay income tax and then transfer the remaining ownership to a third party.

bottom-out = *oversold.*

bottom-up approach the method that searches for outstanding performance of individual stock before considering the general economic trends. ***See***: *top-down approach.*

bottom-up equity management an investment style which selects specific securities within particular sectors. ***See***: *top-down equity management.*

bought deal <1><UK> = *block trade.* <2> = *firm commitment.*

BOUND buy-write option unitary derivative

bourse <French> = *stock exchange.*

Bowie the bond backed by the royalties on copyrights and master recording issued by David Bowie. ***Also***: royalty bond.

box conversion buying call and selling put at one strike, buying call and selling put at another strike.

box option investing in equity options that generate capital gains instead of investing in money market instruments which generate ordinary income.

box ratio trade volume divided by price range.

box short sale = *short sale.*

box size in a *point and figure chart*, the minimum price change that must occur for a given period before a mark is added.

box spread four option positions paired by a granted put matched with a long call at the same strike, coupled with a granted call and a long put at another strike price. ***Also***: box transaction. ***See***: *butterfly spread; condor spread.*

box transaction = *box spread.*

bracket = *distributing syndicate.*

Brady bond the government bond resulting from a debt restructuring, the redemption value of at least some of the bonds has been guaranteed by the US Treasury.

break a sudden rise or drop in price or volatility.

breakeven payment rate the repayment rate of a mortgage-backed security that produces the same cash flow as that of a benchmark.

breakeven point (BEP) in options, the level at which premium income equals the cost of a position.

breakeven spread the spread in a credit default swap at which the present value of premium and the protection legs are equal.

breakeven time the time needed for the convertible security's yield to cover its premium.

break fee <1> a fee paid by a target company to bidders in a merger if a pending deal is terminated. <2> fee paid by one party of a contract to another to cancel legal obligations.

break forward a forward contract with a feature allowing the parties to cancel. ***Also***: Boston option; callable forward; cancellable forward exchange contract; cancellable option; forward break; forward reserve option; forward with optional exit; guaranteed rate on delivery; knock-out forward; trigger forward. **See**: *conditional forward purchase contract*; *conditional forward sales contract.*

break in cross rate difference between two calculated exchange rates from a reference.

breaking a leg an upward price trend followed by a sharp down turn.

breaking the spread a market maker's quoting of the price of a security or other assets below or above the market price.

breaking the syndicate termination of the syndicate formed to underwrite an offering.

breakpoint the minimum investment in a mutual fund that qualifies an investor for a lower sales charge or a discount on the sales fee. ***Also***: breakpoint sales.

breakpoint refund the return of a proposed discount in mutual fund fees to the investors.

breakpoint sales = *break point.*

break-up value in an investment fund or an issue of a holding company, the value of assets available for the issue, taking all the marketable securities at their market value into account.

British savings bond <UK> a savings bond issued by the British Government in 1968 in order to replace the national development bonds.

broad-based index an index based on a wide range of stocks, the gain on the trading of which is taxed at 60% long-term and 40% short term. ***Also***: broad-base index. **See**: *narrow-based index.*

broad-base index = *broad-based index.*

broad index fund a mutual fund which invests in common stocks of companies in all capitalization ranges. ***Also***: core. **See**: *sector fund.*

Broad Index Secured Trust Offering (BISTRO) JP Morgan's preferred derivative that transfers some tranched credit exposure to large, diversified portfolios of loans from the securitizing bank to investors.

broad market = *active market.*

broken convertible the convertible bond sold at a yield competitive with the yields on nonconvertible securities.

broken date the nonstandard date for a foreign exchange forward contract. ***Also***: broken period; cock date; odd date. **See**: *standard date.*

broken date contract a *forward currency contract* with a broken date.

broken lot an irregular amount of shares, less than 100 shares. ***Also***: fractional lot; job lot; odd lot; odd lot of stock; odd share. ***Opp***: *round lot.*

broken period = *broken date.*

brokerage <1> a broker's carrying out of the client's buy or sell orders for a fee. <2> for a fee, bringing together parties interested in buying, selling, exchanging, or leasing real properties. <3> the fee charged by a broker for carrying out the instructions of client. ***Also***: brokerage fee; courtage.

brokerage cost price change from the moment an order is placed with a broker until the order is executed by the broker.

brokerage fee = *brokerage.*

broker/dealer (B/D) a broker engaging in the business of selling and buying securities to or for customers and also trades for his firm's own account. ***See***: *market participant.*

broker/dealer lite a full set of capital, margin, and other regulatory provision by the Securities and Exchange Commission for OTC derivatives dealers.

brokered CD a large denomination certificate of deposit that is sold by a bank to a broker who then divides it into smaller pieces to be sold to the small investors. ***Also***: brokered deposit.

brokered deposit = *brokered CD.*

broker holder of record an investment firm holding stock in its name.

broker loan rate = *call money rate.*

broker's call = *call money rate.*

broker's collateral loan = *call money.*

broker's loan = *call money.*

broker's loan rate = *call money rate.*

brought over the Chinese wall = *brought over the wall.*

brought over the wall the situation in which a research analyst at an investment bank works for underwriting department for the corporate client. ***Also***: brought over the Chinese wall.

Brownian motion a sophisticated random number generator based on a process in small particles suspended in a fluid, discovered by Robert Brown in 1827. ***Also***: Ito process; Markov diffusion process.

brundle a strip of consecutive quarterly Eurodollar futures or option contracts.

Brussels Stock Exchange (BSE) the major stock exchange in Belgium.

B share <1><UK> a stock classified as B, but with voting power. ***See***: *class B stock.* <2> mutual fund share with a unique feature such as *back-end load.*

BTP futures contract based on the Italian Government bond with a 12% coupon and half year maturity.

bubble theory the belief that security prices occasionally rise well above their fundamental values until at some point the bubble bursts and the price drops.

buck in bond quotation, for example if a bond's price range is 97- 98, the quote "28 to 1 buck" means bid 97 28/32 asked 98.

bucket the class of financial instrument separated for analysis and measurement of risk. ***Also***: bin.

buffer stock (BS) inventory maintained to prevent unpredictable shortages. ***Also***: base stock; basic minimum inventory; inventory cushion; margin of safety; minimum stock; perpetual stock; safety inventory.

building air = *doctoring.*

building block approach a risk management method which separates a single security into simple component and then re-aggregates them into portfolios, and manages risk in the separate portfolios.

building materials stocks of companies in the business of building materials.

built-up interest = *accrued interest.*

bulge = *spurt.*

bulge bracket firms in an underwriting syndicate responsible for placing the largest amounts of the issue.

bull <1> one who buys security or other derivatives in expectation of a rise in price. ***Also***: long; long interest. ***Opp***: *bear.* <2> = *buying long.*

bull and bear note a security created by tranching other instruments so that one tranche pays a floating rate which moves in the same direction as the benchmark and the other moves in the opposite direction.

bull-bear bond a bond the principal repayment of which is linked to the price of another bond.

bull buying = *buying long.*

bull call ladder a spread created by buying a lower strike call and selling a higher strike call, and another higher strike call option.

bull call spread the vertical spread created by buying at, in and out-of-the-money call option and selling further out-of-the-money call option profiting from a rise in price. ***Also***: bull spread using calls; call bull spread; call debit spread.

bull campaign action by bulls aimed to push prices up by buying in securities. ***Also***: bulling the market. ***See***: *bear campaign*; *holding the market.*

bull CD a CD that pays a percentage of increase in return on a specified index while guaranteeing a minimum return.

bull combination a combination that is like a bull straddle but with different prices. ***Also***: long combination.

bull-cum-bear option zero-coupon note made up of a deep in-the-money call and a deep in-the-money put, either can be closed out before maturity to convert the position into an option.

bull cylinder buying a call and selling a put with the same strike, profiting from a price rise. ***See***: *bear cylinder.*

bulldog bond <UK> a bond issued by a foreign borrower and sold in the UK. ***See***: *foreign bond*; *Yankee bond.*

bulldog market <UK> = *foreign market.*

bullet <1> a straight debt issue without a sinking fund, but is repaid in a lump-sum at maturity. <2> the mid-duration bond in a butterfly hedge.

bullet bond <1> a bond that is not able to be redeemed prior to its maturity. ***See***: *callable bond.* <2> = *put bond.*

bullet contract *guaranteed investment contract* sold with a single premium.

Bulletin Board a federal agency set up in June 1990 to prevent fraud in the trading of OTC and pink sheet assets.

bullet maturity feature of a bond which pays interest periodically, and repays the entire principal upon maturity.

bullet maturity bond a bond that pays coupon interest and repays principal upon maturity.

bullet proof structure the highly-rated asset-backed debt instrument that will sell for only a modest premium over a similarly rated conventional security.

bullet strategy a strategy in which a portfolio is designed to have securities with maturities that are highly concentrated at a point on the yield curve.

bullet swap the swap set up with a constant notional principal reflecting a constant risk-offset requirement, and the use of a *bullet maturity bond.*

bull floater a floater the yield increases as the floating rates decline. ***Also***: bull floating rate note; indexed inverse floating-rate note; inverse floater; inverse floater note; inverse floating security; maximum rate note; reverse floating-rate note; yield curve note. **See**: *bear floater.*

bull floating rate note = *bull floater.*

bull gut a bull strangle created by in-the-money options. ***Also***: long gut.

bulling the market = *bull campaign.*

bullish factor good news that may push the price up.

bullish spread = *bull spread.*

bull market the market in which prices are going up. ***Also***: long market; rising market. ***Opp***: *bear market.*

bull note an interest rate note or equity-linked note that benefits from rising price or falling interest rates. **See**: *bear note.*

bull position = *long position.*

bull purchase = *buying long.*

bull put ladder a ladder created by buying a lower strike put and selling a higher strike put, and another higher strike put option.

bull put spread a vertical spread created by selling at-, in- or out-of-the-money put and buying further out-of-the-money put profiting from a rise in price. ***Also***: bull spread using puts; put bull spread; put credit spread.

bull spread buying and selling options, profiting if the underlying asset rises. ***Also***: bullish spread. **See**: *bear spread.*

bull spread using calls = *bull call spread.*

bull spread using puts = *bull put spread.*

bull straddle a straddle created by buying both a put and a call with the same strike price. ***Also***: convexity hedge; long straddle; reverse option hedge. **See**: *bear straddle.*

bull straddle writing selling a covered call and an uncovered put option on the same underlying asset. **See**: *bear straddle writing.*

bull strangle buying out-of-the-money puts and OTM calls with a higher strike. ***Also***: long strangle. **See**: *bear strangle.*

bull strategy the strategy based on the belief that the prices will rise.

bull vertical spread buying an option and selling an option with higher strike price. ***Also***: vertical bull spread. **See**: *bear vertical spread.*

bump-up CD a CD which grants the owner the right to increase its yield one time for the remaining term.

bundle commercial loans sold to investors as securities. ***Also***: bale packing.

bundling the creation of securities by combining primitive and derivative securities into one composite hybrid or by separating returns on an asset into different classes. **See**: *unbundling.*

bunny bond a bond with the option to receive additional bonds with the same coupon and maturity or interest.

burning the yield = *yield burning.*

burn rate the rate of negative cash flow, usually monthly, used to measure how long it will take for a startup to reach positive cash flow.

business = *exchange.*

business combination = *merger.*

business day one day of trading, which includes morning and afternoon sessions. ***Also***: market day. **See**: *trade day.*

businessman's investment = *medium grade.*

business paper = *commercial paper.*

busted convertible a *convertible* security the convertibility is worthless because the underlying is low in price. ***Also***: fixed income equivalent.

busted planned amortization class bond a *PAC bond* of a *collateralized mortgage obligation* with prepayment range above the market rates.

busted takeover a highly leveraged takeover, the acquirer's assets must be sold to repay the loan which financed the takeover. ***Also***: bust-up takeover. **See**: *bootstrap sale.*

bust up proxy proposal = *proxy fight.*

bust-up takeover = *busted takeover.*

butterfly a strategy which trades only bonds with medium maturities, excludes short-term or long-term bonds. **Opp**: *barbell strategy.* **See**: *laddered maturity strategy.*

butterfly spread <1> the spread created by the combination of a straddle and a strangle. <2> the bond investment strategy which involves 3 similar bonds with different durations. <3> buying 2 options with high and low strikes and selling 2 options with middle strikes. ***Also***: alligator spread. **Opp**: *sandwich spread.* **See**: *box spread.*

butterfly transaction <Canada> = *divisive D reorganization.*

buy <1> a rating that recommends others to buy a stock. ***Also***: buy rating. <2> = *cash out.*

buy active the futures-spot index premium value at which buy programs should be prevalent.

buy and hold a strategy of accumulating shares in a given company over the year. ***Also***: buy-and-hold strategy; buy and put aside. **See**: *for stock*; *in and out*; *position trader.*

buy-and-hold strategy = *buy and hold.*

buy and put aside = *buy and hold.*

buy-and-write strategy an option strategy which involves buying stocks and then selling covered call options.

buy-at-the-low option = *lookback call.*

buyback (BB) = *bond buyback.*

buy-back clause a clause in a contract allowing the holder to unwind an OTC derivative contract before maturity.

buydown = *point.*

buyer 60 contract a contract under which, the buyer of stock at a higher-than-the-market price with the right to pay for the stock 60 days later. **See**: *forward purchase underwriting.*

buyer of the swap = *swap buyer.*

buyer's call the right given to a buyer to establish a cash price at an agreed number of points above or below the contract price of a predetermined futures month.

buyer's market = *depressed market.*

buyer's option (BO) <1> = *call option.* <2> = *option-delivery contract.*

buyer's right to pay fixed swaption = *payer's swaption.*

buy hedge = *long hedge.*

buying a butterfly = *long butterfly.*

buying basis the difference between the cost of a cash commodity and the futures contract sold to hedge it. ***Also***: basis.

buying hedge = *long hedge.*

buying in <1> when a seller does not deliver the securities, the buyer obtains shares from other sources. <2> closing a short position by buying back what is sold. <3> = *closing purchase.*

buying long buying goods or securities in expectation of price rise. ***Also***: bull; bull buying; bull purchase; for long account; going long; long purchase.

buying offer = *bid.*

buying on margin buying without paying full price. ***Also***: margin buying; on account buying; on balance buying.

buying out the payment of a swap's market value to the net creditor in order to close out the transaction.

buying power = *excess margin.*

buying tender = *takeover bid.*

buying the index = *indexing.*

buy-in management buyout (BIMBO) a form of management buyout under which capital is from the existing managers and outside venture capitalists.

buyout the purchase of the controlling interest in a company. ***Also***: buy up. **See**: *leveraged buyout*; *management buyout.*

buyout fund the fund set up to acquire the entire outstanding shares of a company. ***Also***: LBO fund.

buy program the simultaneous purchase of all the stocks in the index and the sale of the index's futures contract.

buy rating = *buy.*

buy right strategy a strategy of buying a security and then selling an at-the-money call. **See**: *covered call writing.*

buy signal a technical signal that indicates it is a time to buy. ***Also***: signal to buy. ***Opp***: *sell signal.*

buy threshold the minimal futures - spot index premium value at which *buy programs* might be initiated.

buy up = *buyout.*

buy-write = *covered call.*

buy-write option unitary derivative (BOUND) a companion to *LEAPS* proposed to fill the gap created by the expiration of *Humpty Dumpty fund* components. **See**: *Americus trust unit.*

by bidding = *bidding up.*

C c

C <1> abbreviation for March in put option. <2> Nasdaq descriptor meaning exempt from listing requirements. <3> option strike price code for 15.

c bond rating with quality lower than CC.

Ca = *CC.*

Caa = *CCC.*

cabinet bid a deal not made on the floor and that transacts an out-of-the-money option contract for one cent.

cabinet crowd an NYSE members who deal in inactive bonds. ***Also***: inactive bond crowd. ***Opp***: *active bond crowd.*

cabinet security a bond or stock that is listed on a major exchange but not actively traded. **See**: *inactive stock.*

cabinet trade a trade that allows traders to liquidate non-active deep out-of-the-money options by trading at half tick.

cable rate = *short rate.*

cacall = *call on a call.*

CAGR compound annual growth rate

calculation agent a party given the responsibility for ensuring the correct calculation of payment for derivatives.

calculation date the date for calculation of the cash settlement amount.

calculation frequency the intervals at which calculations are made for payment based on an index.

calendar dates of coming new issues.

calendar arbitrage = *arbitrage in time.*

calendar call buying long term call such as LEAP and selling shorter term calls. ***Also***: calendar call spread. **See**: calendar put.

calendar call spread = *calendar call.*

calendar condor the combination of calendar spread and reverse calendar spread in multiple months.

calendar option arbitrage the option arbitrage that involves selling near term options and buying longer term options in different exchanges.

calendar put buying long term put such as LEAP and selling near term put. **See**: *calendar call.*

calendar roll the combination where a position is closed in one month and opened on the same side of the market in a more distant calendar month.

calendar spread = *time spread.*

call <1> the payment demand of stock subscribed. ***Also***: leviation. <2> = *call money.* <3> = *call option.*

callable bond the bond which may be redeemed whenever the issuer wishes. ***Also***: optional bond; redeemable bond. **See**: *bullet bond*; *put bond.*

callable CDS a credit default swap that allows one party to buy a third-party protection against the counterparty's default. ***Also:*** callable default swap. **See**: *protection call.*

callable default swap = *callable CDS.*

callable forward = *break forward.*

callable option a long call or long put subject to a short call retained by the writer of the long option.

callable security a bond or a preferred stock that can be redeemed by the issuer. ***Also***: redeemable security.

callable step-up note a callable debt issue that features one or more increases in a fixed rate or a step-up in a spread over a benchmark in the life of the note. ***Also***: step-up coupon note.

callable swap a swap that can be canceled by participants. ***Also***: collapsible swap. ***See***: *cancellable swap.*

call-adjusted yield = *option-adjusted yield.*

call an option to exercise a call option.

call bear spread = *bear call spread.*

call bull spread = *bull call spread.*

call credit spread = *bear call spread*

call date the day before the maturity on which the issuer demands redemption of a bond. ***Also***: redemption date.

call debit spread = *bull call spread.*

called away <1> an option exercised when writers must surrender the underlying. <2> a bond redeemed before maturity. <3> the delivery required on short sale.

called-up capital <UK> that portion of the *unpaid capital* called to be paid. ***See***: *contributed capital*; *partly paid share*; *uncalled capital.*

call feature = *call provision.*

call IV implied volatility for call options.

call LEAPS the LEAPS to buy. ***See***: *put LEAPS.*

call loan = *call money.*

call loan rate = *call money rate.*

call market an *auction market* in which bids are collected for batch rather than continuous execution. ***Also***: Walrasian market. ***See***: *continuous auction market.*

call monetization realizing the value of a call embedded in a fixed rate security prior to the option's maturity.

call money (CM) a demand loan made to brokers. ***Also***: broker's collateral loan; broker's loan; call; call loan; loan at call; money at call; money at call and short notice; redeemable loan; street loan. ***See***: *demand loan.*

call money rate the market interest rate charged on call money. ***Also***: broker loan rate; broker's call; broker's loan rate; call loan rate. ***See***: *overnight financing rate*; *overnight rate.*

call-money swap = *overnight index swap.*

call of more option = *double option.*

call on a call a call with an embedded option to buy another *call.* ***Also***: ca-call.

call on a put a call option with an option to buy a put option on the same underlying. ***Also***: caput.

call on the maximum an option with a payoff based on the difference between a predetermined strike price and the best performance asset in a portfolio.

call on the worst of n-asset an option to purchase the worst performing asset in a portfolio of assets.

call option (CO) option giving the buyer the right to buy 100 shares of stock or other assets from the writer at a stated price at any time before the deadline in exchange for a premium. ***Also***: buyer's option; call. ***See***: *put option.*

call option buy/sell ratio the call option buying volume divided by the call selling volume.

call option with rebate = *up-and-out call.*

call or put (COP) = *as-you-like option.*

call OTM premium added to the value of out-of-the-money calls to make it above those implied by a smile.

call premium <1> the amount by which the call price exceeds the issue price of a callable bond. ***Also***: redemption premium. <2> the amount that the buyer of a call option has to pay to the option seller.

call price the price at which a callable security may be called for redemption. ***Also***: rate of redemption; redemption price.

call protection the period during which a bond can not be redeemed by the issuer. ***Also***: cushion; hard call protection.

call protection swap a bond swap created from a bond with a shorter call protection to a bond with a longer call protection.

call provision the provision allowing a bond to be redeemed before maturity. ***Also***: call feature; redemption provision. ***See***: *redemption privilege.*

call purchase = *seller's call.*

call ratio backspread the purchase of 2 or more calls at one strike price and the sale of a call option at a lower strike price. ***See***: *put ratio backspread.*

call ratio spread the sale of two or more calls at one strike price and the purchase of one call option at a lower strike price.

call risk the combination of cash flow risk and reinvestment risk.

call spread the spread which consists of partially risk-offsetting long and short positions in at least two different calls on the same underlying asset.

calls underwritten by Swanbrook = *CUBS.*

call swaption = *payer's swaption.*

call warrant a *bond warrant* giving the holder the right to buy the underlying for an agreed price before a given date.

Calmar ratio the ratio calculated as the compounded annual return divided by the maximum drawdown.

cambist an expert on exchange rates. ***Also***: foreign exchange trader.

CAMPS cumulative auction market preferred stock

Canada bond <Canada> a noncallable Government bond with fixed coupon. ***Also***: fixed-coupon marketable bond.

Canada call = *doomsday call.*

Canada note <Canada> a promissory note denominated in US dollars issued by a Canadian firm.

Canada premium bond (CPB) <Canada> a bond issued by the Government which offers an interest rate higher than a *Canada savings bond.*

Canada savings bond (CSB) <Canada> the savings bond issued by a Canadian bank that provides a competitive rate guaranteed for one or more years.

cancellable forward exchange contract = *break forward.*

cancellable option = *break forward.*

cancellable swap a swap which can be canceled by the fixed-rate receiver. ***See***: *callable swap.*

cancellation <1> the termination of a derivative contract with a counterparty. <2> <UK> any payment received from the cancellation of a share option.

can crowd the bond specialists who trade cabinet securities.

cap <1> the highest price at which the underwriters are willing to make an offering. <2> a derivative that ensures a maximum interest rate over a period. <3> the maximum interest rate. ***Also***: ceiling; interest cap; interest rate cap; interest rate condom; rate cap. ***See***: *floor.* <4> = *caption.*

cap and floor = *collar.*

CAPE cash adjusted price/earnings ratio

cap interval the amount between the strike price and the cap price.

capital = *net worth.*

capital adequacy a risk management concept which requires the capital of a company be sufficient to protect its counterparties and depositors from risks.

capital and interest = *accumulated amount.*

capital appreciation bond (CAB) a Z-bond issued by Salomon Brothers, Inc.

capital appreciation fund = *aggressive growth fund.*

capital asset pricing model (CAPM) a model that links together the risk and return of assets.

capital builder account (CBA) Merrill Lynch investment account that allows the owner to access the loan value of securities held.

capital distribution = *return of capital.*

capital dividend the dividend paid out of capital rather than earnings. ***Also***: dividend out of capital; interest out of capital; paid in dividend.

capital duty <UK> a stamp duty on the equity certificate of a company.

capital employed (CE) <UK> = *net worth.*

capital equity = *partner's equity.*

capital gain (CG) the excess of the selling price over its purchase price of a *capital asset.* ***Also***: income of capital.

capital gains yield the return on a stock as a result of price change.

capital guarantee structure an investment product the final value of which has a guaranteed minimum, created with a zero coupon and option spread.

capital in cash = *free capital.*

capital increment the amount by which net value per unit of a fund has increased after being held for a period.

capital instrument an instrument that is issued as a means of raising capital.

capital interest = *dividend.*

Capital International index an index by Morgan Stanley that tracks major stock markets worldwide.

capital issue an issue of shares of stock other than the debt instruments. ***Also***: equity issue.

capitalization <1> the inclusion of the brokerage fee in the cost of an investment in securities. <2> the conversion of a company's retained earnings into its capital, usually by issuing more shares. <3> owner's capital plus debt capital. ***Also***: total capital. <4> = *market capitalization.*

capitalization issue = *bonus issue.*

capitalization method a method under which the manager of a mutual fund purchases blue chip shares in the stock index in proportion to their market capitalization.

capitalization of income the method of determining the value of a business by dividing the present value of future income by the average rate of return. ***Also***: capitalized earnings approach.

capitalization rate = *discount rate.*

capitalization ratios the ratios showing what percentage of capital is debt, preferred stock, common stock, and other equity. ***Also***: financial leverage ratios.

capitalization weighted index the stock index in which each component stock affects the index in proportion to its market capitalization. ***Also***: market value weighted index.

capitalization weighting computing an index that gives more weight to the securities with greater capitalization. ***Also***: value weighting.

capitalized earnings approach = *capitalization of income.*

capitalized option = *contingent premium option.*

capitalized value the estimated value of an asset calculated by reference to its current annual earnings. ***Also***: economic value; present value.

capital leverage the effect on EPS when a large amount of income must be paid for bond interest or for preferred dividends. ***See***: *financial leverage*; *operating leverage*; *Wall Street leverage.*

capital loss excess of the cost price over the selling price of a capital asset.

capital market (CM) a place for raising long term capital, both debt and equity capital. ***See***: *money market.*

capital market line (CML) the tangent line to the *efficient frontier* which represents the relationship between risk and the required return for the *super efficient portfolio.* ***Also***: market line; securities market line; security market line.

capital net worth = *net worth.*

capital position = *financial position.*

capital redemption yield the difference between the cost and the cash received on redemption at par of a stock.

capital risk = *Herstatt risk.*

capital share the share issued by a dual purpose fund, the holders receive long-term capital gains. ***See***: *income share.*

capital stock the capital raised by issuing equity stocks. ***Also***: corporate capital; real capital; stockholder's capital.

capital stock certificate = *stock certificate.*

capital structure <1> the make-up of liabilities and owners' equities of a firm. <2> = *equity-debt ratio.*

capital structure arbitrage an arbitrage that seeks to profit from inconsistencies in the relative pricing of a firm's debt and equity.

capital structure expenditure = *cost of flotation.*

capital turnover = *equity turnover.*

capital turnover rate = *equity turnover.*

capitulation = *unloading.*

caplet <1> an interest rate option to pay a fixed interest in the forward agreement. <2> one call component of a strip of call options. ***Opp***: *floorlet.*

cap option = *capped-style option.*

capped call a call option with maximum payoff equal to the strike price plus a cap interval.

capped floater the *floating rate note* the maximum rate of which is fixed.

capped index option the option with *European style exercise* plus an early exercise price trigger.

capped lookback call a *call option* with a lookback *strike price* and a cap on the settlement price or settlement rate of interest.

capped option = *capped-style option.*

capped put a put option with maximum payoff equal to the strike price less a cap interval.

capped-style option an option that must be exercised before expiration when the underlying asset's price hits a given level. ***Also***: cap option; capped option. ***See***: *automatic exercise.*

capped swap an interest rate swap with an embedded cap on the floating rate leg. ***Also***: rate-capped swap.

capping selling, by a person who has sold calls, of the underlying to depress its value and thus discourage the exercise of the calls sold. ***See***: *mini-manipulation.*

cap rate the strike rate set in a cap option. ***Also***: ceiling rate.

CAPS convertible adjustable preferred stock

caption an option to buy a *cap* to lock in the rate of interest. ***Also***: cap; interest rate caption.

caput <1> = *call on a put.* <2> = *exotic option.*

CAR certificate on automobile receivables

car <1> the amount of a commodity that underlies a future. <2> = *future.*

CARB convertible adjustable rate bond

CARD certificate of amortizing revolving debt

CARP controlled adjustable rate preferred stock

CARPS convertible auction rate preferred stock

carried interest the portion of any gains realized by a mutual fund to which the fund managers are entitled.

carrier bond = *host bond.*

carrot-and-stick bond the convertible bond issued with a low conversion premium.

carry <1> to record a purchase in the books so that it can be matched with a forward sale. <2> the difference between the financing cost and the purchase cost minus the cash yield from securities. ***Also***: cost of carry; net financing cost. **See**: *negative carry; positive carry.*

carry arbitrage = *basis trading.*

carry income and loss the difference between the interest yield of a portfolio and the cost of the funds supporting the portfolio. ***Also***: running margin.

carrying amount the par value of a bond issue less any unamortized discount or plus unamortized premium.

carrying charge <1> the cost of storing the physical commodities. ***Also***: cost of carry; holding cost. <2> = *contango.*

carrying charge market = *contango.*

carrying-over day = *continuation day.*

carrying value = *book value.*

carry-over (CO) delaying of the settlement of a trade from one account day to the next. ***Also***: continuation.

carryover day = *continuation day.*

carry trade borrowing money from one country in one currency and converting funds to invest in securities in another country with higher interest rates.

Carter bond a bond issued in Germany and Switzerland in 1978 as a means of obtaining foreign exchange by the US government.

cartwheel an option spread that is long (or short) a ratio call spread and short (or long) a ratio put spread.

carve-out = *partial spinoff.*

cash adjusted price / earnings ratio (CAPE) the P/E of a company with a lot of cash, adjusted to reflect the value of the cash portion of the stock.

cash and carry a tax avoidance method in which an investor buys and holds a security, and sells short of the same security at a higher price and treats the interests paid as a deductible expense.

cash and carry arbitrage = *basis trading.*

cash and carry trade = *basis trading.*

cash and new the method by which an investor negates the position and returns to it in the next account day.

cash-at-expiry option <UK> the binary option with a payoff equal to a fixed cash amount once the price of the underlying breaches the strike price.

cash-at-hit option <UK> binary option with an immediate payoff equal to a fixed payoff once the price of the underlying breaches the strike price.

cash bond the bond issued by banks of Switzerland in denomination of 500, 1000 and 5000 francs, maturing from 2 to 10 years, bearing an interest rate that is higher than that of bank deposit.

cash callable bond a bond that may be called if the refunding can obtain cash.

cash CDO a collateralized debt obligation (CDO) whose collateral comprises cash positions in bonds, loans, or debts. ***See***: *synthetic CDO.*

cash CDO squared a CDO squared whose collateral comprises tranches of cash CDOs. ***See***: *synthetic CDO squared.*

cash collateral account (CCA) the cash position underlying an asset backed security to facilitate meeting cash flow requirements if pool payments lag and to provide additional collateral. ***Also***: collateral investment account.

cash commodity a commodity traded in the *cash market.* ***Also***: actuals; physical commodity; physicals; spot commodity.

cash contract <1> the sales agreement for either immediate or future delivery of the actual product for a designated price. <2> = *cash sale.*

cash credit bond = *bond of credit.*

cash delivery the settlement of a futures contract by cash instead of delivery.

cash dividend the declared dividend that is payable in cash or by check. ***See***: *dividend in kind; property dividend.*

cash down = *delivery versus payment.*

cash equivalent a marketable security, Treasury bill or a banker's acceptance that is considered cash.

cash extraction strategy a strategy under which a position is exchanged for a risk-equivalent derivative position so that cash can be withdrawn from the account.

cash flow CDO a collateralized debt obligation (CDO) with the contingent payments depending on the adequacy of cash flow of the collateral.

cash flow coverage of debt service = *cash flow coverage ratio.*

cash flow coverage ratio the number of times that debts are covered by the *earnings before interest, taxes, depreciation, amortization and rent.* ***Also***: cash flow coverage of debt service.

cash flow hedge a hedge which uses derivative instruments to hedge the risk to variability in the expected future cash flow. ***See***: *fair value hedge.*

cash flow mapping decomposition of a portfolio's cash flows into the maturity buckets that correspond to the timing of cash flows. ***See***: *duration mapping.*

cash flow matching a risk management method that attempts to buy a portfolio with periodic cash flows equal to expected liabilities. ***Also***: cash matching; dedicated portfolio; dedicating a portfolio. ***See***: *duration matching.*

cash flow option loan = *exotic loan.*

cash flow swap the swap with irregular cash flows generated by the specifically designated instruments or investment.

cash forward a contract whereby the buyer and the seller agree upon the delivery of a commodity at a future date. ***Also***: cash forward contract; cash forward sale; forward cash contract.

cash forward contract = *cash forward.*

cash forward sale = *cash forward.*

cash fraction <UK> a distribution to a shareholder from the proceeds of selling the fractional shares after a merger.

cash-futures swap = *exchange of spot.*

cash in <1> to sell the securities or other assets for cash. ***Also***: sell. <2> = *clear.*

cash-index arbitrage = *index arbitrage.*

cash index participations (CIPs) = *index participations.*

cash in lieu (CIL) cash paid to stockholders of the target company in lieu of the shares from the acquirer.

cash instrument = *primary instrument.*

cashless collar a *collar* created by buying a put and immediately selling out-of-the-money call, with the strike of the call set so that the premium received is enough to pay for the cost of the put. ***Also***: costless collar; costly collar; forward band; worthless collar; zero-cost collar. **See**: *free trade*; *income-producing collar*; *zero cost option.*

cashless exercise converting options into stock that requires no initial cash payment to cover the *strike price.*

cash LIBOR spread the basis point measured from LIBOR in the spot market.

cash loan a loan which commences immediately.

cash management account (CMA) the brokerage account with checking privileges. ***Also***: money market account.

cash management bill the Treasury bill issued in 1975 by the US government to raise short-term fund.

cash market a market place where actual commodities are traded. ***Also***: actual market; physical market; spot market. **See**: *futures market.*

cash market arbitrage the arbitrage in space done in actual commodities in the spot market.

cash matching = *cash flow matching.*

cash offer an offer to acquire a target company by payment in cash. **See**: *exchange offer.*

cash on cash return = *current yield.*

cash-on-cash yield <1> total distribution paid on a trust divided by the market value of trust assets. <2> = *current yield.*

cash on delivery (COD) = *delivery versus payment.*

cash on delivery option = *contingent premium option.*

cash-only instrument a bond that can be redeemed or exercised for cash at the holder's discretion.

cash only market meaning the trading in certain securities is on cash basis, that is payment must be made in cash.

cash-or-nothing binary a binary option that is either *European cash-or-nothing binary* or *American cash-or-nothing binary.*

cash-or-nothing call the option with a fixed payoff if the final price of the underlying asset is above the strike price, if not, the payoff is zero. **See**: *asset-or-nothing call.*

cash-or-nothing put the option whose payoff is set to a specified fixed price if the final asset price is below the strike price, if not, the payoff is set to zero. **See**: *asset-or-nothing put.*

cash or titles option (COTO) <Switzerland> a convertible with an expiration date up to 12 months and the holder has the option to receive a cash dividend or exchange for new shares at a set price.

cash out <1> to invest in the stock market. ***Also***: buy. <2> to get money out when refinancing an existing mortgage.

cash-out call option with rebate = *up-and-out call.*

cash plus convertible the convertible that requires cash on conversion.

cash position the percentage of a fund's assets invested in short-term securities. ***Also***: liquid position.

cash price = *spot price.*

cash sale the deal on the floor of an exchange that calls for delivery of stocks sold the same day. ***Also***: cash contract. ***See***: *regular way trade.*

cash secured put = *covered put.*

cash-settled contract the commodity futures contract that is settled by cash other than by deliver of goods.

cash settled option the option settled for cash the difference between strike price and the market price of the underlying at the time of exercise.

cash-settled put a put enabling holders to receive cash at expiration date.

cash settlement <1> the buyer has to pay on the next day, not the next settlement day. <2> satisfying a future with the cash value of the commodity. <3> = *same day settlement.*

cash transaction a spot transaction to be settled in cash. ***Also***: same day transaction; value today.

cash value option the right of a life insurance policyholder to take the cash surrender value at a given time.

catastrophe bond the bond that pays a lower coupon after a catastrophe. ***Also***: Act-of-Devil bond; Act-of-God bond; disaster bond.

catastrophe call early redemption of a municipal bond because of catastrophe. ***See***: *extraordinary call.*

catastrophe derivative the derivative used to hedge against the natural catastrophes. ***Also***: CAT derivative.

catastrophe insurance option an option the underlying asset of which is a set of loss indexes by Property Claim Services.

CAT derivative = *catastrophe derivative.*

CATS certificate of accrual on Treasury securities

cats and dogs highly speculative stocks that have short histories of sales in the past.

CAT spread a contract traded in CBOT that takes the form of an option on a catastrophe futures contract using a call spread as the basis.

CBO collateralized bond obligation

CBOE Nasdaq Volatility Index (VXN) the volatility index on CBOE, known by its ticker "VXN", a measure of the implied volatility for the Nasdaq 100.

CBOE Volatility Index (VIX) a volatility index for CBOE, it is the weighted average of the implied volatilities from eight calls and puts on the S&P index. ***Also***: Market Volatility Index.

CC the rating of bonds or credit swap that are highly speculative, lower than CCC. ***Also***: Ca.

CCC bond rating that is poor or default, lower than B. ***Also***: Caa.

CDO <1> a credit derivative that transfers the credit risk on a portfolio of collateralized debt obligations. ***See***: *cash CDO; single tranche CDO; synthetic CDO.* <2> collateralized debt obligation.

CDO^2 = *CDO squared.*

CDO^3 = *CDO cubed.*

CDO cubed a CDO on a CDO squared. ***Also***: CDO^3; CDO of CDOs of CDOs; CDO of CDO squared.

CDO equity the equity tranche in a CDO.

CDO^n a CDO cubed or higher.

CDO of CDOs = *CDO squared.*

CDO of CDOs of CDOs = *CDO cubed.*

CDO of CDO squared = *CDO cubed.*

CDO option a credit option to purchase a tranche in a pool of the collateralized debt obligations. ***Also***: option on CDO tranche.

CDO over CDO squared a CDO that is underlied by a CDO squared.

CDO squared a tranche of CDO in which the collateral is made up of a mixture of asset-backed securities and sub tranches of synthetic CDOs. ***Also***: CDO^2; CDO of CDOs; CDOs-squared; two-layer CDO.

CDOs-squared = *CDO squared.*

CDO tranche a class of CDO within a complex structured synthetic CDO structure.

CDR <1> collateralized depository receipt. <2> continental depositary receipt.

CDS <1> contingent deferred swap; <2> credit default swap.

CDS option an option to buy CDS. ***Also***: option on CDS.

CDS portfolio a derivative that enables investors to go long or short a portfolio of CDS in one transaction.

CDS spread the basis point that the credit protection buyer pays the premium leg.

cease and desist order the order from the SEC to halt an ongoing practice against the SEC rules. ***See***: *distringas notice.*

ceiling = *cap.*

ceiling rate = *cap rate.*

Central Registration Depository (CRD) NASD sponsored computerized system for the recording of registration.

cents per share a dividend or a mutual fund's distribution that the shareholder receives for each share owned.

century bond a bond issued by a firm with a maturity of 100 years.

CEO collateralized lease equipment obligation.

certain rate = *forward exchange rate.*

certainty equivalent <1> the amount that would be accepted today in lieu of the chance to receive a higher, but uncertain amount. <2> zero-risk return an investor would trade for a specified larger return with an associated risk.

certificate = *stock certificate.*

certificated stock the inventory of the commodity which has been inspected and proven to be of such quality as to be delivered against futures contracts.

certificateless municipal the municipal bond with no certificate of ownership.

certificate of accrual on Treasury securities (CATS) = *separately traded registered interest and principal securities.*

certificate of amortizing revolving debt (CARD) asset-backed instrument with consumer credit card obligations as the collateral. ***Also***: credit card receivable-backed security.

certificate of beneficial interest (CBI) a statement of shares when such shares have been deposited with a trustee.

certificate of bonds a certificate issued to the holder of registered bonds stating that certain bonds have been registered. ***Also***: bond certificate.

certificate of capital stock = *stock certificate.*

certificate of deposit (CD) a negotiable receipt payable to depositor for funds held in a bank. ***Also***: deposit certificate; deposit receipt.

certificate of government receipts (COUGAR) (COUGR) = *separately traded registered interest and principal securities.*

certificate of indebtedness <1> a short term note issued by a government. <2> an unsecured promissory note, the holder of which has a general creditor's recourse against the issuer's assets.

certificate of inscription a certificate representing ownership in *inscribed stock.*

certificate of interest = *bond coupon.*

certificate of liability = *bond.*

certificate of stock = *stock certificate.*

certificate on automobile receivables (CAR) the pass-through securities that are backed by car loan receivables.

CEV <1> constant elasticity of volatility. <2> credit enhanced vehicle. <3> credit equivalent value.

CEW currency exchange warrant

CFD contract for difference

CFO <1> cancel former order. <2> chief financial officer.

CFTC Commodity Futures Trading Commission

chain weighted index = *Fisher index.*

chameleon option an option which has the ability to change structure should certain predetermined terms be met.

change over = *swap.*

changer member of an exchange which functions as an arbitrageur under special permission, who has the right to buy or sell a given commodity executed on the floor of another exchange.

chaos theory the theory which seeks to forecast the future path of stock prices, including sudden changes that occur in periods of intense market activity.

characteristic portfolio a portfolio that represents particular characteristics.

charge for credit = *interest.*

charge for trouble = *commission.*

charm the change in delta over time.

Chase secured loan trust note (CSLT) a note that offers syndicated leveraged loan return by credit derivatives.

chastity bond a bond designed to prevent unwanted takeovers by maturing at par once a takeover is complete.

cheapest to deliver (CTD) a bond the price of which gives the seller the highest return when he buys it to deliver against a bond future that is expiring soon. ***Also***: best bond to deliver.

cheap option an option the volatility of which is low. ***Also***: option with low volatility. ***See***: *expensive option.*

cheap stock a stock which is sold at a price lower than its true value while the company is still in development stage. ***See***: *penny stock.*

cheat sheet the financial document supplied to a prospective investor by a bank without reporting to the SEC.

checking the market asking a number of firms for their quote on a security to determine the best bid or offer.

check rate = *short rate.*

check trading buying a banker's check and selling it to another person who will get paid in installment basis.

check writing a mutual fund service feature which allows shareholders to write a check to redeem shares.

cherry picking <1> choosing stock that performed well in another portfolio in anticipation that the trend will continue. <2> attempting to have the bankruptcy court honor derivative contracts that benefit the defaulting party.

CHESS Clearing House Electronic Subregister System

Chicago Board of Trade (CBOT) the largest futures exchange in the USA.

Chicago Board Options Exchange (CBOE) the official exchange for the public trading of standardized options.

Chicago Mercantile Exchange (CME) an organization which provides a location for trading futures and options, collects and disseminates market information, maintains clearing mechanism, and enforces trading rules.

chief risk officer (CRO) the person who is responsible for risk management in an organization.

child company = *subsidiary.*

China concept stock the stock of a firm the assets, business activities or earnings of which have significant activities in China.

Chinese arbitrage = *reverse hedge.*

Chinese hedge a hedge in which one is short the convertible security and long the underlying asset, in the hope that the convertible's premium may fall. ***See***: *reverse hedge*; *setup.*

Chinese market a market where traders are willing to buy above the lowest offer, or sell below the highest bid, only in significant quantities.

Chinese trading the method of trading OTC securities under which the trader attempts to negotiate the price for a stock after the price has been set by the market maker.

Chinese wall brokerage firm's invisible works and procedures designed to obstruct the flow of inside information to the public. ***Also***: ethical wall; firewall; green baize door.

Chinese water torture tactic a form of taking over a company by gradually buying a majority interest from the shares purchased on the exchange. ***See***: *toehold purchase.*

CHIPS common-linked higher income participation security.

choice <UK> a price where the bid and ask are the same.

choice LIBOR swap a swap which gives the floating rate receiver the right to receive the higher of LIBOR set at the beginning or at the end of the period.

choice market a market in which the bid equals the ask price. ***Also***: locked market. ***See***: *crossed market.*

choice min-max option the *compound option* giving the holder the right to lock into a rate range by exercising an option to buy an *interest rate collar*, *range forward*, or *equity risk reversal.*

chooser flexible cap a *flexible cap* that lets the holder save caplets for later use if the reference rate is only slightly above the cap rate on an early reset date. ***See***: *auto-flexible cap.*

chooser option = *as-you-like option.*

chooser swap a swap with a range option payout embedded in a floating rate, the receiver has the ability to set the mid-point of the range on each reset date.

chop the bid-ask spread in a chop stock.

chop house a dealer in chop stock.

chop stock micro-cap stock that can be easily manipulated by the speculators. ***See***: *penny stock.*

Christmas tree = *table top.*

chumming the trading between market makers to create false appearance of increasing volume. ***See***: *manipulation.*

churning <1> the excessive buying and selling by a broker in the discretionary accounts to generate commission. ***Also***: churning and burning; overtrading; twisting. ***See***: *in and out.* <2> frequently transferring property in order to increase its value and qualify it for higher depreciation.

churning and burning = *churning.*

CIA collateral investment account

CIF corporate income fund

CINS = *cusip code.*

CIPs cash index participations

circle to contact a client who indicates an interest in buying a new issue. ***See***: *indication of interest.*

circuit breaker the measure used by the exchange to stop trading when the price has fallen a certain percentage in a given period of trading. ***See***: *shock absorber.*

circular trading the fraudulent scheme under which sell orders are entered by a broker who knows that offsetting buy orders have been or will be entered.

circus a derivative created by combining an interest rate swap with a foreign currency swap.

circus option = *cross-currency swaption.*

circus swap a fixed-rate currency swap against a floating rate payment in another currency. ***Also***: combined interest rate and currency swap; fixed-floating swap. ***See***: *cross-currency cross-index basis swap.*

citizen bond a US municipal bond in denominations of $1,000.

CIV collective investment vehicle

class <1> bonds, or stocks having similar features, such as class A stock, preferred stock, etc. <2> = *option class.*

class A share one class of mutual fund share with identical features, such as *front-end load.* ***See***: *A share.*

class A stock a class of common stock which has advantage over the class B stock in terms of voting power. ***See***: *voting stock.* (In UK, *A share* has no voting power, while in the USA class A stock has voting power). ***See***: *series A.*

class B share one class of mutual fund share with identical features, such as *back-end load.*

class B stock a common stock which ranks behind A stock in terms of voting power. ***See***: *B share*; *nonvoting stock.* (In UK *B share* has voting power, in US class B stock has no voting power).

classic bear squeeze = *bear squeeze.*

classified stock an equity stock divided into categories with different rights, e. g. A stock has voting power and B stock does not. ***Also***: multiple voting share.

class of options = *option class.*

class of shares the mutual fund shares with identical features, e. g. A shares may have front-end load and B shares may have back-end load, etc.

class option = *option class.*

clawback = *dividend clawback.*

clawback-equity call a bond indenture clause that allows an issuer to redeem a portion of the bond, at a premium plus accrued interest, with the proceeds of a public equity offering.

clean <1> referring to a price of a stock quoted excluding accrued interest. <2> a deal that matches corresponding buy or sell orders to avoid the block positioner inventory risk. ***Also***: natural.

clean asset swap an asset swap in which one party takes the default risk only. ***See***: *perfect asset swap.*

clean balance sheet balance sheet of a company with very little or no debt.

clean float = *free float.*

clean hedge instrument the derivative that can be hedged with liquid exchange-traded securities so that the market risk remains relatively constant. ***See***: *dirty hedge instrument.*

clean price the newspaper quoted bond price excluding accrued interest. ***Also***: ex interest quotation; flat price; net parity. ***See***: *dirty price.*

clean risk the risk to which an investor is exposed when a contract matures and it pays out according to its own obligations before it is certain that payment by the counterpart will be met.

clean up to buy or sell all the remaining supply of stock in order to have a zero position.

cleanup = *exorbitant profit.*

cleanup call the provision of an asset-backed security that permits the issuer to call it at par when the value of the collateral drops to a specified level.

clean your shirt <verb> to clear prior obligations in a security.

clear <verb><1> to make a profit. ***Also***: cash in. <2> to settle a trade.

clearing <1> exchanging of checks and drafts and settling only the balances at the end of the day. <2> comparison of the details of a transaction for accuracy between two brokers before settlement.

clearing agency a person who acts as an intermediary or agent in making payments or deliveries of securities or both.

clearing association = *clearing house.*

clearing broker = *clearing member.*

clearing fee a fee charged by a clearing house for the clearing services provided in a given period.

clearing house the central office where the commodity, foreign exchange and stock exchange transactions are settled. ***Also***: clearing association.

clearing house fund the fund from the Federal Reserve System that requires 3 days to clear between banks. ***Also***: 3-day fund.

clearing house system a system where everyone deals through clearing house.

clearing margin the deposit to ensure that *clearing members* perform on their customers' open positions.

clearing member a member of a futures exchange who is also a member of the clearing house. ***Also***: clearing broker.

clearing price in a discriminatory price auction, the price from the lowest successful bidder. ***Also***: stop-out price.

clientele effect the tendency of funds or investments to be followed by groups of investors with a similar preference.

cliquet option an option that locks in gains at prescribed time intervals. ***Also***: ratchet option. ***See***: *ladder option.*

CLN credit link note

CLO collateralized loan obligation

cloaked orders = *hidden orders.*

clone fund a *fund* set up in a *fund family* to emulate another successful fund.

close the end of a trading cession.

close combination the combination of corporations whereby the stockholders relinquish the stock to a board of trustees who then issue certificates and cash dividends. ***Also***: trust.

closed-end fund the investment firm with a fixed number of shares issued outstanding traded like stocks issued by companies. ***Also***: closed-end investment trust; closed-end mutual fund; closed-end trust; closed fund; publicly-traded fund. ***See***: *open-end fund.*

closed-end investment trust = *closed-end fund.*

closed-end management company an investment company with only one set of shares or other classes of assets under active management.

closed-end mutual fund = *closed-end fund.*

closed-end preferred fund a closed-end fund that invests in corporate preferred stock only.

closed-end trust <Australia> = *closed-end fund.*

closed-form VAR = *linear VAR.*

closed fund = *closed-end fund.*

closed position a zero position after a *clean up.*

closed trade a trade transacted by selling a security which has been paid for previously or by bear covering.

closed transaction the transaction the amount on a sale can be established, so that a gain or loss can be realized.

close market the active market with a narrow bid-and-asked spread.

closeout date the date on which an option trader closes his position.

close-out netting the *netting* of debt or obligations on derivatives which are expiring earlier.

close period the time between the completion of financial statements and the date of announcement to the public. ***Also***: lock-in period.

closet index fund a fund constructed to track a benchmark index very closely.

closet indexing investing most of the money in stocks which comprise most of stocks in an index.

close-to-the-money option the option with a strike price that is close to the current market value of the underlying asset. ***Also***: near-the-money option.

closing price the price that is completed at the end of one trading day. ***Also***: last price. ***Opp***: *opening price.*

closing purchase the deal in which an investor liquidates a position by buying an option having the same terms as an option he previously sold. ***Also***: buying in.

closing rate exchange rate at the close of a trading day. ***See***: *opening rate.*

closing sale a deal in which an investor liquidates position by selling an option having exactly the same terms as the one bought.

closing trade = *offsetting trade.*

closing transaction termination of an option holder's liability by closing the sale rather than by exercising it or by abandonment. ***See***: *opening transaction.*

CLOU currency-linked outperformance unit

CMBS commercial mortgage-backed securities

CME Chicago Mercantile Exchange

CMMUs convertible money market units

CMO collateralized mortgage obligation

CMO REIT risky REIT which invests in the residual cash flows of collateralized mortgage obligations (CMOs).

CMO swap the swap based on a specific *CMO* with amortization of the notional linked to the principal repayment rate of a mortgage pool.

CMS <1> common message switch. <2> constant maturity swap.

CMT constant maturity Treasury

CMT/CMS swap the yield curve swap in which one leg is linked to CMT rates.

CMT index constant maturity Treasury index

CMT-LIBOR differential note a medium term note which pays the difference between the yield on a CMT and that on LIBOR.

CMT rate constant maturity Treasury rate

CMT swap = *yield curve swap.*

CNS continuous net settlement

CO an exchange code for *Chicago Board Options Exchange*. ***Also***: WQ.

COATS Canadian OTC Automated Trading System

coattail investing making trades that are similar to the trades of successful investors.

COC cost of carry

cock date = *broken date.*

cockroach theory a theory which holds that bad news, such as adverse earnings, tends to be released in bunches.

cocktail bond = *dual option bond.*

cocktail swap the swap which involves another swap contract with a third party in the same contract period.

coco contingent convertible

CODM call option deutsche mark

coefficient of variation (CV) a measure of relative dispersion used in comparing the risk of two or more assets with differing expected returns. ***Also***: unitized risk.

COFI <1> Cost of Funds Index. <2> 11th District Cost of Funds Index

COFI swap cost of funds index swap

coherent market hypothesis the hypothesis that the probability density function of a market may be determined by the combination of group sentiment and fundamental bias.

collapsible swap = *callable swap.*

collar <1> buying at- or out-of-the-money calls, and selling at- or out-of-the-money puts simultaneously. ***Also***: cap and floor; collar trade; conversion spread; fence; fence spread; floor-ceiling agreement; mini-max option; min-max option; spread conversion. <2> the lowest interest rate that the bond buyers may accept. <3> the lowest price that an issuer may accept as guarantee for the underwriting. <4> a price range set by two companies before merger. <5> a long position in a stock, a protective put plus a short call. <6> = *curb.* <7> = *interest rate collar.* <8> = *min-max strategy.*

collar bond a bond the floating coupon of which is tied to a benchmark interest rate and with cap and floor. ***Also***: min-max bond.

collared equity the equity share that is acceptable by the bank as collateral.

collared floater = *collared FRN.*

collared FRN a *floating rate note* with an interest rate collar embedded. ***Also***: collared floater; mini-max floater.

collared offer a tender offer that sets an upper limit and lower limit for a number of shares that will be exchanged for one share of the target company.

collared swap a *swap* with a *collar* set on the floating-rate leg. ***Also***: banded swap; collar swap; min-max swap.

collar swap = *collared swap.*

collar trade = *collar.*

collateral securities or other assets that have been pledged by the borrower to secure a debt.

collateral investment account (CIA) = *cash collateral account.*

collateralized bond obligation (CBO) a bond backed by a large, diversified pool of junk bonds.

collateralized debt obligation (CDO) an investment-grade security backed by a pool of bonds, loans, and other assets. ***Also***: collateralized security.

collateralized depositary receipt (CDR) a financial instrument that is secured by another financial instrument with the issuing depository institution.

collateralized increasable yield note the combination of medium-term notes and commodity futures pool designed to produce a guaranteed minimum return.

collateralized lease equipment obligation (CEO)(CLEO) an equipment loan that has been securitized.

collateralized loan obligation (CLO) <1> a structured note collateralized by a portfolio of commercial or personal loans. <2> a *special purpose vehicle* set up with *securitization* payments in the form of tranches.

collateralized mortgage obligation (C-MO) the mortgage-backed bond that has fixed maturity dates, long-term or short-term and a fixed interest rate.

collateralized security = *collateralized debt obligation.*

collateralized swap a swap where one or both parties post collateral with a third party to insure performance.

collateralized trust note the short-term note secured by the assets held in a trust.

collateral security the asset given in addition to a collateral to guarantee the performance of a contract or other agreement.

collateral trust bond a bond secured by other securities which are placed with the trustee by the issuing firm.

collection float the number of shares of a security issued.

collection gain the gain realized when the creditor is paid in an amount greater than the adjusted basis of the debt.

collective fund a fund which combines tax exempt assets of various individuals and organizations in order to create a well diversified portfolio.

collective investment scheme <UK> = *investment club.*

collective investment vehicle (CIV) <Australia> a widely held fixed trust that operates like a mutual fund.

college and university revenue bond a bond secured by dormitory-room rental, tuition and other revenue of colleges.

color a measure of the change in *gamma* in response to the passage of time.

combination <1> = *combination option.* <2> = *merger.*

combination bond a bond backed by the full faith and credit of a government issuing it as well as by the revenue from the projects funded by it.

combination matching an income immunization strategy that uses cash flow matching over the first few years and duration matching thereafter. ***Also***: horizon matching.

combination option the combination of two long options or short options with different expiration dates or strike price. ***Also***: combination; combo. ***See***: *straddle.*

combination yield curve swap a yield curve swap in which the returns from more than one market are swapped for the returns from one market.

combined interest rate and currency swap = *circus swap.*

combo = *combination option.*

Comex <1> Colorado Materials Exchange. <2> Commodity Exchange, Inc.

coming out = *coming to market.*

coming to market of a new security, will be issued soon. ***Also***: coming out.

commercial finance paper = *commercial paper.*

commercial hedger the company that takes futures positions in commodities so that they can guarantee prices at which it will buy materials or sell products.

commercial mortgage-backed security a security backed by the mortgage on commercial not residential properties.

commercial note = *commercial paper.*

commercial paper (CP) an unsecured short term note issued out of a transaction in the ordinary course of business. ***Also***: business paper; commercial finance paper; commercial note; instrument of trade; mercantile paper; trade note; trade paper. **See**: *finance paper.*

commercial real estate CDO a CDO that is backed by the assets in REIT.

commercial risk = *credit risk.*

commercials the shares that are issued by companies in commercial business. **See**: *industrials.*

commingled fund a mutual fund which consists of assets from several accounts blended together. ***Also***: pooled fund; pooled income fund.

commingling <1> mixing the customer-owned securities with those owned by a firm. <2> providing investment funds of individual accounts with each customer who owns a share of the total fund.

Commission = *Securities and Exchange Commission.*

commission the amount paid to a broker for a securities transaction. ***Also***: charge for troubles; premium; rake off; sales fee.

commitment = *open interest.*

commitments = *open interest.*

Committee on Uniform Securities Identification Procedures (CUSIP) the committee that assigns cusip codes for all listed securities.

commoditization the modification of illiquid financial contracts for trading in more liquid and transparent markets. **See**: *securitization.*

commodity an item of trade or commerce in which contracts for the future delivery may be traded or exchanged.

commodity-backed bond the bond the interest rate of which is pegged to the spot price of a commodity.

commodity currency the currency being traded and priced in terms of a *term currency.*

commodity exchange (Comex) the commodity market where all dealings are made except for auction.

commodity-for-interest swap a swap one party agrees to pay the return on a commodity in exchange for receiving a return on a money market rate.

commodity future = *future.*

commodity future contract = *future.*

commodity futures option = *futures option.*

Commodity Futures Trading Commission (CFTC) a federal regulatory agency that administers the Commodity Exchange Act.

commodity index an index measuring the changes in the prices of commodities in the spot market.

commodity-linked bond a *zero coupon bond* the redemption value of which is linked to the price of a commodity. ***Also***: embedded commodity option; embedded option.

commodity option = *futures option.*

commodity pool the company in which funds contributed by a number of investors are combined.

commodity pool operator (CPO) the person or company who originates a commodity pool with unlimited risk. ***Also***: pool operator.

commodity price risk the risk of loss due to fluctuation in the market price of a commodity.

commodity product spread = *crush spread.*

commodity swap the swap in which the floating rate is linked to the price of a specific commodity, e. g. crude oil.

commodity tax straddle the strategy in which an investor profits from a commodity trading, then looks for a capital loss to offset ordinary income.

commodity trading advisor (CTA) an individual who advises others as to the value of or the advisability of buying or selling derivatives. ***Also***: trading advisor.

common code a 9-digit code issued by Euroclear and CEDEL to replace the earlier CEDEL and Euroclear codes.

common dividend the dividend paid to a stockholder of the common stock. ***Also***: common stock dividend; discretionary dividend. **See**: *preferred dividend.*

common equity percent the percentage of common stock and retained earnings to total capital.

common-linked higher income participation security (CHIPS) a *synthetic preferred equity redemption cumulative stock* issued by an intermediary firm.

common stock a stock which represents the ownership interest in a company. ***Also***: equity share; junior equity; ordinary; ordinary share; share of common. **See**: *preferred stock.*

common stock dividend = *common dividend.*

common stock equivalent = *convertible security.*

common stock fund a mutual fund that invests in common stocks only. **See**: *equity fund*; *pure stock fund.*

common stock ratio <1> a ratio of the value of common stock to total capital of a firm. <2> = *equity-to-assets ratio.*

common trust fund a fund that belongs to several owners that is held by a bank as a trustee and is pooled only for investment purpose. ***Also***: pooled trust fund.

commonwealth security a security issued by the Australia government.

companion bond a CMO the principal of which is paid off first due to falling interest rates. ***Also***: support bond.

company-specific risk = *unsystematic risk.*

comparative advantage the ability of a trader to borrow money in a particular market at a preferential rate to his / her competitors or those he is dealing with.

comparison universe a group of fund managers of similar investment style.

compensation for risk = *risk value.*

compensation fund a fund into which members of the stock exchange pay their shares, used to make good losses suffered by investors when a member firm cannot pay its debts.

compensation stock <UK> a government guaranteed stock given to the shareholder as compensation when certain industries were nationalized.

compensatory stock option a low priced employee stock option as a compensation to its holders. ***Opp***: *proprietary stock option.*

competition ahead a situation under which another OTC dealer has transacted with the investment bank before the bid or ask is made.

competitive bid a bid to buy Treasury bills entered by large brokers.

competitive bidding the process under which buyers submit competing bids to the issuer for the new stocks being offered.

competitive offering an offering of new securities through *competitive bidding.*

competitive trader = *floor trader.*

complement rule a rule that says that if two exotic options are held they would replicate the behavior of a standard option.

complete capital market the market in which there is only one security.

complete market a market in which the complete set of variables on future states can be constructed with existing assets.

complete portfolio the entire portfolio, including risky and risk-free assets.

completion fund the fund that invests in stocks that fill the gaps in a portfolio and improve its performance relative to an index. ***Also***: fulfillment fund.

complex chooser option an *as-you-like option* either the strike price or the maturity date is different.

complex option the option with a strike that can change, e. g. a *quanto option.*

complex structured product a financial instrument that contains some embedded complex derivatives that alter risk and return characteristics in a unique way.

complex swap = *advanced swap.*

compliance department a department in a stock exchange to ensure SEC compliance.

COMPO competition compound interest bond

component bond a *collateralized mortgage obligation* with a combination of non-detachable components.

composite average stock average that combines price changes of industrial, railroad, and utility stocks.

composite hedge a hedge that involves more than one hedging instrument.

composite option = *cross option.*

composite swap an equity-linked swap with the equity return denominated in the natural currency of the market.

composite VAR the weighted average of historic VAR, linear VAR, and simulated VAR. ***Also***: blended VAR.

compound accreted value = *accreted value.*

compound annual return = *internal rate of return.*

compound arbitrage the arbitrage that utilizes four or more markets. ***Also***: indirect arbitrage. ***See***: *simple arbitrage.*

compound average rate option the call option to buy a currency at the average rate of exchange.

compound call a call option on the stock of a leveraged company.

compound derivative the derivative that encompasses more than one contractual provision to hedge different risks.

compound exotic the structured note with one or more embedded equity or interest rate components combined with at least one currency component.

compound interest bond the variant of a zero-coupon bond, with actual interest payments reinvested with a municipal issuer at the bond's yield to maturity.

compound option <1> an option which gives the holder the right to enter into another option, such as a *put on a call, call on a put*. ***Also***: nested option; option on an option. ***See***: *double option*; *split-fee option*. <2> = *exotic option*.

compound option strategy an option trading strategy that provides unique and specific results.

compound spread option an option to enter into a spread option.

comprehensive due diligence investigation the investigation of business in connection with a securities offering to determine if the financial information is disclosed in the prospectus.

compression risk the risk of loss from a decline in the yield that triggers call feature on debt or prepayment on mortgage.

concentrated equity position the large position in stock which is difficult to liquidate by traditional means.

concentrated fund a fund representing a portfolio of 30 stocks rather than 100 stocks held by other funds.

concentrated position a position which makes up 40% or more of the market value of a portfolio when the positions are purchased on margin.

concentration of credit risk = *off-balance-sheet risk*.

concentration risk a risk concentrated in financial conglomerates.

concept stock a stock with a huge market-cap-to-revenue ratio.

concern = *stock*.

concertina swap = *rollercoaster swap*.

concession <1> the adjustment of the difference in the book value between the redeemed and the residual shareholders. <2> = *selling concession*.

concessional rate = *bank-prime interest rate*.

concurrent indicator = *lagging indicator*.

conditional call the feature that allows the issuer of a convertible security to demand an earlier redemption.

conditional call option an option in the event a high-yield bond is called, the issuer will replace it with a non-callable bond of the same life and terms.

conditional forward purchase contract the *break forward* agreement whereby the long side of the contract has a right to cancel the purchase by paying a fee on the maturity date.

conditional forward sale contract the *break forward* agreement whereby the short side of the contract has the right to cancel the agreement by paying a fee on the maturity date.

conditional heteroskedasticity = *stochastic volatility*.

conditional variance the one-period ahead forecast variance that is based on past data. ***Also***: time-varying variance.

condor spread the combination of two vertical spreads one is bull and the other is bear. ***See***: *box spread*.

conduit-type customer an institutional client, who does not disclose the name of the principal for whom it is transacting the trade. ***See***: *blind brokering*.

confederation bond <UK> a debt that is issued by the Swiss government.

confirmation of purchase the contract between a broker/dealer and his client when that client wants to buy shares or other assets.

consecutive Parisian option a Parisian-type option that knocks in or out when the consecutive time spent beyond the barrier exceeds a prescribed value. ***See***: *cumulative Parisian option.*

consensus estimate a prediction of the earnings of a company.

consent dividend a dividend paid at year end and followed by an imaginary contribution of them back to the firm to avoid accumulated profits tax.

consent stock the stock entitled to the residual earnings, e. g. preferred stock on which consent dividends are paid.

consol <1><UK> a bond issued by the UK Government with a yield of 2.5 % and without maturity. ***Also***: consol bond; consolidated loan. <2> = *baby bond.*

consol bond = *consol.*

consolidated bond the bond issued to retire two or more outstanding issues.

consolidated loan = *consol.*

consolidated mortgage bond the bond that covers several units of asset and may refinance separate mortgages.

consolidated note a short-tem note backed by the good faith and assets of several debtors.

consolidated security a security large enough to provide the funds to retire two or more outstanding debts.

consolidation <1> a combination of 2 or more firms into a new entity, the former firms will cease to exist. ***Also***: consolidation merger; fusion; integration; statutory consolidation. <2> the combination of several issues of stocks into one security.

consolidation by merger = *merger.*

consolidation merger = *consolidation.*

consolidation of capital = *split down.*

consolidation of shares = *split down.*

constant dollar plan a plan that invests a fixed amount of money at set intervals. ***Also***: averaging; cost averaging; dollar averaging; dollar cost averaging; monthly investment plan; monthly purchase plan; Pound cost averaging; Rupee-cost averaging. ***See***: *constant-ratio formula; variable-ratio formula.*

constant elasticity of volatility (CEV) a change in volatility resulting from a 1% change in the price of the underlying. ***Also***: volatility elasticity. ***Opp***: *vega.*

constant-growth model a model which assumes a fixed growth rate for future dividends and one discount rate. ***Also***: Gordon-Shapiro model.

constant maturity the maturity used by the *Federal Reserve Board* to quote yields on various Treasury securities, adjusted to an equivalent maturity.

constant maturity swap (CMS) an interest rate swap, whereby the floating interest portion is reset periodically according to a fixed maturity market rate of a product with a duration beyond that of the swap's reset period.

constant maturity Treasury (CMT) = *constant maturity Treasury index.*

constant maturity Treasury index (CMT index) the average yields on Treasury securities adjusted to constant maturities of one year. ***Also***: constant maturity Treasury; constant maturity Treasury rate; constant maturity Treasury yield.

constant maturity Treasury rate (CMT rate) = *constant maturity Treasury index.*

constant maturity Treasury swap (CMT swap) = *yield curve swap.*

constant maturity Treasury yield = *constant maturity Treasury index.*

constant percent plan a strategy which maintains a fixed percent in stock and bonds, when stock prices increase, sell the stock and buy bonds or vice versa.

constant prepayment rate (CPR) the rate of the principal that must be repaid of a mortgage pass-through security package.

constant proportion a strategy that re-balances the assets in a portfolio under *multi-period MVO*. ***Also***: constant ratio asset allocation.

constant-ratio asset allocation = *constant proportion*.

constant-ratio formula the formula for an investment plan under which the dollar ratio between the stocks and the fixed-income assets is adjusted periodically to a predetermined rate. ***See***: *constant dollar plan*; *variable-ratio formula*.

constant volatility = *uniform volatility*.

constructive dividend a dividend that is treated for tax purposes as a distribution even though it has not been declared. ***Also***: disguised dividend.

constructive gain a gain realized on the constructive retirement of bonds. ***Also***: gain on constructive retirement.

constructive loss the loss realized on the constructive retirement of bonds. ***Also***: loss on constructive retirement.

constructive retirement the issuer's purchase of its bond or treasury stock with no intent of reissuing.

constructive sale *appreciated financial position* deemed sold by the IRS when all the possible risk and award have been hedged away.

consumer debenture a bond issued by financial institutions to raise funds.

consumer price index swap = *inflation swap*.

contagion the excess correlation of the equity or bond returns.

contagion effect the tendency for a crisis in one asset class to spread to other classes of assets. ***See***: *domino theory*.

contango <1> a situation where the forward price of a commodity is above the spot. ***Also***: carrying charge market; forwardation. <2> an interest payment for carrying over or continuing a trade from one account to the next. ***Also***: carrying charge; loaning rate on stock; off basis. ***Opp***: *backwardation*.

contango day = *continuation day*.

contango swap a swap that allows the user to lock in a fixed spread between the forward price and the spot price.

contingent annuity an annuity the rents of which depend on future events.

contingent cap a cap for which the buyer pays no upfront premium, but has to pay a predetermined premium if the cap has any value on its effective date. ***Also***: contingent premium cap.

contingent claim an option the maturity value of which is determined by the value of one or more other assets or securities. ***See***: *contingent option*.

contingent claim analysis (CCA) method for determining the price of a security whose payoffs depend on the prices of one or more other assets.

contingent convertible (coco) the convertible bond with the strike price and another price that the stock price must reach before the holder has the conversion right. ***See***: *upside contingency*.

contingent credit swap a credit swap the payoff of which depends on some other event in addition to the credit event.

contingent currency option an option that protects a portfolio from currency losses only when the local return on the underlying portfolio falls below a level.

contingent currency risk the exchange rate risk associated with a transaction which may or may not occur. ***Also***: shared currency option under tender.

contingent deferred swap (CDS) a swap the receipts from the counterparty is deferred to future periods.

contingent exchange option an option to exchange managed portfolio for a benchmark portfolio when the managed one underperforms the benchmark by a prespecified amount and simultaneously drops below a pre-specified hurdle value.

contingent immunization a strategy in which a manager pursues an active bond portfolio until an adverse event drives the then-available potential return down to a safety level. **See**: *safety cushion.*

contingent option an option the buyer only pays a premium when exercised. **See**: *contingent claim.*

contingent payout option an option in which the holder's payout is contingent not only on the behavior of an equity rate or index price but on the behavior of a second financial or economic variable. ***Also***: dual contingency option; equity rate contingency option.

contingent premium cap = *contingent cap.*

contingent premium option an option for which the buyer pays no premium but agrees to pay a fixed amount if the option has value (in the money) at expiration. ***Also***: capitalized option; cash on delivery option; pay later option; pay on exercise option; when-in-the-money option. **See**: *money-back option; mini-premium option.*

contingent premium swaption a contract conferring the right to buy or sell a swap on fixed terms.

contingent surplus note a note issued by an insurance company to raise capital at a predetermined rate of interest.

contingent swap the swap valid only if some designated event occurs, such as an acquisition or an interest rate move.

contingent takedown option = *bond warrant.*

contingent value right (CVR) an instrument issued in an acquisition to give shareholders of the acquired company a stake in the surviving company.

contingent voting power the voting power which enables stockholders to vote when the firm fails to satisfy the agreement with the preferred stockholder.

continual redemption sinking fund = *sinking fund.*

continuation = *carry-over.*

continuation day the day on which the contango rate is fixed. ***Also***: carrying over day; carryover day; contango day; making-up day.

continuation option an option the premium of which is paid periodically and the holder has the right to stop making the payment, thereby terminating the option on the due date of the first missed payment. ***Also***: installment option; pay as you go option.

continued bond a bond the holder of which may present it for payment either on its maturity date or a later date.

continuous auction market an *auction market* the participants' and/or dealers' limit order to buy and sell the subject instrument is executed on a continuous basis. **See**: *call market.*

continuous compound interest a compound interest the frequency with which interest is credited approaches infinity.

continuous market a market with great depth and liquidity and by small price changes between successive trades.

continuous net settlement (CNS) the clearing that eliminates multiple fails in the same securities by using the clearing house to match transactions in securities available in the firm's position resulting in one net receiving or delivery position at the end of the day.

continuous return a rate of return that, when compounded continuously, will cause an investment to grow by a factor equal to 1 plus the periodic return.

contract a unit of trading for a commodity futures contract or an option.

contract amount = *contract value.*

contracted value = *contract value.*

contract for difference (CFD) a contract where the price for delivery in the future is fixed in advance and the counterpart pays the difference between the agreed price and the current price. ***Also***: diff contract; difference contract.

contract frustration the invalidation of a contract by unforeseen circumstances.

contract grade the standard quality of a commodity set as the deliverable item in a futures contract. ***Also***: basis grade; deliverable grade; deliverable name; par; sample grade; tenderable grade.

contraction risk the risk of a security or derivative shortening in duration due to the acceleration of prepayments.

contract life = *life of contract.*

contract market = *futures market.*

contract month = *delivery month.*

contract multiplier the amount which, when multiplied by the price gives the value of a contract. **See**: *futures contract multiplier*; *options contract multiplier.*

contract rate = *floor.*

contract rate of interest = *coupon rate of interest.*

contract size the deliverable quantity of commodities that underly the futures, forward, and options. ***Also***: size.

contractual settlement day accounting (CSDA) a securities custodian and safekeeping arrangement between investor and a custodian.

contractual trust a pure trust.

contract unit the actual amount of the commodity represented under a futures contract.

contract value the face value of a futures contract or derivative. ***Also***: contract amount; contracted value; lot size.

contributed capital the authorized capital paid to the company by its shareholders. ***Also***: paid-in capital; paid-up capital. **See**: *permanent capital*; *unpaid capital.*

contributing share = *partly paid share.*

controlled account = *discretionary account.*

controlled adjustable-rate preferred stock (CARP) = *adjustable-rate preferred stock.*

controlled commodity the commodity the trading of which is federally regulated to prevent fraud.

controlled company a company 51% or more of its voting shares are controlled by another company. **See**: *subsidiary.*

controlling interest = *majority holding.*

control person a person in a position to exert direct influence on the policy or actions of a company. ***Also***: affiliated person.

control-share acquisition law = *super-majority.*

control variate a variance reduction technique that replaces the evaluation of an unknown expected value with the evaluation of the difference between unknown quantity and a related quantity whose expected value is known.

convenience return = *convenience yield.*

convenience yield extra yield from holding a commodity rather than a futures position. ***Also***: convenience return.

conventional auction an auction market for securities where there is only one market maker and many buyers. ***Opp***: *double auction system.*

conventional option an option off the trading floor of an exchange, the strike, expiration and the premium of which can be negotiated. ***Also***: OTC option.

conventional pass-through the pass-through which is guaranteed by a business. **See**: *modified pass-through.*

conventional swap = *plain swap.*

convergence movement of the option price toward the price of the underlying as it is close to expiration.

convergence trading investing in two or more securities the prices of which move in the same direction.

conversion <1> the exchange of a convertible into a fixed number of shares. <2> = *conversion arbitrage.* <3> = *exchange.* <4> = *forward conversion.* <5> = *fund switching.*

conversion arbitrage buying a put, selling a call and buying the underlying asset. ***Also***: conversion; long conversion. **See**: *synthetic spread.*

conversion factor the factor used to calculate how many deliverable bonds are equivalent to one notional bond.

conversion feature the right given to the investor to transform investment from one instrument to another.

conversion formula the formula used to convert puts into calls and calls into puts when the option writers prefer to sell one type and the buyer wants to buy the other type.

conversion parity the stock price at which a convertible bond can be exchanged for the common stock of equal value. ***Also***: market conversion price.

conversion premium the amount by which the conversion price of a convertible security exceeds the market price of stock. ***Also***: bond conversion premium; gain on bond conversion. **See**: *premium over conversion value.*

conversion price the price per share at which the convertible securities can be converted into common stock, as set when they were issued. ***Also***: convertible price.

conversion ratio the number of shares one receives for each share he turned in. ***Also***: basis of exchange; exchange rate; rate of conversion.

conversion spread = *collar.*

conversion stock = *government obligation.*

conversion transaction the transaction the gain of which is due to the time value of money and which involves offsetting positions on the same security.

conversion value the value of convertible security if exchanged for common stock immediately, derived by multiplying a *conversion ratio* by the current market price of the stock. ***Also***: parity value.

converted put = *synthetic long put.*

convertibility clause a clause allowing for repayment of a bond in local currency in a conversion suspension.

convertible = *convertible security.*

Convertible 100 Goldman Sachs index of the 100 convertibles of institutional importance.

convertible adjustable preferred stock (CAPS) the adjustable preferred stock which can be converted into common stock of equal market value of the same issuing firm. ***Also***: variable convertible preferred stock.

convertible adjustable rate bond (CARB) a *floating rate bond*, convertible by the holder on interest reset dates into a variable number of the issuer's shares. ***Also***: secured equity-linked loan.

convertible arbitrage a practice of buying one convertible bond and shorting a percentage of the equivalent value of underlying stock issued by the same company.

convertible auction rate preferred stock (CARPS) an *auction rate preferred stock* that is convertible into the underlying shares.

convertible bond a bond that gives the holder a right to exchange or convert it into the common stock of the issuer under certain circumstance. ***Also***: convertible debenture; convertible unsecured loan stock. ***See***: *interchangeable bond.*

convertible bond fund the mutual fund that invests most of its money in convertible bonds.

convertible bond with a premium put a convertible bond with an embedded put that entitles the holder to redeem it for more than its face value beginning at some future date.

convertible capital note the fixed-term note issued by a bank and convertible into a perpetual preferred stock. ***See***: *equity contract note.*

convertible debenture <UK> = *convertible bond.*

convertible discount the amount below the conversion value for which a convertible is selling. ***Also***: discount.

convertible Eurobond a Eurobond that can be converted into another asset by the exercise of the attached warrants.

convertible exchangeable note a type of *convertible exchangeable preferred stock* with the issuer's exchange option to substitute preferred dividend for the interest payment.

convertible exchangeable preferred stock the *convertible preferred stock* that is exchangeable at the issuer's option for convertible debt with identical yield and conversion terms.

convertible floater a *floating rate note* that is convertible into fixed rate bond. ***Also***: convertible floating rate note.

convertible floating rate note = *convertible floater.*

convertible floating rate preferred stock a type of *convertible preferred stock* with the dividend indexed to a *floating interest rate.*

convertible gilt <UK> government bond with an option to convert into longer authority bonds on specified terms.

convertible hedge selling stock short, when a long position is created in the convertible bonds of the same company.

convertible money market units (CMMUs) a *participating equity preferred stock* not issued by the issuer of the underlying stock. ***Also***: synthetic high-income equity-linked debenture.

convertible option the option sold or acquired through an option dealer rather than on an exchange.

convertible preferred stock a preferred stock which can be converted into the common stock of the issuing company. ***Also***: converting preference share.

convertible price = *conversion price.*

convertible security the security which grants the holder the right to exchange it for the common stock of the issuer. ***Also***: common stock equivalent; convertible. **See**: *exchangeable security.*

convertible stock note a note that pays coupons and principal in the common stock of the issuer.

convertible subordinate note a short-term note that can be changed into the stock and ranks below other loans.

convertible unsecured loan stock (CULS) = *convertible bond.*

convertible zero-coupon bond a bond issued as a zero-coupon bond and the interest of which is reinvested and will be converted into exempt security in 10 years.

converting preference share <Australia> = *convertible preferred stock.*

convex the curve, as in the shape of the outside of a circle, that represents the price-required yield relationship for the *option-free bonds.*

convexity the sensitivity of an instrument to large changes in price or yield, it is the second derivative of the price of a bond with respect to its yield.

convexity cost the component of the *option-adjusted spread* caused by the non-linear relationship between a volatile market factor and the price of an embedded option.

convexity hedge = *bull straddle.*

cooking the accounts = *doctoring.*

cooking the books = *doctoring.*

cooling off period = *cooling period.*

cooling period the 21-day period from the filing of a registration statement to the date when SEC approves the issue. ***Also***: 20-day period; cooling-off period; waiting period. **See**: *quiet period.*

Coppock curve a long term momentum indicator used to recognize major price bottoms in the derivatives market.

COPs covered option security

core = *broad index fund.*

core plus a fixed-income style that permits managers to add instruments with greater risk and return to their *core holding* of investment-grade bonds.

core-satellite strategy an *exchange-traded fund* asset allocation program that uses broad index fund and sector funds in an attempt to enhance portfolio performance or diversification while controlling risks.

cornering <1> = *cornering the market.* <2> = *short-squeeze.*

cornering the market buying securities in large volumes in order to control the price. ***Also***: cornering.

corners = *short squeeze.*

corn yield insurance future a futures contract on corns that allows farmers to hedge against the quantity risk of loss due to low yield.

corporate acquisition indebtedness a bond issued after October 9, 1969, for acquiring the stock or two-third's of the non-cash operating assets of a target company through *leveraged buyout.*

corporate bond (CB) a bond issued by a corporation. ***Also***: bond.

corporate bond equivalent the semi-annual equivalent yield for a security whose interest payments are not on a semi-annual basis.

corporate capital = *capital stock.*

corporate equivalent yield = *equivalent bond yield.*

corporate hedging the risk management for corporations.

corporate income fund (CIF) a fund with a fixed portfolio made up of the highest grade securities and monthly investment income payments.

corporate insider = *insider.*

corporate zero a zero coupon bond that is issued by a corporation.

corporation dividend = *dividend.*

corporation's stock = *stock.*

corporation stock <UK> a fixed interest security issued by the British local authorities with redemption usually at some time between two stated dates.

corpus = *principal.*

correlation the extent to which prices on two different assets move together over time.

correlation product derivative product that consists of two reference entities with correlated default.

correlation swap a swap designed for hedging correlation risk.

corridor purchase of a *cap* and the sale of a similar cap further out-of-the-money to another. ***Also***: interest rate corridor.

corridor accrual swap an *accrual swap* with interest accruing on one side when the index price or rate falls in a range reset at the start of each period. ***Also***: corridor swap.

corridor bond a bond the coupon of which is proportional to the time the price spent inside a given band.

corridor note a note the interest payment of which is proportional to the time an index spent inside a given band. ***Also***: *range note.* **See**: *accrual note.*

corridor option <1> an option that is embedded in a corridor bond that guarantees the minimum coupon. <2> = *accrual option.*

corridor swap = *corridor accrual swap.*

co-sale rights = *tag along rights.*

cost averaging = *constant dollar plan.*

cost-benefit ratio = *present value profitability index.*

costless collar = *cashless collar.*

costly collar = *cashless collar.*

cost of 1000 gamma linear daily decay of a theoretical +1000 gamma option with time to expiration greater than 200 days and strike prices at all points across the conceivable range of the underlying.

cost of carry (COC) <1> the cost incurred while an open position is maintained e. g. interest paid, dividends lost on short margin positions etc. ***Also***: full carry; full carrying charge; interest; premium. <2> = *carry.* <3> = *carrying charge.* <4> = *transfer pricing rate.*

cost of carry arbitrage

cost-of-carry market a futures market in which the price difference between the delivery months equals the cost of carry. ***Also***: full carry; full carrying charge market; full carry market.

cost of default = *swap replacement cost.*

cost of flotation cost of issuing security. ***Also***: capital structure expenditure; cost of issues; floatation cost; floating charge; flotation cost; issuance expense; issue cost.

cost of fund = *interest.*

Cost of Funds Index (COFI) = *11th District Cost of Funds Index.*

Cost of Funds Index swap (COFI swap) an interest rate swap with the floating payment stream linked to the *11th District Cost of Funds Index.*

cost of hedging = *premium.*

cost of issues = *cost of flotation.*

cost-of-living index an index reflecting changes in the cost of living.

cost of money = *interest.*

cost of tender the cost associated with the delivery of commodities underlying a futures contract.

cost recovery period = *payback period.*

COT competitive options trader

COTO cash or titles option

COUGAR certificate of government receipt

COUGR certificate of government receipt

countercyclical stock the stock issued by a corporation the earnings of which fluctuate in the opposing direction of the general economic trend.

counterpart the other party in a derivative transaction. ***Also***: counterparty.

counterpart risk the risk to one party in a contract that the other party will fail to fulfill the obligation in full.

counterparty = *counterpart.*

counter-trend strategy the strategy that attempts to make small gains through a series of trades against the current trend.

country risk = *political risk.*

coupon (CP)(CPN) = *bond coupon.*

coupon bond the bearer bond with a coupon attached. **See**: *bearer bond*; *deep discount bond*; *registered bond.*

coupon equivalent rate = *equivalent bond yield.*

coupon equivalent yield actual interest cost expressed on a *365-days-per-year basis.* **See**: *equivalent bond yield.*

coupon-indexed note a *floating-rate note* with the periodic coupon dependent on the performance of an equity, currency, interest rate, or index option. ***Also***: multi-period strike reset option.

coupon leveraging the amount by which the reference rate is multiplied to determine the floating rate payable by an inverse floater.

coupon margin the margin, expressed in basis points, that is added to each rate reset.

coupon of bond = *bond coupon.*

coupon-only swap = *annuity swap.*

coupon pass canvassing by the desk of major broker dealers to determine the inventory and maturity of the Treasury securities.

coupon rate of interest the interest as a percentage of the face value. ***Also***: bond interest rate; contract rate of interest; nominal interest rate; nominal rate of interest; normal rate of interest; quoted rate of interest; stated interest rate; stated rate of interest. **See**: *effective interest rate.*

coupon rollover date the quarterly or semi-annual date on which a new interest rate will be set for payments on a floating rate note. **See**: *rate fixing date.*

coupon sheet = *bond coupon.*

coupon stripping stripping the coupon from a bond, selling the bond at a lower price and recognizing the loss as tax deduction. ***Also***: bond stripping.

coupon swap an *interest rate swap* the fixed rate payments are traded for floating rate. ***Also***: adjustment swap;

fixed-floating swap; fixed-for-floating swap; fixed-to-floating swap; fixed-to-variable interest rate swap; plain vanilla fixed-floating swap; vanilla fixed-for-floating interest rate swap. ***See***: *basis swap*; *circus swap; plain swap.*

course of exchange = *exchange rate.*

courtage = *brokerage.*

covariance an indicator of the tendency for 2 random variables to move together.

covenant lite bond = *floating interest rate subordinated term securities.*

cover <1> to buy back contracts that are previously sold. <2> to have in hand the physical commodity when a short futures or leverage sale is made. <3> to buy the commodity deliverable on a short sale.

coverage period the interim period in a swap agreement or other periodic reset agreement when a specific set of terms is effective.

cover bear one who closes out a short position by buying the currency or asset sold. ***Also***: protected bear.

cover bid the second highest bid in a competitive offering. ***See***: *winning bid.*

covered arbitrage an *arbitrage* that involves investments denominated in different currencies, using *forward cover* to reduce or eliminate *currency risk*. ***See***: *uncovered arbitrage.*

covered call a call in which the *writer is* holding the underlying asset. ***Also***: buy-write. ***See***: *uncovered call.*

covered call writing buying stock and selling a call against that stock. ***See***: *buy right strategy*; *ratio call writing.*

covered combo holding a stock, then selling both an out-of-the-money call and an out-of-the money put.

covered interest arbitrage the *simple currency swap* where the counterparts exchange currencies at the spot and forward rates simultaneously.

covered margin the interest rate margin between 2 different currency instruments after considering the cost of the forward.

covered option an option in which the seller owns the underlying asset. ***Opp***: *uncovered option.*

covered option security (COPs) <UK> a short-term note with a high coupon and an embedded put that gives the issuer an option to repay principal and interest in US dollars or a foreign currency at a preset exchange rate.

covered option strategy a strategy under which the option seller owns the underlying asset. ***Also***: hedge option strategy. ***See***: *uncovered option strategy.*

covered put a put option in which the *writer* also is short the underlying or has deposited cash. ***Also***: cash secured put; married put. ***See***: *uncovered put.*

covered security a security traded in a stock exchange that enjoys federally imposed exemptions from state restrictions and other regulations. ***Also***: qualified security.

covered short straddle the straddle created by the simultaneous selling of equal number of puts and calls of the same underlying asset, same strike price and expiration month with the calls being covered.

covered short strangle a straddle created by buying a stock and selling both out-of-the money calls and puts at the same expiration date.

covered straddle a straddle created by the simultaneous buying or selling of equal number of puts and calls of the same underlying asset, same strike price and expiration month with the calls being covered.

covered warrant a warrant issued by a third party who holds enough share warrants or convertibles in a company to cover his obligations if the warrant is exercised. ***Also***: synthetic warrant.

covered writer option *writer* who sells against his long position in the underlying asset in order to collect premiums.

cover for dividend = *dividend cover.*

co-volatility the co-movement across volatilities.

Cox-Ingersoll-Ross the option pricing model for interest rate options, which assumes that the short-term interest rate conforms to a square root diffusion model with mean reversion.

Cox-Ross-Rubenstein model (C/R/R) an option pricing model that reduces the possibilities of price changes and arbitrage, assumes perfect markets and shortens the duration. ***Also***: binomial option pricing model; lattice model; tree model.

Cox-Ross-Rubenstein technique the technique developed in 1979 by Cox, Ross and Rubenstein to access the risk that an option will be exercised.

CPB Canadian premium bond

CPIW futures a futures contract based on the urban wage and salary index.

CPS currency protected security.

crack spread <1> the price difference between crude oil and refined products. <2> a spread option created by buying crude oil while selling refinery oil products.

crack swap a swap based on the spread between crude oil and an appropriate basket of cracked and refined products.

cram-down bond = *reset bond.*

crash huge drop in prices. ***Also***: stock market crash. **See**: *blow off*; *dip*; *swoop.*

crash option a put that pays the option holder the value of a decline in the position or portfolio over the option's life.

crawling peg a system for revising the exchange rate by setting a par value and around which the rate can vary up and down to a given percent. ***Also***: gliding parity; sliding parity.

creation unit the minimum unit for the issuance or redemption of the shares in an *exchange-traded fund*, usually $25,000 to $300,000 fund shares.

creative mortgage = *exotic mortgage.*

credit arbitrage an arbitrage that takes advantage of the lower borrowing cost by borrowers with higher credit or good connection with some bankers.

credit card receivable-backed security = *certificate of amortizing revolving debt.*

credit default model the model used to calculate credit losses based on the probability of credit default of the counterparty at various point in time.

credit default risk the risk of loss arising from a counterparty's failure to perform contractual obligations.

credit default swap (CDS) a swap where one party pays a fixed fee, in return, he receives a floating rate payment that depends on the credit of a referenced party. ***Also***: credit risk swap.

credit default swap index a standardized actively traded credit default swap.

credit derivative a derivative instrument where the return depends on a set of risk factors related to credit quality or rating.

credit derivative bond the proposed pass-through product based on pools of low-rated bonds held by AAA- or AA-rated financial institutions.

credit distress a situation that a debt will not be recovered in bankruptcy due to ranking.

credit enhanced debt security a security with special investor protection which gives it a better credit standing than the debt of the issuer would have.

credit enhanced vehicle (CEV) = *derivatives product company.*

credit enhancement a process by which one entity of higher credit quality provides support to another entity or to a specific transaction to reduce credit risk. ***Also***: credit guarantee; direct credit substitute.

credit equivalent value (CEV) value of the credit risk exposure represented by an off-balance sheet transaction.

credit event an event that triggers the payoff in a credit derivative, such as bankruptcy, failure to pay, and debt restructuring.

credit exposure in a swap a reduction in the present value of the net cash flows if the swap must be replaced at current market terms for its remaining life.

credit forward a forward contract based on the credit quality of a debt issuer.

credit guarantee = *credit enhancement.*

credit insurance payment protection so that if credit default happens the insured will recover loss.

credit intermediation swap = *dynamic credit swap.*

credit inventory risk the risk of loss arising from an issuer's financial problem and/or default.

credit linked note (CLN) a note with interest rate reset in the event of a change in the issuer's credit rating. ***Also***: credit linked security; credit sensitive note; rating sensitive note.

credit linked note format a derivative contract format that requires initial payment at par. ***Also***: funded format. ***See***: *swap format.*

credit linked security = *credit linked note.*

credit mark-to-market model a model that is used to calculate the credit losses based on the probability of a counterparty's credit deterioration at various points in time over the life of a credit derivative or other derivatives.

credit option a call or put option on the price of a floating rate note or an asset swap package.

credit overlay a derivative that involves embedding a layer of credit risk into an existing instrument.

credit portfolio model a model used to estimate credit losses in a portfolio.

credit portfolio option a credit option the underlying asset of which is a portfolio.

credit quality = *credit rating.*

credit rating the estimate of the credit standing assigned to a person or entity by a credit rating bureau. ***Also***: credit quality.

credit reserve the money set aside in support of expected credit losses.

credit risk the risk of loss occurred due to the counterpart's credit problem. ***Also***: bankruptcy risk; commercial risk; customer risk; default exposure; default risk; insolvency risk; performance risk; portfolio risk; repayment risk.

credit risk derivative the product that allows banks to pass on the *credit risk.*

credit risk option a put that pays off to the holder if the credit rating of a bond issuer falls below a level. ***Also***: credit spread option; quality spread option.

credit risk swap = *credit default swap.*

credit scoring a system used to calculate the probability that a debt will be repaid.

credit sensitive note = *credit linked note.*

credit sensitive payment the payment under a derivative instrument which adjusts the interest rate on the basis of changed credit rating of the borrower.

credit spread <1> selling high premium options and buying low premium ones resulting in a credit. ***Also***: selling the spread. <2> the difference in the value of 2 options when the value of the one sold exceeds that of the one bought. **See**: *debit spread.* <3> = *bond premium.* <4> = *net credit spread.*

credit spread option <1> an option where one party pays a premium and receives the present value of the difference between the spread prevailing on the exercise date between the yield of the reference debt and a benchmark yield. <2> = *credit risk option.*

credit spread risk the risk of loss arising from a decline in the credit quality of the counterparty.

credit spread strike a yield spread to a Treasury bond or interest rate swap. ***Also***: spread strike.

credit spread swap a swap with a payoff that depends on a credit spread.

credit swap <1> a swap with one side's payment based on the rate of return of an instrument with some credit risk. <2> the option with an upfront or periodic payment by one party in exchange for the right to receive a payment contingent on the default of a designated instrument. ***Also***: default put.

credit tranching creating a multi-layer capital structure which includes senior and subordinated classes.

credit watch an alert or warning issued by a credit rating agency in anticipation of a credit upgrade or downgrade of a given reference entity.

credit watch list a list issued by S&P that lists the names of the companies with unusual behavior in the market.

credit writing bank = *issuing house.*

creeping tender = *Saturday night special.*

creeping tender offer = *Saturday night special.*

CRIB swap cross-index basis swap

crop year the 12-month period in which the planting or harvesting of a commodity occurred.

cross-border carry trade borrowing in a *premium currency* and investing in a *discount currency.*

cross-border transaction a transaction that is made in a financial instrument with a foreign counterparty.

cross-commodity option the option the underlying assets can be two or more commodities.

cross-commodity spread a spread that involves being long a commodity, short another commodity, buying a call on the long commodity, selling calls on the short commodity.

cross-currency arbitrage the arbitrage that involves three currencies.

cross-currency asset swap a swap that change foreign currency fixed-rate bond into local currency floating rate bond.

cross-currency basis swap a *basis swap* with both parties as the floating-rate payers in their currencies.

cross-currency cap an option setting a cap on the spread between two reference index rates in two different currencies.

cross-currency convertible bond the bond denominated in one currency, and is convertible into the shares denominated and traded in a second currency.

cross-currency coupon swap a currency swap involving one fixed interest stream and one floating interest stream.

cross-currency cross-index basis swap (XCRIBS) a swap to which one party pays the index rate in the base currency and the other pays a floating rate based on the same index rate in a different currency. ***See***: *circus swap.*

cross-currency exposure a situation in which a firm's debt service in a currency is not covered by its revenue-generating abilities in that currency.

cross-currency floor the *floor* on the spread between two reference index rates denominated in different currencies.

cross-currency forward a forward contract in two currencies for the protection of assets in the 3rd currency.

cross-currency hedge a hedge that involves three currencies.

cross-currency interest rate swap = *cross-currency swap.*

cross-currency option <1> the option struck at an exchange rate between two currencies, with the premiums in a third currency. <2> = *quanto option.*

cross-currency option bond a bond with an embedded outperformance option struck at the rate of exchange between 2 currencies.

cross-currency pair a *currency pair* that is comprised of one foreign currency and another non-US currency.

cross-currency swap the swap of loan payments in two different currencies. ***Also***: cross-currency interest rate swap; differential swap.

cross-currency swaption an option to pay or to receive a fixed rate in a cross-currency swap. ***Also***: circus option.

cross-currency warrant a *currency warrant* where neither of the two currencies determining the payout is the US dollar.

cross-default clause a clause in a swap which states that default by a party will be deemed a default for the swap.

crossed market the market in which the bid is higher than the lowest offer or vice versa. ***See***: *choice market.*

crossed quote the asked price of one market participant which is the same or lower than the bid submitted by another market participant. ***Also***: locked quote.

crossed sale = *manipulation.*

crossed trade = *manipulation.*

cross hedge a hedge the underlying of which does not match the subject being hedged. ***See***: *direct hedge.*

cross-hedge risk = *cross-hedging.*

cross hedging the selling of a forward Treasury bill to hedging against the risk of corporate bonds which have no future contracts. ***Also***: cross-hedge risk.

cross holding a listed company's holding of the securities issued by another *listed company.*

cross-index basis swap (CRIB swap) = *cross rate swap.*

cross margining the procedure for margining related securities, options and futures jointly when different clearing houses clear each side of the position.

cross option an option on a foreign index, security, or basket struck at a value of the underlying in the investor's local currency and priced and paid in the base currency if it is exercised. ***Also***: composite option; joint option.

cross-option agreement an agreement that gives a deceased partner's estate the option to sell shares, and surviving partners the option to buy shares. ***Also***: double-option agreement.

crossover bond a bond ranked BBB by one rating agency and BB by another. ***Also***: 5B bond.

crossover fund a mutual fund which invests in both publicly traded stock and private equities.

crossover rate the *rate of return* at which two alternative projects have the same *net present value*.

crossover refunded a refund pledged to secure stocks being refunded for paying off debt on the refunded stock.

cross rate an exchange rate between 2 currencies expressed in terms of a 3rd currency. ***Also***: currency cross rate.

cross-rate option an option on a currency pair not standard in the market. (e. g. a sterling/DM option is cross-rate option in the US.)

cross-rate swap a swap with one of the rates denominated in a different currency than the principal currency. ***Also***: cross-index basis swap; currency coupon swap; currency protected swap; currency rate swap; dual swap; index differential swap; interest rate index swap; LIBOR differential swap; quantoed swap; quanto swap. **See**: *diff swap*.

cross-sectional approach an approach that uses a statistical formula for the valuation of stocks.

cross-sectional volatility the volatility within a pool of assets at a given time.

cross shareholding two or more firms holding the shares in each other.

cross trading the trading for equal amount of the same month of a future or option at the same price.

crowd buying in a rising market and selling in a declining market. ***Also***: following the market.

crowding out the displacement of some private investment by the increases in the government expenditures which is financed by debt issues.

crown jewel defense a strategy used to thwart a hostile takeover by selling to a third party the most valuable assets, thus making it less attractive. ***Also***: selling the crown jewels.

crown jewel option the provision in the bylaws of a corporation or a takeover agreement that gives a friendly party a favorable option to buy the corporation's most attractive assets or operations.

C/R/R Cox-Ross-Rubenstein model

crude oil knock-in note a note issued with upside potential on the principal payback contingent upon prices of the crude oil.

crush margin money a processor earns from selling the derivatives of a product, minus the cost of the product.

crush spread a spread option involving 2 derivative commodities and soybeans, e. g. buying soybean futures and selling soybean oil and soybean meal, profiting from price fall. ***Also***: bean, oil and meal spread; BOM spread; commodity product spread; Paris spread; source spread; ***Opp***: *reverse crush spread*.

crystallization the act of selling and buying stocks almost instantaneously to increase or decrease book value.

CSB Canada savings bond

C share a family of multi-class mutual funds, the class with a constant load structure throughout the life.

CSLT Chase secured loan trust note

CTD cheapest to deliver

CUBS <1> a call the holder of which

receives the face price of bonds that are underwritten by Swanbrook company. ***Also***: calls underwritten by Swanbrook. <2> customized upside basket security.

CULS convertible unsecured loan stock

cum coupon of bonds with a coupon attached that soon becomes due.

cum distribution = *cum dividend.*

cum dividend a share which is sold with a dividend declared out but not yet paid. ***Also***: cum distribution; dividend in; dividend on; with dividend.

cum drawing of bonds, soon due to be drawn with rights that may come with the drawing such as profit or premium.

cum interest words meaning a coupon bond carries accrued interest. ***Also***: with interest. **See**: *ex interest.*

cum new with the rights issue or the scrip issue. **Opp**: *ex new.*

cum rights the buyer has the right to buy a specified amount of stock that is yet to be issued. ***Also***: right on; with rights. **Opp**: *ex rights.* **See**: *rights on.*

cumulative abnormal return (CAR) the difference between the expected return on a stock and the actual return.

cumulative auction market preferred stock (CAMPS) preferred stock issued by Oppenheimer & Co in Dutch auction.

cumulative discount privilege a way for the mutual fund shareholders to qualify for a reduced sales charge by combining the investments in different mutual funds of the same fund family made at the same time into a single transaction.

cumulative dividend the dividend that must be paid before making distributions to common shareholders.

cumulative Parisian option a Parisian-type option that knocks in or out when the total time spent beyond the barrier exceeds a predetermined value. **See**: *consecutive Parisian option.*

cumulative preferred stock the stock with a right to have the omitted dividend paid before the common dividend is paid.

cumulative trust preferred security = *trust originated preferred security.*

cumulative voting the voting for directors of a corporation in which shareholder's number of votes is equal to the number of shares held times the total number of candidates. **See**: *majority voting.*

cum warrant words meaning warrants are to accompany the securities referred to. ***Also***: with warrant. **See**: *ex warrant.*

CUPS currency protected swap

Curb = *American Stock Exchange.*

curb <1> the restriction on program trading whenever the DJIA moves 50 points higher or lower than the previous closing price. ***Also***: collar. **See**: *trading curb.* <2> = *over-the-counter market.*

Curb Exchange = *American Stock Exchange.*

curb exchange <1> a trade that is made outside the stock exchange with the assistance of a member of the exchange. ***Also***: ex-pit transaction; kerb exchange; off-board trading; trading on the curb. <2> = *over-the-counter market.*

curb market = *over-the-counter market.*

currency the money of a country that is in general use as cash, passing from person to person or as a means of payment.

currency annuity swap the *swap* which does not call for exchange of principal in different currencies at maturity.

currency arbitrage the arbitrage which involves buying foreign exchange in one market and selling it in another. ***Also***: exchange arbitrage; foreign exchange arbitrage; illegal procurement of foreign exchange.

currency average rate option = *average price option.*

currency basket options = *basket options.*

currency call option the option which gives the holder the right to buy a currency at a specified exchange rate within a specific period of time.

currency carry trade borrowing funds in a foreign market and the purchase of an offsetting position in some fixed income securities in the domestic market.

currency cocktail a unit of account on several different currencies.

currency coupon swap = *cross rate swap.*

currency cross rate = *cross rate.*

currency depreciation decline in value of a currency. ***Also***: depreciation.

currency devaluation the planned reduction in the value of a monetary unit. ***Also***: devaluation.

currency diversification the placing of investments in different currencies.

currency exchange warrant (CEW) the cash settled *American option* which entitles the holder to a cash payment at exercise if the spot rate in the target currency exceeds the strike rate.

currency exposure method (CEM) the method used to calculate the credit risk of a swap, which involves a factor for future credit exposure and replacement cost of the swap.

currency forward = *forward currency contract.*

currency future = *foreign currency future.*

currency hedge a hedge against foreign exchange fluctuations.

currency-hedged foreign bond a foreign bond the coupon and the principal payments of which are in the investor's domestic currency, but the coupons are sensitive to foreign interest rates.

currency index warrants a basket of currencies each of whose inclusion and representation in the group is determined by its inclusion in an index.

currency insurance a risk management strategy created either through dynamic hedging in cash or futures or using a sequence of short-term currency options to replicate the longer-term options.

currency-linked note a note with the returns partly determined by a change in the currency rates and, by interest rate differentials across currencies.

currency-linked outperformance unit (CLOU) a note with its return tied to an embedded *outperformance option* which increases in value in proportion to the relative change in two currencies.

currency option = *foreign currency option.*

currency overlay the outsourcing of the currency risk management to a specialist, known as *overlay manager.*

currency pair two currencies that are traded in pair in the spot foreign exchange market, such as US dollar and Japanese Yen.

currency protected instrument the contract under which the return from a foreign market or an instrument is translated back to the investor's home currency at an embedded rate.

currency protected option = *quanto option.*

currency protected security (CPS) the *structured note* with value at maturity linked to the percentage change in the value of a foreign equity security in the investor's home currency.

currency protected swap (CUPS) = *cross rate swap.*

currency put option an option to sell certain amount of a currency at an agreed rate at some future time.

currency quantity adjusting option = *quanto option.*

currency quanto = *quanto option.*

currency rate swap = *cross rate swap.*

currency risk = *exchange risk.*

currency swap = *foreign exchange swap.*

currency-translated option = *quanto option.*

currency warrant a warrant that grants the holder the right to exercise it into a prespecified amount of another currency at a specific exchange rate.

current assets ratio = *acid-test ratio.*

current coupon an interest coupon on a bond that gives a yield close to current rates on comparable instruments.

current-coupon issue = *on-the-run issue.*

current delivery the delivery of the commodities to be made now or in the next few months.

current delivery month = *nearby month.*

current distribution a distribution other than a liquidating distribution.

current dividend a dividend paid out of profits and earnings from the normal operations. ***See***: *liquidating dividend.*

current exercisable value = *intrinsic value.*

current exposure method a method of calculating cost of default as the replacement cost of all marked-to-market contracts currently *in-the-money*, plus the credit risk of potential changes in the prices of the underlying asset.

current face the remaining principal on a mortgage security.

current interest rate = *going rate of interest.*

current issue the most recently auctioned issue of Treasury securities.

current market value = *fair market value.*

current maturity time interval between the present date and the maturity date of a bond. ***See***: *original maturity.*

current note = *short-term note.*

current paper = *short-term note.*

current price the real time price of a security traded on an exchange. ***Also***: real-time quote.

current return = *dividend yield.*

current sinker the bond with a sinking fund obligation set up and is presently operative.

current yield the yield that equals the annual return of an investment divided by the price paid for it. ***Also***: actual yield; cash-on-cash return; cash-on-cash yield; current return; running yield. ***See***: *indicated yield.*

curtailment the partial prepayments of an asset-backed security because borrowers are repaying more principal.

cushion <1> the amount by which the revenue bond's revenues exceed the operating costs and the maintenance cost and debt service, usually 20%. ***Also***: 20% margin. <2> = *call protection.*

cushion bond a high interest rate bond of top quality that sells at a premium level (20%) *above par.*

cushion theory a theory which holds that a stock's price will rise if many short positions have been built.

cusip code the 9-character alphanumeric for identifying issues, such as IBM's cusip is 45920QEQ3. ***Also***: CINS; ***See***: *stock symbol.*

custodial account an account in which the securities or other assets are held under a safekeeping agreement on behalf of one or more customers.

custody-only trading system in which shares must be registered to the holder and only be traded in its physical form.

customary payout ratios the range of payout ratios that is typical according to an analysis of comparable companies.

customer picking prices the customer is firm on prices without allowance.

customer risk = *credit risk.*

customer segregated account the special account that is used to hold and separate clients' assets from the assets of the brokerage firm.

customer's net debit balance the total amount of credit given by an NYSE member firm to its customers.

customer-type indicator codes (CTI) the system that uses four different codes to indicate the types of transactions.

customized benchmark the benchmark designed to meet the client's requirements and long-term objectives.

customized CDO = *single-tranche CDO.*

customized off-exchange derivative = *over the counter derivative.*

customized swap a swap which is tailored to the need of the participants.

customized upside basket security (CUBS) an *equity-linked note* the payout of which is contingent on the average value of an underlying portfolio.

cut-off date the date on which the stock goes from *cum rights* to *ex-rights.*

cut-off point = *hurdle rate.*

cut-off rate = *hurdle rate.*

cut-off time = *exercise cut-off time.*

cut-off yield the bond yield at which or below which the bids are accepted.

cutting a melon additional distribution of profits by means of *dividend.*

CV coefficient of variation

cyclical stock a stock that goes up and down with the trend of business, e. g. housing stock. ***Opp***: *noncyclical stock.*

cylinder <1> buying a series of puts at the same strike price but with different maturities, and simultaneous writing of a series of calls at a lower strike price. ***Also***: risk reversal. ***See***: *equity risk reversal.* <2> = *range forward.*

D d

D <1> bond rating of the lowest quality. <2> the month abbreviation for April in puts. <3> Nasdaq descriptor meaning a new issue or a reverse split. <4> option strike price code for 20.

daily adjustable tax-exempt security (DATES) the variable-rate municipal re-marketed daily at the clearing rate.

daily earnings at risk (DEAR) the measure of value at risk for a 24-hour period using a 95% confidence level.

daily settlement the settlement of futures positions at the end of a trading day.

daily time decay = *theta.*

daily time effect the profit or loss per day on a particular option position.

daisy chain (DC) = *manipulation.*

DARTS Dutch auction rate transferable security

DAT direct access trading

dated date = *date of value.*

dated security the security which bears a specific redemption date on it.

date due <1> = *due date.* <2> = *maturity date.*

date forward = *post date.*

date generation determination if the reset cycle is computed backwards from the expiration date or forwards from the effective date.

date of declaration <1> the date on which the company declares dividends. ***Also***: declaration date; dividend declaration date. <2> = *expiration date.*

date of delivery = *delivery date.*

date of expiration = *expiration date.*

date of issue <1> the date on which a bond is issued. ***Also***: issuing date. <2> the date on which the securities are actually sold and delivered. ***Also***: D-day; offering date.

date of maturity = *maturity date.*

date of record the date on which the shareholder must own shares to be entitled to a dividend, usually the fourth day after ex-dividend date. ***Also***: holder of record date; record date.

date of value date from which accrued interest is calculated on bonds or loans. ***Also***: dated date; initial day; interest date. ***See***: *value date.*

DATES daily adjustable tax-exempt security

date sensitivity risk the risk associated with a derivative portfolio from mismatches in floating-rate reset dates on two sides of a dealer's derivatives book.

dating the method of extending credit beyond the time it was originally given, e. g. 90 days instead of 60. ***Also***: seasoned dating; special dating.

dating ahead giving a document a date earlier than the actual date on which it was signed to make it effective from the earlier date. ***Also***: back dating.

dating forward = *post dating.*

DAX 30 an index of the 30 most heavily traded stocks in Germany.

DAX 100 the price-weighted index of the 100 heavily traded stocks in Germany.

day-after option an option that gives buyers the right to cancel after 24 hours.

day count basis = *money market yield.*

day count note = *accrual note.*

daylight exposure = *open position.*

daylight trade = *day trading.*

day of delivery = *delivery day.*

day of due date <1> = *due date.* <2> = *maturity date.*

day of maturity = *maturity date.*

day of reckoning = *account day.*

day-of-the-week effect = *weekend effect.*

days to cover aggregate *short interest* on a stock for the month divided by the average daily trading volume. ***Also***: short interest ratio.

day-to-day option the option for only one day but renewable from one day to the next if both parties agree.

day-to-day repo repurchase agreement callable on a 24 hours notice.

day-to-day volatility the price change in one trading day.

day trader one who buys and sells in one day. **See**: *in-and-out trader.*

day trading buying and selling securities, futures or options in one day. ***Also***: daylight trade. **See**: *in and out*; *jobbing*; *swing trading.*

day trading buying power four times the equity in a margin account.

DD <1> the rating of bonds which are questionable, lower than DDD. <2> deep discount. <3> delayed delivery.

D-day = *date of issue.*

DDD rating of bonds that are in default or in arrears, lower than C.

DDM <1> discounted dividend model. <2> dividend discount model.

DDN documented discount note

dead cat bounce the price recovers and comes back up.

dead hand provision a defense method used by companies to protect against a takeover by another company.

dead market a market with little trading, or open interest. **See**: *inactive market.*

dead money the investment in stocks which have dropped in value.

deadweight the percentage of a portfolio which matches the underlying index.

deadwood effect the phenomena that traders tend to contribute stocks they do not want, so the mutual fund may contain weak shares.

deal <1> the temporary reduction in the price of an asset. ***Also***: bargain. <2> = *securities transaction.*

dealer agreement = *agreement among underwriters.*

dealer bank the investment bank that specializes in dealing with government securities. ***Also***: government securities dealer.

dealer equity option the equity option bought in the normal course of activity of dealing in options by a dealer.

dealer loan an overnight loan made to securities dealers from the money market banks.

dealer market = *dealer's market.*

dealer option a futures option written by a company which deals in the underlying cash commodity.

dealer paper the commercial paper purchased by a broker-dealer who sells it to institutional investors. ***Also***: dealer-placed paper. **See**: *direct paper.*

dealer-placed paper = *dealer paper.*

dealer profit the difference between the asked price and the bid from a dealer.

dealer's discount = *underwriter's discount.*

dealer's market a market whereby market makers buy and sell for both their own account and client accounts by telephone or by computers. ***Also***: dealer market.

dealer spread = *bid-ask spread.*

dealing day = *trading day.*

dealing desk = *trading desk.*

dealing for the new time = *account dealing.*

dealing in differences the practice of ordering the broker to buy a security, then selling it within the period of a single account and settling the difference. ***Also***: speculating in differences.

dealing in futures = *forward business.*

dealing within the account the purchase or sale or a short sale executed in the same account period. **See**: *account dealing.*

deal stock the stock of a company that is rumored to be a takeover target.

deal to deal broker = *inter-dealer broker.*

DEAR daily earnings at risk

death-backed bond the bond backed by the loans of a policyholder against the value of a life insurance policy.

death future an investment in which the death benefit of a terminally ill person is purchased in a lump-sum. ***Also***: viatical settlement.

death play a strategy that buys stock on the belief that a key executive will die, the company find a replacement executive and the stock will have a higher price.

death put the redemption feature on a bond that allows the estate of the bond beneficiary to sell it back to the issuer in the event of the beneficiary's death. ***Also***: survivor's option.

death spiral <1> an investor who lends money in exchange for the convertible debt of a company which needs money desperately. <2> = *toxic convertible.*

death spiral convertible = *toxic convertible.*

death valley curve the period before a new company starts generating revenues, when it is difficult to raise money.

debenture <1> = *bond.* <2> = *public bond.* <3> = *unsecured bond.*

debenture coupon = *bond coupon.*

debenture discount = *bond discount.*

debenture rate debenture interest rate.

debenture stock <1> the stock of a firm with all or part of its assets promised as security. <2><UK> a bond which refers to debt issues as stock, no individual instrument will be issued.

debenture to bearer = *bearer bond.*

debit the cost of securities or commodities covered by the credit extended by a broker. ***Also***: debit balance.

debit balance = *debit.*

debit paper = *short-term note.*

debit spread <1> the buying and selling of puts and calls of the same class, the premiums paid exceed the premiums received, resulting in a debit entry in the client's margin account. ***Also***: front spread. <2> difference in the value of 2 options, when the value of the one purchased exceeds the value of the one sold. **See**: *credit spread.*

debt/bond fund a *mutual fund* that invests in fixed income instruments like bonds, debentures and various money market instruments.

debt calling = *early extinguishment.*

debt ceiling the maximum amount of money that a bond issuer can owe.

Also: debt limit.

debt discount = *bond discount.*

debt/equity hybrid = *hybrid security.*

debt-equity ratio the financial relationship between debt to outsiders and the owners' capital. ***Also***: debt-net worth ratio; debt-to-capital ratio; debt-to-equity ratio; debt-to-net worth ratio; equity gearing; ratio of debt to capital; ratio of liabilities to net worth.

debt-equity swap <1> the issuing company's using of distribution facilities of the broker/dealer to exchange a newly registered issue of stock for outstanding bonds of the same issue. ***See***: *debt-for-equity swap.* <2> buying debt from a commercial bank at a discount, and exchanging it with the central bank for local currency and using the money to buy local equities. ***Also***: debt swap. <3> a swap that converts a debt into equity.

debt exchangeable for common stock (DECS) = *automatically convertible enhanced security.*

debt factor = *leverage ratio.*

debt financed corporate takeover = *leveraged buyout.*

debt for debt exchange satisfying an old debt by issuing a new debt.

debt-for-debt swap = *bond swap.*

debt-for-equity swap a swap to exchange equity for debt or vice versa over a prearranged period. ***Also***: debt-for-stock swap. ***See***: *debt-equity swap.*

debt-for-stock swap = *debt-for-equity swap.*

debt instrument IOU, CD, bill, bond, or commercial paper which represents the money borrowed. ***Also***: debt security.

debt leverage = *leverage.*

debt limit = *debt ceiling.*

debt-net worth ratio = *debt-equity ratio.*

debt option a non-equity option the underlying asset is a debt instrument.

debt-paying ability = *solvency.*

debt-reducing exchange offer (DREO) an offer of equity securities to holders of a company's bond or other debt to extinguish the debt.

debt retirement complete *repayment* of a debt instrument or bond issue. ***Also***: extinguishment.

debt security = *debt instrument.*

debt service the schedule for repayment of principal and interest of a debt.

debt-serving capacity = *solvency.*

debt shelf the shelf registration for a bond offering.

debt swap = *debt-equity swap.*

debt-to-capital ratio = *debt-equity ratio.*

debt-to-equity ratio = *debt-equity ratio.*

debt-to-net worth ratio = *debt-equity ratio.*

debt type the form of a credit obligation.

debt warrant = *bond warrant.*

debt with springing warrants a deep discount bond with *springing warrants* attached.

decay = *theta.*

decimalization switching reporting and quotation of prices from fractions to decimal numbers. ***Also***: decimal pricing; decimal trading.

decimal pricing = *decimalization.*

decimal trading = *decimalization.*

declaration <1> announcement to pay dividends by a corporation. ***Also***:

dividend announcement; dividend declaration. <2> = *exercise.*

declaration date (DD) <1> = *date of declaration.* <2> = *expiration date.*

declaration day = *expiration date.*

declared capital = *stated capital.*

declared dividend the dividend declared by the company. ***Also***: dividend declared.

declining call schedule a stepped call structure in a bond in which each call date has a lower call price.

declining market <1> = *bear market.* <2> = *down market.*

decompounded rate a scale-down rate used for a stub in a swap.

deconstructing segregating components of a security into categories.

decoupling a departure from the observed relationship between 2 prices or indexes.

decoupling trade the trade designed to profit from a sudden change in the spread between two indexes or two rates.

DECS dividend enhanced convertible stock

dedicated capital = *nominal capital.*

dedicated portfolio = *cash flow matching.*

dedicated short bias a *hedging* strategy under which the hedge fund manager is required to have more short positions than long positions.

dedicating a portfolio = *cash flow matching.*

dedication strategy *cash-flow matching* in more than one period.

deed of trust <1> a document conveying title to an asset to a designated person. ***Also***: trust deed. <2> = *indenture.*

deemed benefit <Canada> the amount by which the actual cost of a share under the option is less than the fair value of the share or unit on its date of acquisition.

deemed dividend the dividend deemed to be paid to shareholder on redemption, acquisition or cancellation of share of stock.

deemed risk <1> the estimate of the loss arising from the replacement of a contract at an unfavorable exchange rate. <2> = *fractional exposure.*

deep bid a bid or offer of a significant size somewhat away from the market.

deep discount bond the bond issued at a par value of $1,000, sold at a discount of more than 20%, the interest rate of which fluctuates frequently. ***See***: *coupon bond*; *discount bond.*

deep in the money (DITM) so far *in the money* that it is unlikely to go *out of the money* prior to expiration.

deep out of the money so far *out of the money* that it is unlikely it may go *in the money* before expiration. ***Also***: under water; wing out.

deep pocket a firm or an individual of wealth. ***Also***: mogul; tycoon.

deer an investor who wants to buy and sell stock in a short period and will go away after making a profit.

default <1> failure to pay the interest or principal on an obligation. <2> failure of a dealer to deliver the securities sold or to pay for securities bought. <3> failure of the holder of a futures contract to meet a margin call or make or take a delivery.

default adjusted price the present value of default impaired cash flows discounted at the nominal yield of a bond or loan.

default basket swap = *basket credit default swap.*

default contingent swap = *default swap.*

default correlation the tendency of two or more reference assets in the basket to default together. ***Also***: default event correlation.

defaulted security fixed income security unable to make interest payments or unable to pay the principal.

default event correlation = *default correlation.*

default exposure = *credit risk.*

default-free security = *gilt-edged security.*

default option an option that pays off a fixed amount upon default of the reference asset.

default payment <1> the payout value of a credit derivative, which equals the *mark-to-market* decline in the value of the underlying asset. <2> payment of par on the instrument in return for physical delivery. <3> a fixed percentage of the notional value of the instrument.

default premium the premium in yield that compensates investors for the *credit risk.*

default probability the likelihood that a debt instrument will default in a given period of time.

default put = *credit swap.*

default rate <1> the weighted average probability for all bonds held in a portfolio to default within one year. <2> the probability of the tendency of bonds of given ratings to default in one year.

default risk = *credit risk.*

default swap <1> a credit swap under which one leg pays a fixed amount periodically and the other pays nothing unless a default occurs. ***Also***: default contingent swap. <2> a swap in which one party failed to perform.

default swap basis the difference between the CDS spread and the cash LIBOR spread.

default swaption the option that gives the option holder a right to enter into a credit default swap.

defeased bond/equity swap the swap used by guarantors of some industrial development bonds to pre-refund the bond, and swap its common stock for the US Treasury securities.

defense bond <UK> the savings bond issued by the UK Government from 1939 to 1964 to raise money for military purpose.

defensive buy investment with low risk.

defensive security the low-risk security providing predictable and safe return to the investors.

defensive stock a stock issued by a firm with stable earnings even when market is weak.

deferred annuity an *annuity* that delays payments of *rents* until the investors elect to receive them in the future. ***Also***: annuity in arrears; deferred-payment annuity. **See**: *annuity due*; *ordinary annuity.*

deferred bond the bond the interest rate of which is low at the start but will gradually increase to its full rate in later periods. **See**: *deferred interest bond*; *deferred payment bond.*

deferred call the clause that prohibits the company from calling the bond before a certain date.

deferred coupon bond a bond that pays no interest for a fixed period and then pays interest at a relatively higher rate.

deferred coupon swap = *forward swap.*

deferred delivery (DD) an agreement by a buyer of shares that he or she will not press for delivery but will allow extra time for the jobber to get the shares.

deferred dividend the dividend that is declared to be paid at some future date.

deferred future the futures contract of a more *distant month.*

deferred interest bond the bond which pays interest at a later date, e. g. a zero-coupon bond. ***See***: *deferred bond.*

deferred interest certificate = *arrear certificate.*

deferred interest warrant = *arrear certificate.*

deferred payment-American option an option the holder of which can freeze the underlying price at which it will exercise before maturity. ***Also***: Boston option; deferred-payment option; deferred-payout option; lock-in option.

deferred-payment annuity = *deferred annuity.*

deferred payment bond the bond the payment to the issuer is deferred for a fixed period until the buyer can obtain finance. ***Also***: fixed assurance note. **See**: *deferred bond.*

deferred payment note an equity-linked note issued with an embedded *deferred payment American option.*

deferred payment obligation a market discount bond, short-term note, US savings bond or annuity.

deferred-payment option = *deferred-payment American option.*

deferred-payment swap a swap where some or all payments are delayed for tax purpose. **See**: *forward swap.*

deferred-payout option = *deferred-payment American option.*

deferred pay security a security the value of which accrues for some time before the issuer has to pay with cash.

deferred premium the premium that must be paid following the policy's statement date, but prior to the policy renewal.

deferred premium option an option with premium paid at expiration.

deferred profit sharing the portion of profits allocated to employee's trust.

deferred rate-setting swap a fixed-for-floating interest-rate swap the coupon of which is not set until a later day, usually referenced to the US Treasury rate. ***Also***: delayed rate-setting swap; spreadlock; spreadlock swap; swap spreadlock.

deferred sales charge = *back-end load.*

deferred serial bond a serial bond in which the first installment does not fall due for at least 2 years after issuance.

deferred share <1> a share of stock that receives no right to the remaining assets of the company in the event of bankruptcy until all other shareholders have been paid. <2> <UK> = *founder's share.*

deferred start option an option traded before its effective term begins, usually before the strike price and other terms are set.

deferred-start swap = *forward swap.*

deferred stock a stock the dividends of which are not paid until a stated date or until a specified event has occurred in the future.

deferred strike option an option which allows the buyer to set the strike price at some date after it is traded.

deferred swap = *forward swap.*

defibrillator an option that pays off when the market makes an extreme move.

deficiency the excess of liabilities over assets because of operating losses.

Also: deficit net worth; negative net worth.

deficit net worth = *deficiency.*

defined portfolio the fixed basket of securities underlying some limited function unit trusts and trust issued receipts.

definitive bond a permanent document given in exchange for a bearer scrip when all the installments have been paid.

definitive note a note representing the obligation that can be delivered, either a fixed rate or a floating rate note.

degenerate swap a swap or a *forward rate agreement* or a simple variation that is based on only one forward rate.

degree-day index an index published by Energy Information Administration on daily changes in temperature.

degree-day swap a swap which pays a floating coupon that is proportional to the change in the *degree-day index* over a fixed period in return for a fixed fee. ***Also***: temperature swap.

degree of financial leverage (DFL) the percentage change in the earnings available to common shareholders associated with a given percentage change in the earnings of the company.

degree of financial risk = *gearing ratio.*

de-hedging commodity producer's buying back of long-term futures contracts to hedge against future price increase, often to save cost.

delayed of quotes or news, not current. ***Opp***: *real-time.*

delayed barrier option a barrier option which will be knocked in or knocked out certain days after the barrier is reached.

delayed cap a floating rate note with a cap, but the cap does not take effect until a later date.

delayed convertible a *convertible bond* that cannot be converted now due to some limitation.

delayed delivery (DD) the delivery later than the scheduled date. ***Also***: delayed settlement. ***See***: *overdue delivery.*

delayed delivery, interest to run the words meaning delivery on the bonds will be delayed and therefore the interest will not be set to the settlement date, but to the delivery date.

delayed double-barrier option the double barrier option that is knocked out certain days after the knock-out window.

delayed drawdown swap = *forward swap.*

delayed ending a situation when the buy and sell orders accumulate at the close of a day's trade.

delayed issuance pool the *mortgage backed securities* which, at the time of issuance were collateralized by the seasoned loans originated prior to the *date of issue.*

delayed LIBOR-reset swap = *LIBOR in arrears swap.*

delayed option = *forward-start option.*

delayed rate-setting swap = *deferred rate-setting swap.*

delayed reset swap = *arrears swap.*

delayed settlement = *delayed delivery.*

delayed start swap = *forward swap.*

delayed-strike option a normal option with the strike price to be set at some future date before expiration. ***See***: *forward-start option.*

deleverage the reduction of instruments or borrowed capital previously used to increase the return of an investment. ***Opp***: *leverage.* ***See***: *deleveraging.*

deleveraged constant maturity-linked floater the *floating-rate note* with the interest payment set relative to a constant maturity swap or sovereign rate.

deleveraged floater the fixed-income investment with a floating rate tied to a specific index. ***See***: *leveraged floater.*

deleveraged instrument a note, swap or an option, in which the participation rate in an interest rate or other index change is less than 100%.

deleveraging the process of decreasing the proportional use of debt in the capital structure. ***See***: *deleverage.*

deliverable bill <1> a Treasury bill that fulfills a set of guidelines set forth by the exchange. <2> = *Treasury bill.*

deliverable bond a bond which is listed by an exchange as being acceptable in the settlement of a bond future.

deliverable grade = *contract grade.*

deliverable instrument the asset in a forward contract that will be delivered in the future at an agreed-upon price.

deliverable name = *contract grade.*

deliverable stock the commodities for which receipts may be used in making delivery on futures contracts.

delivery <1> the seller's transmission of securities to the broker. <2> the tender and receipt of a commodity in the settlement of a futures contract. <3> the transfer of deed in a real estate sale.

delivery against cash (DAC) = *delivery versus payment.*

delivery against payment (D/P) = *delivery versus payment.*

delivery date the date on which a delivery is made. ***Also***: date of delivery.

delivery day <1> the first day of a month on which delivery is to be made under a futures contract. ***Also***: day of delivery. <2> = *account day.*

delivery factor a coefficient multiplied by the settlement price of a futures contract to obtain the invoice price for a specific deliverable instrument.

delivery instrument a document used to effect delivery on a futures contract, e. g. a warehouse receipt.

delivery mechanism the specified process for the delivery of a commodity.

delivery month the month in which the futures or options contracts are to be delivered. ***Also***: contract month.

delivery on spot the delivery of securities soon after the contract.

delivery option the provision of a futures contract available to the seller, including the *quality option*, *timing option*, and *wild card option.*

delivery point the location at which the underlying commodity in the futures contract must be delivered.

delivery price actual price invoiced in the futures delivery, including freight and related cost.

delivery risk the risk that a counterpart will not be allowed to complete his or her side of the deal though willing to do so. ***Also***: settlement risk.

delivery specifications the provisions of a future, a forward, or an option contract that detail the characteristics of the financial instruments or commodities that are accepted as *good delivery.*

delivery versus payment (DVP) the delivery of the securities to the buyer's bank for payment. ***Also***: cash down; cash on delivery; delivery against cash; delivery against payment; for cash; for money; pay cash; receive versus payment; wanted for cash. ***Opp***: *free delivery.*

delta <1> measure of how much the option premium will change if a point move occurs in the price of the *under-*

lying asset. ***Also***: delta value; hedge ratio; neutral hedge ratio. **See**: *option elasticity.* <2> the inactive and stable shares that are traded on the *third market.*

delta 100 *delta* multiplied by 100.

delta cross-hedge a futures hedge which has both maturity and currency mismatches with an underlying risk exposure.

delta differential the difference between the delta of the option bought and that of the option sold.

delta-gamma approximation using the delta and the gamma to approximate the change in the derivative price due to a change in the price of the underlying.

delta-gamma hedge a hedge which neutralizes the market risk of an asset or a position in an instrument with embedded options.

delta-gamma-kappa-rho hedge any complex hedge involving at least two options with different expiration dates.

delta-gamma-theta approximation the formula using delta, gamma and theta to approximate the change in the price of derivative due to a change in the price of the underlying and the passage of time.

delta hedge = *dynamic hedging.*

delta hedging = *dynamic hedging.*

delta hedging derivative the derivative used in delta hedging.

delta neutral calendar spread a time spread with a neutral delta.

delta neutrality the strategy used to create a hedged portfolio with a delta of zero, i.e. with offsetting positive and negative deltas. ***Also***: delta neutral position; delta spread; neutral position; neutral spread.

delta neutral position = *delta neutrality.*

delta-normal VAR = *linear VAR.*

delta of a call the sensitivity of the value of a call option to the changes in the underlying asset's price.

delta of a put the sensitivity of the value of a put option to the changes in the underlying asset's price, it is always negative.

delta of CDO the notional of CDS for that credit which has the same market change as the tranche for a small movement in the credit's CDS spread curve.

delta risk <1> the risk of a loss due to a positive or negative delta of an option or option portfolio. <2> = *directional disk.*

delta spread = *delta neutrality.*

delta value = *delta.*

delta variable the likelihood of an option being exercised.

demand loan a short-term loan that is repayable on demand. ***Also***: floating loan. **See**: *call money.*

demand rate = *short rate.*

dematerialization the process by which physical stock certificates are converted into an equivalent number of shares in the electronic format and credited on account. **See**: *rematerialization.*

dematerialzed securities the securities in electronic format rather than the traditional paper certificates.

demerger to sell off subsidiaries or divisions of a company. ***Opp***: *merger.* **See**: *reverse merger.*

de minimis exemption <1> the SEC exemption under which mistaken bids or purchases by a distribution participant of less than 2% of the ADTV of the security being offered are exempt from trading restrictions. <2> = *3-cent de minimis exemption.*

demutualization a conversion in which a mutually owned company becomes a shareholder-owned company.

denomination = *face value.*

depositary trust company (DTC) the company providing asset management, settlement, and clearing services to the broker/dealers.

deposit certificate = *certificate of deposit.*

depository preferred stock an issue of high par value preferred stock deposited with a bank, which in turn issues more shares of a lower par value.

depository receipt a negotiable financial instrument issued by a bank to represent a foreign company's securities.

deposit receipt = *certificate of deposit.*

Deposit/Withdrawal at Custodian (D-WAC) an automated system for the deposits and withdrawals of securities or other assets from the depository trust company.

depreciation = *currency depreciation.*

depressed market the market situation when prices are falling because supply is much greater than demand. ***Also***: buyer's market; flat market; soft market. **See**: *seller's market.*

depressing news any news that is bad for investors and leads to falling prices because there are few buyers.

depth of market the degree to which the market can absorb substantial trading volume without any wild price fluctuations.

deregulation the removal of government rules and regulations, which allows the market to function with more freedom.

derivative <1> a financial product that derives its value from the value of another asset. ***Also***: derivative financial product; derivative instrument; derivative product; derivative security; financial derivative. ***Opp***: *primary instrument.* <2> the rate of change at which the strike slope changes with every ten point increase in the call delta in the intra-month skew.

derivative deposit the deposit created when a person borrows money from a bank by depositing it into an account.

derivative financial product = *derivative.*

derivative gain the gain from holding a financial derivative.

derivative instrument = *derivative.*

derivative loss the loss from holding a financial derivative.

derivative portfolio a portfolio of position in the derivative products.

derivative product = *derivative.*

derivatives accounting = *accounting for derivatives.*

derivatives book-runner a bank or a brokerage firm specializing in structuring and trading derivatives.

derivatives disclosure rule an SEC rule that requires financial risks must be disclosed to the investors before they can open accounts for trading derivatives.

derivative security = *derivative.*

derivatives operating subsidiary the entity that is established to avoid some regulatory and capital restrictions that its bank or investment bank parent might face in certain markets of financial derivatives.

derivatives policy group (DPG) a group representing six large non-bank OTC derivatives dealers who worked with CFTC and SEC to design the oversight and procedures for OTC derivatives.

derivative pricing theory the body of financial theory used for the valuation of derivatives.

derivatives product company (DPC) a financial company which serves as a the counterpart for swaps and other credit-sensitive financial derivatives. ***Also***: credit enhanced vehicle. ***See***: *bankruptcy remote entity; special-purpose vehicle.*

derivatives trading manager (DTM) <1> the manager of a futures fund or a hedge fund specializing in derivatives. <2> the manager of a derivatives trading desk.

descending yield curve = *inverted yield curve.*

designated sale a sale of security under which only certain members participate. ***Opp***: *group sale.*

designated time net settlement (DTNS) the funds settlement used in Japan where net settlements are debited or credited to the accounts of participating banks.

designer stock = *tracking stock.*

desktop ticker the software that provides real time or delayed quote data directly on a computer screen.

desperate debt a debt of a desperate firm.

destructured asset swap a structured note combined with a swap contract that converts it to a simple floating-rate note.

detachable warrant the warrant that entitles the holder to purchase a given number of shares of the issuing company at a specified price. ***See***: *non-detachable warrant.*

deterministic interest rate = *fixed interest rate.*

deterministic volatility function model = *implied tree model.*

devaluation = *currency devaluation.*

diagonal bear spread the purchase of a relatively long-term option contract and the sale of a shorter-term contract with a lower strike price.

diagonal bull spread a spread created by selling an option and buying another option with a further expiration date and a lower strike price.

diagonal calendar call spread buying in-the-money LEAP and selling at-the-money or out-of-the-money near term calls. ***Also***: diagonal time spread using calls.

diagonal call = *diagonal spread using calls.*

diagonal credit spread diagonal spread with the premium received higher than the premium paid.

diagonal debit spread diagonal spread with the premium paid higher than the premium received.

diagonal option spread = *diagonal spread.*

diagonal put = *diagonal spread using puts.*

diagonal reverse spread = *reverse diagonal spread.*

diagonal spread buying an option with longer expiration date and selling one with a shorter expiration date and different strike price. ***Also***: diagonal option spread. ***See***: *horizontal spread; vertical spread.*

diagonal spread using calls buying a call with a lower strike price in a further month, and selling a call with a higher strike in a near-term month. ***Also***: diagonal call.

diagonal spread using puts buying a put with a higher strike price in a further month, and selling a put with a lower strike price in a near-term month. ***Also***: diagonal put.

diagonal time spread selling an at-the-money or out-of-the-money near term option and buying options with a different strike in a deferred month.

diagonal time spread using calls = *diagonal calendar call spread.*

diff = *Euro-rate differential future.*

diff contract = *contract for difference.*

difference the difference between the market price and the theoretical value of an option. ***See***: *option-adjusted spread.*

difference check the difference in interest payments paid to a swap party in *net settlement.* ***See***: *termination payment.*

difference contract = *contract for difference.*

difference from S&P a mutual fund's return minus the change in the price of the S&P 500 index.

difference option (diff option) <1> an option on the *forward interest rate differential* between two comparable financial instruments denominated in two different currencies. <2> a spread or an out-performance option with a payout linked to the price difference between two underlying assets. ***Also***: spread option.

difference swap = *diff swap.*

differential <1> = *interest rate differential.* <2> = *odd-lot differential.* <3> = *swap rate differential.*

differential disclosure <1> preparing different set of financial statements for different users. <2> a public firm's reporting of conflicting or significant information in official statements such as annual reports, 10-Ks and 10-Qs.

differential equation a continuous time equation that contains derivatives of a function.

differential option an *outperformance option* the payout of which is based on the value of an index determined by the relative performance of two instruments.

differential swap <1> = *cross-currency swap.* <2> = *diff swap.*

diff option difference option

diff swap a swap under which both the floating rates are applied to one single currency only. ***Also***: difference swap; differential swap; rate differential swap. ***See***: *cross-rate swap.*

diffusion index a statistical measure of the overall behavior of a group or series of economic time series.

diffusion process the way the price of a security changes that assumes that the price takes on all intermediate values.

digested security a security purchased by an investor who is likely to hold it for quite a long time.

digital gap option an option with the payoff equal to the asset value less the gap value, depending on the underlying asset finishes above or below the strike price.

digital option (DO) = *binary option.*

digital option pricing the pricing of a digital option, done by separating the option into several components.

digits deleted the first digit of a price dropped because of heavy trading, for example 35 ½, 35 3/8, 35 1/8 becomes 5 ½, 5 3/8, 5 1/8. ***See***: *points quote.*

diluted earnings per share = *fully diluted earnings per share.*

diluted shares the new number of shares outstanding after all dilutive shares have been accounted for. ***Also***: diluted shares outstanding.

diluted shares outstanding = *diluted shares.*

dilution the effect of a drop in earnings per share caused by the potential conversion of securities or by the potential exercise of warrants or options. ***See***: *ownership dilution.*

dilution protection a change in the *conversion ratio* in the case of a stock dividend or extraordinary distribution to avoid *dilution* of a convertible bond-holder's potential equity.

dilutive effect the result of a transaction that decreases the earnings per share.

dilutive security a stock warrant, right, convertible security, preferred stock, etc. the exercise or conversion of which would lower the earnings per share of the issuing company. ***Also***: residual security.

dingo a government bond with coupons stripped off. ***Also***: felines.

dip a slight drop in the securities prices after a sustained uptrend. ***Also***: plunge; reaction. **See**: *crash*.

direct access trading (DAT) the trading which allows a trader to trade directly with another trader.

direct arbitrage = *simple arbitrage*.

direct credit substitute = *credit enhancement*.

directed shares = *friends and family shares*.

direct equity option the option under which investors can invest capital lump sums in securities.

direct exchange = *forward exchange rate*.

direct financing raising capital without the assistance of underwriters. ***Opp***: *indirect financing*.

direct hedge a hedge the underlying asset of which matches the subject being hedged. **See**: *cross hedge*.

directional movement index (DMI) an index developed by J Welles Wilder for identifying when a trend is present, or if it is trending or not.

directional risk the exposure to the direction of a market or reference. ***Also***: delta risk.

directional strategy a compound option strategy that seeks to take advantage of market direction rather than volatility.

directional trading the strategy used by investors who believe that they are able to predict the movement of price, then take positions to take advantage of it.

directly placed paper = *direct paper*.

direct market = *primary market*.

direct offering = *public offering*.

direct paper the commercial paper sold to the investors directly by the issuer. ***Also***: directly placed paper. **See**: *dealer paper*.

direct placement = *private placement*.

direct public offering (DPO) the public offering of shares by small companies without an underwriter. ***Also***: blue-sky securities offering.

direct purchase program the program which enables a company to sell shares directly to the investors. ***Also***: direct stock plan; direct stock purchase plan.

direct quote the foreign exchange quote expressed as variable units of domestic currency against a fixed unit of foreign currency. ***Also***: American terms; direct rate; direct term; giving quote; North American terms; pence rate. **See**: *indirect quote*.

direct rate = *direct quote*.

direct share program (DSP) a program which allows employees and other parties with a relationship to the company to buy stock as part of a public offering.

direct stock plan (DSP) = *direct purchase program*.

direct stock purchase plan (DSP plan) = *direct purchase program*.

direct term = *direct quote*.

direct yield the yield of a foreign bond calculated by dividing the annual interest income by its original purchase price.

dirty bond a bond *cum dividend* and is close to the interest payment date.

dirty float floating exchange rate system in which a government may intervene to change the value of its currency. ***Also***: managed float; managed floating rate.

dirty hedge instrument a financial derivative the risk of which cannot be fully hedged with the liquid exchange-traded securities. **See**: *clean hedge instrument.*

dirty price the quoted bond price which includes the accrued interest since the last payment. ***Also***: full price; gross parity. **See**: *clean price.*

dirty stock a stock which does not meet the requirements for *good delivery.*

disappearing basis rule a rule that the original investment in a stock cannot be treated as taxable distribution when that stock is redeemed.

disaster bond = *catastrophe bond.*

disbursing agent = *paying agent.*

disclaimer the statement made to free oneself from any liability. ***Also***: *hedge clause.*

disclosure risk the risk that disclosure of company information will put it at a disadvantage in the future.

disclosure statement the document that must be provided to and signed by customers before an account is opened.

disco = *discount bond.*

discomfort index the annual inflation rate plus the unemployment rate.

discontinuity risk the risk from failure of market prices or rates to follow a smooth path. ***Also***: market gapping.

discontinuous barriers characteristic of a barrier option when there is a gap.

discontinuous lookback the lookback option which is based on the periodic samples such as daily price fixing.

discontinuous look-forward the look forward option based on the periodic samples such as daily price fixing.

discount <1> the amount by which the forward exchange is less than the spot rate. ***Also***: discount on exchange; exchange discount; swap cost. <2> the amount by which a security sells below its par. ***Also***: discount payment. <3> the conversion of the future value to present value. ***Also***: discount back to present. <verb><4> to sell the note for less than its face value. <5> a reduction in price. <6> a reduction in the mutual fund fee. <7> = *convertible discount.*

discount arbitrage an arbitrage in which a discount option is purchased and an opposite position is established in the underlying asset.

discount back to present = *discount.*

discount basis = *discount yield.*

discount bond a bond that is sold at a discount, and is below its redemption value. ***Also***: disco; discounted bond; pure discount bond. **See**: *deep discount bond*; *zero coupon bond.*

discount currency a currency which has a higher interest rate relative to another currency. **See**: *premium currency.*

discount curve a curve showing discount factors for different maturities.

discounted basis the method of issuing bond at a price below its maturity value.

discounted bond = *discount bond.*

discounted by the market any unannounced information that is widely accepted, and is taken into account in the market price of the stock. ***Also***:

anticipated by the market; discounted in the market.

discounted cash flow (DCF) future cash flows multiplied by the discount factor.

discounted dividend model (DDM) = *dividend discount model.*

discounted gross benefit-cost ratio = *present value profitability index.*

discounted in the market = *discounted by the market.*

discounted investment an investment the return of which is guaranteed by a government.

discounted note = *note discounted.*

discounted payback the length of time needed to recover the cost of an investment discounted to present value.

discounted payback period rule the decision rule in which cash flows are discounted and investment with shortest payback period will be chosen.

discounted present value (DPV) = *present value.*

discounted security = *relevant discounted security.*

discounted stock option an option the exercise price of which is below the market value of the underlying shares on the date of the stock option grant.

discounted value = *present value.*

discount from asset value of an investment trust, the difference between the asset and the stock price expressed as a percentage of the asset value.

discounting the market taking into account of anticipated financial events so that the present stock prices are affected rather than the future prices.

discount instrument <1> a debt instrument that pays no periodic interest but trades at a discount. <2> fixed-rate bond sold with a below market coupon. <3> = *discount security.*

discount issue an issue of securities at a price below the par or redemption value. ***Opp***: *premium issue.*

discount margin the return earned in addition to the index underlying the floating rate security.

discount method the method of paying interest by issuing a security at less than its par and repaying the par value at maturity.

discount note unsecured corporate debt issued at a discount and matures at par.

discount on bonds = *bond discount.*

discount on creditors = *bond discount.*

discount on exchange = *discount.*

discount on stock difference between the par value of stock and the actual amount contributed by the stockholders. ***Also***: excess of par value over issuing price of stock.

discount payment = *discount.*

discount period time interval between the date a bill is discounted and its maturity date. ***Also***: term of discount.

discount point 1% of the account balance.

discount rate (DR) <1> the interest rate which banks are charging for discounting the bills of exchange. ***Also***: maturity interest rate; rate of discount. <2> the interest rate used to discount future value to the present value. ***Also***: capitalization rate. <3> = *hurdle rate.*

discount risk the risk of loss when the discount on mutual fund shares widens.

discount security the security selling at less than its expected or theoretically fair value. ***Also***: discount instrument; original issue discount security.

discount swap <1> a *non-par swap* with one or both of the equivalent securities that are underlying the swap payments selling below parity. ***See***: *premium swap.* <2> a swap that uses the coupon of a discount bond as the payment reference.

discount yield actual yield on a security sold at a discount, it is calculated as: discount ÷ face amount × 360 × days until maturity. ***Also***: discount basis.

discrete barrier option = *partial barrier option.*

discrete process the stochastic process with terms associated with each integer under consideration.

discrete variable a random variable that is countable, e. g. the number of trades.

discretionary account (DA) the account giving a bank the power to invest at its discretion. ***Also***: controlled account; managed account.

discretionary cash flow the cash flow available for paying dividend, retiring debt and repurchasing stock.

discretionary dividend <1> the dividend that is based on the operating results of the company. ***See***: *non-discretionary dividend.* <2> = *common dividend.*

discretionary fund investment money placed with a bank at discretion. ***Also***: advisory fund; flexible trust; general management trust; in-house fund. ***See***: *feeder fund*; *master fund.*

discretization the process of discrete-time approximation of stochastic continuous time series.

discriminatory cross-rate a situation where the par of exchange and the official exchange rate differ between two countries.

disguised dividend = *constructive dividend.*

disintermediation the shifting of funds away from financial intermediaries into Treasury bills and other securities for higher interest rates.

disinvestment the decision or action of whether to terminate an investment or operation.

disparity = *premium disparity.*

disposable capital = *idle money.*

disposition effect the tendency of the investors to sell stock in which they have a profit rather than those in which they have a loss.

distance to default the measure of how close a debt is to a defaulting.

distant month a month in the future during which a futures contract is to be settled. ***See***: *furthest month.*

distressed exchange the exchange of debt for other securities during debt distress in bankruptcy.

distressed security a security of a firm undergoing bankruptcy.

distressed trading a trade in notes and securities of a company undergoing a financial difficulty.

distress sale urgent sale of securities at a significantly reduced price.

distress selling the selling of securities on margin to avoid hurting the equities in the position held.

distributing syndicate a group of investment bankers that come together to facilitate the distribution of a large block of securities. ***Also***: banking syndicate; bracket; distribution syndicate; guerilla group; investment banking group; investment banking syndicate; public syndicate; purchase group; selling group; selling syndicate; syndicate; underwriting group.

distribution <1> the sale of a large block of stock in such a manner that the price is not adversely affected. ***Also***: dumping. <2> = *dividend.* <3> = *public offering.*

distribution area <1> the price range within which a stock trades for a long time. <2> the price range within which sellers sell shares of a stock.

distribution bond a bond that makes distribution of dividend twice a year without affecting the value of the principal.

distribution by coupon classification of a portfolio's securities according to the *coupon rate of interest.*

distribution by maturity classification of securities by their maturities, the longer the maturity, the more risk.

distribution cost a cost for the promotion of mutual fund shares.

distribution date the date on which a dividend, mutual fund distribution, or bond interest payment is made. ***Also***: payable date; payment date.

distribution of shares = *public offering.*

distribution participant a party involved in the public offering of a new security, such as underwriter, broker, dealer and affiliated purchaser.

distribution period the time between the *date of declaration* and the *record date*, usually a few days.

distribution plan a mutual fund's plan to charge some distribution costs such as advertising to investors as an additional load.

distribution stock part of a block of stock sold over a period of time in order to avoid upsetting the market price if sold in a larger volume.

distribution syndicate = *distributing syndicate.*

distributive share the partner's share of partnership income, loss, deduction and tax credit.

distringas notice a notice to suspend the dealings in certain securities for a limited period with the approval of a court. ***See***: *cease and desist order.*

DITM deep in the money

ditto in newspapers, meaning a company is offering a different class of security.

diversifiable risk = *unsystematic risk.*

diversification spreading of investments among a wide variety of assets, from bonds, stocks, CDs to derivatives.

diversified common stock fund a fund which has substantially all of its assets invested in a portfolio of the common stocks of companies engaged in a wide varieties of industries. ***Also***: diversified fund; diversified investment company.

diversified fund = *diversified common stock fund.*

diversified investment company <UK> = *diversified common stock fund.*

diversified portfolio a portfolio of assets that consists of many different specific assets of the same type.

diverstiture the sale or liquidation of a subsidiary. ***See***: *spin-off.*

divestment the transfer of fund or assets to another corporation through a sale or spin-off.

divided account = *severally but not jointly.*

dividend <1> a portion of the earnings that has been declared for distribution to stockholders. ***Also***: capital interest; corporation dividend; distribution; divvy; interest on capital; profit on stock; stock interest. <2> = *interest.*

dividend announcement = *declaration.*

dividend appropriation setting aside the *retained earnings* for the payment of dividend.

dividend arbitrage selling a stock right before the ex-dividend day, and buying it back on or after the ex-dividend day. ***See***: *dividend capture.*

dividend capitalization model a formula used to calculate *cost of equity.* COE = (dividend per share ÷ market value of stock) + dividend growth rate.

dividend capture buying stock before ex dividend day, selling it on ex dividend day after receiving dividend. ***Also***: dividend play; dividend rollover plan; dividend trade; dividend trade roll; roll order. ***See***: *dividend arbitrage.*

dividend claim requesting registered holder for the amount of dividend for the trade made before the ex-dividend date.

dividend clawback a plan in which the sponsors of a project agree to use prior dividends received to cover subsequent cash deficiencies. ***Also***: clawback.

dividend clientele the shareholders who want the company to follow a specific dividend policy, usually for tax-saving reasons.

dividend cover the ratio equal to net profits available for distribution as dividend ÷ dividends actually declared. ***Also***: cover for dividend.

dividend credit = *dividends received deduction.*

dividend crossover method a method used to estimate the date on which the rising common stock dividend will equal the convertible coupon.

dividend declaration = *declaration.*

dividend declaration date = *date of declaration.*

dividend declared = *declared dividend.*

dividend discount model (DDM) the formula used to estimate the intrinsic value of stock of a company by the present value of all future dividends. ***Also***: discounted dividend model.

dividend distribution the mutual fund's distribution of dividend that it receives from other companies.

dividend drag an SEC rule that the cash dividends received by a trust not to be reinvested in portfolio stocks, and that must be accumulated and paid out to the investors periodically.

dividend enhanced convertible stock (DECS) a preferred stock issued with an embedded short put and long call and an above-market dividend rate. ***Also***: preferred redeemable increased dividend equity security; stock appreciation income-linked securities; yield enhanced stock. ***See***: *automatically convertible enhanced security.*

dividend equivalent a dividend imputed on options, which if vested, is charged to retained earnings, if not vested, to the compensation expense.

dividend exclusive = *ex dividend.*

dividend growth model the model for estimating the cost of equity by dividing the expected dividend by the difference between the required rate of return and the expected growth rate in dividends.

dividend in = *cum dividend.*

dividend in arrears unpaid dividend on preferred stock which must be paid before any dividends can be paid to the common stockholders. ***Also***: arrearage; passed dividend. ***See***: *accumulated dividend; omitted dividend.*

dividend in kind a dividend paid in the form of tangible assets. ***Also***: noncash dividend. ***See***: *cash dividend; property dividend.*

dividend in scrip = *scrip dividend.*

dividend limitation the bond covenant that restricts in some way the company's ability to pay cash dividends.

dividend notification the requirement that public companies should notify Nasdaq's Uniform Practice Department at least 10 days in advance of the determination of the *record date.*

dividend off = *ex dividend.*

dividend on = *cum dividend.*

dividend option an option given to the holder of a with-profits life insurance policy that concerns the way the dividend is paid, either in cash, or be used to pay the future premium.

dividend order the stockholder's letter ordering the company to pay dividends to a named person.

dividend out of capital = *capital dividend.*

dividend paid on short sales = *in lieu of dividend.*

dividend-paying stock the stock which pays dividends regularly.

dividend payout proportion of earnings that is paid to common stockholders in the form of dividend.

dividend payout ratio the percentage of earnings paid to the shareholders in the form of dividend. ***Also***: dividend-to-earnings ratio; payout ratio.

dividend play = *dividend capture.*

dividend rate the annual dividend paid per share of *common stock* or *preferred stock.*

dividend reinvestment plan (DRIP) (DRP) a plan which allows stockholders to use the dividends to purchase more shares directly from the issuer.

dividend requirement annual earnings a company needs in order to be able to pay the specified dividends to holders of its *preferred stock.*

dividend return = *dividend yield.*

dividend right a shareholder's right to receive per-share dividends.

dividend rollover plan = *dividend capture.*

dividend scrip = *scrip.*

dividend shares the shares that company stockholders received as *stock dividend.*

dividends per share (DPS) the dividend paid to the shareholder per share of stock owned.

dividends received deduction the tax deduction granted to the shareholders for dividends received from domestic corporations. ***Also***: dividend credit.

dividend stock = *bonus share.*

dividend stock scrip = *scrip.*

dividend stripping a practice by which one company buys control of another company and arranges matters so that income is distributed in dividends and then sells the company. ***Also***: dividend washing; stripping.

dividend swap a transaction in which the investor exchanges an underlying stock or index's current dividend for increased upside equity participation.

dividend-to-earnings ratio = *dividend payout ratio.*

dividend trade = *dividend capture.*

dividend trade roll = *dividend capture.*

dividend warrant the order by a company to its bank to pay a stated sum of money as dividend to a named stockholder. ***Also***: sub-share.

dividend washing = *dividend stripping.*

dividend yield the annual dividend paid divided by the market price per share. ***Also***: current return; dividend return.

dividend yield risk the risk of changes in stock dividend yields.

diving board effect the tendency of forward price or yield to go up or down near delivery than more distant delivery. ***Also***: horizontal tornado.

divisive D reorganization company A's transfer of half of its assets to B, followed by A's distributions to its shareholders the stock and other assets received from B. ***Also***: butterfly transaction. **See**: *acquisitive D reorganization.*

divisor = *index divisor.*

divvy = *dividend.*

diworsification the process of adding to one's portfolio in such a way that the risk-return tradeoff is worsened.

DJIA Dow Jones Industrial Average

DKI option double knock-in option

DKO option double knock-out option

DMA daily moving average

DMI <1> directional movement index. <2> direct member input.

DO digital option

doctoring artificially increasing income to maintain the price of stock. ***Also***: building air; cooking the accounts; cooking the books; parking; window dressing.

documentation risk the risk due to the unforeseen aspect of certain legal documentation behind the financial derivative contract.

DOEA Designated Options Examining Authority

dogs of the Dow <1> the 10 top-yielding stocks in the Dow Jones Industrial Average. <2> a strategy that advocates buying the 10 DJIA stocks with the highest yields. ***Also***: *Dow dividend theory.*

do-it-yourself fund = *folio.*

dollar at risk (DAR) the value at risk denominated in dollars.

dollar averaging = *constant dollar plan.*

dollar bear a trader who capitalizes on a falling dollar by buying foreign currency directly.

dollar BILS dollar bond index-linked securities

dollar bond <1> the municipal revenue bond denominated in US dollars. ***Also***: dollar-pay bond. <2> a bond issued in Europe but denominated in US dollars. <3> bond denominated in US dollar and is sold in the US by a foreign the companies.

dollar bond index-linked securities (dollar BILS) the floating-rate, zero-coupon notes with an interest rate that measures the total return on a long-term bond.

dollar cost averaging = *constant dollar plan.*

dollar-denominated delivery = *virtual currency option.*

dollar duration the *modified duration* multiplied by the initial issue price of a security.

dollar equivalency hedging = *tail hedging.*

dollarized bull note fixed-rate medium-term note denominated in dollars, but with principal payments linked to the performance of a non-dollar rate note.

dollarized yield curve rate (DYCN) the medium-term note with an embedded rate differential swap agreement.

dollar-pay bond = *dollar bond.*

dollar pool <UK> the total amount of US dollars and dollar securities held by the UK residents.

dollar premium <UK> the extra cost of buying US investment dollars before the removal of the exchange control in 1979. **See**: *investment premium.*

dollar price of a bond the percentage of the face value of a bond quoted.

dollar return the return on a portfolio for a given period.

dollar roll a special type of repurchase agreement under which the security transferred to the investor as collateral is a *mortgage-backed security*.

dollar safety margin the dollar equivalent of the safety cushion for a portfolio of assets in a *contingent immunization* strategy.

dollar value of a basis point (DV01) = *price value of a basis point*.

dollar volume of options (DVO) the average options trading volume of the last 5 trading days.

dollar weighted put/call ratio a put-call ratio which is derived by using the dollar weighted volumes in put and call options.

dollar weighted return the rate of return that discounts a portfolio's terminal value and interim cash flow back to its initial value.

dolphin = *stag*.

domestic bond a bond which is issued and traded in the domestic market.

domestic series a series of non-marketable interest and non-interest bearing securities issued by the US Treasury.

domino theory a notion which holds that a default or financial stress at one firm will precipitate more defaults or financial stress in all other firms. ***See***: *contagion effect*.

donated stock a paid up stock donated by the stockholder to the company.

donated surplus the credit in a stockholder's equity account when the stockholder donates stocks back to the company.

Donoghue Average the weekly average index of all major money fund with 7- to 30-day yields, published in daily newspaper by Donoghue Co.

donor advised fund private fund managed by a third party and created for the purpose of charitable donations by an organization or individual.

do-nothing option an option the payout of which is linked to the realized range of the underlying asset's price, the payout will increase as the price range of the underlying asset decreases.

do not increase (DNI) instruction on a good-till-canceled order to prevent the order increase in the case of a stock split or stock dividend.

do not reduce (DNR) the instruction on a limit order to buy or on a stop order to sell, meaning not to reduce the order when the stock goes ex-dividend.

doomsday call the provision added to fixed income securities allowing for early redemption by the issuer. ***Also***: Canada call.

doomsdayer strategy = *raging bull strategy*.

dormant capital = *idle money*.

dot-com stock the stock issued by a company that embraces the Internet as the key component in its business.

double A S&P or FIS's second highest credit rating of bonds. ***Also***: AA.

double auction the auction of Treasury bills where, unlike traditional auction with one auctioneer and many buyers, there are many sellers and buyers.

double auction market the system by which the listed securities are traded through brokers. ***Also***: 2-sided market.

double auction system the securities trading system with many buyers and sellers. ***Opp***: *conventional auction*.

double barreled bond the municipal revenue bond whose principal and interest are guaranteed by a municipal entity.

double-barreled offering the security offering which involves both the primary elements, e. g. the issuer selling to the general public, and secondary elements, such as shareholders selling shares to each other.

double-barreled quotation = *two-way quotation.*

double-barrier knock-in option double barrier option with knock-in feature that pays off if the price hits the upper limit. ***Also***: double knock-in option; one touch knock-in option.

double-barrier knock-out option the double barrier option with knock-out feature that pays off if the price of the underlying does not touch either the upper or the lower limit. ***Also***: double knock-out option; one touch knock-out option.

double-barrier option an option with two barriers: one below the current market price of the underlying and one above. **See**: *knock-in option*; *knock-out option.*

double-barrier step option a double-barrier option the barriers of which are set in simple or arithmetic steps. **See**: *double-barrier step option.*

double diagonal an option strategy that consists of short calls and puts in one expiration month, and long calls and puts in another expiration month.

double dip the dividend roll in which the dividend capturer already owns the stock with dividend.

double dipping financing constructions by issuing industrial revenue bonds.

double exemption bond = *double tax exempt municipal bond.*

double gearing two firms using shared capital to buffer against risk occurring in separate entities without the proper documentation of exposure.

double hedging simultaneous hedging of a cash market position by both a future and an option position.

double knock-in option (DKI option) = *double-barrier knock-in option.*

double knock-out option (DKO option) = *double-barrier knock-out option.*

double lockout option an option which pays out a fixed amount if the underlying asset stays within a predetermined range.

double-named paper = *two-named paper.*

double-no-touch option barrier option that expires if the underlying touches the lower end or breaks the upper end of a range before expiration.

double-one-touch option an option with a range, and pays a fixed amount if the market touches the lower end or breaks the upper end before expiration.

double option <1> an option with the right to buy or sell at a given strike price. ***Also***: call of more option; put and call option. **See**: *compound option.* <2> the operation of a bond sinking fund, the issuer is permitted to buy the mandatory number of bonds for the sinking fund at par. ***Also***: option to double.

double-option agreement = *cross-option agreement.*

double tax exempt municipal bond the municipal bond the interest of which is exempt from both state and federal income taxes. ***Also***: double exemption bond.

double touch knock-in (DTKI) double barrier option, if both the upper and lower barriers are breached, the holder is knocked-in to a call or put option.

double touch knock-out (DTKO) a double barrier option, if both the upper and lower barriers are breached, the holder is knocked-out and loses the option.

double witching hour time between 3 to 4 p.m. when arbitrageurs have their final chance to close out stock index options and futures. ***Also***: witching hour. **See**: *triple witching hour.*

doubling option the clause that allows the repurchase of twice the required number of bonds at the predetermined call price.

doubling up purchasing a first lot of securities, then buying another lot of an equal amount with unrealized loss, and holding them for 30 days to avoid the IRS wash sale rule.

doubling up forward conversion the hedging strategy by buying twice the original amount of shares, and buying a put on the new shares and selling a call with the same strike as the put on the new shares.

Dow dividend theory = *dogs of the Dow.*

Dow Jones bond average daily price average of 10 first grade rail bonds, 10 2nd grade rails, 10 utilities, 10 industrials and a composite of all 40 bonds compiled by Dow Jones & Co.

Dow Jones Composite the index that combines the DJIA, DJTA, and DJUA. ***Also***: 65-Stock Average.

Dow Jones Industrial Average (DJIA) the average of the closing prices of 30 industrial stocks, including American Express and AT&T, computed at the end of the day on the NYSE.

Dow Jones put and call option = *DOWPAC.*

down <1> the total price decline of the futures price of a commodity within 10 days. **See**: *up.* <2> with lower option strike price.

down-and-in option a *barrier option* that comes into existence if the price of the *underlying asset* touches a predetermined price level during its life. ***Also***: drop in option. **See**: *down-and-out option.*

down-and-in price (ID) a *knock-in price* set below the barrier when the contract was initiated. **See**: *up-and-in price.*

down-and-out Parisian option a Parisian option with down-and-out feature embedded.

down-and-out option knock-out option that becomes worthless if the price of the underlying asset declines by a predetermined amount prior to expiration. **Opp**: *down-and-in option.* **See**: *up-and-out option.*

down-and-out price (OD) the *knock-out price* set above the barrier price when the contract was initiated. **See**: *up-and-out price.*

downgrade negative change in ratings for a security. **See**: *upgrade.*

downgrade risk the risk that an issuer's debt ratings will be lowered by the rating bureau or analyst because of a deterioration in its financial condition.

downgrade trigger a drop in credit rating that can terminate a derivative contract.

down market the trend of declining market prices. ***Also***: declining market.

downscale buying buying securities at set intervals as the price declines. **Opp**: *pyramiding.*

downside the potential for financial loss for a given investment or portfolio.

downside protection a cushion, often a hedge or other protection against any possible loss in covered call writing.

downside put = *out-of-the money put.*

downside risk an estimate that a security will decline in value and the extent of the decline. ***Also***: Morningstar risk.

downside volatility market volatility that is measured when prices are going down.

downstairs trade a trade in the listed securities that is executed through the stock exchange system. ***Also***: listed trade. ***Opp***: *upstairs trade.*

downstream exchange the company's exchange of its outstanding bond for new common stock or preferred stock.

downtrend the downward movement in price. **See**: *uptrend.*

down under bond a bond denominated in Australian or New Zealand dollar.

downward sloping yield curve = *inverted yield curve.*

DOWPAC put and call options that are underlied by one of the Dow Jones averages. ***Also***: Dow Jones put and call option.

Dow theory a theory which holds that a major trend in the stock market must be confirmed by a similar move in *DJIA, DJTA* or *DJUA.*

DPC derivatives products company

DPO direct public offering

DPS dividends per share

drag along right the right that enables a majority shareholder to force a minority shareholder to sell the stock.

dragon bond a US dollar bond issued in Asia.

drawdown <1> a decline in the account value after a trade or series of trades. <2> a percentage drop in the price of a mutual fund from its peak net asset value to the lowest net asset value.

drawdown swap = *accreting swap.*

drawn bond <UK> a bond redeemable by drawings at set intervals. **See**: *serial bond.*

drawn pricing the spread paid on the outstanding balance under a revolving credit facility.

drawn securities the securities which have been called for redemption by the issuer.

DREO debt reducing exchange offer

dressed option the short futures option that is collateralized by a risk-offsetting position in the underlying future. **See**: *uncovered option.*

dressing up = *window dressing.*

Drew's odd-lot theory a theory which advises investors to sell if odd-lotters were buying, and to buy if odd-lotters were selling. ***Also***: odd-lot theory.

drill bit size range the price range of a low priced stock, in this case a fraction of a dollar.

drill-bit stock the shares that are now trading for prices less than one dollar. **See**: *penny stock.*

DRIP dividend reinvestment plan

drop down the transfer of asset or stock of a target company to one or more subsidiaries after the reorganization is completed.

drop in option = *down-and-in option.*

drop-lock fixing the interest rate on a floating rate note if it falls to a set level.

drop-lock floating-rate note a *floating-rate note* that will be converted into a fixed-rate note when the reference index rate drops below a preset level.

drop-lock security a floating rate security with interest payments pegged to the changes in a popular inter-bank loan rate e. g. LIBOR.

drop-lock swap a swap with the clause that resets the fixed-rate payment if the market rates change by an agreed level.

drop-out price = *outstrike price.*

drought sale a farmer's sale of more animals than in a typical year because of the poor weather conditions.

drying up of an active market, which is losing investor interest, resulting in lower volume and prices.

DTCC Depositary Trust and Clearing Company

DTKI double touch knock-in

DTKO double touch knock-out

DTM derivatives trading manager

DTNS designated time net settlement

dual class stock dual stock issued by a firm with varying classes indicating the different voting rights and dividends.

dual contingency option = *contingent payout option.*

dual coupon swap a coupon swap with an option giving one party the right to have periodic settlements in another currency if the exchange rate is against him. ***See***: *reverse zero-coupon swap*; *zero-coupon swap.*

dual credit spreads the combination of two credit spreads of the same contract month.

dual currency bond the bond with an embedded option where the principal is repaid in dollars but the coupon is paid in another currency. ***Also***: dual currency issue. ***See***: *foreign currency bond.*

dual currency issue = *dual currency bond.*

dual currency option an option that consists of two standard *foreign currency options* of which only one is exercisable at expiration, the other one will expire. ***See***: *alternative currency option.*

dual currency swap the swap created to hedge a *dual currency bond* by using an option to transfer the unwanted features of the bond from the issuer to an agent or intermediary which will disaggregate and reassemble the components.

dual exchange rate the system with a fixed official exchange rate and an illegal market-determined exchange rate.

dual index floater a note with coupon rates linked to the difference between two market indexes, typically a *constant maturity Treasury rate.*

dual listing the listing of a security on more than one exchange.

dual option (DUOP) <1> a futures call option matched with a put option which involves the same underlying commodity. <2> a stock warrant that contains two options that enables the holder to subscribe to either common stock or preferred stock of the issuer. <3> = *outperformance option.*

dual option bond a bond issued with an option giving the holder a choice of the currencies for both its interest and the principal payments. ***Also***: cocktail bond.

dual purpose fund a closed-end fund that issues capital and income shares. ***Also***: leveraged investment company; split investment company.

dual rate system an exchange control system that has two rates, one for trade items and another for non-trade items.

dual reverse calendar spreads = *reverse calendar strangle.*

dual series zero-coupon debenture two distinct series offered by the same issuer at the same time in an endeavor to appeal to different segments.

dual-strike option an interest rate option with one rate for part of the option's life, one for the rest of its life.

dual swap = *cross-rate swap.*

dual syndicate offering equity offering split into two branches, domestic and international, each is managed by a separate *managing underwriter.* ***Also***: dual syndication.

dual syndication = *dual syndicate offering.*

dual trading the practice of a broker who acts as an agent by executing orders for his clients, and also for his own account. **See**: *market participant.*

due bill an instrument that evidences the transfer of rights to any dividends pertaining to stocks contracted for.

due date (DD) <1> the date on which a debt must be repaid. ***Also***: date due; day of due date. <2> = *maturity date.*

due diligence the process by which a potential acquirer is allowed to closely examine the target company's financial statements and operations.

duet bond the bond with principal and interest payments linked to the exchange rate between two currencies on the date of payment.

dull market = *inactive market.*

dumbbell = *barbell strategy.*

dumping <1> the sudden offering of large blocks of stock with little or no concern for the market effect. ***Also***: undercutting an offering. ***Opp***: *distribution.* <2> the foreign exporter's selling of goods in foreign market at a price lower than that in the domestic market.

DU-OP dual option

Dupir-Derman-Rubinstein model a non-standard option hedging model by Bruno Dupir, Emanuel Derman and Rubinstein, which focuses on the volatility smile and the term structure of interest rates. ***Also***: Rubinstein-Dupir-Derman model.

duplicative portfolio a basket of stocks that imitates the price movement of an index. **See**: *equity-linked note.*

duration <1> time left until a bond is due. ***Also***: remaining maturity; term to maturity; time to maturity; time until maturity. **See**: *basic time*; *tenor*; *time to expiration.* <2> the average maturity of all payments on a note weighted by the discounted value of payments. <3> the sensitivity of the value of an instrument to change in its *yield to maturity.*

duration-based hedge ratio the number of second bonds to be purchased so that the risk of the first bond will be hedged.

duration bogey the level of asset or liability duration.

duration-convexity matching = *duration matching.*

duration gap an interval that measures the magnitude of the exposure to the stockholders if interest rates move in an adverse direction. ***Also***: gap; maturity gap. **See**: *positive duration gap.*

duration mapping setting of a portfolio into time buckets that correspond to durations. **See**: *cash flow mapping.*

duration matched hedge risk offsetting position that is constructed from a long position in one instrument, and a short position in another, which has a different maturity, coupon, yield to maturity and equivalent life to the first but which has an equal and opposite duration.

duration matching selecting portfolios that make the *duration* of assets match the duration of liabilities. ***Also***:

duration-convexity matching. ***See***: *cash flow matching.*

duration neutral <1> the situation in which a bond strategy has a duration of zero on a net-net basis. <2> of a balance sheet, the dollar duration of assets is equal to that of liabilities.

duration risk management the use of modified duration measurement for a group of assets or liabilities to quantify and control the exposure to rate risk.

duration-weighted swap a swap with one of the payment streams dependent on the effective rate at more than one point on the yield or swap curve.

Dutch auction an *auction* technique of US Treasury bills in which the prices are gradually lowered until it meets a bid.

Dutch auction preferred stock the preferred stock the dividend of which is set in a Dutch auction every 7 weeks.

Dutch auction rate transferable security (DARTS) = *auction rate preferred stock.*

DV 01 dollar value of a basis point

DWAC Deposit/Withdrawal at Custodian

dwarf a pool of mortgage-backed securities by FNMA with a maturity of 15 years.

DYCN dollarized yield curve note

dynamic asset allocation the allocation of assets in response to changing market condition. ***See***: *dynamic hedging.*

dynamic asset replication = *dynamic replication.*

dynamic credit swap a credit swap with the notional linked to the market price of another swap or portfolio of swaps. ***Also***: *credit intermediation swap.*

dynamic delta hedging = *dynamic hedging.*

dynamic hedging continual rebalancing a portfolio to maintain delta neutrality status. ***Also:*** delta hedge; delta hedging; dynamic delta hedging; portfolio insurance; synthesizing. ***See***: *dynamic asset allocation*; *portfolio insurance.*

dynamic overwriting a call writing strategy that requires an increase in the strike price of a short call position as the price of the underlying rises.

dynamic portfolio management the management of portfolio by continuous assessment and periodic adjustment of the portfolio components.

dynamic replication *portfolio replicating* that requires portfolio revision over time. ***Also:*** dynamic asset replication. ***See***: *static replication.*

dynamic simulation a simulation of the financial performance of a portfolio of transactions using various scenarios generated by a computer.

E e

E <1> the abbreviation for May in put options. <2> Nasdaq descriptor meaning it has not yet met the SEC requirements. <3> the option strike price code for 25.

EAFE Index Europe, Australia, and Far East Index

early distribution premature withdrawal from a tax-deferred retirement account. ***Also***: premature distribution.

early exercise the exercise that may result in an early assignment, when an option holder chooses to buy or sell before the expiration date.

early exercise date the date on which the holder of a *Bermuda option* can be exercised before expiration.

early exercise price trigger = *trigger option.*

early extinguishment the issuing firm's open market purchase of its own bonds before maturity. ***Also***: debt calling; retirement of debt.

EARN expected to accrue return on nominal warrant

earned surplus = *retained earnings.*

earning rate = *earnings yield.*

earnings announcement date the date on which the next earnings is to be released by a public company.

earnings effect factor a factor derived by dividing the volatility by a forecast volatility of an asset.

earnings forecast the projection of earnings per share (EPS) or earnings of a public company by the management or an independent security analyst. ***Also***: forecast.

earnings momentum the increase in EPS from one period to another.

earnings multiple = *price/earnings ratio.*

earnings multiplier the estimated P/E ratio, adjusted for the current level of interest rates for valuation purposes.

earnings per share (EPS) the earnings allocated to each outstanding share of stock. ***Also***: basic earnings per share; net income per share of common stock. ***See***: *primary earnings per share*; *fully diluted earnings per share.*

earnings per share fully diluted = *fully diluted earnings per share.*

earnings price ratio (EPR)(EP ratio) = *earnings yield.*

earnings rate of stock price the ratio calculated as: $(\text{interest} + \text{discount} - \text{premium}) \div \text{redemption period}) \times 2 \times (\text{present value} + \text{face value})$.

earnings report <1> a report issued by a company showing its earnings over a given period. <2> = *income statement.*

earnings response coefficient (ERC) the ratio of unexpected stock price response to an *earnings surprise*, e. g. if a \$ 0.10 earnings surprise leads to \$ 2.00 stock price change, the ERC is 20.

earnings retained = *retained earnings.*

earnings retention reinvestment of the net earnings rather than paying dividend. ***Also***: plowback; profit reinvestment.

earnings retention ratio the percentage of earnings reinvested. ***Also***: plowback ratio. ***See***: *reinvestment rate.*

earnings warning a warning made by a firm before its earnings announcement that earnings will fall short of the expected levels. ***Also***: profit warning.

earnings yield the ratio of profit available for distribution to the market value of common stock. ***Also***: earning rate; earnings price ratio; income yield; market capitalization rate; price-earnings reciprocal; yield on shares.

EARN option = *accrual option.*

EASD European Association of Securities Dealers

easier = *faded.*

easier market the stock market when prices are lower in quiet trading.

Eastern account = *jointly and severally.*

easy-come, easy go option the option that will knock out if it is in the money, and knock in when out of the money.

eating stock being forced to buy stocks when an underwriter is not able to find enough buyers.

eat out allowing a person to pay for about half the cost of the acquisitions in stock and the balance in 5 years, depending on the buyer's earnings.

EBITDA earnings before interest, taxes, depreciation and amortization

EBITDA volatility change of EBITDA as a result of the operating performance.

ECE eligible commercial entity

ECHO Exchange Clearing House

economic exposure the risk arising from changes in the market not tied to any item in the financial statements.

economic growth rate the annual rate of change in the GNP.

economic hedge <1> a *currency hedge* to offset the factor of production cost advantage of a competitor with a currency that is depreciating. <2> a hedge based on statistically measured sensitivity to a risk factor.

economic risk exposure to the changes in exchange rates and local regulations.

economic surplus <1> the excess of the fair market value of the assets over the liabilities. <2> = *net worth.*

economic value = *capitalized value.*

economic value added (EVA) <1> the increment in the monetary value of an entity at the end of a period over the monetary value at the beginning. <2> of a company, after-tax earnings minus the opportunity cost of capital.

Econophysis area of study trying to apply physical methods to the financial market.

ECP eligible contract participant

EDF <1> estimated default frequency. <2> expected default frequency.

EDGAR an SEC system that allows public companies to file electronically. ***Also***: Electronic Data Gathering, Analysis, and Retrieval; SEC EDGAR.

edge <1> the difference between option premium and the theoretical price under a model. <2> a dealer's profit.

EDPC enhanced derivatives product company

EDR European depository receipt

EDSP exchange delivery settlement price

effective annual percentage cost = *effective annual yield.*

effective annual yield annual measure of an effective yield. ***Also***: annual yield; effective annual percentage cost.

effective call price the strike in a market redemption provision plus the accrued interest to the redemption date.

effective convexity <1> the convexity of a bond calculated with cash flows which change with the yield. <2> the convexity of a bond with consideration of the convexities of embedded options. ***Also***: option-adjusted convexity.

effective date <1> the date on which the registration of a new security filed with the SEC becomes effective. <2> date on which the interest rate swap begins to accrue interest. ***Also***: value date.

effective duration the duration of the bond with an embedded option when the value includes the expected change in the cash flow caused by the option as the interest rates change. **See**: *modified duration*; *option-adjusted duration.*

effective exchange rate the exchange rate at which a jobber agrees to buy or sell. ***Also***: actual exchange rate; trade-weighted exchange rate. **See**: *real effective exchange rate.*

effective hedge = *efficient hedge.*

effective interest rate <1> the bond the coupon interest rate is determined by its expected income, market price and face value. **See**: *coupon rate of interest.* <2> the interest rate that takes into account opportunity cost. ***Also***: actual interest rate. **See**: *real interest rate.*

effectiveness = *hedge effectiveness.*

effective par the par value of preferred stock that would ordinarily correspond to a given dividend rate.

effective price the round-lot sales price on which an odd-lot price is based.

effective rate = *effective yield.*

effective spread the gross underwriting spread adjusted for the impact on price by the announcement of a new offering.

effective volatility the function of the mean reversion of the spot rate which is determined by the time derivative of the lognormal short rate volatility.

effective yield a rate of return realized by an investor who buys a security and later sells it. ***Also***: effective rate.

efficiency <1> the degree of risk reduction provided by a hedge relative to the cost of the hedge. <2> = *yield.*

efficient capital market the market in which new information is very quickly reflected in the price.

efficient frontier a set of portfolios with the highest rates of returns for a given level of risk. ***Also***: efficient loci; efficient set; Markowitz efficient frontier; Markowitz efficient portfolio; mean-variance efficient portfolio.

efficient hedge a hedge that achieves a given level of risk reduction at minimum cost. ***Also***: effective hedge.

efficient loci = *efficient frontier.*

efficient market a market in which new information is immediately available to all investors and potential investors.

efficient market hypothesis the theory which holds that a stock's price is the same as its investment value, and everything is reflected in the price.

efficient market theory (EMT) a theory that holds that if all assets are correctly priced then there will be no bargains.

efficient portfolio the portfolio the risk-return characteristics of which fall on the *efficient frontier*, i. e. at a given risk, it does not have a higher expected return, and for a given expected return it does not have a lower level of risk.

efficient set = *efficient frontier.*

e-flex = *flex option.*

EFS exchange of futures for swap

either-or option = *alternative option.*

either way both the buy side and the sell side in a quote.

either-way market a market in which the bid and offered rates are identical.

elasticity of option = *option elasticity.*

election period the period in which the holder can extend an extendible bond, or retract a retractable bond.

election warrant a warrant the ultimate payoff or redemption value of which depends on the results of an election.

electricity swap a swap that is based on energy commodity index or electricity price.

Electronic Data Gathering, Analysis, and Retrieval = *Edgar.*

electronic EE bond the new EE bond introduced in 2003 that is not issued at a discount. **See**: *paper EE bond.*

eleven bond index = *11 bond index.*

ELF-X equity-linked foreign exchange option

eligible dividend a dividend paid out of a company's earnings.

eligible stock a stock in which charities and financial institutions can invest.

eligible swap participant (ESP) a party permitted to enter into swaps under CFTC rules. **See**: *swap participant.*

ELKS equity-linked security

ELRB equity linked real bond

embedded commodity option = *commodity-linked bond.*

embedded derivative a derivative that is a component of a hybrid instrument which includes a non-derivative host contract. **See**: *free-standing derivative.*

embedded loss = *unrealized loss.*

embedded option <1> an option that is an inseparable part of another instrument. <2> = *commodity-linked bond.*

embedded swing option sale of swap with the purchase of a swing option from the same party.

embedding attaching a *derivative*, insurance contract, or any other asset or liability with another financial derivative, insurance contract, asset, or liability.

emerging market fund a fund investing a majority of its assets in the emerging markets of developing countries.

E-mini an index that is 25% the size of the full-size counterpart.

employee stock option (ESO) = *option grant.*

employment cost index (ECI) US index on the growth of compensation.

EMTN Euro medium-term note

end date = *maturity date.*

end/end rule a rule, if the value date of the spot rate is at the end of a month, then the value date of all forward exchange will be at the end of a month.

end-of-month option an option given to the short seller of bonds to announce 7 days before the end of a month which bond to deliver.

end-of-the-week liquidation the increased selling of stocks on Fridays.

endorsed bond = *guaranteed bond.*

endowment option a call where the strike grows at the prevailing interest rate but also decreases in line with dividends paid by the underlying stock.

endowment warrant long-term margined stock warrant.

end user a counterpart in a derivative or swap other than a derivatives dealer.

energy derivative a derivative on crude oil and natural gas.

energy stock the stock issued by an energy company e. g. an oil company.

energy swap an average price swap on energy futures.

English auction the auction where bidder submits a bid for a specific quantity of the issue, the issuer sells the securities to many bidders. ***Also***: multi-price auction.

enhanced coupon = *accrual note.*

enhanced derivatives product company (EDPC) AAA-rated subsidiary of a low-rated *derivatives product company.*

enhanced indexing a modified indexing that attempts to exceed the return of a benchmark. ***Also***: indexing plus.

enterprise multiple a ratio that equals the *enterprise value* divided by EBITDA.

enterprise value (EV) measure of what the market believes a company's ongoing operation is worth, it is equal to the market capitalization + debt + preferred stock - cash and cash equivalents.

entry price a price at which a position is established.

environmental fund a mutual fund that invests strictly in stocks of companies that are environmental friendly. **See**: *green investing.*

environmental risk a risk that can not be controlled by a business e. g. price.

EOF exchange of options for physicals

EPS <1> earnings per share. <2> equity participation note.

equal dollar swap a swap that involves selling stock in one company and reinvesting the proceeds in as many shares of another type of stock issued by the same company or same type of stock issued by another company. **See**: *equal shares swap.*

equalizing dividend a special dividend paid in order to correct the existing unequal dividend benefits among stockholders.

equalizing the dividends supplementing a dividend payment from reserved cash, or deducting a possible dividend to permit a transfer to reserves to maintain a dividend at consistent level.

equal shares swap selling the underlying shares and reinvesting the proceeds in as much of the convertible as can be converted into the number of shares of stock sold. **See**: *equal dollar swap.*

equated maturity = *average due date.*

equilibrium exchange rate the rate of exchange at which the demand for a currency is equal to the supply of that currency.

equilibrium market price of risk the slope of the *capital market line.*

equilibrium position = *no position.*

equilibrium rate the correct exchange rate in foreign exchange intervention policy. ***Also***: reference rate.

equilibrium rate of interest the interest rate which clears the market. ***Also***: trade-clearing interest rate.

equipment trust certificate the security issued by a railroad company to pay for the purchase or construction of new equipment.

equity <1> value of a margin account if all positions were liquidated. ***Also***: account equity. <2> in futures trading, cash plus all open positions *marked to market.* <3> = *net worth.* <4> = *stock.*

equity base = *market capitalization.*

equity basket option an option on a portfolio consisting of more than one stock or stock market index.

equity call swap a swap that receives

value as the market price of an index rises above the strike.

equity cap the agreement in which one party, for a premium, agrees to pay the other at a specific period if a benchmark reaches a predetermined level.

equity carve-out = *partial spinoff.*

equity collar the purchase of equity cap and equity floor at the same time.

equity contract note a note issued with mandatory convertibility into common stock of the issuer. ***Also***: exchangeable capital security; exchangeable capital unit. **See**: *convertible capital note.*

equity-debt ratio the ratio of owners' equities to debts. ***Also***: capital structure; equity-to-debt ratio; net worth to debt ratio; ratio of capital to liabilities; solvency ratio.

equity derivative a derivative based on stock, equity baskets or equity index.

equity enhanced dedication the risk management that uses a dedicated bond portfolio as reserve asset and common stock or index futures as risky asset.

equity financing the corporation's raising of capital by issuing capital stock.

equity flex option = *flex option.*

equity floor an agreement in which one party, for a premium, agrees to pay the other at a specific period if a benchmark falls below a predetermined level.

equity forward a forward contract for the purchase and sale of an equity instrument or index at a future date.

equity fund a fund which holds stocks and bonds, both earning high dividends and interest. ***Also***: equity income fund. **See**: *common stock fund.*

equity funding <1> the investment in a life insurance policy and a mutual fund. <2> borrowing money with equity in a house as collateral.

equity gearing = *debt-equity ratio.*

equity holder = *shareholder.*

equity income fund = *equity fund.*

equity index an aggregation of the market prices of a group of equities.

equity-indexed annuity (EIA) an annuity the returns of which are based on the performance of an equity index.

equity index embedded derivative an embedded derivative the payments of which are derived from an equity index.

equity index swap a swap that is based on a range of equity instruments.

equity index warrant = *index warrant.*

equity issue = *capital issue.*

equity kicker a debt security convertible to the common stock of the issuer.

equity leg the cash flow based on the rate or index of the stock in an equity swap.

equity-linked bond a five-year bond linked to the performance of a stock.

equity-linked CD a tradable certificate of deposit with its redemption value linked to an underlying asset or index. ***Also***: market-linked CD; market participation deposit.

equity-linked foreign exchange option (ELFX) an option the face value of which is linked to a foreign asset or benchmark. ***Also***: portfolio currency protection option.

equity-linked forward a forward contract under which the quantity to be purchased or sold depends on the performance of a stock or a benchmark index.

equity-linked note a note the return of which is tied to a stock, a hedge fund or an equity market index, such as S&P 500. ***Also***: equity participation note; market-indexed note; portfolio income note; protected equity note; stock index growth note; stock index return security; stock-linked note. **See**: *automatic common exchange security*; *duplicative portfolio*; *recovery note.*

equity-linked real bond (ELRB) equity-linked guaranteed instrument with the minimum return based on the performance of an inflation-linked bond.

equity-linked security (ELKS) security issued by Salomon Smith Barney, that is exchanged for the underlying stock with mandatory conversion.

equity-linked swap <1> a *swap* linked to the performance of a basket of selected shares. <2> = *equity swap.*

equity market = *stock market.*

equity market neutral the hedge fund strategy that seeks to exploit the differences in prices by being long and short in stocks in the same sector, market, industry, or country.

equity multiplier total assets divided by total common stockholders' equity. **See**: *asset/equity ratio.*

equity note a note that will automatically become a share of common stock of the same issuing company after a set period of time. ***Also***: equity purchase contract.

equity option an option which gives the holder the right to buy or sell common stock. ***Also***: equity warrant; stock option. **See**: *non-equity option.*

equity participation note (EPS) = *equity-linked note.*

equity premium the average return on the overall stock market minus the return on riskless government bonds, such as the US Treasury bonds.

equity purchase contract = *equity note.*

equity put swap a swap that receives value as the market price of an index drops below the strike price.

equity range note a stock or stock index range note with the payout dependent on the behavior of a stock or stock index relative to a given price range.

equity rate contingency option = *contingent payout option.*

equity ratio = *equity-to-asset ratio.*

equity redeemable bond = *participating equity preferred stock.*

equity REIT an REIT that assumes ownership in the properties, enabling investors to earn rental income and appreciation of the properties.

equity return risk the risk associated with rate of return from equity securities.

equity return swap = *equity swap.*

equity risk the risk of unexpected loss to an entity arising from a change in the market price of equity securities.

equity risk premium the extra return that the stock market provides over the risk free rate to compensate for the risk taken by the investor.

equity risk reversal the contract that provides a payoff pattern in a stock that is similar to an interest rate collar or range forward in the fixed-income and currency market. ***Also***: hedge wrap; zero cost hedge. **See**: *cylinder*; *interest rate collar*; *range forward.*

equity security an ownership interest or right to acquire ownership interest and dispose of ownership interest in a firm. **See**: *equity-type security.*

equity share <1> an equity interest unit in a credit union. **See**: *non-equity share.* <2> = *common stock.*

equity substitutes the amounts that are added to or subtracted from the reported common equity to reflect the actual economic value invested in a company by the shareholders.

equity swap <1> a swap under which a party pays a return on equity security in exchange for receiving a fixed or floating rate. ***Also***: equity-linked swap. <2> a swap under which two parties exchange payments based on price, dividend, and the cost of carrying the security. ***Also***: equity return swap.

equity-to-assets ratio the ratio of the owners' equities to total value of assets. ***Also***: common stock ratio; equity ratio; solvency ratio.

equity-to-debt ratio = *equity-debt ratio.*

equity tranche the class in a synthetic CDO that takes the greatest risk. ***See:*** *first tranche, mezzanine tranche.*

equity turnover total sales divided by the stockholders' equity of a company. ***Also***: capital turnover; capital turnover rate.

equity-type security the security that is neither a common stock nor a preferred stock but is capable of conversion, subscription, or exercise for either of them. **See**: *equity security.*

equity value = *market capitalization.*

equity warrant = *equity option.*

equity yield enhancement security (EYES) an equity-linked instrument with a single stock as the underlying asset, a coupon in excess of the dividend paid on the underlying, and a capped return.

equivalent bond yield the yield on the government discount bonds measured with yields on corporate bonds. ***Also***: bond equivalent yield; corporate equivalent yield; coupon equivalent rate. **See**: *coupon equivalent yield.*

equivalent position a position that is the same as another position in some way.

equivalent shares the new number of common shares if the convertible securities are converted to stock.

equivalent taxable yield the taxable yield on the corporate bond that equals tax-exempt yield ÷ (1 - marginal tax rate). ***Also***: yield equivalence.

ERC earnings response coefficient

ERM enterprise risk management

escalating rate swap = *setup swap.*

escalating swap = *accreting swap.*

escrowed bond a bond the debtor has deposited Treasury bonds with escrow to secure the payment of principal and interest.

escrowed to maturity (ETM) holding of proceeds from a new bond issue in an escrow account to be used to pay off an existing bond issue at its maturity.

escrowed to maturity bond a municipal bond the proceeds of which are held in escrow to meet all coupon and principal payments. ***Also***: ETM bond.

escrow receipt a bank document that evidences the existence of collateral to be used as the underlying asset for an option.

e-shares the shares issued by the companies engaged in e-commerce.

ESP eligible swap participant

essential purpose bond = *public purpose bond.*

estimated default frequency (EDF) the number of credit defaults of a company in a given period. **See**: *expected default frequency.*

ETF exchange-traded fund

ethanol calendar swap a swap based on the price of the ethanol futures contract.

ethical fund a fund that will not invest in the companies having interests in socially unacceptable markets. ***Also***: socially conscious mutual fund.

ethical investing = *green investing.*

ethical investment = *green investing.*

ethical wall = *Chinese wall.*

ETL expected tail loss

ETM bond = *escrowed to maturity bond.*

ETO exchange traded option

Eurex a European derivatives exchange formed in 1998.

Eurobond the bond issued outside the jurisdiction of any single country.

Euro CD a CD issued by a foreign branch of a US bank or a foreign bank located outside the US.

Euroclear a computerized settlement and depositary system for the safe custody, delivery and payment of Euro-bonds.

Euro-commercial paper a short-term note with maturity of up to 360 days issued in foreign money markets.

Eurodollar bond a bond with interest and principal payment in Eurodollars.

Eurodollar futures the futures contracts on Eurodollars.

Eurodollar futures strip the position in multiple Eurodollar futures with some in a series of sequential dates of delivery. ***Also***: Eurostrip.

Euroequity <1> an equity denominated in a currency differing from that of the country in which it is traded. <2> an IPO that occurs simultaneously on more than one national market.

Euroequity issue a security sold in the Euromarket.

Euromarket a short-term Eurocurrency, medium term *Euro-credit* or the long-term *Eurobond* market.

Euro medium-term note (EMTN) the flexible rate medium-term note issued and traded outside of Canada and USA.

Euronext the pan-European exchange founded on Sep 22, 2000.

Euro note short- to medium-term note sold in the Eurocurrency market.

Europaper <UK> a note issued through American brokers in the London Stock Exchange in 1960 when the US restricted the export of capital.

European barrier option <1> a barrier option which becomes live when the underlying trades above or below a set level at maturity. ***Also***: European reverse knock-in option; kick-in at the end. <2> = *point barrier option.*

European cash-or-nothing binary the binary option that pays a fixed amount if it expires in-the-money. **See**: *American cash-or-nothing binary.*

European depositary receipt a Europe issued depositary receipt evidencing ownership of a non-European security.

European option an option which can be exercised only on its predetermined expiration date. ***Also***: European style option. **See**: *American option*; *Bermuda option.*

European Parisian option a Parisian option that can only be exercised on the expiration date.

European reverse knock-in option = *European barrier option.*

European style exercise the exercise of an option on the expiration date. **See**: *American option.*

European style option = *European option.*

European terms = *indirect quote.*

Euro-rate differential future an interest rate differential traded on the Chicago Mercantile Exchange structured to allow US-based investors to hedge non-US interest rates. ***Also***: diff.

Euro straight a Eurobond with a fixed-rate coupon.

Eurostrip = *Eurodollar futures strip.*

Eurowarrant a stock warrant traded in the Euromarkets, originally in London and Zurich, but now in Asian.

Euroyen bond Eurobond denominated in Japanese yen.

even basis swap the sale of one fixed income security and the purchase of another effected without any change in the yield on the portfolio.

even lot (EL) = *round lot.*

even par swap the sale of one block of bonds and the simultaneous purchase of the same nominal principal amount of another block of bonds.

even spread a spread of which the premium paid and the premium received are the same.

event arbitrage an arbitrage that counts on a specific event, such as a judicial decision to change the price or rate relationship of two or more financial instruments for a profit.

event driven strategy a strategy where the hedge fund manager takes significant positions in a certain number of companies with special situations.

event-linked swap the swap with a contingent payment attached on one side that is determined by a triggering event, usually a catastrophe such as an earthquake.

event risk the risk that the bond rating or the credit quality will drop due to a particular event that is not related to the general market.

evergreen option an employee option plan that grants additional shares to the plan every year.

evolution the change of the implied volatility over time.

EW ex warrant

exact matching finding the lowest cost portfolio that can generate cash inflows exactly equal to cash outflows being financed by the investment.

exact replicating portfolio the portfolio that follows an index or a basket of financial instruments without error.

ex all of the price of a security, without dividends, stock rights or stock warrants.

ex ante return the expected return of a portfolio, calculated from a proportional weighting of expected returns.

ex bonus (x.b.) = *ex capitalization.*

ex-by-ex exercise-by-exception

ex capitalization without the bonus stock about to be issued. ***Also***: ex bonus; ex scrip.

excepted exchange a tax free exchange of foreign stocks.

exceptional return residual return plus benchmark return. ***See***: *active return.*

excess = *excess margin.*

excess cash accumulation = *undue retention.*

excess kurtosis the distribution of the financial time series, showing density of probability mass in the "tail" and "head" distribution that lies beyond the normal distribution. ***Also***: fat tail; heavy tail; leptokurtosis; power-law distribution.

excess margin an equity in a brokerage account, that is above the minimum or maintenance requirement, available for new trades. ***Also***: buying power; excess; gross power; surplus equity.

excess of par value over issuing price of stock = *discount on stock.*

excess present value index = *present value profitability index.*

excess return the difference between the return on a portfolio and the return which could have been raised by investment of the same amount of fund in a risk-free asset.

excess share the new share in a rights issue, allotted to the shareholder with rights. ***See***: *bonus share.*

excess spread <1> remaining net interest payments from the underlying assets of an asset-backed security, after all the payables and expenses are covered. <2> the difference between the premium received from a C credit default swap portfolio and the tranche liabilities.

excess volatility puzzle the unexplained behavior that the volatility of equity exceeds the variance implied by the present value formula. ***Also***: volatility puzzle.

exchange (X change) <1> changing the currency of one country into that of another. ***Also***: business; conversion; money exchange. <2> = *exchange rate.* <3> = *foreign exchange.*

Exchange, The = *New York Stock Exchange.*

exchangeable auction rate preferred stock an auction rate preferred stock which is exchangeable at the issuer's option for auction rate notes on a dividend payment date.

exchangeable bond the bond in which the holder has the option to convert from a fixed rate to a floating rate or from a floating rate to a fixed rate.

exchangeable capital security (X-cap) = *equity contract note.*

exchangeable capital unit = *equity contract note.*

exchangeable note <1> an open-ended debt obligation that resets every few years to a new interest rate based on negotiations between the issuer and the investor. <2> a note with an embedded option that gives the issuer or the holder the right to terminate or extend the maturity of the note at a specified rate of interest on one or more exercise dates. ***Also***: resettable note.

exchangeable security a bond or note that grants the holder the right to convert the bond or note into the common stock of another company. **See**: *convertible security.*

exchange acquisition a method of filling an order to buy a block of stock on the floor of an exchange, by lumping together all the orders to sell and then crossing with the buy order. ***Also***: special bid. **See**: *exchange transaction.*

exchange against actuals = *exchange of spot.*

exchange arbitrage = *currency arbitrage.*

exchange cover the act of buying foreign exchange when others sell.

exchange delivery settlement price (EDSP) the price at which the delivery or cash settlement takes place.

exchange discount = *discount.*

exchange for futures transfer of a cash commodity into a long futures position. **See**: *exchange of spot.*

exchange for physicals (EFP) an alternative to *physical settlement* by private negotiation between two parties. **Also**: exchange of futures for physicals.

exchange for swap a swap under which the dealer takes the banker's futures positions into its own account and swaps the commodity return for a rate.

exchange fund = *swap fund.*

Exchange Fund account <Canada> a fund maintained by the Government of Canada for promoting the order and stability of the Canadian dollar.

exchange future = *foreign currency future.*

exchange market = *stock exchange.*

exchange of assets = *acquisition of assets.*

exchange of borrowings a currency swap under which each counterpart obtains funds from the third party lenders and then exchanges the funds.

exchange offer <1> an offer to acquire a target company by an *exchange-of-shares.* ***See***: *cash offer.* <2> a method allowing limited partners to exchange their interests for marketable securities of a listed company on a tax-free basis. <3><UK> offer to exchange one equity security for another.

exchange of futures for cash = *exchange of spot.*

exchange of futures for physicals = *exchange for physicals.*

exchange of futures for swap (EFS) <UK> a variant of an *exchange of spot* transaction in which the parties offset their respective sides of a futures contract and establish a swap agreement.

exchange of options for physicals (EOF) a variant of an *exchange of spot* in which the parities offset their respective sides of an option in exchange for a transfer of a related commodity or financial instrument.

exchange-of-shares acquisition the acquisition by a company in exchange of its own shares for the shares of the target company. ***Also***: reorganization exchange; stock-for-stock exchange; stock-for-stock swap; stock swap; Type B reorganization. ***See***: *purchase acquisition.*

exchange of spot the exchange of cash commodity for an equivalent quantity of futures contract. ***Also***: against actuals; cash-futures swap; exchange against actuals; exchange of futures for cash; exchange versus cash; ex-pit transaction; transfer trade; versus cash. ***See***: *exchange for futures.*

exchange option = *Margrabe option.*

exchange parity = *par of exchange.*

exchange position the difference between the buying and selling amounts of a foreign exchange. ***Also***: foreign exchange position.

exchange premium <1> = *agiotage.* <2> = *premium.*

exchange privilege the right of the holder of mutual fund shares to switch from one fund to another fund without fees.

exchange quotation = *par of exchange.*

exchange rate <1> the exchange price of one currency to another. ***Also***: course of exchange; exchange; foreign exchange rate; rate of exchange; rate of foreign exchange. <2> = *conversion ratio.*

exchange rate agreement (ERA) a forward rate agreement that increases or decreases in value as the spread between two forward exchange rates changes.

exchange rate differential = *premium.*

exchange rate mechanism (ERM) the commitment on the part of the members of the European Monetary System to maintain exchange rates within the specified range.

exchange rate option = *foreign currency option.*

exchange rate quotation = *foreign exchange quotation.*

exchange rate risk = *exchange risk.*

exchange risk the risk that movement in the exchange rate between the home currency and the currency in which assets are held moves against the trader. ***Also***: currency risk; exchange rate risk; foreign exchange risk.

exchange risk factor the delta value of an option as computed daily by the stock exchange on which it is traded.

exchange-traded contract standardized options and futures contract that is listed and traded on an organized exchange.

exchange-traded derivative standardized derivative product that is traded on an exchange.

exchange-traded fund (ETF) a mutual fund traded on an exchange, which is a combination of an open-end and a close-end fund. ***Also***: EXTRA fund. **See**: *basket deposit receipt; optimized portfolio as listed securities.*

exchange-traded option = *listed option.*

exchange transaction the transaction done when somebody who wants to sell a large block of stock can get a broker to solicit and bunch a large number of buy orders. **See**: *exchange acquisition.*

exchange versus cash = *exchange of spot.*

exchequer bill = *Treasury bill.*

exchequer stocks <UK> the gilt-edged securities issued by the UK Government. E. g., 12% 2013.

ex claim = *ex right.*

excluded commodity an interest rate, exchange rate, currency, credit risk or measure, debt instrument, measure of inflation, or other macro-electronic index or measure.

excluded dividend <Canada> a cash dividend paid by a company to a shareholder who holds a substantial interest.

excluded stock the stock not counted in determining if a shareholder owns 50% or more of the total voting power.

exclusionary self-tender <UK> the company's offer to buy a given amount of its own shares while excluding targeted shareholders.

exclusive having sole possession of the customer order, not in competition with other dealers.

ex coupon without the interest on the coupon soon due for payment.

excursion level = *barrier price.*

ex date = *ex dividend.*

ex distribution = *ex dividend.*

ex div. ex dividend

ex dividend without the next dividend soon due to be paid. ***Also***: dividend exclusive; dividend off; ex date; ex distribution; without dividend.

ex-dividend date the date from which the dividend becomes payable to the new owner of the stock, often three days before the record date in New York Stock Exchange.

execution cost the unfavorable difference between the price at which an order is executed and the market price at the time of decision.

execution gain the favorable difference between the price at which an order is executed and the market price at the time of decision.

executive equity swap an *equity swap* in which one of the parties is the insider of a public company.

executive stock option an option that is issued to the executives only.

exempt commodity a commodity that is not an excluded commodity or an agricultural commodity.

exempted dealer <UK> a dealer who is permitted to buy and sell securities on their accounts without a broker.

exempt facilities bond a bond issued to finance the privately-owned or privately used facilities that are eligible for the tax-exempt financing.

exempt foreign firm a foreign firm that does business with US customers only on foreign exchanges and is exempt from registration with CFTC.

exempt interest dividend the dividend paid by the regulated investment companies that is exempt from taxation.

exemption waiver of formal registration procedures with the SEC for a new issue of securities. ***See***: *Rule 504 exemption*; *Rule 505 exemption*; *Rule 506 exemption.*

exempt security a security not required to be registered under the provisions of the SEC, e. g., governmental and municipal bond.

exempt swap agreement a swap done between two eligible swap participants.

exercisable value = *intrinsic value.*

exercise to buy securities from or sell them to the option writer at a set price at predetermined time. ***Also***: declaration; exercise an option; put an option.

exercise an option = *exercise.*

exercise assignment = *assignment notice.*

exercise-by-exception (ex-by-ex) the procedure used by the *Options Clearing Corporation* to exercise expiring in-the-money options to protect their holders.

exercise cut-off time the time frame in which the holder of an option must exercise the option. ***Also***: cut-off time.

exercise date the date on which an option can be exercised.

exercise limit a limit on the number of options of any one class which can be exercised in 5 business days.

exercise notice = *assignment notice.*

exercise price = *strike price.*

exercise ratio the number of shares of common stock that would be received for one warrant exercised.

exercise value amount of advantage over a current market transaction provided by an in-the-money option.

exhaust price the price at which a broker is forced to sell a security that was margined and subsequently declined in price because the client failed to meet the margin call. ***See***: *famine price.*

ex interest (x. int.) without the next interest payment soon due, e. g. a bond in default. ***Also***: flat; selling flat; with no interest; without interest. ***See***: *cum interest.*

ex interest date the date on which an income bond sells *ex interest*, following a declaration of interest.

ex interest quotation = *clean price.*

existing position total amount of *open positions.*

exit bond a modified or rescheduled bond issued by a low-rated sovereign borrower to a long-term creditor.

exit cost = *back-end load.*

exit fee = *back-end load.*

exit load = *back-end load.*

exit strategy the way an investor plans to exit a position under a given market condition. ***Also***: liquidity event.

ex-legal the municipal bond issue without any legal opinion of the bond attorney.

ex new (x.n.)(X new) without the scrip issue or rights issue soon due. ***Also***: new share off. ***Opp***: *cum new.*

exorbitant profit a profit that is beyond all reasonable limits. ***Also***: cleanup; sudden huge profit.

exotic convertible a convertible bond with unusual terms.

exotic currency a foreign currency that is not widely traded.

exotic derivative a derivative containing more than one instrument or feature. ***Also***: nonstandard derivative. **Opp**: *vanilla derivative.*

exotic loan an adjustable rate mortgage loan with different monthly payment options. ***Also***: cashflow option loan; option loan.

exotic mortgage a mortgage with unusual terms such as zero down payment, interest payment only, reverse amortization etc. ***Also***: creative mortgage.

exotic option the option on an unusual underlying asset, with unique option pricing model. ***Also***: caput; compound option; non-standard option; second generation option; specialty option; third generation option. ***See***: *vanilla option.*

exotic swap a swap the return of which is derived from a formula that may include numerous factors which are not found in a plan vanilla swap. ***Also***: non-generic swap; nonstandard swap.

exotic warrant a complex warrant with unusual risk and payoff structure. ***Also***: nonstandard warrant.

expanding face option = *gradual knock-in option.*

expectational analysis an analysis that takes into account both the technical and fundamental facts to analyze a stock.

expected credit loss the credit loss calculated by a combination of expected credit exposure, probability of credit default and recoveries.

expected default frequency (EDF) the measure of credit weakness based on the probability that a firm will default. **See**: *estimated default frequency.*

expected dividend yield total amount of dividends received for holding a stock in one year.

expected earnings the earnings of a public company reported by an analyst for the upcoming quarter or year. **See**: *forecasted earnings.*

expected exposure the expected value of credit exposure in a future time.

expected portfolio return the average expected return of a portfolio of assets.

expected return an estimation of the return on a risky investment or a venture, usually the *benchmark return* multiplied by the beta of investment. **See**: *bogey.*

expected shortfall = *expected tail loss.*

expected tail loss (ETL) the average portfolio loss assuming that it exceeds a given level. ***Also***: expected shortfall.

expected to accrue return on nominal warrant (EARN) = *accrual option.*

expected utility the axiomatic extension of the ordinal concept of utility to uncertain payoffs. ***Also***: von Neumann Morgenstern utility.

expected volatility <1> = *forecasted volatility.* <2> = *implied volatility.*

expected yield the amount of money an investor expects to earn from a specific security divided by the investment value.

expendable trust fund the governmental fund restricted by an expendable trust.

expensive option an option the premium is high because the volatility of which is high. ***Also***: option with high volatility. **See**: *cheap option.*

expiration an option becoming worthless at the end of contract. ***Also***: lapse. ***See***: *abandonment.*

expiration cycle a sequence of expiration dates on which options expire, such as *January cycle, February cycle* etc. ***Also***: option cycle; option lifetime.

expiration date a date on which an option expires, often the last day on which the holder may declare if he exercise it or not, often the day before the account day. ***Also***: date of declaration; date of expiration; declaration date; declaration day; expiry day; last trading day; maturity date; option expiration date.

expirationless option = *perpetual option.*

expiration time the time at which an option expires on the *expiration date.*

expiration value the value of an option at expiration.

expiry date <UK> = *expiration date.*

ex-pit transaction <1> = *curb exchange.* <2> = *exchange of spot.*

explicit interest rate the rate of interest obtained by dividing the interest by the principal value. ***Also***: force of interest; monetary rate of interest; money rate of interest; nominal cost of money; nominal interest rate; nominal rate of interest.

exploding call = *up-and-out call.*

exploding delta a wide variation in an at-the-money option's hedge ratio just prior to expiration. ***Also***: pin risk.

exploding option <1> a reverse knock-out barrier option with the rebate equal to the intrinsic value at the barrier. <2> a European style call spread with an early exercise trigger. ***Also***: one-touch option. <3> = *up-and-away option.*

exponential barrier the barrier price that is exponential. ***See***: *flat barrier.*

exponential step option = *proportional step option.*

exposure total risk faced by an investor.

exposure limit the risk limit based on some exposure metric of risk.

exposure netting offsetting exposures in one currency with the exposures in the same or another currency.

expunge to remove any trace of an order or cancelled transaction.

ex rights (x.r.) words that means without the rights issue soon due. ***Also***: ex claim; without rights. ***Opp***: *cum rights.*

ex rights date the date on which the buyer of common stock is no longer entitled to the rights that has been declared.

ex scrip (x.s.) = *ex capitalization.*

ex-stock dividends the time interval between the announcement and payment of a stock dividend.

extendible bond the bond issue with a maturity which can be extended to a longer period at the option of the issuer.

extendible convertible bond the convertible bond with a maturity that can be extended to a future date at the option of the holder.

extendible debt security the debt security which allows the holder to continue to hold it for another period.

extendible note <UK> the note with a maturity that can be extended by an agreement between the issuer and the investor.

extendible option an option the date of expiration of which may be extended.

extendible swap the swap one or both parties to which have an option to extend the original maturity. ***See***: *puttable swap.*

extension date the date on which the first option expires or is extended.

extension risk the risk of a security lengthening in duration because of the deceleration of prepayments.

extension swap <1> the sale of a bond with a short maturity for the purchase of another bond with a longer maturity. ***Also***: maturity swap. **See**: *refunding*. <2> forward swap whose start date coincides with the termination date of an existing swap and which will automatically extend the original swap.

external market = *international market.*

external return = *opportunity cost.*

extinguishable option = *knockout option.*

extinguishing option = *knockout option.*

extinguishment = *debt retirement.*

extinguishment fund = *sinking fund.*

extra dividend a dividend in addition to regular dividend. ***Also***: bonus dividend; extraordinary dividend; special bonus dividend; special dividend.

EXTRA fund = *exchange-traded fund.*

extraordinary call early redemption of a bond due to the elimination of revenue source. **See**: *catastrophe call.*

extraordinary dividend = *extra dividend.*

extraordinary redemption the provision which gives a bond issuer the right to call the bonds, due to a one-time occurrence as specified in the prospectus.

extreme the price or volatility level that is abnormally high or low.

extreme dependent option an option with a value dependent on extreme values of the underlying asset passing a level.

extrinsic value the component of the option value which comes about purely by virtue of the time remaining before expiration. ***Also***: premium over current exercisable value; time value; time value of option. **See**: *intrinsic value.*

ex warrant (EW) meaning since the security is sold, the buyer is no longer entitled to the stock warrant attached to it. ***Also***: sans warrant; without warrant. **See**: *cum warrant.*

eye beam the common stock of IBM. ***Also***: big blue.

EYES equity yield enhancement security

F f

F <1> the month abbreviation for January in futures and call options. <2> Nasdaq descriptor meaning the issue is a foreign stock issue. <3> option strike price code for 30.

FAB spread five against bond spread

face amount <1> amount printed on a bond, which is paid when it is retired. <2> amount stated on the face of the policy that will be paid in case of death.

face amount certificate a promissory note the holder of which makes periodic payment to the issuer who promises to pay the face value at maturity.

face amount certificate company the investment firm that issues *face amount certificates.*

face capital = *nominal capital.*

face par = *face value.*

face value the nominal value of a security as distinguished from market value. ***Also***: denomination; face par; nominal price; nominal value; par; par value; principal; principal of instrument.

face value flat yield = *flat yield.*

factor constant value of a minimum price fluctuation for a given commodity, which when multiplied by the price and quantity of futures, will result in the value of a contract.

factor portfolio a portfolio of assets that is constructed to have a beta of 1.0 on one factor and a beta of zero on other relevant factors.

factory orders total orders of durable and non-durable goods of a reporting period, usually a quarter.

faded of a bid, meaning the previously quoted bid has been withdrawn or revised downward. ***Also***: easier.

fail position undelivered securities due to the failure of short sellers to deliver.

fail to deliver the situation in which the short seller has not delivered securities to the buyer.

fail to receive the situation in which the buyer of a contract has not received any delivery from the seller.

fair market price = *fair market value.*

fair market value (FMV) the price that an interested but not desperate buyer would be willing to pay and the interested but not desperate seller would be willing to accept. ***Also***: current market value; fair market price; justified price.

fairness opinion professional opinion of an investment banker regarding the fairness of the price offered in a merger.

fair price the equilibrium price for a derivative. ***Also***: arbitrage-free price; benchmark price; theoretical futures price.

fair value <1> the futures - spot index premium value at which the futures and the markets are in equilibrium. <2> = *theoretical value.*

fair value basis the difference between the forward or futures price and the spot price that offers no opportunity for arbitrage at current carrying costs.

fair value hedge the hedge against the exposure to changes in the fair value of a recognized asset or liability or a firm commitment. ***See***: *cash flow hedge.*

fair value model a model used to generate the fair value of a financial instrument.

fair value premium = *forward intrinsic value.*

fair value pricing assigning a price that may differ from the reported prices of a fund to a portfolio component under rules set by the directors of the fund.

fair value spread the spread paid by a credit risky asset, it is the probability of default times the loss upon default.

fairway bond = *accrual note.*

fairway note = *accrual note.*

fairway option = *accrual option.*

falcon a covered warrant with the issuing company's obligation collateralized by enough shares to deliver the underlying stock upon exercise.

fallen angel a bond of investment grade when issued, but which is of much lower quality now. ***See***: *rising star.*

fallen angel credit the reference of credit of a fallen angel firm in a credit derivative.

fall out of bed sudden drop in a stock's price resulting from poor earnings.

fall's fall = *October effect.*

Fama & French 3-factor model a model that considers the fact that value and small-cap stocks outperform markets on a regular basis.

family = *fund family.*

family of funds = *fund family.*

famine price the price under conditions that securities are difficult to find in the exchange. ***See***: *exhaust price.*

FAN <1> five against note. <2> fixed assurance note.

fancy paper = *blue chip.*

Fannie Mae = *Federal National Mortgage Association.*

Fannie Maes the shares issued by the Federal National Mortgage Association. ***Also***: FNMA stock.

FAN spread five against not spread

Farmer Mac Federal Agricultural Mortgage Corporation

far month = *furthest month.*

far option that side of a stock spread option position that will expire after the other side of the near term option.

farther in an option maturing in July is said to be "farther in" than the option maturing in October.

farther out an option maturing in October is said to be "farther out" than the option maturing in July.

FAS 133 financial accounting standards for recording and reporting transactions in financial derivatives and hedging. ***Also***: Accounting for Derivative Instruments and Hedging Activities.

fashion shares the shares which are in demand by investors for a short period.

FAST fast automated screen trading

fastest-pay tranche a tranche on a CMO which is currently scheduled to receive principal.

fast market the market that experiences heavy *trading volumes* and wide price fluctuations within a short period of time. ***Also***: fast moving market. ***See***: *subject market.*

fast market rule <UK> a rule that permits the market makers to trade outside the range where real time quote is impractical in a *fast market.*

fast moving market = *fast market.*

fast-pay preferred stock a high-coupon instrument designed to pay a partially tax-sheltered dividend that, in effect, liquidates the principal before the payment drops to a nominal level and the issuer is recapitalized. ***Also***: step-down preferred stock.

fat tail = *excess kurtosis.*

fault free security = *gilt-edge security.*

favorite fifty = *nifty fifty.*

F/C <1> first call date. <2> first coupon date.

FCO foreign currency option

FD (f/d) <1> forward delivery. <2> full disclosure.

FE <1> foreign exchange. <2> futures exchange.

feasible portfolio a portfolio which can be constructed from the assets currently available in the market.

February cycle the *expiration cycle* of options in February, May, August and November throughout the year. ***See***: *January cycle*; *FMAN*; *March cycle.*

federal agency issue = *federal agency security.*

federal agency security debt issued by an agency of the federal government, e. g. FNMA, having high safety ratings. ***Also***: federal agency issue.

Federal National Mortgage Association (FNMA) a publicly-owned government sponsored company, chartered in 1938 to purchase the mortgages from banks and resell them as securities to the public. ***Also***: Fannie Mae.

feeder fund the mutual fund that accounts all of its investment through a *master fund.* ***See***: *discretionary fund.*

feeding the duck selling a security or a futures contract as the market price is going up.

feed ratio the relationship of the cost of feed, expressed as a ratio to the selling price of animals.

felines = *dingo.*

fence = *collar.*

fence sitter a retail client or a portfolio manager who is unable to make decision about the merits of an investment.

fence spread = *collar.*

Fibonacci a series of numbers, each is the sum of the two numbers preceding it.

fictional principal = *notional principal.*

fictitious capital the capital in the form of securities that can produce income, such as equity share.

fictitious credit the credit balance in a client's margin account, from proceeds of short sale and margin requirement.

fictitious payee = *bearer.*

fiduciary call a call the present value of its strike is invested in the securities that are placed in escrow to cover the cost of possible exercise.

fiduciary principal = *principal.*

fiduciary put a put sold with aggregate strike price invested in the securities that are placed in escrow to assure that cash will be available in the event of exercise.

FIELD fixed-income equity-linked debt

fifo first-in, first-out

FIGS future income growth securities

figure = *handle.*

figure the tail to calculate the yield at which a future security is purchased when that future security is created by buying an existing instrument.

filter rule <1> the rule under which the stop loss price is increasing. <2> a stipulation as to when the security should be bought or sold to trade profitably.

filter system the system that buys stocks that have moved up by more than 5% from their low and hold them until they move down 5% from their high.

final dividend the dividend declared by the company in the annual general meeting in addition to the interim dividends paid.

finality risk the risk that the transfer of funds or securities can be rescinded.

final settlement date the *delivery date* of non-cash settling futures or other financial derivative contracts.

final transfer an irrevocable transfer of funds or securities.

final value = *future value.*

finance paper unsecured promissory note issued by a *financial institution.* ***See***: *commercial paper.*

financial asset securitization trust (FAST) a vehicle that is established to facilitate securitization of a variety of illiquid assets.

financial bond a bond issued by a bank or other financial institutions.

financial buyer an investment company that uses high levels of leverage to fund their acquisitions and operations.

financial derivative = *derivative.*

financial elasticity = *beta coefficient.*

financial engineer an expert in financial engineering. ***Also***: rocket scientist.

financial engineering the creation of new and improved financial products through innovative design or repackaging of some existing products.

financial future a futures contract that is based on interest sensitive financial instruments such as T-bills, CDs, and GNMA pass-throughs.

financial house a finance company.

financial instrument a future or option which is not based on an agricultural commodity or a natural resource.

Financial Instrument Exchange = *Finex.*

financial leverage <1> the ratio of debt and capital to net worth. <2> the ratio that shows the relationship between earnings before interests and tax and the earnings per share. ***See***: *capital leverage.*

financial leverage ratios = *capitalization ratios.*

financial position the source of funds and their application of a business. ***Also***: capital position; financial standing; position.

financial pyramid the risk structure the foundation of which is built on liquidity and safety investment, then income and long-term growth securities, then the speculation on top.

financial rand proceeds from the sale of South African securities. ***Also***: blocked rand; securities rand.

financial risk <1> a risk that the returns to the owner's equity will decrease due to the payment of interest on debts. ***See***: *operating risk.* <2> the buyer's concern that the stock considered for purchase is priced too high.

financial simulation using historical data or Monte Carlo method to project the future returns of an asset. ***Also***: simulation.

financial solvency = *solvency.*

financial spread betting = *spread betting.*

financial standing = *financial position.*

Financial Times Actuaries Index = *FT Actuaries Index.*

financing cost the cost of borrowing to buy and hold a specified asset position or a portfolio.

finder = *jobber.*

fine paper (FP) = *risk-free security.*

fine rate = *bank prime interest rate.*

Finex a division of the NYCE for trading financial futures and options. ***Also***: Financial Instrument Exchange.

finite difference method the method used to estimate a derivative instrument's price by converting a differential equation into a set of difference equations.

finite insurance a financial product that insurers sold to their customers who are looking for ways to smooth their net earnings or improve their accounting numbers.

finite-life REIT (FREIT) the REIT which plans to liquidate all of its holdings by a specified date to realize the capital gains.

FIP fixed income security options permit

FIPS fixed income pricing system

firewall <1> the legal barrier between the bank and broker/dealer operations in a financial institution created to prevent the exchange of inside information between the two institutions. <2> = *Chinese wall.*

firm bid a valid offer to sell a security at a definite price.

firm commitment the arrangement under which investment bankers make an outright purchase of the whole issue of the securities from the issuer ***Also***: back-stopped deal; bought deal; firm commitment underwriting.

firm commitment underwriting = *firm commitment.*

firm market active and steady market.

firm offer valid offer to sell a security at a definite price.

firm price the price at which a trader is willing to trade a derivative for a limited period of time.

firm quote round lot bid or offer price of a security stated by a market maker as the price at which he is willing to trade. **See**: *nominal quote.*

firm-specific risk = *unsystematic risk.*

firm trading market the market when a trader simultaneously fixes a bid to buy and also an offer to sell a security.

FIRST fixed interest rate substitute transaction

first board the first of delivery dates of futures contracts as established by the exchange.

first call <1> the start of a cash flow cycle for the cash flow window. <2> gathering research notes and earnings estimates from analysts by a public company.

first call date (FCD) the earliest date at which the issuer of a debt security or the preferred stock may call the security for premature redemption.

first-coupon date (F/C) the first interest paying date of a bond.

first fixing the fixing of the gold price at 10:30 a. m. by two representatives of the London Gold Market.

first-in, first-out (fifo) the method of settling and offsetting positions in which a given buy or sell transaction will offset the earlier trade date of the given commodity month sell or buy on file for a given client. **See**: *last-in, first-out.*

first loss swap a credit swap where the protection seller commits to indemnify the protection buyer for a predefined amount of losses upon a credit event.

first loss tranche the loss in an exotic credit derivative affecting the equity.

first market = *primary market.*

first notice day the first day on which the notice of intent to deliver a commodity in fulfillment of an expiring future can be given by the clearing house to the buyer. **See**: *last notice day.*

first passage option an option that has a random payoff at a random time, such as a stock option that pays its intrinsic value when the price of the underlying reaches a prescribed level.

first preferred stock a preferred stock having preferential claims on dividends and on assets over other preferred issues. ***See***: *second-preferred stock.*

first round the stage of venture financing following the startup stage. ***See***: *mezzanine level stage.*

Firsts floating interest rate subordinated term securities

first sinking fund date the earliest date at which the issuer of a bond obligates itself to begin making sinking fund payment.

first-tier penalty a penalty for violation of the Securities Exchange Act 1933 which shall not exceed the greater of the following: <a> $5,000 for a natural person or $50,000 for other person, or <b> gain as a result of the violation.

first-to-default a derivative feature that stops and the investor no longer bears the credit risk after the first credit event.

first-to-default swap a credit swap where the protection seller takes on exposure to the first entity suffering a credit event.

first tranche the class in a synthetic CDO that takes the lowest risk. ***Also***: senior tranche. ***See***: *equity tranche, mezzanine tranche.*

IS Fitch Investor's Service, a New York based financial service firm that rates corporate bonds. ***See***: *Moody's*; *Standard & Poor's.*

fiscal agent an agent who performs the functions relating to the issue and payment of bonds.

fisher effect all other things being equal, a rise in the country's expected inflation rate will cause an equal rise in the interest rate, then the exchange rate of its currency. ***Also***: international fisher effect.

Fisher index the measure of change in economic data calculated from a moving average of current observations of prices. ***Also***: chain-weighted index; Fisher price index.

Fisher price index = *Fisher index.*

Fisher's separation theorem a notion that a company's choice of investments is separate from its owner's attitudes toward investments. ***Also***: portfolio separation theorem.

FITE five-year note over ten-year note

fitted yield curve a yield curve which is formed by fitting a curve through many points representing the yields that are associated with the bonds of different maturities.

five against bond spread (FAB spread) a spread in the futures markets created by taking offsetting positions in futures for 5-year Treasury bonds and long-term Treasury bonds.

five against note spread (FAN spread) a spread in the futures markets created by taking offsetting positions in futures for the 5-year Treasury notes and 10-year Treasury notes.

five-year interest rate swap an interest rate swap with a five-year term, and a notional principal amount of about $200,000 or more.

five-year note over bond (FOB) a note over bond spread where the note is 5-year note.

fixed-adjustable rate preferred stock (FRAP) the variation on the adjustable-rate preferred that increases the dividend rate if the inter-corporate dividend exclusion rate is lowered in the future.

fixed annuity the annuity in which the payment to the annuitant are fixed. ***Also***: period-certain annuity.

fixed assurance note (FAN) = *de-*

ferred payment bond.

fixed base period = *base period.*

fixed bond = *term bond.*

fixed coupon a bond coupon the rate of which is fixed.

fixed coupon capital guaranteed credit link note a credit derivative the notional is guaranteed, but the coupon stops if a credit event occurs.

fixed-coupon marketable bond = *Canada bond.*

fixed dates the standard period for which Euro securities are traded.

fixed debenture <UK> a debenture that is secured by a specified asset of the issuing firm. ***Also***: secured debenture. **See**: *floating debenture.*

fixed delta the delta which does not change with the change in the underlying asset, e. g. the delta of a futures contract.

fixed-dollar obligation the conventional dollar bond the coupon of which is fixed.

fixed-dollar security the non-negotiable debt which can be redeemed at the holder's option for a dollar value set forth in a schedule of fixed prices.

fixed exchange rate the exchange rate of a country that is tied to another currency, gold or a basket of currencies. ***Also***: fixed rate of exchange; stable rate of exchange.

fixed exchange rate foreign equity option = *quanto option.*

fixed-fixed currency swap a currency swap both parties to which are fixed-rate payers in their respective currencies.

fixed-fixed swap the *circus swap* where both payment streams are at a fixed rate. ***Also***: fixed-for-fixed swap; fixed rate swap.

fixed-floating rate bond the bond issued with a fixed rate in early years which changes to a floating rate at a later date.

fixed-floating swap <1> = *circus swap.* <2> = *coupon swap.* <3> = *pay-fixed /receive floating swap.*

fixed-for-fixed swap = *fixed-fixed swap.*

fixed for floating swap = *coupon swap.*

fixed hedge a hedge under which the quantity being hedged is matched by the quantity to buy or sell by the option used as hedging instrument.

fixed income arbitrage a strategy that attempts to profit from the opportunities in fixed interest rate securities due to market price changes or convexity shifts.

fixed-income equity-linked debt (FIEL-D) = *automatically convertible enhanced security.*

fixed income equivalent = *busted convertible.*

fixed income pricing system (FIPS) an NASD system which centralizes trade reporting for the high-yield and other debts.

fixed income security = *fixed interest security.*

fixed income term structure the spot curve, forward curve or yield curve that describes the time value of money at a given point of time.

fixed interest rate the interest rate that is fixed at the time the fixed income bond is issued. ***Also***: deterministic interest rate.

fixed interest rate substitute transaction (FIRST) the two-tranche floater structure where one tranche is a traditional floater and the other is a reverse floater.

fixed interest security a security with fixed interest coupon. ***Also***: fixed income security.

fixed-interval hedging the hedging that is done in set intervals.

fixed investment trust = *unit investment trust.*

fixed leg the fixed payment portion of a swap. **See**: *floating leg.*

fixed lookback option a lookback option that pays the difference between the fixed strike price and the maximum reached by the underlying asset price in the life.

fixed par of exchange par of exchange maintained by the government. ***Also***: absolute par of exchange.

fixed price basis an offer of securities to the public at a fixed price.

fixed price method the method of closing stock position by selling stock after its price has jumped up a given range.

fixed-price tender offer one-time offer to buy a fixed number of shares at fixed price, at a premium over the market.

fixed-rate capital security the security which has a $25 par value and offers features of bonds and preferred stock.

fixed rate of exchange = *fixed exchange rate.*

fixed rate payer <1> the issuer of a fixed coupon note or bond. **See**: *floating-rate payer.* <2> = *swap buyer.*

fixed-rate swap <1> a foreign currency swap with two fixed rate legs. ***Also***: fixed-to-fixed currency swap. <2> = *fixed-fixed swap.*

fixed rate system the monetary system in which the exchange rate of each currency is fixed in terms of another currency. ***Also***: rigidly fixed rate system.

fixed strike ladder option the ladder option sold with a prescribed strike price. ***Also***: modified ladder option. **See**: *floating strike ladder.*

fixed strike lookback option a lookback option with a pre-set strike price.

fixed strike shout option an option that locks in gains to the larger of the difference between the terminal value and the strike price or the terminal value and the price chosen by the buyer in the life of the option. ***Also***: modified shout option. **See**: *floating strike shout option.*

fixed-to-fixed currency swap = *fixed-rate swap.*

fixed-to-floating swap = *coupon swap.*

fixed-to-variable interest rate swap = *coupon swap.*

fixed trust <UK> a trust that consists of securities agreed upon at the time of investment and never change.

fixing setting the gold price in London by the five representatives of the London Gold Market. ***Also***: gold fixing. **See**: *first fixing*; *second fixing.*

fixing date = *rate fixing date.*

flat <1> of a trade executed for no profit. <2> of stocks, borrowed without interest. <3> of a bond, = *ex interest.*

flat barrier the barrier price that is fixed. **See**: *exponential barrier.*

flat bond a bond the purchase price of which does not reflect any accrued interests. ***Also***: bond bought flat.

flat forward = *par forward.*

flat income bond the bond the quoted price of which includes all the unpaid accrued interest when it is in default.

flat market = *depressed market.*

flat outright forward method = *outright method.*

flat price = *clean price.*

flat price risk taking a position either long or short without spreading.

flat rate = *flat yield.*

flat scale a situation in which shorter and longer term yields show little difference over the maturity range of a new serial municipal bond issue.

flat trade a trade in bond where the price does not include accrued interest.

flat volatility the same volatility used to value each of the component caplets that collectively make up a cap.

flat yield the yield earned by the fixed-interest bond expressed as a percentage of the investment, without recognition of gain or loss. ***Also***: face value flat yield; flat rate.

flat yield curve a chart showing the yields of bonds with short maturities are equal to those of bonds with longer maturities. ***Also***: humped yield curve.

flex = *flex option.*

flexible auction rate preferred stock = *auction rate preferred stock.*

flexible bond = *managed bond.*

flexible cap a *cap* with fewer *caplets* than there are periods from the first to the last reset date. ***Also***: mulligan cap. **See**: *auto-flexible cap*; *chooser flexible cap.*

flexible exchange option = *flex option.*

flexible exchange rate the exchange rate that could fluctuate within certain limits. ***Also***: movable rate.

flexible fund = *flexible mutual fund.*

flexible mutual fund a fund that invests in a variety of securities in varying proportions to maximize shareholder returns. ***Also***: flexible fund.

flexible put option the put option some terms of which can be negotiated.

flexible trust = *discretionary fund.*

flex option the option which allows the traders to customize terms, including the strike prices and expiration dates. ***Also***: e-flex; equity flex option; flex; flexible exchange option.

flier a speculative investment made by an individual who does not usually speculate or actively trade in the market with knowledge that the investment is risky. ***Also***: taking a flier.

flip = *in-and-out.*

flip bond the bond with an embedded *Bermuda swaption.*

flip flop the investors in floating rate note could flip out into a future year bond, or flop back from the bond to the note at the discretion of the holder.

flip-flop note a note which enables the investors to switch between two different kinds of debt.

flip over the provision set by a target company under which preferred stockholders are granted the privilege of conversion into the common share of the company or of the acquiring company.

flipper = *scalper.*

flipping <1> buying a stock at close with the intent of selling it at the opening to capture a gap opening. <2> purchasing shares in an initial public offering and immediately selling them for a profit.

flip side the opposite side to a position.

float <1> a portion of outstanding shares expected to be traded actively in the stock market. ***Also***: floating securities; public float; publicly floated shares. <2> of the exchange rates, to vary in line with the market forces.

floatation <UK> = *initial public offering.*

floatation cost = *cost of flotation.*

floater <1> a debt security the interest on which is tied to some external index such as the prime rate. <2> = *bearer stock.* <3> = *floating rate note.*

floating bond = *short bond.*

floating capital (FC) = *idle money.*

floating cash reserve = *idle money.*

floating charge <1> the creditor's right extending to all the company's assets. <2> = *cost of floatation.*

floating coupon the coupon the interest rate of which is reset periodically based on a set formula.

floating debenture <UK> bond secured by the assets of the issuer generally, not by a particular asset. ***Also***: naked debenture. **See**: *fixed debenture.*

floating debt <1> continuously refinanced *short-term debt* for a company's ongoing operation. <2> the short-term obligation of a government.

floating exchange rate the exchange rate determined by the market supply and demand. ***Also***: float rate; fluctuating rate of exchange; free exchange rate; variable exchange rate.

floating-fixed swap = *pay-floating/ receive-fixed swap.*

floating-floating swap = *basis swap.*

floating-for-fixed swap a swap that allows floating rate payer to exchange payment with fixed rate payer.

floating-for-floating swap =*basis swap.*

floating interest rate subordinated term securities (Firsts) a hybrid debt instrument that combines features of a securitized loan and a high-yield bond. ***Also***: *covenant lite bond.*

floating leg the floating rate payments of an interest rate swap. **See**: *fixed leg.*

floating loan = *demand loan.*

floating lookback option a lookback option that pays the difference between the price of the underlying asset at expiration and the minimum price of the underlying in the life of the option.

floating money = *idle money.*

floating price the price on a fixed-for-floating swap or a floating-for-floating swap or on a floating-price cash transaction.

floating rate an interest rate adjusted up or down according to a benchmark index. ***Also***: adjustable rate; variable interest rate; variable rate.

floating rate bond a bond on which the interest payable is variable.

floating rate CD (FRCD) the CD the coupon of which is variable and linked to the market rate. ***Also***: variable rate CD.

floating-rate contract a contract the interest rate of which is tied to a benchmark.

floating-rate debt the debt on which the interest rate is reset periodically. ***Also***: adjustable-rate debt; variable-rate debt.

floating-rate enhanced debt security (FRENDS) a securitized note which is backed by the participation in a leveraged buyout loan.

floating rate note (FRN) <1> the note issued in the Eurosecurities market for 5 to 15 years, and carries a fixed spread over six-month LIBOR with provision for a minimum rate of interest. ***Also***: floater; variable rate-note. <2> = *adjustable rate note.*

floating-rate payer <1> the issuer of a floating-rate note or an *adjustable-rate preferred stock.* **See**: *fixed rate payer.* <2> = *swap seller.*

floating rate preferred (FRP) = *floating rate preferred stock.*

floating rate preferred stock (FRPS) a preferred stock the dividend of which is changing. ***Also***: floating rate preferred. **See**: *adjustable rate preferred stock.*

floating-rate rating sensitive note the floating-rate note in which the quarterly reset is based on a variable spread over the reference index rate.

floating rate securities the bonds, bank loans, or other securities with coupon rates that adjust periodically based on a specified reset mechanism.

floating rate system the monetary system under which the rate of exchange is determined by the market.

floating securities <1> securities held in the broker's name, purchased to make profits in a short period. <2> outstanding stock that is trading on an exchange. <3> = *float.*

floating spread the difference in basis points above or below a benchmark.

floating stock that part of a company's stock which is on the open market for speculation.

floating strike Asian option = *average strike option.*

floating strike ladder a ladder option with no prescribed strike price. **See**: *fixed strike ladder.*

floating strike lookback option the look-back option which settles based on a strike that is set equal to the optimal value achieved by the underlying over the life of the option.

floating strike option = *average strike option.*

floating strike reset option the exotic option for which the strike price is continuously reset to equal the highest or lowest market price to date.

floating strike shout option an option without strike price, that locks in gains between the terminal value and the price chosen by the buyer in the life of option.

floating supply <1> total dollar amount of municipal bonds for sale as offered in the Blue List. <2> number of shares of a stock available for sale.

floating to floating swap = *basis swap.*

float rate = *floating exchange rate.*

floor <1> the trading area in the stock exchange. ***Also***: trading floor. <2> an OTC instrument that is equivalent to buying a series of interest rate puts with different expiration dates, but the same strike. <3> the lowest interest rate of a floating rate instrument. ***Also***: contract rate; interest rate floor. **See**: *cap.* <4> a financial derivative which offers protection against the declining interest rates.

floor-ceiling agreement = *collar.*

floor-ceiling swap a swap with a built-in interest rate collar which constrains the floating-rate payment between the floor and ceiling rates as in a separate interest rate collar structure.

floor committee a committee empowered by an exchange for the purposes of resolving disputes and supervising the conduct and practices of the members and others on the floor.

floor dealer = *floor trader.*

floored put a put option position with a maximum payout limited by the terms of the option contract. ***Also***: limited put. **See**: *reverse equity risk reversal.*

floorlet <1> one of the interim period floors in a multiple period floor agreement. <2> one component put option of a strip of floor options. ***Opp***: *caplet.*

floorless convertible = *toxic convertible.*

floor rate the rate serving as the strike rate in an interest rate floor option or a foreign exchange floor option.

floortion an option giving the holder the right to buy a floor at a certain strike for a specified premium before expiration. ***Also***: flotion; option on a floor.

floor trader (FT) the member of a stock exchange who buys and sells for his own account. ***Also***: competitive trader; floor dealer; local trader; registered competitive trader; registered trader.

flotation cost = *cost of flotation.*

flotion = *floortion.*

flower bond a Treasury bond which can be applied to the payment of estate taxes at par when held by and included in the estate of a deceased.

flow-through share <Canada> the share issued by mining, petroleum and certain energy companies to finance the exploration and project development, the tax deductions flow through to investors.

fluctuating rate of exchange = *floating exchange rate.*

fluctuation the change in the market price. **See**: *point.*

flurry a significant volume increase in a specific security or derivative.

flush-out warrant a warrant that permits the issuer to lower the strike price for short periods during the life of the option.

FMAN the abbreviation of four quarterly expiration months of options: February, May, August, and November. **See**: *February cycle.*

FNMA stock = *Fannie Maes.*

FOB five-year note over bond

focused fund the fund which holds large positions in a small number of stocks.

focused ranged accumulation note the variant of the range accumulation note for investors who have more faith in their ability to predict short-term rates during the preceding period than in their forecasting ability on longer term rates.

FOF futures and options fund

folio an unstructured basket of stocks that represents an index or actively-managed portfolio. ***Also***: do-it-yourself fund.

following the market = *crowd.*

follow-on offering after an initial public offering. ***Also***: primary seasoned offering; seasoned public offering; subsequent offering. **See**: *secondary offering.*

footsie = *FT Actuaries Index.*

for cash = *delivery versus payment.*

forced conversion = *forcing conversion.*

force of interest = *explicit interest rate.*

forcing conversion forcing holders of convertible securities to convert their holding to common shares of the issuing company. ***Also***: forced conversion. **Opp**: *stimulating conversion.*

forecast <1> = *earnings forecast.* <2> = *whisper number.*

forecasted earnings the earnings of a future period reported by a public firm. **See**: *expected earnings.*

forecasted transaction the transaction for which there is no firm commitment. ***Also***: anticipated transaction.

forecast volatility an individual investor's perception of market volatility. ***Also***: expected volatility; future volatility. **See**: *actual volatility*; *historical volatility*; *implied volatility*; *relative volatility.*

foreign bond the bond issued by a domestic borrower to raise money in the foreign market in the foreign currency. ***Also***: tranche. **See**: *bulldog bond*; *Yankee bond.*

foreign bond fund a fund which invests in foreign bonds.

foreign crowd the NYSE members who trade on the floor in foreign bonds.

foreign currency bond a bond with the interest paid in a different currency than the proceeds of issuance. **See**: *dual currency bond.*

foreign currency contract = *foreign currency future.*

foreign currency exchange = *foreign exchange.*

foreign currency forward contract = *forward currency contract.*

foreign currency future a futures contract for the delivery of certain amount of one currency in exchange for another currency on or before a specific date at a set exchange rate. ***Also***: currency future; exchange future; foreign currency contract; foreign exchange future. **See**: *forward currency contract.*

foreign currency hedge a hedge that is set up to manage the risk of fluctuations in the exchange rates for given foreign currencies.

foreign currency option (FCO) an option the underlying asset of which are the packages of foreign currencies. ***Also***: currency option; exchange rate option; foreign exchange option. **See**: *international options.*

foreign exchange <1> instrument used for international payments, including cash, checks and bills. ***Also***: exchange. <2> the exchange of currency of one country for that of another. ***Also***: foreign currency exchange.

foreign exchange arbitrage = *currency arbitrage.*

foreign exchange dealer a dealer who buys foreign exchange from one party then sells it to another.

foreign exchange future = *foreign currency future.*

foreign exchange linked cap a cap that is linked to a foreign currency chosen by the contract parties.

foreign exchange market an OTC market where buyers and sellers trade foreign exchange.

foreign exchange official rate the foreign exchange rate derived by the ratio of the price indices between two countries and the *official exchange rate.*

foreign exchange option (FX option) = *foreign currency option.*

foreign exchange position = *exchange position.*

foreign exchange quotation the official rate of foreign exchange quoted by a bank. ***Also***: exchange rate quotation.

foreign exchange rate = *exchange rate.*

foreign exchange risk = *exchange risk.*

foreign exchange swap (FX swap) the OTC swap where two parties exchange an amount of one currency for another currency for a period. ***Also***: currency swap; principal currency swap.

foreign exchange trader = *cambist.*

foreign futures or options secured amount the cash, securities and other assets that an FCM must maintain in a separate account to cover or satisfy all of its current obligations to customers.

foreign holding the percentage of a portfolio represented by stock and SDR that are issued by the foreign firms.

foreign investment company stock the stock issued by a foreign company which was deemed by the IRS as an investment company during the period the shareholder owned the stock.

foreign issue = *foreign security.*

foreign market the domestic market for issuing and trading foreign securities. ***Also***: bulldog market; samurai market.

foreign premium the difference in price between the shares owned by foreign investors and the shares which must be held by the domestic investors.

foreign rho = *vega.*

foreign security the security issued by a foreign company. ***Also***: foreign issue.

foreign stock fund a fund that invests in securities issued by the foreign entities. ***Also***: international stock fund.

foreign-targeted issue the US notes sold between October 1984 and February 1986 to foreign institutions.

forestalling = *forward buying.*

forex foreign exchange

forfeited share the share of stock forfeited by the issuing company when the holder of which cannot meet the call on any unpaid amounts.

for long account = *buying long.*

Form 10K a detailed *annual report* of a public company, to be filed 90 days after the end of the fiscal year.

Form 10Q the quarterly report required by the SEC of every issuer of a registered security.

formation a technical chart pattern.

for money = *delivery versus payment.*

Form S-1 = *Registration Statement.*

formula basis the method of selling new issue of stock whereby the SEC declares effective on the basis of a pricing formula rather than on a specified range.

formula investing investment based on a predetermined asset allocation model, when the value of one asset changes, buy or sell that asset to maintain the same proportion. ***See***: *constant-dollar plan*; *constant-ratio formula*; *dollar averaging*; *program trading*; *variable-ratio formula.*

formula method a method of determining damages on early termination of a swap by using a formula.

for short account = *selling short.*

for stock the bond buyer is going to hold the bonds purchased in inventory for resale at some future time. ***See***: *buy and hold*; *going away.*

for the account to be paid for the next *account day.* ***See***: *account dealing.*

Fortune 500 Index common stock index that tracks the stock prices of the Fortune 500 companies.

forward <1> with a further expiration date. <2> = *future.*

forwardation = *contango.*

forward averaging a method of treating lump-sum distributions as if they have occurred over a 5- or 10-year period.

forward band = *cashless collar.*

forward based derivatives contract an instrument which can be analyzed as a portfolio of forwards, such as futures contracts and swaps.

forward break = *break forward.*

forward business buying and selling of futures. ***Also***: dealing in futures.

forward buying buying commodities in advance for future use or profit when prices are rising. ***Also***: forestalling.

forward cap an interest rate cap with a deferred start date.

forward cash contract = *cash forward.*

forward commitment the trading of a security at a set price with delivery and settlement at a specified future date.

forward contract a contract to buy or sell an underlying financial instrument at a specific future date for a price currently fixed. ***Also***: advance contract; forward exchange contract.

forward conversion the arbitrage in the currency option market when the options and forwards become mispriced relative to one another. ***Also***: conversion. **See**: *forward reversal.*

forward cover buying a cash commodity in order to cover the obligation of a forward contract.

forward currency contract a contract to buy or sell a currency at a specific price in a fixed period, 30, 60 or 90 days. ***Also***: currency forward; foreign currency forward contract; outright forward. **See**: *foreign currency future.*

forward currency swap a *foreign exchange swap* with a forward start on terms agreed upon in advance.

forward curve the interest rate yield curve that consists of a series of forward rates implied by a yield curve of spot rates. ***Also***: forward strip.

forward dating = *post dating.*

forward delivery the settlement on a specified date in the future by delivery.

forward derivative a derivative that involves a forward agreement.

forward difference $\Delta f(x) := f(x+1) - f(x)$ is called the forward difference of f.

forward differential the percentage difference between the *forward rates* and *spot rates* of a zero-coupon Treasury.

forward discount the amount by which the forward price is lower than the spot.

forward exchange the foreign exchange with settlement and delivery at a future date. ***Also***: future exchange. **See**: *spot exchange.*

forward exchange agreement (FXA) an agreement the maturity value of which is based on the differences between the forward currency exchange rate on the start date and the spot rate at the settlement date.

forward exchange contract = *forward contract.*

forward exchange rate exchange rate set today for a foreign currency transaction with payment or delivery at the future date. ***Also***: certain rate; direct exchange; forward rate.

forward exchange transaction a foreign exchange transaction with settlement and delivery at a future date.

forward Fed fund trading in Fed funds for future delivery.

forward foreign exchange contract an agreement that obligates an investor to deliver certain amount of one currency in return for a specified amount of another currency.

forward-forward an agreement between two parties for selling an underlying financial instrument in the future which is agreed with a delayed starting date.

forward-forward arbitrage = *arbitrage in time.*

forward-forward deal a deal done for a future date in an instrument that matures on a further forward date.

forward-forward interest rate = *forward rate.*

forward/forward volatility the volatility that changes with different strikes and expiration dates. ***Also***: forward volatility; successive volatility; variable volatility. **See**: *uniform volatility.*

forward hedge the hedge which uses the favorable forward exchange rate. ***Also***: lender arbitrage. **See**: *spot hedge.*

forward implied volatility the implied volatility of forward rates. ***See***: *implied forward rate.*

forward induction a method that uses forward in time to determine how much a dollar at a particular node contributes to the price of a contingent payout.

forward interest rate = *forward rate.*

forward intrinsic value the *intrinsic value* of an option plus the *fair value basis* on the forward contract that underlies the option. ***Also***: fair value premium.

forward LIBOR rate the log normal LIBOR interest rate under a forward contract.

forward loan a loan that begins on some future date based on the current terms and rate of interest.

forward-looking multiple = *forward P/E.*

forward-looking P/E = *forward P/E.*

forward margin = *premium.*

forward market the informal trading of commodities to be delivered at a future date. ***See***: *futures market.*

forward multiple = *forward P/E.*

forward option an option to buy or sell certain amount of foreign currency.

forward outright foreign exchange deal that matures on any day past the spot delivery date.

forward outright rate the exchange rate used in a forward outright.

forward parity a notion which holds that the *forward rate* is the unbiased predictor of future spot exchange rates.

forward P/E a P/E ratio based on the forecast of next year's earnings. ***Also***: forward-looking multiple; forward-looking P/E; forward multiple.

forward plus = *participating range forward.*

forward point a number that is added to or subtracted from the spot currency rate to calculate the forward price.

forward point agreement a swap under which one party pays the fixed forward points and the other party pays floating forward points based on the relative interest rates in the two currencies.

forward position the difference between the forward exchange bought and the forward exchange sold.

forward premium = *premium.*

forward price the price of a security for delivery at an agreed date in the future. ***Also***: futures price. ***See***: *spot price.*

forward pricing the SEC requirement that open-end funds, the share price of which is determined by the net asset value of the outstanding shares, base all incoming buy and sell orders on the next valuation of fund shares.

forward purchase the purchase of a commodity for deferred delivery.

forward purchase underwriting the underwriting whereby a company can raise capital by issuing stock at a price higher than the prevailing levels if the company will defer its sales revenue until a later day to boost future net earnings. ***See***: *buyer 60 contract.*

forward rate <1> the interest rate specified now for a debt obligation in the future. ***Also***: forward-forward interest rate; forward interest rate. ***See***: *spot rate.* <2> = *forward exchange rate.*

forward rate agreement (FRA) the contract in which one party receives a fixed interest rate while paying a floating rate for one single fixed future period.

forward rate bias = *prediction bias.*

forward rate bracket = *range forward.*

forward rate curve = *forward yield curve.*

forward reserve option = *break forward.*

forward reversal simultaneous sale of a currency forward and purchase of a call option and writing of a put option to realize a risk-free profit. ***Also***: reversal; reverse conversion. **See**: *forward conversion.*

forward sale a sale of actual commodity for deferred delivery.

forward settlement the settlement of a transaction on a future date after the spot settlement.

forward short rate a forward rate that is for a short period of time.

forward-spot parity relation relationship between the forward price and the price of its underlying asset.

forward spread the difference between any two forward rates or prices.

forward spread agreement <1> a specialized forward rate agreement which settles at the index rate at the time of settlement plus or minus an agreed spread. <2> a forward settling at the basis between two agreed-upon rates on the settlement day.

forward-start option an option with contractual feature determined until a future date before expiration. ***Also***: delayed option. **See**: *delayed-strike option.*

forward starting swap = *forward swap.*

forward start swap = *forward swap.*

forward strip = *forward curve.*

forward surprise a return on a currency that exceeds the rate of return implied by the forward rate.

forward swap a swap in which some payments are deferred for a preset period after they have been calculated and become due. ***Also***: deferred coupon swap; deferred-start swap; deferred swap; delayed draw-down swap; delayed start swap; forward starting swap; forward start swap.

forward trade the trade for which the settlement occurs on a future date after the spot settlement.

forward trading = *front running.*

forward triangular merger the merger whereby the acquiring company, which is a subsidiary, receives substantially all of the assets of the target company in exchange for the stock of the acquiring company, a parent company. **See**: *reverse triangular merger.*

forward value date account day for the settlement of forward exchange.

forward volatility = *forward/forward volatility.*

forward volatility agreement a contract that settles at a value determined by the spread between the contractual volatility determined on the trade date and an implied or actual volatility determined on the settlement date.

forward with optional exit (FOX) = *break forward.*

forward yield curve the interest rate curve derived point by point from the traditional yield curve, used to price interest rate derivative instruments. ***Also***: forward rate curve.

founder's share the share of a stock taken by founders of the company which ranks after the common stock, and carries a fixed rate of interest, and receives residual earnings only. ***Also***: deferred share; promoter's share.

fourchette option an option the payout of which is subject to spread or range.

four-point arbitrage = *4-point arbitrage.*

fourth market buying and selling unlisted securities directly among investors with the assistance of computers.

FOX <1> forward with optional exit. <2> Futures and Options Exchange.

FRA forward rate agreement

fractional Brownian motion = *random walk process.*

fractional exposure the estimate of an institution's maximum potential mark-to-market exposure to a specific party between the calculation date and the date of maturity of all open contracts. ***Also***: deemed risk; pre-settlement risk; time-to-decay risk.

fractional lot = *broken lot.*

fractional pricing the use of fractions in quoting the prices of stocks under $1.

fractional share a unit of stock less than one full share. **See**: *half stock.*

fractional strike a fraction (1/8) of the strike price of an option. ***Also***: strike price fraction.

franchise P/E surplus the amount by which the *price/earnings ratio* of a company exceeds the *basic P/E.*

franchise value the present value of a company's prospective new investments, representing its ability to earn an above-market rate of return on a given level.

franked dividend a dividend on which income tax has been paid.

FRAP fixed-adjustable rate preferred stock

fraption an option that gives the holder a right to enter into a forward rate agreement. ***Also***: interest rate guarantee.

fraud the intentional misrepresentation or concealment of information to deceive or mislead. **See**: *collusion; gold brick.*

FRCD floating rate CD

free asset ratio (FAR) the total fair market value of an insurance company's assets in excess of its policy liabilities.

free capital <1> the capital in the form of cash, or short-term money. ***Also***: capital in cash; liquid capital; monetary capital; non specific capital. <2> = *authorized capital stock.*

free cash flow (FCF) the cash flow which remains after deducting the funds a firm must commit to continue in operation. ***Also***: free cash flow for the firm.

free cash flow for the firm = *free cash flow.*

free cash flow per share *free cash flow* divided by the number of shares.

free collar zero net premium cost *interest rate collar* or *equity risk reversal.*

free currency the currency that can be converted into foreign currency without any restriction.

free delivery a practice whereby delivery of the securities sold is made to the buyer's bank without cash collection. **Opp**: *delivery versus payment.*

freedom shares the US saving notes sold from 1967 through the mid '70s.

freed up when members of a syndicate are no longer bound by the agreed upon price, thus free to trade in the security.

free exchange foreign exchange which can be paid to a third party without any restriction. **See**: *bilateral exchange.*

free-exchange rate = *floating exchange rate.*

free float the exchange system without government intervention. ***Also***: clean float; freely floating system.

free index an index by Morgan Stanley which measures the market capitalization weights indicating the degree to which a security can be purchased by foreigners. ***Also***: investible index.

freely flexible exchange rate = *freely floating rate.*

freely floating rate an exchange rate with no government intervention. ***Also***: freely flexible exchange rate.

freely floating system = *free float.*

free market = *active market.*

free market price = *market price.*

free range option = *nonpath dependent option.*

free riding the practice by which a member of the underwriting syndicate withholds a portion of new issue and later resells it at a higher price.

free right the right to transfer securities from one name, e. g. street name, to another, investor's name, without a fee. ***Also***: free right of exchange.

free right of exchange = *free right.*

free-standing derivative the derivative such as a future, a forward, a swap or an option. **See**: *embedded derivative.*

free stock a fully paid stock not pledged in any way as collateral.

free supply the supply of a commodity available to commercial entities as opposed to government agencies.

free trade buying close-to-the-money options at low volatility, then when the underlying asset price moves up, selling further out-of-the money options having higher volatility. **See**: *cashless collar.*

freeze out <verb> to force a minority shareholder to sell the shares after a merger.

FREIT finite-life REIT

French OAT obligations assimilables du Tresor, bond issued by the government.

FRENDS floating-rate enhanced debt security

fresh buying the purchase of a stock not for covering short position. **See**: *open selling.*

frictional cost the difference between an index fund return and that of the index that it represents.

frictions time, effort, money, and tax effects involved in trading derivatives.

friendly takeover a *takeover* supported by the management of the *target company.* **See**: *hostile takeover.*

friends and family offering the offering of stock to friends and family members of a pre-IPO start-up for seed money.

friends and family shares the shares in an initial public offering or secondary offering allocated to certain persons at the request of the issuer. ***Also***: directed shares.

frivolity theory a theory that holds that future market trends can be predicted by looking at the percentage of earnings Americans spend on eating and drinking. (If it is above 36% or below 33% of income, market will drop).

FRN floating rate note

frogs floating-rate notes with coupons reset quarterly or semi-annually to the coupon on the current 30-year Treasury bond. **See**: *yield curve swap.*

front contract the near month futures contract. ***Also***: front month contract.

front-end fee = *front-end load.*

front-end load a fee charged by open-end mutual funds at the time new securities are purchased by the investor. ***Also***: front-end fee; loading charge;

purchase fee; upfront fee; upfront sales charge. ***See***: *back-end load.*

front-end loading the practice of mutual funds in which administrative expense, selling expense, brokerage and other fees are deducted from initial deposit.

front fee a fee paid by the buyer upon entering a *split-fee option* contract.

front month = *nearby month.*

front month contract = *front contract.*

front running an illegal practice whereby a trader with advance knowledge of block transaction which will influence the price of a stock, enters into option positions to profit from the trading. ***Also***: forward trading; trading ahead of the client. ***See***: *beating the gun.*

front spread <1> a strategy in which the number of options purchased is less than the number of options sold. ***Opp***: *back-spread.* <2> = *debit spread.*

front stub period the first coupon period on a floating rate note that is shorter than a normal full coupon period. ***See***: *back stub period.*

FRP floating rate preferred

FRPS floating rate preferred stock

F.S. futures spread.

FSF first sinking fund date

FT 500 Share Index <UK> an index of 500 stocks compiled by the Financial Times.

FTABX Fidelity Spartan Tax-Free Bond Fund

FT Actuaries Index <UK> an index of stock prices compiled by the Financial Times in association with the Institute of Actuaries of London, the base period is April 1962. ***Also***: footsie; Financial Times Actuaries Index; FTSE.

FT All-Share Index <UK> the index of all stock prices compiled by the Financial Times.

FT Government Securities <UK> an index of government securities compiled by the Financial Times

FTSE = *FT Actuaries Index.*

FTSE 100 <UK> an index of 100 stocks by the Financial Times.

fugit the risk-neutral expected time of an American option.

fulcrum = *bottom.*

fulfillment fund = *completion fund.*

full = *handle.*

full capital structure synthetic a synthetic CDO structured using securitization under which the sponsoring bank will enter into a portfolio default swap with a special purpose vehicle.

full carry <1> = *cost of carry.* <2> = *cost- of-carry market.*

full carrying charge = *cost of carry.*

full carrying charge market = *cost-of-carry market.*

full carry market = *cost-of-carry market.*

full charge the event in which a futures contract holder pays a carrying charge that is adequate enough to cover the entire amount of expenses incurred.

full coupon bond the bond the coupon rate of which is near the current market interest rate.

full fungibility a right of options ownership in which the buyer is free to sell his contract before the expiration date.

full lot = *round lot.*

full price = *dirty price.*

full-service fund the fund in which the dividends are automatically reinvested rather than distributed.

full stock a stock the face value of which is $100. ***See***: *half stock.*

full volatility the volatility measured at all times, including upside and downside markets. ***See***: *semi-volatility.*

fully-diluted earnings per share earnings per share figure calculated after all the convertible bonds, preferred stocks, options and warrants are assumed to have been converted or exercised. ***Also***: diluted earnings per share; earnings per share fully diluted. **See**: *primary earnings per share.*

fully distributed issue a new offering of securities which has been completely resold to the public, not dealers. **See**: *absorbed securities.*

fully funded account asset management account the balance of which is equal to or in excess of the positions held. ***Also***: funded account. **See**: *nominally funded account.*

fully invested portfolio a portfolio the assets of which are all securities, with no cash.

fully modified pass-through = *modified pass-through.*

fully paid share the share that has been paid in full. ***Also***: all-square share; paid-up share. **See**: *called-up capital*; *uncalled capital*; *partly paid share.*

fully participating preferred stock the preferred stock that in addition to receiving preferred dividends, will participate in the excess dividends on a rate based on the total par value of common and preferred stock. **See**: *partially participating preferred stock.*

fully tax-exempt security = *triple tax-exempt security.*

fully valued stock a stock the value of which is recognized by the marketplace and factored into its market price. **See**: *overvalued stock*; *undervalued stock.*

functional currency the currency of the primary economic environment in which a firm operates, generates and expends cash. ***Also***: non-base currency. **Opp**: *reporting currency.*

function bond = *public purpose bond.*

fundamental beta the product of a statistical model used to predict the fundamental risk using not only price data but also other market and financial data.

fundamental value the value of a stock based on fundamental analysis.

fund assets the net market value of a portfolio's assets minus outstanding debts.

fundatechnician a trader who uses both fundamental analysis and technical analysis.

funded account = *fully funded account.*

funded debt <1> a debt due after one year and is formalized by the issuing of bonds or long-term notes. ***Also***: long-term debt. **See**: *unfunded debt.* <2> a bond issue whose retirement is provided for by a sinking fund.

funded format = *credit linked note format.*

fund family a mutual fund which offers many shares for various objectives. ***Also***: family; family of funds; mutual fund family.

fund for retirement of bonds = *bond sinking fund.*

funding the substitution of long-term for short-term debt.

funding loans <UK> gilt-edged securities issued by the British Government, e. g. 4% 1960 to 90, 5.5% 1982 to 84, 3.5% 1999 to 2004 etc.

funding risk = *interest rate risk.*

funding system issuing bonds to defray the expenses of government, and creating a sinking fund designed to lower interest expense and repay principal.

fund of funds <1> a mutual fund which also invests in other mutual funds. ***Also***: multi-manager vehicle. <2> a commodity pool which invests in other commodity pools.

fund open ended = *open-end fund.*

fundoscope the mutual fund statistical service, which provides historical data and analysis.

fund scandal = *market timing 2.*

funds lying idle = *idle money.*

fund switching transfer of mutual fund shares without charge from one mutual fund to another. ***Also***: conversion.

fungibility the interchangeability of traded contracts between exchanges.

fungible securities the securities which are normally substitutable for other similar ones in offsetting trades or liquidating a position.

funnel sinking fund the sinking fund in which the issuer has combined the payments from several issues so the profits can be used to retire the most expensive issues.

funny money <1> options, convertible bonds, preferred stocks, and warrants with characteristics of the common stock but did not reduce reported EPS before 1969. <2> = *unsecured bond.*

furthest month delivery month furthest away from the spot or nearby delivery month. ***Also***: back month; far month; most distant month. **See**: *distant month*; *nearby month.*

fusion = *consolidation.*

future a contract for the delivery of a commodity at a future time at a preset price. ***Also***: car; commodity future; commodity futures contract; forward; futures contract.

future amount = *accumulated amount.*

future exchange = *forward exchange.*

future investment opportunity more valuable investment opportunity that results from a current investment.

futures call the purchase of commodities by exercising a call option on futures.

futures contract (FC) = *future.*

futures contract multiplier the number set by an exchange which when being multiplied by the futures price, gives the dollar value of a futures contract.

futures equivalent the number of futures contracts associated with a speculative option position.

futures exchange an official marketplace where buyers and sellers meet to trade futures and options on futures.

Futures Industry Association (FIA) a national trade association for futures commission merchants.

futures market a place on which futures contracts are traded. ***Also***: contract market; terminal market. **See**: *cash market*; *forward market.*

futures month abbreviations = *standard futures month.*

futures on index futures contract the underlying asset of which is an index.

futures option an option to enter into a futures contract in some future time at a given price. ***Also***: commodity futures option; commodity option; option on futures. **See**: *option on physicals.*

futures option month the month abbreviations in options trading, e. g. for calls: F = Jan, G=Feb, H=Mar, J=Apr, K=May, M = Jun, N=Jul, Q=Aug, U=Sep, V=Oct, X=Nov, Z=Dec; for puts: A=Jan, B=Feb, C=Mar, D=Apr, E=May, I=Jun, L=Jul, O=Aug, P=Sep, R= Oct, S=Nov, T=Dec.

futures option pair two options on the same commodity or two commodities traded at the same time.

futures overlay converting an investment in asset A into asset B by entering into a short futures position on A and a long futures position on B.

futures price =*forward price.*

futures spread difference between the prices of two related futures contracts.

futures strip an option consisting of two put options and one call option on the same commodity with the same strike price and expiration date.

futures strips a series of futures contracts in succeeding contract months. ***Also***: strips.

futures style option an option the buyer of which does not pay premium, but buyers and sellers post margin, as in a futures contract, and the option premium is marked to the market daily.

future sum the amount that a borrower agrees to repay for an obligation.

future value the equivalent value at a future date based on the time value of money. ***Also***: final value; future worth. **See**: *present value*; *time value of money.*

future volatility =*forecast volatility.*

future worth =*future value.*

G g

G <1> abbreviation for February in futures and call option. <2> a Nasdaq descriptor meaning an issue is the first convertible bond. <3> the option strike price code for 35.

gain = *profit.*

gain on bond conversion = *conversion premium.*

gain on constructive retirement = *constructive gain.*

GAINS partial strips from Goldman Sachs

gamma a measurement of how fast *delta* changes, given a unit change in the underlying asset price, it is the derivative of *delta.* ***See***: *omega*; *theta.*

gamma hedge a hedge taken by initiating option positions to reduce the risk of change in delta in response to changes in the price of the underlying asset.

gamma neutral an asset or investment portfolio whose delta rate of change is set to zero. ***See***: *negative gamma*; *positive gamma.*

gamma risk the risk that option market-makers are exposed to because of a positive or negative gamma.

gap <1> the price movement when one day's trade range does not overlap the next day's. ***Also***: price gap. <2> the bank rate-sensitive assets minus rate-sensitive liabilities. <3> a mismatch between assets and liabilities. <4> = *duration gap.*

gap option an option in which the strike price determines the size of the payoff, but a different constant determines if the payoff is to be made.

garbatrage the rising prices and volume throughout an industry sector due to a major takeover or merger between two big companies. ***See***: *rumortrage.*

GARCH Generalized Auto-Regressive Conditional Heteroskedasticity

GARCH effect = *volatility clustering.*

Garman-Kohlhagen model currency option evaluation model that is similar in structure to the Black-Scholes model with separate terms for foreign and domestic interest rates. ***Also***: Biger and Hull model.

GDR global depository receipt

gearing = *gearing ratio.*

gearing ratio the relationship between the capital and fixed interest capital, derived by dividing (preferred stock + loan capital) by common stock. ***Also***: degree of financial risk; gearing. ***See***: *leverage ratio.*

geisha security = *shogun security.*

GEM growing equity mortgage

GEMM gilt-edged market maker

GEMX German Equity Market Index

general annual meeting = *annual meeting.*

general cash issue = *public offering.*

general cash offer = *public offering.*

general collateral a repo in which the borrower can supply Treasury securities as collateral.

Generalized AutoRegressive Conditional Heteroskedasticity (GARCH) a time series modeling technique that uses past variances.

general management trust <UK> = *discretionary fund.*

general mortgage bond a bond secured by a mortgage on the issuer's real property.

general obligation bond the municipal bond backed by the full faith and credit of the municipality government. ***Also***: GO bond.

general stock ownership corporation a corporation formed under state laws, which invests in other corporations.

generic credit spread the bond spread quoted for a given credit rating and expiration.

generic swap = *plain swap.*

genus = *spider.*

geographic arbitrage = *arbitrage in space.*

geometric mean frontier rebalanced portfolios with greater geometric mean return than other with the same or lesser risk, and lesser risk than others with the same or greater geometric mean return.

geometric mean return = *time-weighted rate of return.*

geometric return = *log return.*

geometric step option = *proportional step option.*

Geske-Johnson model an option pricing model created by Robert Geske and Herbert Johnson for American puts.

gestation repo a reverse repo between mortgage banks and securities dealers.

GFOF geared futures and options fund

G-hedge an interest rate collar with an upfront premium and a symmetrical range on either side of the forward rate.

ghosting *collusion* among two or more market makers to manipulate the price.

GIC <1> guaranteed investment certificate. <2> guaranteed investment contract.

gigabite a sudden, billion-dollar drop in net worth. ***See***: *megabite.*

gilt-edge bond the bond issued by a blue chip company, usually with AAA rating. ***Also***: gilt-edged security.

gilt-edged <UK> = *gilt-edged security.*

gilt-edged security <1> <UK> a UK government security the risk of which is minimum. ***Also***: default-free security; fault free security; gilt-edged; gilts; government security. <2> = *gilt edge bond.*

gilt fund a mutual fund that invests in several different types of medium and long term government securities.

gilts = *gilt-edged securities.*

Ginnie Mae <1> stock and bonds issued by GNMA. <2> = *Government National Mortgage Association.*

Ginnie Mae I the mortgage-backed securities issued by Ginnie Mae, that are single-issuer pools. ***Also***: GNMA II.

Ginnie Mae II a pass-through issued by Ginnie Mae, based on a group of mortgage pools with differing interest rates and maturities. ***Also***: GNMA II.

Ginnie Mae pass-through = *pass-through security.*

giver = *issuing house.*

give-up the reduction in yields resulting from the sale of bonds and the purchase of other bonds with a lower yield.

giving quote = *direct quote.*

glamor stock the stock classified by a higher earnings growth rate with a wide public following.

gliding parity = *crawling peg.*

global bond the bond issued on a temporary basis with a face value equal to the amount of borrowing, until such time as the individual bonds are printed.

global depository receipt (GDR) <1> a bank certificate issued in more than one country for shares issued by a foreign firm. <2> the financial instrument used by private market participants to raise capital denominated in US dollars or Euros.

Global Electronic Exchange = *Globex.*

global fund a mutual fund investing in securities throughout the world. ***Also***: international fund; international mutual fund; world fund.

global hedge the hedge covering the unwanted risks of a portfolio by taking advantage of any natural risk offsets and using broad hedging instruments.

global hedging = *macro hedging.*

global macro strategy the strategy of holding long and short positions to profit from the changes in global economies.

global registered share the share issued and registered in the global markets.

Globex an electronic trading platform for derivatives and futures developed by CME, Reuters, CBOT, and MATIF. ***Also***: Global Electronic Exchange.

GMC guaranteed mortgage certificate

GNMA Government National Mortgage Association

GNMA I = *Ginnie Mae I.*

GNMA II = *Ginnie Mae II.*

GNMA option an option based on the GNMA pass-through or mortgage bond.

GNMA standby a put option based on GNMA securities.

gnomes the 15-year-fixed-interest-rate pass-through securities issued by the FHLMC.

gobble = *merger.*

GO bond = *general obligation bond.*

godfather offer the aggressive takeover from a big company that management of the *target company* cannot refuse.

go-go fund a mutual fund that invests in risky and aggressive growth securities. ***Also***: performance fund.

going around communicating with the primary dealers in order to establish a market of bids and offers.

going away <1> the bond buyer is going to immediately resell the bonds purchased. **See**: *for stock.* <2> = *blowout.*

going-concern value company value in terms of continuing operations.

going long = *buying long.*

going longer = *switching.*

going rate of interest the current yield rate of bond interest. ***Also***: current interest rate; prevailing rate of interest.

going short = *selling short.*

gold arbitrage an arbitrage that takes advantage of the gold price inefficiency.

gold bond a bond which bears a clause promising the payment of interest or principal (if the bonds were redeemable) in gold coin of a standard fineness.

goldbrick share a stock with only the appearance of quality and worth, when actually it is worth very little.

goldbug an analyst who recommends gold as an investment or hedge.

gold-carry trade borrowing gold selling it to buy securities that pay more in interest than the cost of borrowing the gold.

golden handcuffs rewards and penalties designed to discourage key employees from leaving a company.

golden handshake large payment to a senior executive upon termination of employment before the contract ends.

golden life jacket the compensation package an acquiring company offers to the top executives of the target company.

golden parachute cash paid to the high officials of the target company. ***Also***: gold parachute. **See**: *silver parachute.*

golden ratio 0.618, the ratio of any two consecutive numbers in the Fibonacci sequence. ***Also***: phi.

golden share a type of share that gives its shareholder veto power over change to the company's charter.

gold fixing = *fixing.*

gold-linked note the promissory note with interest rates indexed to the gold prices.

gold parachute = *golden parachute.*

gold silver ratio the number of ounces of silver required to buy one ounce of gold at current spot price.

good delivery the securities delivered in proper form per terms of a contract.

good delivery and settlement procedures the Uniform Practices such as cutoff times on delivery of securities and notification, allocation and endorsement of derivative contracts.

good faith deposit a deposit, 25% of a deal, required by some securities firms of investors not known to them.

Good-Ship-Lollipop stock a stock the price of which will not crash in a long period of time. ***Opp***: *Titanic stock.*

good volume actively traded volume on an exchange, e.g. 25,000,000 shares per hour on NYSE is considered active.

Gordon-Shapiro model = *constant-growth model.*

gorilla stock the stock issued by a company which holds so many assets that it may become a *target company* soon.

government debt the debt issued by a government. ***Also***: national debt; official debt; public borrowing; public debt; public fund.

Government National Mortgage Association (GNMA) a government-owned company acting as an agent of the US Department of Housing and Urban Development, which buys mortgages from banks and sells them as securities to the public like Ginnie Mae I. ***Also***: Ginnie Mae.

government obligation the debt such as Treasury bill, bond, note, savings bond, etc. issued and pledged to repay by the Federal Government. ***Also***: conversion stock. **See**: *government security.*

Government of Canada Treasury bill <Canada> a promissory note issued by the Bank of Canada on behalf of and guaranteed by the Federal Government.

government securities dealer = *dealer bank.*

government security <1> the security issued by a government agency, such as FHLB. ***Also***: agency security. **See**: *government obligation.* <2> = *gilt-edged security.*

GPM graduated payment mortgage

grade certain quality of a commodity or credit instrument.

grading certificate a document, issued by the inspectors or approved graders, that signifies the quality of a commodity.

gradual knock-in option a step option the value of which depends on the time the price of the underlying asset spent inside of the corridor. ***Also***: expanding face option.

graduated call writing selling covered call at incrementally rising strikes so that the seller can profit more as price increases.

graduated payment mortgage (GPM) a fixed-rate mortgage the payments will get larger at a designated point in time.

graduated rate coupon a coupon with pre-set payment dates but the payment amounts vary. ***Also***: multiple coupon.

graduated security a security the listing of which has been upgraded, that is moving to the more famous exchange or from regional to national exchange.

Graham and Dodd method a method that buys the stock of a company with undervalued assets.

Graham-Harvey Measure 1 a measure developed by John Graham and Camp-bell Harvey to lever the fund's portfolio to match the volatility of the S&P 500.

Graham-Harvey Measure 2 a measure developed by John Graham and Camp-bell Harvey to lever the S&P 500 portfolio to match the volatility of the fund.

grand average IV the overall average implied volatility of all options of the same asset for a given period.

grandfathered share <Canada> a share issued after 6/18/1987 and before 1988.

granny bond <UK> a savings bond that may be bought only by investors who receive pension or government benefit.

grant of option <UK> = *option grant.*

grantor = *writer.*

grantor trust a trust established for taking collateral for mortgage-backed securities.

grave dancer = *bottom fisher.*

graveled = *oversold.*

graveyard market the bear market like a graveyard, those who are in can not get out (short sellers facing great losses), those who are out do not want to get in (potential investors prefer to keep their cash). **See**: *roach motel.*

gravy = *profit.*

gray chip the stock issued by a smaller and mid-size company.

gray knight the second bidder in a takeover bid who attempts to take advantage of the problems between the target and the initial bidder.

gray list a list of stocks traded by the block desks, not in risk arbitrage.

gray market an unofficial market where new issues of shares are bought and sold before they officially become available for trading on the stock exchange.

Greeks the Greek letters used in options trading, such as delta, theta and vega.

green baize door = *Chinese wall.*

green investing an investment in the socially responsible companies. ***Also***: ethical investing; ethical investment; investing for the green; socially conscious investing; socially responsible investing. **See**: *black investing; environmental fund.*

greenmail the cash paid by the *target company* to the raider company to buy back the shares acquired by it. **See**: *anti-greenmail.*

green shoe a clause in an underwriting agreement which, in the event of exceptional public demand the issuer, will authorize additional shares to be issued. ***Also***: green shoe option; over-allotment provision.

green shoe option = *green shoe.*

Greenspan put psychological insurance against drops in the market since Alan Greenspan, former Chairman of the Federal Reserve Board, will take actions in preventing significant and sustained market downturns.

gross capitalization = *market capitalization.*

grossed-up net redemption yield <UK> the yield on a security divided by the rate of marginal income retained by the investor after tax.

gross negative fair value total fair value on all contracts on which one party owes money to another without *netting* by what the other party owes him.

gross parity <1> the price of an international security, including fees, stamp duty, commissions, taxes, and other transaction costs. ***See***: *net parity.* <2> <of a convertible bond> = *dirty price.*

gross positive fair value total fair value on all contracts on which one party owes money to another without any *netting* by what the first party owes any 3rd parties.

gross power = *excess margin.*

gross processing margin (GPM) the amount by which a dealer's sales of oil and meal exceed his cost paid for the soybean in a *crush spread.*

gross return the market price divided by the previous closing price. ***See***: *total return.*

gross spread (GS) the difference between the offering price of a new issue and cash price the issuer actually received after deducting underwriting fees and issuing costs. ***Also***: spread; underwriting spread.

gross yield to redemption <UK> yield on a security plus the annual capital gain if it is held to redemption.

ground floor = *laggard.*

grounding of stock prices, touching the bottom. ***See***: *oversold.*

group averages the entire industry's average of the market prices, price-earnings ratios, and earnings per share.

group rotation the tendency of stocks in one sector to outperform and then underperform other industries.

group sale the sale of securities to institutional investors by every member of the syndicate. ***See***: *designated sale.*

group sales the amount of a block sale of securities to an institution investor that must be apportioned by all members of the syndicate group.

growing equity mortgage (GEM) the graduated payment mortgage in which each payment is larger than the last one. ***Also***: rapid-payoff mortgage.

growth fund the mutual fund invested in growth stocks. ***See***: *value fund.*

growth manager a money manager who seeks to buy stocks with a high P/E.

growth stock <1> a stock invested for an increase in value rather than for income payments. ***Also***: performance stock. <2> a stock that is much favored by investors because its earnings in the future may grow faster than others.

GRS guaranteed return structure

guaranteed bond a bond the principal or income or both are guaranteed by a third party. ***Also***: assumed bond; backed bond; endorsed bond; indorsed bond. ***See***: *double-barreled bond; recovery note.*

guaranteed exchange rate option = *quanto option.*

guaranteed income bond a single premium insurance bond that pays a fixed income annually and returns the original sum invested at the end of a given period.

guaranteed interest contract (GIC) = *guaranteed investment contract..*

guaranteed investment certificate (GIC) <Canada> an investment security issued by a bank or investment trust that offers a fixed rate of return.

guaranteed investment contract (GIC) debt instrument issued by an insurance company, the interest is guaranteed. ***Also***: guaranteed interest contract.

guaranteed mortgage certificate (GMC) an instrument issued by Freddie Mac in 1975 representing undivided interest in Freddie Mac loans.

guaranteed rate on delivery (GUARD) = *break forward.*

guaranteed return structure (GRS) the structured product that guarantees the minimum value at maturity or a minimum return based on levels reached by the underlying during the contract life. **See**: *principal protected product.*

guaranteed spread excess of a broker-dealer's agreed price to buy securities over the cost prices in *overtrading.*

guaranteed stock <1> a stock on which dividends are guaranteed by a third party. <2><UK> the stock issued by some nationalized industries, the interest on which is guaranteed by the government.

guaranteed stock market bond a bond that pays income based on the performance of the stock and guarantees the principal of investment.

guaranteed warrant an index warrant issued by a government or a company.

guarantee letter a letter by a bank that guarantees the payment of the strike of the put when an *assignment notice* is presented to the option writer.

guaranty fund a fund of last resort set up by local government to protect consumer interest.

guaranty stock the share issued by a mutual insurance company.

GUARD guaranteed rate on delivery

guerilla group = *distributing syndicate.*

gung-ho investor an investor who paid too much for a security or derivative.

gun jumping = *beating the gun.*

gunning the market = *manipulation*

gunslinger <1> the aggressive manager who makes risky investment in search of high returns. <2> = *speculator.*

gut an option strategy created by selling an in-the-money put at the same time buying an in-the-money call. ***Also***: gut spread; gut strangle. **See**: *strangle.*

guts = *mambo combo.*

gut spread = *gut.*

gut strangle = *gut.*

gypsy swap the exchange of restricted shares for freely exchangeable shares between two separate parties.

H h

H <1> in securities listings of newspaper, meaning declared or paid after a stock dividend or split-up. <2> the month abbreviation for March in futures and calls. <3> Nasdaq descriptor meaning the issue is the second preferred bond. <4> option strike price code for 40.

habitat = *spider.*

haircut reduction from the market value in the valuation of securities for the purpose of calculating the broker-dealer's net capital, for example gilt-edged securities could have 0% haircut, while equities could have 30%, and failed positions 100%.

half-hedge option the option sold by a writer who holds only 50% of the value of the underlying stock. ***Also***: 2-against-1 ratio writing; 2-against-1 writing.

half-life the point in time when half the principal has been repaid in a mortgage backed security issued by GNMA, FNMA or FHLMC.

half stock a fractional share having a par value of $50. ***See***: *fractional share; full stock.*

hammering the market the intense short selling of stocks by those who think the prices will decline. ***See***: *bear campaign*; *holding the market.*

HAMSTER hope for a market stabilization in a given range

hamster option = *accrual option.*

handle the first few digits of a quote. ***Also***: big figure; figure; full.

hands-off investor an investor who has a large holding of stock in a company, but does not wish to participate in daily management.

hands-on investor an investor who has a large stock in a company, and takes an active role in management.

hard call date the date on which the hard call protection ends.

hard call protection = *call protection.*

hard commodity a commodity which is mined, such as silver and gold. ***See***: *soft commodity.*

hard currency freely convertible currency of a country not expected to drop in value in the foreseeable future. ***Also***: specie. ***See***: *soft currency.*

hard dollar cash given in exchange for an equity in a transaction for real estate. ***See***: *soft dollar.*

hardening <1> the price of futures contracts that is gradually stabilizing. <2> the futures market that is slowly advancing.

harmful warrant a warrant detached from its *host bond* with the right to buy a bond other than an indentured bond. ***See***: *host bond.*

harmless warrant a warrant giving the holder the right to purchase bonds by surrendering a bond with similar terms. ***Also***: wedding warrant.

harmonized index of consumer price swap = *inflation swap.*

has-been a stock or asset that has lost its popularity.

hat trick high bid for a *target company.*

hawkish favoring an increase in interest rate.

headline earnings reported earnings including all the tax-adjusted profits and losses from the disposal of assets and sale or discontinued operations.

headline earnings per share (HEPS) headline reported earnings divided by the number of shares outstanding.

heart attack futures the official futures contracts traded on the CME (Chicago Mercantile Exchange).

Heath-Jarrow-Morton (HJM) the formulation of Treasury bond in terms of forward rates resulting in a two-dimensional Gaussian quantum field theory.

heavy offering available in large volume and bids do not seem to be developing fast enough to absorb the supply.

heavy selling = *unloading.*

heavy tail = *excess kurtosis.*

heavyweight the stock of a company with at least 100 million shares outstanding.

hedge counter balancing a present sale or purchase by a purchase or sale of the similar foreign exchange or securities, for delivery at some future date. ***Also***: hedging; hedging transaction.

hedge against inflation a hedge to avoid loss due to inflation.

hedge bond the bond issued to hedge another bond.

hedge clause = *disclaimer.*

hedged fund the fund that constantly uses hedging techniques to protect its investments.

hedge diagram chart showing immediate changes in the underlying asset price into the resulting profit and loss from a position.

hedged inverse floater the combination of an *inverse floater* based on a foreign rate and a *foreign exchange swap* to hedge currency exposure.

hedged portfolio a portfolio consisting of a long position in the stock and a long put position on the same stock.

hedged swap unmatched swap where the dealer has undertaken transactions to offset interest rate or other risks.

hedged tender selling short a position of shares being tendered at a takeover bid to hedge against a price drop in the event that all shares tendered are not accepted by the *acquiring company.*

hedge effectiveness the degree to which a hedge can offset the risk being hedged. ***Also***: effectiveness.

hedge efficiency the success of a hedging transaction in reducing risk exposure, as measured by 80 to 120 percent.

hedge fund a fund that uses aggressive strategies such as short selling, leverage, swaps, arbitrage, and derivatives.

hedge fund strategy the strategy used by a hedge fund to hedge against risk.

hedge impairment = *ineffectiveness.*

hedge interval the amount that a price is allowed to move between adjustments of the underlying for delta hedging.

hedge letter a letter signed and dated by a client stating the commodity in which he qualifies for hedge privileges.

hedge option strategy = *covered option strategy.*

hedge quality R-square in a regression of spot rate changes on the futures price changes.

hedger an investor engaged in reducing an exposure to a risk by *hedge.*

hedge ratio (HR) <1> the ratio of the value of futures contracts purchased or sold to the value of the cash commodity being hedged. <2> = *delta.*

hedge-to-arrive contract the contract whereby a producer agrees to sell a product to the intermediary, with cash settlement linked to the futures price.

hedge wrap = *equity risk reversal.*

hedge wrapper a strategy under which a trader is holding the underlying stock buys an out-of-the-money put and sells an out-of-the-money call.

hedgie a hedge fund operator.

hedgilator <1> one who is a hedger in one direction and an option-holder-speculator in the other. <2> one who delays hedging hoping that a hedge is not necessary.

hedging = *hedge.*

hedging demand a demand for securities to hedge particular consumption risk beyond the mean-variance diversification motivation.

hedging derivative the derivative that is designated as hedging against risk.

hedging strategy a strategy used to hedge against risk.

hedging transaction = *hedge.*

Heisenberg uncertainty principle the indicator that becomes too popular will lose its effectiveness.

held-to-maturity (HTM) a debt intended to be held to maturity. ***See***: *available-for-sale securities*; *trading securities.*

hemline theory a theory which holds that stock price will rise when short skirts are in fashion, and fall when long dresses are in fashion. ***See***: *yellow color theory.*

herding using the same strategies by other investors. ***Also***: herd instinct.

herd instinct = *herding.*

hermaphrodite option = *as-you-like option.*

Herstatt risk the risk in foreign exchange trading that a party will deliver foreign exchange but the counterpart defaults. ***Also***: capital risk; settlement risk.

Heston model an option pricing model under which instantaneous variance of stock return follows a mean-reverting square root process.

H-H page *Quotron* display page showing new listed inquires and orders received after the block call. ***Also***: I-I page.

hidden load sales charge not explicitly disclosed in the fine print of a mutual fund prospectus.

hidden orders a market system which permits participants to place a bid or offer for a larger amount than they are willing to expose. ***Also***: cloaked orders.

highballing the dealer's purchase of securities from a customer above the current price.

high beta index an index composed of companies with high betas trading on the NYSE.

high-coupon bond refunding replacing a high-coupon bond with a bond with lower coupon.

high-coupon swap an *interest rate swap* where a fixed-rate payment is above the market. ***See***: *low-coupon swap.*

high current income fund a fund the main purpose of which is high income rather than growth by investing in high-risk stocks.

higher barrier = *upper barrier.*

higher-of floater a floating rate note with the interest rate stated as the higher of two different formulas. ***See***: *lower-of floater.*

highest-in, first-out (HIFO) an accounting procedure for mutual fund shares, whereby shares with highest costs are sold first.

high-expense fund a mutual fund that charges investors high management fees, more than 1% of asset value for a stock fund, 0.8% for a bond fund and 0.6% for a money-market fund.

high flyer = *yo-yo stock.*

high-grade bond a bond rated AAA, or AA. ***See***: *low-grade bond.*

highjacking <Japanese> = *takeover.*

high-low floater a floating-rate note with a premium rate up to a cap level on the reference index rate.

high-low index (hi-lo index) <1> an index calculated by dividing the weekly number of highs and lows by the actual number of total issues traded. <2> moving average of industrial stocks that reach new highs and new lows each day.

high-low option a cash settled call with payout equal to the spread between the high and low prices or rates touched in a period, times the contract multiplier.

high low range volatility (HLRV) = *Parkinson's historical volatility.*

high P/E stock the stock with a high P/E ratio, 20 or above, often with low yield and risky. ***See***: *low P/E stock.*

high-premium convertible debenture a bond with long-term high premium stock conversion right and a relatively high interest rate.

high price = *inflated price.*

high risk stock a stock with a volatile price, usually selling with a high *price-earnings ratio* and a small and thin capital structure.

high speculation security a security from a company that has a high *price-earnings ratio.*

high-tech stock the stock of companies involved in high technology industries, (computers, bio-technology, etc.)

high watermark <1> high point of value that an investment fund has reached. <2> the previous relative high value of account that is subject to incentive fee arrangement.

high yield of an investment, with a high rate of return but often lower credit rating.

high-yield bond a bond with a high rate of return, but may be risky. ***See***: *junk bond.*

high-yield bond fund a mutual fund that invests in bonds that are rated below Baa.

hi-lo index high-low index

hi-low option the combination of two lookback options or 2 path-dependent options.

hindsight currency option the option giving the buyer the retroactive right to buy a currency at its low point (call) or to sell a currency at its high point (put) in the entire option period. ***Also***: hindsight option. ***See***: *lookback option.*

hindsight option = *hindsight currency option.*

HIPER high interest principal protection with extendible redemption

historical data past data about a company or its historical price information.

historical volatility (HV) the volatility that is calculated by using historical data. ***Also***: actual volatility; realized volatility; statistical volatility. ***See***: *forecasted volatility*; *implied volatility*; *relative volatility.*

historical yield the past performance yield provided by a mutual fund over a specific period.

historic VAR the value at risk calculated by using historic data.

HITS high income trust securities

HJM Heath-Jarrow-Morton

HLRV high low range volatility

Ho and Lee model = *Ho-Lee model.*

hold <1> the rating that recommends

others to hold the stock. <2> not to sell a stock owned.

holder = *option holder*.

holder extension option an option that grants the holder the right to extend the expiration date.

holder of non-voting stock the person who is both the owner and record holder of a non-voting stock.

holder of record a holder of a security as recorded in the books of the issuer or a transfer agent on a particular day, usually the record day.

holder of record date = *date of record*.

holding the number of shares held.

holding company <UK> = *controlling corporation*.

holding company bailouts the practice whereby the stock issued by companies with large earnings are transferred to a new holding company, which could not pay dividend for lack of earnings.

holding cost <1> the cost associated with maintaining an ongoing position in a stock or market, including the *custodian cost* and tax. <2> = *carrying charge*.

holding period the length of time an asset was held, the time between the date of the purchase and the date of the sale.

holding period return the return from holding an asset, it is equal to the gain and income plus price appreciation in a given period divided by the initial cost of investment. ***Also***: holding period yield.

holding period yield = *holding period return*.

holding the market entering the market with large block of buy orders in order to support price. **See**: *bull campaign*; *hammering the market*.

holding value <1> the weighted average price of the securities in a portfolio. <2> the assumed value of an option for holding one more period.

HOLDR the security issued by Merrill Lynch that bundles together a portfolio of selected stocks in a given sector.

Ho-Lee model a model developed by Ho and Lee in 1986 for making the derived option prices consistent with the prices of default-free zero-coupon bonds. ***Also***: Ho and Lee model.

home asset bias the tendency of small investors to invest in the assets of their own country.

homemade dividend the sale of some shares to get cash in an amount similar to that of a cash dividend.

homemade leverage the substitution of risks to move from overpriced shares in highly leveraged firms to the unleveraged companies by borrowing in personal accounts.

home run <1> a potential takeover bid, which results in a price spurt. <2> in 80s, a successful high-yield bond issue.

hope for a market stabilization in a given range (HAMSTER) = *accrual option*.

horizon matching = *combination matching*.

horizon return <1> the investment return over a set horizon. <2> = *total return*.

horizontal bear spread the horizontal spread in which the holder is long the near month and short the back month.

horizontal bull spread the horizontal spread in which the holder is long the back month and short the near month.

horizontal calendar call spread buying at-the-money LEAP call options and selling at-the-money near term call options against the LEAP.

horizontal credit spread a horizontal spread created with the premium received higher than the premium paid, resulting in a credit.

horizontal debit spread the horizontal spread with the premium paid higher than the premium received.

horizontal reverse spread = *reverse horizontal spread.*

horizontal spread a *time spread* which is established by buying an option with longer expiration and selling an option with shorter expiration. ***See***: *diagonal spread*; *vertical spread.*

horizontal tornado = *diving board effect.*

hospital revenue bond the bond that is issued to finance the construction of a hospital by a municipal or state agency.

host bond a debt instrument originally issued with detachable warrants. ***Also***: bond with attached warrant; bond with warrant; carrier bond. ***See***: *harmful warrant.*

hostile takeover a takeover that is not supported by the target company. ***Also***: unfriendly takeover. ***See***: *friendly takeover.*

host security the security to which a warrant is attached.

hot deal an initial public offering the shares of which are being sold at a price below their market value.

hotelling principle the principle which states that the price, net of extraction cost, of an exhaustible resource should rise over time as long as it pays to extract some of the resource and leave some unextracted.

hot issue <1> an issue where securities, after their initial sale to the public, are resold in the open market at the prices much higher than the original offering price. <2> = *blowout.*

hot money the money that flows between financial markets in search for highest short term interest rates.

hot stock <1> the stock which has been stolen. <2> a newly issued stock which rises quickly in price.

house = *stock exchange.*

house of issue = *issuing house.*

house's money amount of loss which has been recovered by the gain from a recent rise in price.

housing bond the bond issued by local housing authorities to finance the construction of housing.

housing starts the reported number of new housing units on which construction has started.

HPR holding period return

HR <1> hedger ratio. <2> here.

HTM held-to-maturity

Hull-White model a model for interest rate derivatives developed by John Hull and Allan White in 1990. ***See***: *control variate.*

humped yield curve <1> a yield curve that rises with maturity in some period but declines maturity thereafter. ***Also***: hump shape. <2> = *flat yield curve.*

hump shape = *humped yield curve.*

Humpty Dumpty fund the five-year fund set up in 1980, when AT&T was split down, into which an AT&T shareholder could deposit certain number of shares and receive a fractional interest in the fund. ***Also***: Americu's trust.

hung convertible a convertible bond or preferred stock issue whose conversion cannot be forced by the issuer.

hurdle derivative a derivative the payoff of which depends on the time spent by an index below a given level.

Also: range derivative; switch derivative.

hurdle rate the minimum rate of return acceptable by investor for an investment. ***Also***: base interest rate; benchmark interest rate; cutoff point; cutoff rate; discount rate; limit rate; lowest acceptable rate of return; minimum acceptable rate; minimum attractive rate of return; minimum cutoff criterion; minimum required rate of return; required rate of interest; required rate of return; vest charge. **See**: *bogey*; *maximum return criterion*.

hurricane bond a bond with so high risk that will blow the investors away.

HV <1> have. <2> historical volatility.

hybrid package of two or more risk management instruments.

hybrid bond a structured security that includes callable bonds and puttable bonds.

hybrid CDO a CDO with the character of a cash CDO and a synthetic CDO.

hybrid collar a collar that writes discrete equity call options against a passive portfolio and buys lower priced index put options.

hybrid contract a contract that possesses the characteristics of a forward, future, option, debt and interest.

hybrid credit derivative a derivative that combines credit risk with market risks.

hybrid debt the combination of a debt instrument and an equity, a currency, or a commodity forward, option or swap.

hybrid fund a mutual fund that invests in market-neutral stocks.

hybrid instrument <1> a derivative that contains an embedded financial derivative which otherwise would require bifurcation. <2> = *hybrid security*.

hybrid loan a loan with a combination of fixed and floating rates.

hybrid REIT a REIT which generates income from rent and capital gains, as well as interest.

hybrid security a security which combines features of both debt and equity, i. e. of both bond and stock. ***Also***: debt-equity hybrid; hybrid instrument.

hypothecation pledging of securities as collateral for any debit balance in a margin account.

hysteresis the failure of an effect to reverse itself as the underlying cause is reversed.

I i

I <1> paid this year, dividend omitted, deferred or no action taken at the meeting. <2> the abbreviation for June in put options. <3> Nasdaq descriptor meaning the 3rd preferred bond. <4> option price code for 45.

IAN <1> index amortizing note. <2> indexed amortization note. <3> interest arrears note.

IBEX-35 a capitalization weighted index of 35 most liquid Spanish stocks.

IBEX-35 future a futures contract that is underlied by the IBEX-35.

I-bond Treasury savings bond with a 30-year maturity indexed to account for inflation. ***Also***: Series I bond.

ICC Intermarket Clearing Corporation

ichimoku chart the chart that provides a one look glance of the equilibrium prices for specified securities.

icing stock the reservation of stock under an agreement with a stock lender in anticipation of borrowing it.

ICON indexed currency option note

ID <1> immediate delivery. <2> income debenture. <3> interim dividend.

IDB industrial development bond.

ideal portfolio the perfect portfolio that an investor would hold if all of his or her assets were available to be invested without restriction.

identical securities stocks received by the lender which are identical, of the same class and issue, to those lent out.

identified hedging a hedge transaction for risk management or hedging purpose. ***See***: *arbitrage hedge.*

identified share a stock or mutual fund share the purchase price and date are identified for capital gains tax purpose.

identified straddle the straddle clearly identified on the investor's records.

idiosyncratic risk = *unsystematic risk.*

idle fund = *idle money.*

idle money the cash held in idle balance, such as uninvested available fund, and inactive bank deposit. ***Also***: disposable capital; dormant capital; floating capital; floating cash reserve; floating money; funds lying idle; inactive money; unemployed capital.

IDR international depository receipt

IEF <1> individual equity future. <2> interest earning facility.

IFOX Irish Futures and Options Exchange

IFX options = *international options.*

I-I page <in OTC trading> = *H-H page.*

illegal procurement of foreign exchange = *currency arbitrage.*

illiquid security = *non-marketable security.*

immediacy cost the cost associated with a decision to trade quickly, rather than by entering a limit order.

immediate annuity = *immediate payment annuity.*

immediate payment annuity an annuity bought with one payment and has a specified payment plan that starts immediately. ***Also***: immediate annuity.

immediate settlement the delivery and settlement of securities in five business days after the transaction.

IMM swap a swap which is priced using the IMM's Eurodollar futures strip as the reference.

immunization the construction of asset and liability of portfolio to offset any changes in market value. ***Also***: income immunization; portfolio immunization. **See**: *cash flow matching*; *duration matching*.

immunized portfolio a portfolio that is structured under immunization.

impact forward a forward contract with collar.

imperfect hedge the hedge that is less than the full amount of the subject being hedged. ***Opp***: *perfect hedge*.

implied 20-day an estimate of the front-month at-the-money implied volatility, usually 20 days.

implied call a borrower's right to repay a loan.

implied duration the duration of a deliverable bond or underlying bond.

implied forecast a forecast of where the implied 20-day will be in 20 days.

implied forward price the forward price implied in the price of at-the-money options based on the put-call parity.

implied forward rate the interest rate for a specific forward period calculated from the incremental period return in adjacent instruments on the zero-coupon yield curve. **See**: *forward implied volatility*.

implied interest rate the forward rate calculated by using all the default-risk free bonds available in the market.

implied repo rate the maximum cost of financing a position consistent with or discounted by the return available from a cash/futures arbitrage position. ***Also***: return to hedged portfolio.

implied spread the expected yield spread between two debt instruments indicated by a yield matrix model.

implied strike a strike price that would make the *market price* the *theoretical value* when the *historical volatility* of the underlying asset is used as a function input.

implied tree model the financial model which assumes that future volatilities will be a deterministic function of time and the value of the underlying asset. ***Also***: deterministic volatility function model; local volatility model.

implied volatility (IV) the theoretical value representing the volatility of the asset underlying an option that has been built in the price. ***Also***: expected volatility; market's opinion of volatility; market volatility. **See**: *actual volatility*; *forecast volatility*; *historical volatility*; *relative volatility*.

implied volatility index (IV index) the weighted average of implied volatilities of all options on a stock. ***Also***: average implied volatility.

implied volatility puzzle the bias in implied volatility as a forecast of the subsequent realized volatility.

implied volatility smile the relationship between the implied volatility and the strike price of an option.

implied zero-coupon swap curve the *yield curve* for zero-coupon notes derived from the traditional yield curve to value fixed-rate swap payments.

improvement bond a bond issued for the improvement of existing facilities.

imputed interest the interest deemed paid to bondholders through discount, even though no cash bas actually been paid. ***Also***: interest imputed; unstated interest.

imputed principal amount the total sum of the present values of all payments of principal and interest due under a promissory note.

inactive bond crowd = *cabinet crowd*.

inactive market the market with very less trades. ***Also***: dull market; listless market; narrow market; thin market. ***See***: *active market*; *dead market*.

inactive money = *idle money*.

inactive stock issue of stock traded on an exchange or in the OTC market in which there is a relatively low volume of trades. ***See***: *cabinet security*.

in and out the purchase and sale of the same security in one trading session. ***Also***: flip; round trip trade; round turn trade. ***See***: *buy and hold*; *churning*; *day trading*; *swing trading*.

in-and-out cost = *round trip cost*.

in-and-out trader one who buys or sells the same security in one trading session. ***See***: *day trader*; *scalper*.

in-arrears swap = *arrears swap*.

"in" barrier = *knock-in price*.

"in" barrier option = *knock-in option*.

in between of a price which is higher than the *bid* but lower than the *offer*.

incentive fee = *performance fee*.

incentive shares the shares issued to high executives on advantageous terms, e. g. deep discount, convertible etc.

incentive stock option (ISO) the stock option issued to employees for a term less than 10 years. ***See***: *non-incentive stock option*.

incentive trade the trade that a broker may share in any gain from a better than average order execution and to be penalized for an inferior execution.

inception the beginning of an option.

incestuous share dealing buying and selling each other's shares by two companies to create a tax advantage due to corporate exemption.

inchoate instrument an incomplete instrument that can be perfected by the addition of a payee's name.

"in" clearing checks, bills of exchanges etc. received by a bank after clearing at the clearing house. ***See***: *"out" clearing*.

income <1> earnings from any source. <2> = *net income*.

income basis a way of figuring out the rate of return by dividing cost by the income in a given year.

income bond <1> <UK> the fixed interest bond issued for 5, 10 or 15 years, which consists of an immediate and a deferred annuity. ***Also***: adjusted bond; adjustment bond; insurance bond. <2> the bond guaranteed as to principal, but interest payment is contingent.

income dividend the amount paid to fund investors, with dividends, interest, and short-term capital gains earned and paid from the fund's portfolio.

income equalization the distribution of realized capital gains to shareholders of a fund when redeeming shares, so that the capital gain can be divided between the leaving shareholders and the remaining shareholders.

income fund a mutual fund whose target is to maximize current income.

income immunization = *immunization*.

income investment company an investment fund that tries to provide the highest income possible to its holders.

income of capital = *capital gain*.

income-producing collar a collar that is structured to generate cash flow. ***See***: *cashless collar*.

income return the annual gain from an investment or the percentage ratio found by dividing annual gain by total cost.

income risk the risk of loss that income provided by a fund or a floating rate note will reduce due to interest rates changes.

income share a class of shares issued by a dual purpose mutual fund, which pays both dividends and interest income of the fund to its shareholders. ***See***: *capital share.*

income statement the financial statement that shows revenues earned, expenses incurred in earning revenues and the net profit or loss in a given period. ***Also***: earnings report; profit and loss statement.

income stock a stock that pays a large dividend.

income warrant a stock warrant paying interest while remaining the ownership rights to the dividend.

income yield = *earnings yield.*

in competition an indication that the client has revealed trading interest to multiple brokers and that the trade will take place with the firm having the highest bid or the lowest offer.

in-competition compound interest bond (COMPO) = *zero-coupon bond.*

increasing rate note (IRN) a note on which the coupon rate increases by the predetermined amounts at specified time intervals.

incremental share the number of shares converted by the option minus the number of treasury stock that can be bought by the proceeds.

indefinitely dated stocks <UK> the securities without a fixed maturity, but is redeemable any time as the government wishes after a specified date.

indemnification method the method for assessing damages on early termination of a swap.

indemnity option given to a shareholder who has lost his dividend check to buy or sell a specific quantity of a stock at a stated price in a given period.

indemnity letter the letter sent to a stockholder who lost the dividend check with a statement protecting the company from liability if it issues a duplicate check and the first was cashed.

indenture a written agreement of issue and sale for bonds which contains the maturity date, interest rate etc. ***Also***: bond indenture; deed of trust.

index statistical yardstick expressed in terms of percentages of a base year.

index allocated principal bond (XAC bond) a bond the principal of which is allocated based on an index.

index amortizing note (IAN) a structured note whose payment schedule is determined by the behavior of interest rates. ***Also***: indexed amortization note.

index amortizing rate swap = *index amortizing swap.*

index amortizing swap a swap whereby the notional principal amount of the agreement is amortized according to the movement of an underlying rate. ***Also***: index amortizing rate swap; indexed principal swap.

index arbitrage the arbitrage on the temporary discrepancies between the prices of the stocks comprising an index and the price of a future on that index. ***Also***: cash-index arbitrage; stock index futures arbitrage.

indexation the linking of prices, wages, income, interest rates or loan values to an index. ***Also***: index-linking.

index bond = *indexed bond.*

index call a clause in which the issuer can retire the bond at a price connected to the Treasury bond rate.

index differential swap = *cross-rate swap.*

index divisor the total market value of a component stock in an index divided by the index value. ***Also***: divisor.

indexed amortization note (IAN) = *index amortizing note.*

indexed bond a bond of which the rate of interest and the repayment amount are based on the changes in CPI. ***Also***: index bond; stabilized bond.

indexed coupon note the note with a fixed principal due at maturity, but with coupons that vary with the behavior of an interest rate, equity, currency, commodity, inflation, or other index. ***Also***: indexed rate bond.

indexed currency option note (ICON) a note with all payments in one currency but principal payment indexed to an exchange rate at maturity.

indexed debt obligation <Canada> the debt providing for an adjustment to the amount payable by reference to the consumer price index.

indexed employee stock option an employee stock option the exercise price of which is linked to a broad market index or the index of peer companies or the index chosen by the company.

indexed inverse floating-rate note = *bull floater.*

indexed note the combination of a zero-coupon bond and an embedded index option with the present value of what would be the annual yield on the zero-coupon bond.

indexed principal swap (IPS) = *index amortizing swap.*

indexed rate bond = *indexed coupon note.*

indexed security = *Treasury inflation protected security.*

indexed security investment plan (ISIP) <Canada> a plan which offers savings of capital gains by adjusting the cost basis in listed shares by inflation.

indexed strike cap the cap which gives customized interest rate protection at reduced cost, with a *knock-in option* or a *knock-out option.*

index floater = *accrual note.*

index fund a mutual fund that tries to mirror the performance of an index, e. g. S&P 500. ***Also***: *tracker fund.*

index fund arbitrage an index fund holder's exploiting the disparities between the spot and futures markets to take the opportunity to boost returns.

index future a futures contract based on an index, such as a stock index futures contract.

index hugger a mutual fund that tends to perform very similar to a benchmark index like the S&P 500.

indexing <1> a strategy under which all investments are weighted in line with one of the major stock indices. ***Also***: bond indexing; buying the index. <2> buying shares in an index fund.

indexing plus = *enhanced indexing.*

index-linked bond a bond the redemption price of which is linked to an index.

index-linking = *indexation.*

index model a model used to measure the returns that uses a market index to represent the common or systematic risk factors.

index of capital growth a measure of the success of a mutual fund or hedge fund in accumulating capital gains over a period of years.

index option a call and put on the stock indices. ***Also***: stock index option.

index participations the instruments that provide small investors with a low cost way to obtain an index equivalent portfolio, replaced by the *exchange-traded funds.* ***Also***: cash index participations.

index portfolio a portfolio designed to track the performance of an index.

index principal swap a swap the notional principal amount of which declines through a prescribed barrier levels, resulting in decreasing payments. **See**: *amortizing swap; reverse index principal swap.*

index program = *basket trading.*

index range note = *accrual note.*

index range option = *accrual option.*

index rate a benchmark of interest rates.

index risk the yield curve risk based on the difference between the coupon rate paid to bondholders and the yield of the underlying securitized receivables.

index share an index-based share that represents the entire portfolio of stocks in one single security, such as QQQQ.

index swap a swap of an index for some other assets. **See**: *stock index swap.*

index tracking the correlation between a portfolio's return and the return on a benchmark index.

index warrant an index option issued by a company as part of an offering, and guaranteed by the option clearing house. ***Also***: equity index warrant.

indicated order = *indication of interest.*

indicated yield coupon or dividend rate as a percentage of the market price. **See**: *current yield.*

indication of interest a note issued by a dealer or an investor showing his or her interest in buying securities still in registration. ***Also***: indicated order. **See**: *circle.*

indication rate exchange rate offered by a dealer for information only. ***Also***: info quote.

indicative optimized portfolio value (IOPV) calculation of the approximate intra-day asset value of an optimized index *exchange-traded fund,* based on the intra-day value of the creation basket.

indicative per share portfolio value (IPSPV) the intra-day net asset value of an exchange-traded fund based on nearly real-time pricing of the portfolio after the close of the a trading day.

indicative price <1> an estimate of the price at which a financial instrument may be created. <2> = *nominal quote.*

indicative swap pricing schedule the quoted price schedule for the swaps in which a swap dealer makes a market.

indirect arbitrage = *compound arbitrage.*

indirect financing issuing bonds with the aid of a bank or the underwriters. ***Opp***: *direct financing.*

indirect quote a foreign exchange quote expressed as a fixed unit of home currency in variable units of foreign currency. ***Also***: European terms; indirect rate; rate in foreign money; receiving quote. **See**: *direct quote.*

indirect rate = *indirect quote.*

indirect stockholding holding the controlling interest in a third company by a subsidiary.

individual equity future (IEF) a futures contract based on individual stocks.

individual investor <1> a natural person investor. ***Also***: retail investor. <2> = *small investor.*

indorsed bond = *guaranteed bond.*

industrial aid bond = *industrial revenue bond.*

industrial development bond (IDB) = *industrial revenue bond.*

industrial rate of return = *internal rate of return.*

industrial revenue bond (IRB) the bond issued by a state to finance plants and facilities that are then leased to private businesses. ***Also***: industrial aid bond; industrial development bond.

industrials the stocks issued by the industrial companies. ***Also***: industrial stock. **See**: *commercials.*

industrial stock = *industrials.*

industry bet a mutual fund manager's increasing (or decreasing) holdings in an industry.

industry stock group a group of stocks representing the same industry.

ineffectiveness the failure of a hedge in protecting against risk. ***Also***: hedge impairment.

inefficient hedge a hedge that can not offset the risk exposure at the lowest cost.

inefficient portfolio the portfolio that delivers an expected return that is too low for the amount of risk it requires, or a portfolio that requires too much risk for a given expected return.

in-favor stock a stock currently favored by investors. **See**: *wallflower.*

infinite ATM IV = *long-term IV.*

infinite forecast the forecast of *infinite volatility* that the asset will revert to.

infinite ladder option a *ladder option* sold without cap or limit on the number of rungs.

infinite volatility a volatility based on the assumption that the variance increases indefinitely.

inflated price an overvalued stock price in terms of its earnings. ***Also***: high price; soaring price.

inflation adjusted principal an adjusted principal amount of a security, derived by multiplying the par amount by the inflation index ratio.

inflation derivative an instrument with the producer or consumer price index used as the basis for swap or other index payment. ***Also***: inflation-linked debt; real yield security.

inflation hedge a hedge that is designed to protect against inflation risk.

inflation-indexed embedded derivative an embedded derivative that alters the payments based on an inflation index.

inflation-indexed security the security that promises a higher return than the rate of inflation if the security is held to maturity.

inflation-linked debt = *inflation derivative.*

inflation risk the risk of the rate of return being lower due to inflation. ***Also***: price-level risk.

inflation swap a swap one party pays the consumer price index while the other pays a fixed amount. ***Also***: consumer price index swap; harmonized index of consumer price swap; retail price index swap.

inflection point the point on a chart that marks the beginning of a significant price move, either up or down. ***Also***: turning point. **See**: *reversal.*

inflos inverse floating security

info quote = *indication rate.*

information coefficient (IC) the correlation between the forecasted return and the actual stock returns used to measure the accuracy of a financial analyst.

informationless trade a trade initiated for reasons other than short-term earnings expectations or risk control. **See**: *information motivated trade.*

information motivated trade a trade in which an investor believes that he or she has the information not reflected in the stock's price.

in house fund = *discretionary fund.*

initial charge = *initial performance bond.*

initial coverage an indication to cover short position by buying back the underlying stock.

initial day = *date of value.*

initial filing = *Registration Statement.*

initial market value the market value of the shares determined on the date on which the shares were appropriated to the participant concerned.

initial offering date the date on which a mutual fund is first available for sale to the public.

initial performance bond the money required when a futures position (or a short option on futures position) is initiated. ***Also***: initial charge. **See**: *maintenance performance bond.*

initial public offering (IPO) the first registered sale of new stock to the public. ***Also***: floatation; new issue. **See**: *primary offering.*

initial reserve the *self-insurance fund* at the beginning of a year. **See**: *terminal reserve.*

initial sales charge sales charge paid by the investor at the time of purchase of mutual fund shares on the IPO.

in-kind distribution = *in-kind redemption.*

in-kind redemption the sales of large block of fund or ETF shares to an arbitrager, specialist, market maker or an affiliate. ***Also***: in-kind distribution.

in lieu of dividend payment to lender of borrowed stock to make a short sale in lieu of the dividends while the short position is maintained. ***Also***: dividend paid on short sales; in lieu of payment; manufactured dividend; premium.

in lieu of payment = *in lieu of dividend.*

in line <1> order of market in a specific security within the *inside market.* <2> of earnings, that is very close to Wall Street expectation.

in-line buyer the buyer of a significant quantity of security who is willing to deal at prevailing price levels.

inner CDO the CDO inside an outer CDO in a CDO squared. **See**: *outer CDO.*

innocent purchaser a person or entity who in good faith does not expect hidden defects to appear when buying the stock.

innovative financial instrument = *new financial instrument.*

in option = *knock-in option.*

in play rumored to be vulnerable to a takeover attempt.

inscribed stock <UK> the government security for which no stock certificates are issued, but a certificate of inscription is issued, stating that the holder's name is inscribed at the Bank of England. ***Also***: registered stock.

inside barrier a barrier option in which the same asset's price serves as both the underlying's price and the barrier price. **See**: *outside barrier.*

inside bid the highest price at which an investor is willing to buy a security, a futures contract or an option.

inside buildup the increase in a policy's cash value which has not been borrowed by the insurance policy holder. ***Also***: unborrowed policy cash value.

inside day a day in which the total price range of a security is entirely within the previous day's range.

inside debt a debt in the form of a loan. **Opp**: *outside debt.*

inside information corporate affairs not yet been made public. ***Also***: asymmetric information; insider information; tips. ***See***: *nonpublic information.*

inside market <1> bid or asked between dealers trading for their own investors. ***Also***: inter-dealer market; wholesale market. <2> = *market maker spread.*

inside offer the lowest price at which an investor is willing to sell a security or enter into a derivative contract.

inside quote <1> the bid and asked price of an unlisted stock among the broker-dealers. <2> = *market maker spread.*

insider one who has business knowledge not available to the public. ***Also***: corporate insider.

insider dealing = *insider trading.*

insider information = *inside information.*

insider trading <1> unfair secret buying and selling of shares by insiders. ***Also***: insider dealing; short swing trading.

inside spread = *market maker spread.*

inside the fees the situation when the securities are selling at a price that allows the underwriter to make a profit. ***Opp***: *outside the fees.*

insolvency risk = *credit risk.*

installment bond = *serial bond.*

installment option = *continuation option.*

institutional broker the broker who buys and sells securities for banks, mutual funds, pension funds, insurance or other institutional clients.

institutional fund a mutual fund which targets pension funds, endowments and other high net worth investors.

institutional market short-term investments and commercial paper market for institutional investors.

institutional pot that percentage (often 20%) of an offering of an issue which is set aside by underwriters for large institutional investors. ***Also***: pot.

institutional share a mutual fund share available to institutional investors only. ***Also***: Y share.

instrike = *instrike price.*

instrike price the price at which a *barrier option* becomes a standard option. ***Also***: instrike. ***See***: *outstrike price.*

instrument = *security.*

instrument of trade = *commercial paper.*

insubstantial quantity the allocation of hot issues of 2,000 or fewer shares, or $25,000 face value of bonds.

insurable risk a risk that can be hedged by insurance policies.

insurance bond = *income bond.*

insurance derivative a derivative, such as futures or structured note, for which the underlying is an index of property and casualty insurance policies.

insurance dividend an annual dividend paid to policyholders participating in cash value life insurance policies.

insured bond a municipal bond insured against default risk by insurance.

insured portfolio the portfolio which is managed to produce insurance payoff, especially the *floor* and *upside capture.*

integrated volatility = *realized volatility.*

integration = *consolidation.*

integrity risk the risk when delivery of a portfolio contains one or more illiquid positions that increase execution cost.

intellectual risk the risk that the employees capable of controlling the business will leave the company.

intensity model a model that uses given intensity and uncertain time horizon to estimate the time of credit default.

interactive mutual fund a mutual fund in which shareholders can view portfolios online.

interbank rate = *LIBOR.*

interbank swap a swap between 2 swap dealers.

interchangeable bond a bond, such as a bearer bond, a coupon bond, etc. that can be converted into registered bonds without charge. **See**: *convertible bond.*

intercommodity spread a spread which consists of a long and a short position in two different but related commodities. **See**: *interdelivery spread.*

intercompany note the promissory note issued from one affiliate company to another or to the parent company.

intercrop spread buying and selling of the commodity on the same exchange with one position in one crop year, and the other in another crop year.

intercurrency spread the simultaneous buying and selling of two currencies.

interday call the margin call requested in the trading session against a position known to be held at the close of the previous day.

inter-dealer broker (IDB) <1> a broker operating in bonds or OTC derivatives market who acts as an intermediary between major dealers to facilitate *inter-dealer trades.* ***Also***: deal to deal broker; intermediary dealer broker. <2> <UK> a member of London Stock Exchange who is only permitted to deal with market makers, rather than the public.

interdealer market = *inside market.*

interdealer trade the transaction made between two dealers.

interdelivery spread a spread which consists of a long position and a short position in different delivery months of the same underlying commodity. **Also**: inter-month spread; intracommodity spread. **See**: *intercommodity spread.*

interest <1> price paid for the borrowed use of money. ***Also***: charge for credit; cost of fund; cost of money; dividend; interest charge; interest on money; premium; price of capital; price of money. <2> = *cost of carry.*

interest accrued = *accrued interest.*

interest agio the difference between the interest rates of two countries.

interest arbitrage money speculation by using favorable difference between two rates of interest. ***Also***: arbi loan; interest rate arbitrage; money arbitrage.

interest arrears note (IAN) the note the issuer of which can not pay interest.

interest bond a bond that is used as a payment in lieu of the interest due on other bonds.

interest cap = *cap.*

interest charge = *interest.*

interest coupon = *bond coupon.*

interest date = *date of value.*

interest earning facility (IEF) a private investment company operated by the Chicago Mercantile Exchange to help its clearing members to earn interest in the variable restricted asset accounts.

interested shareholder the shareholder with beneficial ownership of substantive voting stock to affect corporate decisions. ***See***: *majority shareholder.*

interest imputed = *imputed interest.*

interest on capital <1> interest paid to partners on their capital contributed to the partnership. <2> = *dividend.*

interest only (IO) meaning having the coupon interest payment as the payoff. ***See***: *principal only.*

interest-only strip (IO strip) <1> the contractual right to receive interest due on. <2> a security with cash flows based on the monthly interest payments received from a mortgage pool. ***Also***: interest-only tranche.

interest-only tranche = *interest-only strip.*

interest on money = *interest.*

interest out of capital = *capital dividend.*

interest parity a theory which holds that if there is an instrument with identical risk and maturity in two countries, the difference in interest rates will be reflected in the forward exchange rate. ***Also***: interest rate parity.

interest rate percentage of *interest* on the amount of money lent. ***Also***: rate; rate of interest.

interest rate arbitrage = *interest arbitrage.*

interest rate cap = *cap.*

interest rate caption = *caption.*

interest rate collar the combination of an interest rate cap and interest rate floor. ***Also***: collar. ***See***: *equity risk reversal*; *range forward.*

interest rate condom = *cap.*

interest rate-contingent option the call or put option on an equity, physical commodity, or foreign exchange rate that is contingent on a particular interest rate being above or below a certain level, or within a certain range.

interest rate corridor = *corridor.*

interest rate derivative (IRD) a derivative the underlying of which is the right to pay or receive the notional amount of money at a specified interest rate.

interest rate differential a yield spread between 2 otherwise comparable debt instruments denominated in different currencies. ***Also***: differential.

interest rate driven <UK> a point in the economic cycle when interest rates are dropping, bond prices are rising.

interest rate floor = *floor.*

interest rate future a futures contract the underlying of which is a debt obligation.

interest rate guarantee (IRG) = *fraption.*

interest rate index swap = *cross rate swap.*

interest rate margin = *interest rate spread.*

interest rate of return = *present value profitability index.*

interest-rate option (IRO) a put or call in which the underlying is specific bills, notes or bonds issued by the Treasury or CD with a fixed face value.

interest rate parity = *interest parity.*

interest rate reset note a note the interest on which is reset several years after the issuance to the greater of the initial rate or a rate sufficient to give the note a market value that is greater than its face value.

interest rate risk the possibility that the trader will incur loss or extra cost due to a rise in interest rate. ***Also***: funding risk; market risk; termed money risk.

interest rate spread <1> the excess of the yield on 10-year US Treasury bond over the *index rate.* <2> excess of the interest rate on a loan over the *index rate.* ***Also***: interest rate margin; interest spread; margin.

interest rate swap conversion of interest calculation method by two borrowers from fixed rates to flexible rates or vice versa.

interest rate swaption an option that gives the holder the right to enter into an interest rate swap.

interest ratio interest expense as a percentage of income.

interest rebate = *rebate.*

interest sensitive stock a stock the price of which is sensitive to changes in the interest rates.

interest spread = *interest rate spread.*

interest warrant a company's demand of payment of interest due on note or debt.

interest yield nominal rate of interest or dividend per share.

interest yield equivalent the rate of return on a security sold on a discount basis, assuming actual number of days to maturity and a 360-day year.

inter-exchange spread = *intermarket spread.*

interim certificate = *scrip.*

interim dividend a partial dividend that could be declared by the corporate board of directors before the closing of accounts at the year end.

interim report a report sent to the stockholders to keep them informed concerning activities of the company in intervals between annual reports.

inter-market arbitrage = *arbitrage in space.*

intermarket front running the trading in one market with knowledge of a trade in a related market which can be expected to have an immediate favorable impact in relation to trading in the first market.

intermarket sector spread = *intermarket spread.*

intermarket spread the spread involving the same commodities at different exchanges. ***Also***: inter-exchange spread; intermarket sector spread; sector spread. **See**: *inter-commodity spread; inter-delivery spread.*

intermarket spread swap a swap in the bond market done in anticipation of a change in the yield spread between two issues from different market sectors.

intermediary dealer broker (IDB) = *inter-dealer broker.*

intermediated market a financial market in which some situation stands between the parties to a transaction.

intermediate rally = *spurt.*

intermediation <1> pooling and supplying of fund by a financial intermediary like a broker, for investment in securities, loan, mortgages, or government debts. <2> the execution of derivative transaction by another party rather than the user.

inter-month spread <1> = *inter-delivery spread.* <2> = *time spread.*

internal derivative a financial derivative the counterparts of which are within the same control group of companies.

internal market the market for issuing and trading derivatives in a country.

internal measure the number of days a company can finance operations without additional cash flows. **See**: *out-of-cash date.*

internal rate of return (IRR) the rate of discount that can make an investment equal to the present value of future net cash flows. ***Also***: actuarial rate; adjusted rate of return; compound annual return; industrial rate of return; time-adjusted rate of return; true rate of return.

internal reserve = *retained earnings.*

international arbitrage simultaneous buying and selling of foreign securities and ADRs to capture profit potential created by time, currency, and inconsistencies in the settlement that vary across internationally.

international bond a bond that is issued outside the country of the borrower, e. g. Euro-bond, foreign bond.

international currency a currency that is recognized and accepted in the payment of debt worldwide. ***Also***: key currency.

international depositary receipt (IDR) a depositary receipt issued by Morgan Guaranty in the 1970s to help international trading of stocks and shares.

international finance subsidiary the subsidiary incorporated in the United States and issues securities in overseas market to foreign investors.

international fisher effect = *fisher effect.*

international fund = *global fund.*

international market the market exists outside a country. ***Also***: external market; offshore market.

International Market Index (IMI) an index that tracks the performance of 20 ADRs on Amex, NYSE and Nasdaq.

International Monetary Market (IMM) a division of CME, found in 1972, for the trading in financial futures.

international mutual fund = *global fund.*

international options fungible *foreign currency options* traded on Philadelphia or London Stock Exchange. ***Also***: IFX options; PFX options.

international securities identification number (ISIN) the numbering system for financial instruments, designed by the United Nation's International Organization for Standardization.

International Security Market Association (ISMA) a Swiss association for all participants on the Eurobond markets.

international spread option = *spread option.*

international spread warrant = *spread warrant.*

international stock fund = *foreign stock fund.*

international stock-returns swap a swap where one party exchanges the return from domestic stock for the return from international stock with a foreign swap counterpart.

International Swap and Dealers Association (ISDA) = *International Swaps and Derivatives Association.*

International Swaps and Derivatives Association (ISDA) the association of dealers and other organizations acting in the international OTC derivatives market. ***Formerly called***: International Swaps and Dealers Association.

Internet stock the stock issued by a company which generates most of its sales revenue from Internet-based business.

interpolation a method of estimating an unknown price or yield of a security, by using other related known values located in sequence with unknown value.

interruptible supply contract an energy supply contract where the supplier can exercise the call option whenever the spot price exceeds the strike price, effectively canceling the forward contract at the time of delivery.

inter-temporal volatility = *term volatility.*

interval fund a mutual fund that is open for sale or redemption during pre-determined intervals.

intervention rate <1> the interest rate or exchange rate recommended by the government. <2> the exchange rate used in *intervention.*

in the box a dealer having a wire receipt for securities, proving the delivery.

in-the-money (ITM) of an option, the strike of which is below the market price for call, or above for put. ***See***: *deep in-the-money*; *out-of-the-money.*

in-the-money call a call option with a strike price below the market price of the underlying asset. ***See***: *out-of-the money put.*

in-the-money debit spread the spread created by buying in-the-money option and selling the further out-of-the-money options simultaneously.

in-the-money forward the option when the spot price or rate of the underlying is in the holder's favor as compared to the forward price or rate.

in-the-money loan value of a commodity, the difference between the strike and the futures settlement price and multiplied by the factor and the quantity.

in-the-money lookback option a look-back option that pays off based on the better of an initial in-the-money strike or a more profitable strike reached in the life of the option.

in-the-money put the put option with a strike above the market price of the underlying. ***See***: *out-of-the-money call.*

in-the-money spot an option with positive intrinsic value with respect to the prevailing market spot rate.

in the penalty box the situation when a company's stock price is in the doldrums and has yet to rebound because of poor earnings, new regulation or other reason.

intracommodity spread = *inter-delivery spread.*

intracompany trade the trade among the subsidiaries which are under the control of the same parent company.

intra-contract spread a spread of a long position in a commodity expiring in one month and a short position in the same commodity expiring in another month.

intra-crop-year spread buying and selling the same commodity on one exchange with both positions lying within one crop year.

intraday limit set price range in a day.

intraday position open position run by a dealer within one day.

intramarket arbitrage = *arbitrage in time.*

intramarket sector spread = *intramarket spread.*

intramarket spread the purchase of an option and sale of the same of a different contract month or of a different option of the same or a different month, both are traded on the same market. ***Also***: intra-market sector spread.

intrastate offering a securities offering limited to the residents of one state.

intrinsic value <1> the value of a firm based on an underlying perception of the value, calculated as EPS ÷ expected rate of return. ***Also***: absolute value. <2> the amount an option is in the money, or the value of an option if it were to be exercised immediately. ***Also***: current exercisable value; exercisable value; parity. ***See***: *extrinsic value.*

inventory securities bought and held by a dealer for resale, or the net long or short position of a broker-dealer or an expert.

inventory cushion = *buffer stock.*

inverse floater = *bull floater.*

inverse floater note = *bull floater.*

inverse floating rate swap = *reverse floating rate swap.*

inverse floating security (inflos) = *bull floater.*

inverse numerical order a series of bonds redeemable before maturity starting with the ones farthest from maturity and back toward the nearest.

inverse problem the market's risk-neutral probabilities depend on the price of the derivatives.

inverted market = *backwardation.*

inverted scale a serial bond where earlier maturities have higher yields.

inverted yield curve the curve showing the yields for short bonds are higher than those on long-term bonds because those who commit funds for longer periods are taking more risk. ***Also***: abnormal yield curve; descending yield curve; downward sloping yield curve; kinked yield curve; negatively sloping yield curve; negative yield curve.

investible index = *free index.*

investing for the green = *green investing.*

investment adviser <1> a licensed person or an organization that makes the day-to-day decisions regarding the portfolio investments. ***Also***: portfolio manager. <2> = *underwriter.*

investment banker = *underwriter.*

investment banking group = *distributing syndicate.*

investment banking syndicate = *distributing syndicate.*

investment basis adjustment the annual adjustment used by parent companies to adjust the basis in common and preferred stock of the subsidiaries in order to account for their operations.

investment bill a bill of exchange that the holder has bought at a discount and will hold as investment until maturity.

investment bond the bond issued to substitute the managed bond and the insured bond. ***Also***: Treasury bonds investment series.

investment certificate a certificate that evidences amount invested in a savings and loan association with no voting rights and shareholder liability. ***Also***: mutual capital certificate.

investment climate the general economic conditions that are affecting the markets.

investment club a group of investors who collectively pool their money and knowledge to make big investments, research and diversify the investments based on research. ***Also***: collective investment scheme.

Investment Company Act of 1940 the law created in 1940 that defines the responsibilities and limitations placed upon companies that offer investment products to the public.

investment contract <Canada> a debt instrument excluding income bonds the income of which is included in taxable income annually.

investment currency <UK> a limited pool of funds that is derived from overseas investments. ***Also***: security dollar.

investment fraud using false and/or misleading information to induce investors to buy low-grade securities.

investment fund an entity that invests its funds mainly in securities, bonds and stocks.

investment grade a grade of bond ratings that is suitable for purchase by prudent investors e. g. AAA to BBB.

investment grade bond a bond which is relatively safe, having a high rating such as BBB or above. ***Also***: angel.

investment in securities investment for dividend or interest income only. ***Also***: portfolio investment; securities investment.

investment letter the letter of interest from the buyer stating that he is going to buy new issue as an investment, not for resale, to avoid SEC registration.

investment letter stock = *letter stock.*

investment management = *money management.*

investment portfolio = *portfolio.*

investment premium <1><UK> the excess of investment dollar rate over the official exchange rate. **See**: *dollar premium.* <2> the premium over the investment value at which a convertible security trades.

investment pyramid an investment strategy which allocates all investable assets based on safety and soundness.

investment quality stock = *blue chip.*

investment reserve = *terminal reserve.*

investment site a web site for investors. ***Also***: investorville.

investment skeleton the securities that become worthless or were purchased contrary to the investment goal, or that failed to meet one's expectations.

investment stock the stock the issuer of which has a good record of earnings, and is good for long term investment.

investment strategy a strategy used by an investor in deciding how to allocate the resources or capital among several alternatives.

investment style indicator of a mutual fund's investment emphasis.

investment trigger price the price at which an investment can produce the optimal return.

investment trust <1> <UK> a publicly traded investment company whose gain is exempt from tax. <2> a *closed-end fund* regulated by the Investment Company Act.

investment trust fund the government fund used to account for the investment activities.

investment value the estimated price at which a convertible security would be valued by the market place if it had no stock conversion feature. ***Also***: straight value.

investment yield amount equal to a life insurance company's gross investment net income less investment expense, depreciation and non-insurance and business deduction.

investor one who buys shares for long-term profit. **See**: *speculator.*

investor control rule a rule that holds if the policyholder has sufficient control over his segregated account in the insurance company, he will be taxed on the earnings. **See**: *segregated account.*

investor fallout the risk incurred by the originators of mortgage collateral in the pipeline period when the originator of the loans commits the loan terms to the borrowers and obtains financial commitment from the investors at application.

investor registration option (IRO) the registration of equity ownership which permits an investor to establish a book entry position in his name directly with the transfer agent.

investor's equity the balance of a margin account. **See**: *margin loan.*

investorville = *investment site.*

investor warrant the warrant given to film and motion movie investors that, in case of a failure, guarantees the investor of 110% of the original investment.

invisible supply uncounted stocks of a commodity in the hands of wholesalers, manufacturers and producers which can not be identified accurately.

invoice price the price that the buyer of a futures contract must pay the seller when a Treasury bond is delivered.

inward arbitrage the conversion of the foreign currency into the home currency since the interest rate in the home country is higher. ***See***: *outward arbitrage.*

in-warehouse the method of settlement under which commodity is delivered in a warehouse at a stated location.

IO bond an interest only CMO bond.

IOM Index and Option Market

IOPV indicative optimized portfolio value

IOSCO International Organization of Securities Commissions

IO strip interest only strip

IOU = *promissory note.*

IPE International Petroleum Exchange

IPO initial public offering

IPO lockup = *lockup.*

IPO spinning setting aside portions of the share in an IPO for senior management of the issuing company.

IPS indexed principal swap

IPSPV indicative per share portfolio value

IRB industrial revenue bond

IRD interest rate derivative

Irish dividend = *split-down.*

IRN increasing rate note

IRO <1> interest rate option. <2> investor registration option.

iron butterfly a limited risk, and limited return strategy that consists of a long or a short position in a straddle including a strangle on the same underlying asset. ***Also***: bondor.

iron condor a condor that is created by buying and holding four different options with different strike prices, it is a combination of the long and short positions in two different strangles.

irrational call option the implied call option which is embedded in mortgage-backed securities.

irredeemable bond = *annuity bond.*

irredeemable gilt <UK> a bond issued by the Government with no maturity date but redeemable with 3-month's notice after a specified date has passed.

ISDA <1> International Swaps and Dealers Association. <2> International Swaps and Derivatives Association.

ISEQ Irish Stock Exchange Equity Index

iShares index funds that are traded like shares on a stock exchange, each share represents a proportion of ownership in each stock that makes up an index.

iShares COMEX Gold Trust = *iShares Gold Trust.*

iShares ETFs an array of exchange-traded funds issued by iShares.

iShares Gold Trust a trust that issues shares that represents the assets in gold bullion to match the day-to-day movement of the price of gold bullion. ***Also***: iShares COMEX Gold Trust

iShares Lehman TIPS a bond fund that is held by Lehman.

iShares silver trust a trust that issues shares that represents the assets in silver.

ISIN international securities identification number

ISIP indexed security investment plan

island reversal the trading range where there is an exhaustion gap down, then prices trade in a narrow range, then there is a breakaway gap up.

ISO <1> incentive stock option. <2> Internet securities offering.

issuance expense = *cost of flotation.*

issue flotation of a company's security or government bonds.

issue cost = *cost of flotation.*

issued and outstanding = *outstanding shares.*

issue day settlement the settlement on the *date of issue* of stocks traded before their issuance.

issued capital stock = *outstanding shares.*

issued shares = *outstanding shares.*

issued stock the authorized stock that has been actually sold to subscribers.

issue price the price at which shares or bonds are sold on issue.

issuer an entity that issues securities.

issuer exposure the credit risk to the issuer of an instrument.

issues traded the number of classes of stock traded during a market session.

issuing date = *date of issue.*

issuing house a merchant bank or other financial concern specializing in finding buyers for new issues. ***Also***: credit writing bank; giver; house of issue.

itayose the clearing method used by Japanese commodity exchanges, like an auction market in which the time of the order entry is not distinguished, as all buys or sells are batched together.

ITM in the money

Ito process = *Brownian motion.*

ITS Intermarket Trading System

IU up-and-in price

IV implied volatility.

IV index implied volatility index

J j

J <1> the month abbreviation for April in futures and call options. <2> the Nasdaq descriptor that means the issue is the voting stock of the issuer. <3> the option strike price code for 50.

jack-in-the-box swap a swap that does nothing until finally the price jumps to a level that creates a favorable margin for the investor.

JAJO the abbreviation of four quarterly expiration months of options: January, April, July and October.

James bond Treasury bonds maturing in 2007, 007 in which is similar to the name of a British Agent James Bond.

January barometer the belief that the overall stock market rises in the year when the S&P 500 is up in the month of January and drops when that index for that month is down.

January cycle option *expiration cycle* in January, April, July, and October. ***See***: *February cycle*; *March cycle*.

January effect <1> the tendency of the stock market to rise between December 31 and the end of the first week in January. ***See***: *Santa Claus rally*. <2> the tendency for the stocks of the large growth firms to outperform stocks of small firms in the month of January. ***See***: *anomaly*.

Japanese option the stock index option traded on Tokyo Stock Exchange and Osaka Stock Exchange which can be exercised each Thursday during the life of the option. ***See***: *American option*; *Bermuda option*; *European option*.

Jasdaq Japanese Association of Securities Dealers Automated Quotation

JB junk bond

jelly roll spread the combination of a long call and a short put, together with a short call and a long put with a different expiration date. ***See***: *long jelly roll*.

Jensen index = *alpha*.

JGB Japanese government bond

jobber an exchange member who deals in securities, buying for himself from and selling to the broker and jobbers shares of the classes in which he specializes. ***Also***: finder; stock jobber.

jobber's turn the profit made by a jobber often the difference between his buying or offer price and his selling or bid price. ***Also***: turn of the market.

jobbing continually trading securities, futures or options. ***See***: *day trading*.

jobbing backwards inducing investors to purchase additional shares by stressing the past performance.

job lot = *broken lot*.

joining = *merger*.

joint account (JA) <1> the investment account owned by two investors. <2> an agreement to share in the purchase, sale or ownership of securities with equal or proportionate risk and financial participation.

joint and several bond a bond that has more than one obligator or is guaranteed by a party other than the issuing company. ***Also***: joint bond.

joint and survivor annuity the annuity contract under which the payments are made to 2 or more annuitants so long as one of them remains alive.

joint annuity an annuity contract under which payments are made to 2 or more annuitants but only so long as they all remain alive. ***Also***: joint life annuity.

joint bond = *joint and several bond*.

joint clearing member the member firm that clears more than one stock exchange.

joint life annuity = *joint annuity.*

jointly and severally the municipal bond underwriting where the issue is divided and members are responsible for all unsold bonds in proportion to their participation rate. ***Also***: Eastern account; several and joint agreement. **See**: *severally but not jointly.*

joint option = *cross option.*

joint probability the probability of each possible joint credit quality.

joint venture tender two or more companies pooling capital to take over the target company.

Jones model a hedge fund investment strategy created by A. W. Jones, which buys stocks that will increase in price and sells those that will drop in price in the same sector. ***Also***: long-short strategy.

Jonestown defense an extreme kind of *poison pill* used by a company trying to avoid a hostile takeover, that threatens the company's ability to survive.

jumbo CD the CD with a minimum face value of $100,000 traded by large banks or institutions.

jump the periodic increase in the coupon rate of the *step-up cap.* ***Also***: periodic coupon increase.

jump ball <1> a deal *in competition,* no brokerage firm is exclusive. <2> there is no preference in picking a buy or sell side of a stock as profile.

jump diffusion process the process, by Robert Merton, in which the price of the underlying neither jumps nor follows a pure diffusion process but moves by a jump followed by continuous diffusion.

jumping the gun = *beating the gun.*

jump process the stochastic process for movements of price of the underlying, created by John Cox and Stephen Ross.

junior bond a bond which falls subordinate to other bonds from the same issuer if that issuer defaults or becomes subject to financial claims.

junior capital pool (JCP) the corporate structure whereby companies can issue shares to the public before establishing a line of business.

junior common stock plan a plan under which a company issues common stock that is subordinate to its presently outstanding common stock, often to its high executives.

junior debt = *subordinated debt.*

junior equity <1> = *common stock.* <2> = *junior stock.*

junior refunding issuing new securities to refinance an existing government debt that matures in one to five years.

junior security the security with lower priority claim than a senior security.

junior stock shares issued to employees, that are usually subordinate to common stock. ***Also***: junior equity. **See**: *mixed shares; preference stock.*

junior swap = *short-term swap.*

junk bond (JB) a bond with lower credit standing, and the risk of repayment of both principal and interest is higher than the investment grade bond. ***Also***: below-investment-grade bond; non-investment grade bond; speculative grade bond. **See**: *high yield bond; worthless security.*

justified price = *fair market value.*

K k

K <1> the month abbreviation for May in futures and call options. <2> the Nasdaq descriptor that means the issue has no voting rights. <3> the option strike price code for 55.

kangaroo bond the Eurobond, payable in Australian dollars.

kangaroos Australian stocks.

kappa = *vega.*

Keltner channel volatility-based indicator which measures the movement of market price to an upper and lower moving average band.

kerb exchange = *curb exchange.*

key currency = *international currency.*

key rate duration (KRD) the sensitivity of a security or the value of a portfolio to a 1% change in yield for a given maturity.

kickback illegal or secret payment made in return for a referral which resulted in a transaction or a contract.

kicker added feature of a debt instrument, e. g. convertibility to stock if the prices of shares of the same company reach certain price level. ***Also***: bell and whistle; sweetener. ***See***: *bond warrant.*

kick-in at the end = *European barrier option.*

kick-in option a *knock-in option* with the instrike in the money.

kick it out <verb> to liquidate a position without regard to price.

kick-out option the *knockout option* with the outstrike price that is in the money.

kind arbitrage the purchase and sale of substantially identical securities in the same market, based on the price differences prevailing in the separate trading values.

kinked yield curve = *inverted yield curve.*

kitchen sink bond the bond issued by a secured trust formed to provide an outlet for less popular *collateralized mortgage obligation* tranches.

kite flying drawing an accommodation bill and discounting it at a bank.

kiting driving the stock prices to the high levels by manipulative trading such as creating artificial trading activity by the buyer and seller working together.

kitty money invested by more than two investors.

kiwi bond a Eurobond, payable in New Zealand's currency.

kiwis five-year floating rate notes issued by Sallie Mae in the secondary markets.

knife nickname of the New York Futures Exchange. ***Also***: NYFE.

knocked down price the seller's asking price that has been reduced.

knock in the process in which a barrier option becomes active as the underlying asset price is in the money.

knock-in barrier = *knock-in price.*

knock-in cap option the path-dependent option that pays off only if the underlying rate changes by a fixed amount before rising through the cap strike.

knock-in digital call option a digital call option which kicks in when the price crosses a barrier.

knock-in digital put a digital put option which kicks in when the price crosses a barrier.

knock-in option an option which kicks in when a price crosses a barrier, such as the *down-and-in option* and *up-and-in option*. ***Also***: "in" barrier option; in option; trigger option; twin-in barrier option. ***See***: *double-barrier option*.

knock-in premium cap the cap set on a floating rate with the cap strike price substantially above the current rates.

knock-in price the barrier when reached will activate the knock-in option. ***Also***: "in" barrier; knock-in barrier. ***See***: *down-and-in price*; *up-and-in price*.

knock-in risk reversal the *equity risk reversal* or comparable structure in the currency markets with one or more *knock-in option* components.

knockout (KO) share of Coca Cola Co.

knockout agreement a secret agreement by a group of dealers at an auction not to bid against each other.

knockout barrier = *knockout price*.

knockout digital call option a digital call option which expires when the price crosses a barrier.

knockout digital put the digital put option which expires when the price crosses a barrier.

knockout forward = *break forward*.

knockout option an option that expires worthless when a price crosses a barrier, such as *down-and-out option* and *up-and-out option*. ***Also***: extinguishable option; extinguishing option; out option; twin-out barrier option. ***See***: *double-barrier option*.

knockout premium cap the cap set on a floating rate with a premium trigger knockout rate below current rates.

knockout price the barrier price when reached will deactivate the rights of certain *knockout options*. ***Also***: knock-out barrier; "out" barrier.

knockout rate the percentage of change in the principal of a step barrier option.

knockout seagull a *seagull* structure with knockout options on the down-swept portion of the seagull's wings.

knockout swap a swap that terminates if a designated instrument or index moves above or below an agreed level.

knockout window minimum occupation time outside of the range required to reduce the step option principal to zero.

KO knockout

Kondratieff Wave the economic theory created by Kondratieff stating that the economies of the western world are susceptible to major up-and-down super cycles lasting from 50 to 60 years.

KRD key rate duration

kurtosis the size of the tail of a price or volatility distribution as compared to a normal distribution bell shape.

L l

L <1> in listings of newspapers, meaning listed. <2> M3 plus liquid assets. <3> the month abbreviation for July in put. <4> Nasdaq descriptor meaning the issue is the 3rd class preferred stock warrant, 6th class preferred stock, foreign preferred or preferred when issued stock. <5> option strike price code for 60.

labour-sponsored fund <Canada> the mutual fund designed to provide venture capital to emerging companies.

LABS liquid asset-backed securities

ladder = *laddered maturity strategy.*

ladder cap the *step-up cap* the *jump* in which is based on the highest rate level yet achieved, rather than the rate at the previous reset date.

laddered maturity strategy a method that invests equal amounts in all maturities of bonds. ***Also***: ladder; ladder strategy. **See**: *barbell strategy; butterfly; staggering maturities.*

laddering the promotion of inflated pre IPO prices for obtaining a greater allotment of the offering.

ladder option an extended option which settles and resets its strike at the level of the underlying for a limited number of times once prescribed values are reached. ***Also***: lockstep option; step-lock option. **See**: *cliquet option; look back option.*

ladder periodic cap a periodic cap that depends on LIBOR at the end of the previous period, but on the highest or lowest level of the ladder of LIBOR.

ladder strategy <1> spread with an extra leg. <2> = *laddered maturity strategy.*

ladder trade = *table top.*

Lady Macbeth strategy the strategy under which a third party poses as the white knight in a takeover bid, and joins forces with an unfriendly bidder.

laggard a security the price of which is lower. ***Also***: ground floor; pup.

lagging indicator the market indicators that shows the general direction of the economy. ***Also***: concurrent indicator.

lambda = *vega.*

lapse = *expiration.*

lapsed option = *abandoned option.*

large cap over $ 5 billion capitalization. **See**: *micro cap; mid cap; small cap.*

large cap stock the shares issued by companies with large cap.

large CD the certificate of deposit with a face amount over $100,000.

large trader a trader who holds or controls a position in one futures contract or option expiration series of a commodity on one market equaling or exceeding the CFTC- or exchange-specified level.

last = *last trade.*

last day of trading = *last trading day.*

last delivery day final day on which the long can receive delivery and the short must make delivery of the commodity to remain in compliance with the rules and regulation.

last-in, first-out (lifo) a method of settling and matching two offsetting positions under which a given buy or sell trade will offset the latest trade of the given commodity. **See**: *first-in, first-out.*

last notice day the last day on which trading may occur in a given futures or options contract. **See**: *first notice day.*

last price = *closing price.*

last sale <1> the most recent trade in a trading session. <2> the price of the final trade after the market closes.

last sale reporting an electronic entry, to the Nasdaq, of the amount and price of shares involved in a transaction's not less than a *round lot.*

last split a recent stock split.

last tender day the last day a notice of intention to deliver a commodity may be issued.

last trade the trade just completed, and the price. ***Also***: last.

last trading day <1> the last trading day on which a futures or options contract may be settled. ***Also***: last day of trading. <2> = *expiration date.*

late-day trading = *market timing 2.*

latent call option an option retained by the issuer of a convertible which permits the issuer to redeem it for a set value or to convert it to common stock.

latent warrant a warrant embedded in a convertible bond or convertible preferred stock that gives them convertibility.

late trading = *market timing 2.*

lattice model = *Cox-Ross-Rubenstein model.*

law day = *maturity date.*

law of average covariance given a portfolio with the dollar value weighted equally among component securities, its variance will tend to the average covariance of components as the number of securities in a portfolio increases.

law of one price a rule that in an efficient market a security must have one price.

layoff the strategy to reduce the risk in a standby commitment under which the bankers agree to buy and resell to the public any portion of a stock issue that is not subscribed to by shareholders.

LBO leveraged buyout

LBO fund = *buyout fund.*

LDT leveraged derivatives transaction

leader a stock at the forefront of the rise and fall. ***Also***: leading stock.

leading indicator a market indicator that signals the economy state for the future.

leading lipstick indicator the indicator, created by Leonard Lauder, which states that the lipstick sales will increase in times of an economic recession.

leading stock = *leader.*

leading the market moving in advance of the market as a whole, up or down.

lead manager = *managing underwriter.*

lead month the contract month during which delivery may be made.

lead underwriter = *managing underwriter.*

LEAN LIBOR-enhanced accrual note

LEAPS the stock options or index options with expiration up to 3 years away. ***Also***: long-term equity anticipation securities. ***See***: *warrant.*

leaps long the long-term LEAPS with expiration up to two and a half years or more.

ledger cash the cash balance shown in the balance sheet. ***Also***: book cash.

LED spread the differential between the LIBOR and the Eurodollar interest rates.

left-hand side the price of a foreign currency a bank is willing to sell. ***See***: *ask*; *right-hand side.*

leg <1> one side of a hedge or an option spread. <2> the fixed or floating side of a swap. ***Also***: side.

legal capital = *stated capital.*

legal defeasance the deposit of cash into an irrevocable trust sufficient to enable the bond issuer to discharge its debts from its books.

legal list = *approved list.*

legal risk <1> the risk that a derivative contract is not enforceable due to some legal restrictions. <2> a risk which certain clients may not be suitable for certain investments by law.

legal security the stock or bond which can be purchased by a fiduciary and held for the beneficiaries.

legal settlement rate the rate of return that equals the difference between the discounted receivable rate and payable rate of a swap .

legend restrictions placed upon certain stock certificates describing the terms and conditions of sale and ownership.

legging into creating offsetting position in a security by executing one side now and waiting until some later time to execute the other side of the trade.

legging out = *lifting a leg.*

legging up buying or selling one leg of a straddle separately rather than at the same time.

leg in the air a futures market situation where a trader is looking to complete a straddle by doing one leg first, leaving the other leg to be done in a later date.

leg type the fixed or floating character of the leg of a swap. ***Also***: swap type.

Lehman Investment Opportunity Note = *Lion.*

lemming losing by following the *crowd.*

lender arbitrage = *forward hedge.*

lender insurance the insurance, maintained by an issuer of mortgage-backed securities, which will pay off the loan and accrue interest upon a default by a borrower and environmental condition at the collateral property.

lender option <1> the floor on a floating-rate agreement. <2> a put option on a forward rate agreement.

lender option commitment the agreement that gives a lender the option to deliver loans to a guarantor or repackager by a certain date at agreed-upon terms when the borrower defaults.

lender's option-borrower's option (LOBO) a floater which allows the lender to nominate a revised rate at periodic reset dates, and the borrower has the option to decide whether to pay the revised rate or redeem note.

lending asset <Canada> a bond, note, debenture, mortgage, hypothecary claim, or a *prescribed security.*

lending at a premium one broker lends stocks to another to cover the client's short position and charges a fee.

lending stock the stock lent to another broker to make a short sale. ***Also***: loan stock; securities loan; stock loan. **See**: *borrowed stock.*

leptokurtosis = *excess kurtosis.*

lettered stock = *tracking stock.*

letter of comment SEC letter suggesting changes to the registration statement.

letter of free credit the statement from one broker-dealer to another on behalf of a buyer attesting to the availability of the funds to fully pay for the securities.

letter of guarantee a letter from a bank to a brokerage firm stating that a client who sold options owns the underlying asset.

letter of intent (LOI) a written promise by a mutual fund shareholder to invest a fixed sum of money monthly for a year for a lower sales charge.

letter of rights = *stock warrant.*

letter security = *letter stock.*

letter stock <1> the stock not registered with the SEC, and for which the buyer supplies a letter stating that the purchase was for investment only. ***Also***: investment letter stock; letter security; unregistered stock. <2> = *tracking stock.*

letter stock fund a mutual fund which invests in letter stocks.

level 1 quotes the real-time quotes of the best bid and ask prices for a given stock. ***See***: *real-time.*

level 2 quotes real-time quotes of the bid and ask prices for a given stock, futures contract or option.

level 3 quotes the level 2 quotes plus the ability to enter quotes, execute orders and transmit other information.

level-coupon bond the bond with a stream of coupon payments which remain unchanged during the life of the bond.

level load mutual fund sales charge that does not vary depending on how long the investor held the investment. ***Also***: level sales load.

level of margin = *margin level.*

level-payment fixed-rate mortgage the conventional fixed rate mortgage under which the principal amortizes over the life of the mortgage in a way that each periodic payment is identical.

level payment swap one that converts cash flows from an amortizing debt into a fixed payment plan.

level sales load = *level load.*

leverage the ability to control a large position with a small amount of money. ***Also***: debt leverage. ***Opp***: *deleverage.* ***See***: *capital leverage*; *operating leverage*; *Wall Street leverage.*

leverage contract = *long leverage.*

leveraged beta the degree of leverage in a company's capital structure.

leveraged buyout (LBO) the takeover of a corporation by using borrowed money. ***Also***: debt financed corporate takeover; short tender. ***See***: *management buyout.*

leveraged capped floater a floating rate note with a short cap on the amount greater than the face amount of the note.

leveraged equity the stock in a company that operates mainly relying on financial leverage.

leveraged floater the variable-rate note with the floating rate set at a multiple of the reference index rate less a fixed rate or spread. ***See***: *deleveraged floater.*

leveraged hedge the investment which produces unproportionately high profit compared to its original cost price.

leveraged inverse floater inverse floating rate note with coupon leverage of higher than 1.

leveraged investment company <1> a fund permitted to borrow capital from a bank. <2> = *dual-purpose fund.*

leveraged option the option granted to an employee, the number of shares exercised increases based on the price movement or financial performance.

leveraged portfolio a portfolio which includes some risky assets that are purchased with borrowed funds.

leveraged recapitalization a strategy in which a company takes on significant additional debt by either paying a large dividend or repurchasing shares.

leveraged stock a stock acquired by financing with credit as in a margin account.

leveraged swap <1> a swap embedded in a structured note, under which the payments are expressed relative to a multiple of its face value. ***Also***: levered swap. <2> swap the fixed-rate receiver receives an above-market fixed rate and pays a multiple of the floating rate index. ***Also***: power swap; ratio swap.

leverage ratio the measure of the degree to which the owners or the creditors have financed a firm, usually the total debt divided by total assets. ***Also***: debt factor. **See**: *gearing ratio.*

levered portfolio the investment at least partially financed by borrowing.

levered swap = *leveraged swap.*

leviation = *call.*

LGD loss given default

liability-based swap a swap which is driven by the floating-rate borrower's decision to switch from a floating-rate liability into a fixed-rate liability, or fixed-rate borrower's decision to swap for a floating rate.

liability dividend = *scrip dividend.*

liability funding strategy the investment strategy that selects assets so that the net cash flows will equal or exceed total liability of the client.

liability hedge the strategy used by a bank or a firm to protect its liabilities against the fluctuation of interest rates.

liability swap an interest rate swap that is used to alter the cash flow characteristics of an institution's liabilities so as to provide a better match with the cash flow of its assets.

LIBID London Inter-Bank Bid Rate

LIBOR London InterBank Offered Rate, the interest rate on the dollar-denominated deposits, *Eurodollars*, traded between banks in London. ***Also***: inter-bank rate.

LIBOR-based swap a swap the interest rate of which is based on LIBOR.

LIBOR differential swap = *cross rate swap.*

LIBOR-enhanced accrual note (LEAN) a type of range floater with LIBOR as the reference rate.

LIBOR in-advance swap a swap in which the LIBOR rate is reset at the beginning of the previous period except for the first period during which LIBOR is set at the beginning of the corresponding period as in a conventional swap transaction.

LIBOR in-arrears swap an *arrears swap* with LIBOR as the floating rate. ***Also***: arrears rate reset swap, delayed LIBOR reset swap.

LIBOR range note = *accrual note.*

LIBOR ratchet a path-dependent product sensitive to the serial or auto-correlation of successive LIBORs.

LIBOR spread basis point measured from LIBOR. ***Also***: spread to LIBOR.

LIBOR^2 swap the coupon swap with the floating rate calculated by squaring the LIBOR expressed as a percentage, e. g., $(3.0\%)^2 = 9.0\%$. ***Also***: turbo swap.

licensed warehouse a warehouse that is approved by a futures exchange from which a commodity may be delivered on a futures contract.

LIED loss in the event of default

life cycle fund an investment fund that offers investors a portfolio of cash, bonds, and stocks structured to achieve a reasonable return over a given time span. ***Also***: life style mutual fund.

life insurance bond a bond backed by life insurance policies.

life insurance stocks the stocks issued by companies engaged in underwriting and marketing life insurance products.

life of contract the period between the beginning of the trading in a particular futures contract and the expiration of trading. ***Also***: contract life.

life of delivery the period between the first and last day of trading in futures.

life style mutual fund = *life cycle fund.*

lift the rise in securities market prices as measured by the DJIA.

lifting a leg closing one side of a hedge leaving the other side as a long or short position. ***Also***: legging out; taking off a leg.

light bid a bid which is not equal to or better than the best bid.

lighten up selling portion of a position in a portfolio to realize capital gains or losses or increase cash.

light trading low volume of transactions, under 100 million shares on NYSE.

LIMEAN the mid-point between *LIBID* & *LIBOR*

limitation on conversion termination of the right to convert before redemption date.

limit down maximum price movement allowed in a trading day when the price is falling. ***Also***: stop down. ***See***: *limit up.*

limited discretion the authority given to the broker to make trades without consulting the client, e. g. to sell an option position that is near expiration.

limited exercise option = *Bermuda option.*

limited put = *floored put.*

limited risk the risk in buying an option contract which is limited to premiums only. ***See***: *unlimited risk.*

limited risk derivative a derivative with predetermined downside potential.

limited risk spread a spread consisting of buying a near month of a given commodity and selling the distant month at a premium and the difference between the spread and the carrying cost is the risk.

limited tax bond the government bond secured by a special tax or a specified percentage of the real estate tax.

limited-tax general obligation bond the *general obligation bond* of a government that is backed by specified or constrained revenue sources.

limit option = *barrier option.*

limit rate = *hurdle rate.*

limit up the maximum price movement allowed in one day when the price is rising. ***Also***: stop up. ***See***: *limit down.*

LIMOS partial strips from Merrill Lynch.

linear derivative a derivative the payoff of which shows a linear relationship, e. g. forward. ***Opp***: *nonlinear derivative.*

linear VAR the VAR measure using linear transformation. ***Also***: closed-form VAR; delta-normal VAR; parametric VAR; variance-covariance VAR.

line bottom a bottom price pattern that takes a longer period. ***Also***: long base.

linkage ability to buy (sell) a contract on one exchange and sell (buy) it on another exchange.

Lintner's observation John Lintner's work suggesting that dividend policy is related to a target level and the speed of the adjustment of the change in the dividends.

Lion the note that is issued by Lehman Brothers Kuhn Leon. ***Also***: Lehman Investment Opportunity Note. **See**: *separately traded registered interest and principal securities*; *Tiger*.

Lipper mutual fund industry average the average performance level of all mutual funds, as reported by the Lipper Analytical Service of New York.

liquid asset-backed securities (LABS) securities backed by the liquid assets of the issuer.

liquidating a position closing off a position by simply selling a security or by offsetting transaction or by holding it until expiration.

liquidating dividend a dividend that will reduce the paid-in capital of a company. ***Also***: liquidation dividend. **See**: *current dividend*; *nondividend distribution*.

liquidating REIT the REIT formed by a bank or other company into which were transferred mortgages and real property.

liquidating value asset value that can be realized when a company is going out of business. ***Also***: auction value. **See**: *liquidation value*.

liquidation <1> winding up a business by converting its assets into cash, paying off its debts and distributing the remaining assets. <2> the forced sale of a client's securities or commodities after failure to meet a margin call. ***Also***: sell-out.

liquidation dividend = *liquidating dividend*.

liquidation right the right of creditor or shareholder to get paid in the event of a liquidation.

liquidation value <1> the value per share that will be paid to the preferred stockholders upon liquidation of the company. **See**: *liquidating value*. <2> = *abandonment value*.

liquid capital = *free capital*.

liquidity diversification the purchase of bonds with maturities range from short to medium to long term, thus helping to protect against interest rate fluctuation.

liquidity event = *exit strategy*.

liquidity preference <1> the argument that the greater the liquidity the more valuable the investment. <2> a theory which holds that the forward rate exceeds the future interest rate.

liquidity premium extra yield required to compensate for the lack of liquidity for a security. ***Also***: liquidity spread.

liquidity ratio the measure of the trading volume of a security associated with a 1% change in its price.

liquidity risk the possibility that the investor will not be able to buy or sell a commodity or security quickly enough or in sufficient quantity because the volume is limited. ***Also***: marketability risk.

liquidity spread = *liquidity premium*.

liquidity theory a theory which holds that the implied forward rates will not be a pure estimate of the market's expectation of future interest rates because they embody a liquidity premium.

liquidity trap the situation in which the prevailing interest rates are lower than the savings rates.

liquid market the market with many bid and ask offers.

liquid position = *cash position*.

liquid security = *marketable security*.

Liquid Yield Option = *LYON*.

liquid yield option note = *LYON*.

listed CIV <Australia> a CIV, collective investment vehicle, listed on a national exchange.

listed company a company the stock of which is traded in an exchange. ***Also***: quoted company.

listed futures a futures contract listed on an exchange.

listed option a put or call option that an exchange has authorized for trading. ***Also***: exchange-traded option.

listed security the security that has been admitted for trading on a national stock exchange and complied with listing and other requirements. ***Also***: admitted to dealings; on-board security; quoted security.

listed stock = *quoted share.*

listed trade = *downstairs trade.*

listless market = *inactive market.*

LKI lower barrier knock-in

LKO lower barrier knock-out

LKO 2 lower barrier knock-out 2

LMV long market value

load the fee added to the purchase or the sales price of mutual fund shares and annuities. ***Opp***: *no-load.* ***See***: *back-end load; front-end load.*

load-adjusted return the return of the investment on a mutual fund adjusted downward to reflect load charge.

load curtailment contract a utility sells a lower price swap to industrial users and gets the right to not deliver power fixed number of times in a fixed period of time.

load fund a mutual fund sold for a sales charge by a brokerage firm or other sales person. ***See***: *no-load fund.*

loading charge = *front-end load.*

load spread option the method of allocating annual load on mutual funds, in the first four years of the contract, up to 20% of one year's contributions may be credited against the load.

loan at call = *call money.*

loan commitment <1> a commitment to provide a loan to the borrower. <2> = *written loan commitment.*

loaned flat of securities lent interest-free between brokers to cover short sales.

loaned stock a stock lent from a broke to an investor who is selling short to cover delivery of the shares.

loan equivalent the practice of translating *off-balance sheet commitment,* such as swaps and other financial instruments, into the credit equivalent exposure represented by a loan.

loaning rate on stock = *contango.*

loan on securities a loan lent out with securities as collateral. ***Also***: securities loan.

loan stock <1> <UK> = *bond.* <2> = *lending stock.*

loan stock debenture = *bond.*

loan value the maximum percentage of the value of securities that a broker can lend to a margin account customer.

LOBO lender's option-borrower's option

lobster trap the strategy of prohibiting conversion into common shares by a holder of the convertible if the holder owns 10% or more of the voting shares.

local the member of an exchange trading for his own account. ***Also***: pit broker.

local clearing the exchanging of clearing balance with the local banks.

local expectations hypothesis (LEH) the theory that bonds which are similar in all aspects except maturity will have the same holding-period rate of return.

local expectations theory a theory which holds that the rate of returns on bonds of different maturities will be the same over a short-term investment horizon.

local trader = *floor trader.*

local volatility model = *implied tree model.*

locational basis the difference between two prices is attributable to the cost of moving the physical commodity between two markets.

LOCH London Options Clearing House

lock to make a market on both ways, bid and ask.

lock-box system a banking service entailing holding a customer's securities and, as agent, receiving and depositing income such as dividends

locked-in <1> the situation where an investor who wants to qualify for capital gains tax treatment can not sell a security until it has been held long enough to qualify. <2> the commodities position in which the market has an up or down limit day, and investors cannot get in or out of the market. <3> of a yield that has been assumed for a length of time through an investment, such as a fixed rate bond or certificate of deposit.

locked-in trade a transaction in which all of the terms and conditions are accepted by the buyer and the seller unconditionally.

locked-in yield the profit or yield on the securities which have been protected through hedging.

locked market <UK> = *choice market.*

locked quote = *crossed quote.*

lock-in option <1> a *binary option* used primarily in the currency markets that pays off as long as the underlying asset price stays within the designated range throughout the life of the option. <2> = *deferred payment American option.*

lock-in period = *close period.*

lock limit a limit when the trading price of a futures contract arrives at the exchange predetermined limit price.

lock-out <1> the period of time in which prepayment of a loan is prohibited. <2> the time before which the sinking fund for a PAC bond becomes effective.

lockout bond a collateralized mortgage obligation which receives the principal payments similar to a sequential pay bond, until the first PAC bond begins paying its scheduled principal payments. ***Also***: non-accelerating senior bond.

lockout option the *binary option* used in currency markets that pays off only if the underlying breaches the upside or the downside barrier at least once.

lockout period the time interval during which a call option, conversion feature, or some other provision is not operative.

lock-step option = *ladder option.*

lockup <1> a secret sales agreement between the principal stockholders and the raider who intends to take over the target company, such stock is not allowed to be sold freely. ***Also***: lock-up agreement. <2> a restriction on the secondary market sales of insider and venture capital shares in IPO. ***Also***: IPO lockup.

lockup agreement = *lock-up.*

lockup CD a CD issued with a clause that the buyer will not trade the CD.

lockup option the privilege offered to a friendly acquirer by a target company to buy its assets or additional equity to discourage other hostile takeover. ***See***: *Shark repellent.*

lockup period the period (180 days) in which insiders cannot sell their shares.

lockups stock issues of small companies that are not registered with the SEC.

log-normal distribution a statistical distribution that is skewed to the right.

LOGO low outlay geared option

log option an option the payoff of which can be modified by the difference between the log functions of the fixed strike price and the maturity strike.

log return the natural log of gross return. ***Also***: geometric return.

lollipop tactic the strategy to thwart the takeover bid by giving all the current shareholders the right to tender share at a premium.

Lombard Street <UK> the center of the money market in London.

London InterBank Bid Rate = *LIBID.*

London InterBank Offered Rate = *LIBOR.*

long <1> holding an asset in the hope of a price rise. ***Also***: long interest. ***Opp***: *short.* <2> = *bull.*

long account an account used by brokers for recording buyer's securities.

long backspread selling one *near-the-money option* and buying 2 or more out-of-the-money options in the same expiration and on the same underlying asset. **See**: *short back-spread.*

long base = *line bottom.*

long biased of an investment strategy, which tends to hold more long positions than short positions.

long bond the investment bond which matures in more than 10 years. ***Also***: long range maturity; long-term bond.

long box a long synthetic future and a short synthetic future.

long butterfly buying one lower strike option, selling 2 middle strike options and buying a higher strike option. ***Also***: buying a butterfly.

long calendar butterfly spread the spread that is comprised of one long calendar spread and one long butterfly spread.

long calendar condor spread a spread that is comprised of one long calendar spread and two long butterfly spreads.

long call a call option held by the investor who expects the price to rise. ***Also***: purchased call.

long call butterfly a strategy which involves buying one low strike call, selling two middle strike calls with the same strike price, and buying a higher strike call.

long call condor a strategy which involves buying one low strike call option, selling two middle strike calls with different strike prices, and buying a higher strike call.

long call synthetic straddle a synthetic straddle created by shorting a stock and buying twice the number of calls.

long combination = *bull combination.*

long conversion = *conversion arbitrage.*

long cost-of-carry the cost of carry paid for long positions.

long coupon <1> the coupon of a long bond. <2> the first interest payment that covers a period longer than the remaining payment periods.

long-dated forward a forward contract with a settlement date more than one year in the future.

long-dated option the option with an initial life of more than a year, usually three to five years.

long-dated securities the securities in the form of debt, e. g. gilt-edged securities, with a maturity of over ten years.

long-dated shorts a forward purchase and sale with a brief uncovered position. ***Also***: long short dates.

long-dated swap a swap that has a long maturity, usually longer than one year.

long-dated transaction the transaction with a final maturity more than one year.

long end one of the serial bonds that matures last.

long exchange rate = *long rate.*

long forward the party to a forward contract who has the obligation to buy the underlying asset. **See**: *short forward.*

long gut = *bull gut.*

long hedge <1> buying futures contract to protect against a rise in the price of the spot commodities in the future. ***Also***: buy hedge; buying hedge. **See**: *short hedge.* <2> a futures contract or a call bought in anticipation of a drop in the interest rates to lock in the present yield on a fixed income security.

long interest <1> = *bull.* <2> = *long.*

long iron butterfly the combination of a bull put spread and a bear call spread, or a narrow short strangle with a wide long strangle, under which the higher strike put has the same strike price as the lower strike call, but the middle strike prices are the same.

long iron condor the combination of a bull put spread and a bear call spread but the higher strike put is lower than the low strike call, with different middle strikes.

long jelly roll an option strategy involving the sale and purchase of 2 calls and two puts, each with different expiration dates to profit on time value spread. **See**: *jelly roll spread.*

long leg part of an option spread that represents the commitment to buy the underlying asset.

long leverage the deal in which a client contracts to buy a metal by putting down partial payment and using the margin for the rest. ***Also***: leverage contract.

long market = *bull market.*

long market value the market value of a security, excluding options, as of the close of the last business day.

long option a put or call option held by an investor who hopes the price to rise. **See**: *short option.*

long position holding a security in the hope of an increase in price. ***Also***: bull position; net long position; overbought; under the belt. **Opp**: *short position.*

long purchase = *buying long.*

long put a put option held by an investor who hopes the stock price to drop. ***Also***: purchased put.

long put butterfly a strategy which involves buying a low strike price put, selling two middle strike puts with the same strike price, and buying a put with higher strike price.

long put condor a strategy which involves buying one lower strike put, selling two middle strike puts with different strike prices, and buying a higher strike put.

long put synthetic straddle a strategy that involves buying two at-the-money put options for every 100 shares owned.

long range maturity = *long bond.*

long rate <1> the discount rate of a foreign long bill. ***Also***: long exchange rate. <2> interest rate of a long-term bond to its face amount.

long short dates = *long-dated shorts.*

long-short equity a hedge fund strategy that involves buying certain stocks long and selling others short.

long-short strategy = *Jones model.*

long squeeze the situation in which investors who hold long positions feel the need to sell into a falling market in order to cut losses, that may lead to a further decline in prices. ***Opp***: *short squeeze.*

long stock a stock that an investor buys because he believes the price will go up.

long straddle = *bull straddle.*

long strangle = *bull strangle.*

long strip a strip that two puts and one call are held long. **See**: *short strip.*

long synthetic future a futures position created by buying call options and selling the same amount of put options with the same strike price and the same expiration date.

long synthetic straddle = *synthetic straddle.*

long-term bond = *long bond.*

long-term debt = *funded debt.*

long-term debt offsets = *sinking fund.*

long-term equity anticipation securities = *LEAPS.*

long-term forward contract a contract with an exchange rate at which a given currency can be exchanged at a future date.

long-term IV an estimate of the very long-term at-the-money implied volatility of options. ***Also***: infinite ATM IV.

long-term loan <UK> = *Treasury bond.*

long-term option an option with more than a few months until expiration e. g. LEAPS.

long-term swap a swap with an early termination date of more than one year. ***Also***: senior swap.

long the basis a dealer who is long in the cash market, is short hedged by selling a futures position. **See**: *short the basis.*

long vega <1> the situation in which the volatility is extremely low thus causing investors to buy options, profiting from a rise in volatility. **See**: *short vega.* <2> = *long volatility.*

long volatility a position structured to profit from an increase in the volatility. ***Also***: long vega.

look-ahead bias the use of information in a simulation which will not be available in the time being simulated, resulting in an upward shift of the results. **See**: *survivorship bias.*

lookback call a call which enables the holder to buy at the most lowest price available. ***Also***: buy-at-the-low option.

lookback option an option that enables the holder to select the lowest (call) or highest (put) price available in the life of the option as the strike. ***Also***: best price option; best strike option; look-back strike option; no regrets option; sell-at-the-high option; sell-at-the-max option. ***Opp***: *look-forward option.* **See**: *hindsight currency option; ladder option*; *cliquet option*; *Russian option.*

lookback put the put which enables the holder to sell at the most highest price available during the life of the option. **See**: *lookback option.*

lookback strike option = *lookback option.*

look-forward option the option which gives the buyer the right to the difference between the strike price at the beginning of a period and its high (call) or low (put) over that period. ***Opp***: *look-back option.*

look-through earnings the way Warren Buffett judges a security by the market price movement, accounts for the share of reported earnings as if it had been distributed.

loss given default (LGD) the fraction of credit exposure that will not be recovered in the event of default on a debt or credit derivative. ***Also***: loss in the event of default.

loss in the event of default (LIED) = *loss given default.*

loss on bond conversion the excess of the common stock delivered over the carrying value of a convertible bond after conversion.

loss on constructive retirement = *constructive loss.*

loss on delivery loss on a futures contract when the price is against the holder on the delivery date.

loss on redemption of stock the excess of the redemption price of a stock over the market price.

lot <1> $1,000 dollar in foreign exchange. <2> = *block.*

lot size = *contract value.*

lottery bond a bond issued with a rate of return dependent on the payout of a lottery game.

lottery option = *binary option.*

low-basis stock a stock which is bought for a price way lower than its current market price.

low-coupon bond refunding the refunding of a low-coupon bond with a new, higher-coupon bond.

low-coupon swap an *interest rate swap* with fixed-rate payments below current market rates. ***See***: *high-coupon swap.*

low-delta option an option or portfolio of options with a low delta.

lower barrier the lower barrier price in a double barrier option. ***See***: *upper barrier.*

lower barrier knock-in (LKI) a double barrier option, if the lower barrier is breached before the upper barrier, the holder receives a call or put.

lower barrier knock-out (LKO) any double barrier option, if the lower barrier is breached before the upper barrier, the option is terminated; if the upper is breached before the lower barrier, the option has payoff.

lower barrier knock-out 2 (LKO 2) a double barrier option, if the lower barrier is breached before the upper barrier, the option is terminated; if the upper is breached before the lower barrier, the option has payoff; if neither of the barrier is breached, the holder gets nothing.

lower break-even point the strike price minus the total debit paid for the straddle. ***See***: *upper break-even point*

lower-of floater a floater with an interest rate stated as the lower of two different formulas. ***See***: *higher-of floater.*

lowest acceptable rate of return = *hurdle rate.*

lowest call price the maturity call price of a PERCS or the cap.

lowest price = *minimum price.*

low exercise price option (LEPO) the option that has a strike price very close to zero, and hence provides all features of stock ownership except voting rights and dividends.

low-grade bond a bond rated of B or lower. ***See***: *high-grade bond.*

low load fund a mutual fund that charges a sales commission of 3.5% or less.

low outlay geared option (LOGO) the low premium call option which offers gradually declining upside participation.

low-par-value stock a stock with a very low par value.

low P/E effect the tendency of portfolio of stocks with a low P/E ratio to outperform portfolios of stocks with high P/E ratios. ***Also***: P/E effect.

low P/E stock a stock with a low price-earnings ratio, 20 or lower, usually with high yields. ***See***: *high P/E stock.*

LTP limited two-way payment

lucky buy <1> buying at a low price. <2> the acquiring cost of a subsidiary is lower than its net worth.

LYON callable zero-coupon bond issued by Merrill Lynch, with a three-year put option. ***Also***: Liquid Yield Option; liquid yield option note.

M m

M <1> the month abbreviation for June in futures and call options. <2> a Nasdaq descriptor meaning the 4th class of preferred shares. <3> the option strike price code for 65.

Macaroni defense a tactic involving the issuance of a large number of bonds that must be redeemed at a higher value if the company is taken over or is the target of a takeover bid.

Macaulay duration a weighted-average *term to maturity* of a bond's cash flows, based on the present value of each cash flow divided by the market price. ***See***: *modified duration.*

MACR modified and combinable REMIC

macroeconomic option = *macro option.*

macroeconomic swap = *macro swap.*

macro fund a managed fund that takes positions in foreign currencies or bases securities holdings on global trends.

macro hedge a hedge designed to reduce the risk of a portfolio of assets rather than that of an individual asset. ***See***: *micro hedge.*

macro hedging the hedging taken to offset the residual risk between assets and liabilities of an organization. ***Also***: global hedging. ***See***: *micro hedging.*

macro option an option the underlying or reference index of which is a macro-economic index, such as the GDP. ***Also***: macroeconomic option.

macro swap a swap at least one leg of which is pegged to a macroeconomic index like GDP or a broad price index like CPI. ***Also***: macroeconomic swap.

Mae West spread the spread that is the combination of a short straddle and a long strangle.

Maginot spread = *BOAT spread.*

maintaining a market market maker's *making a market* for a long time.

maintenance level the monetary value to which original margin requirement may decline and still be considered satisfactory to carry the position.

maintenance performance bond the sum, smaller than, but part of, the initial performance bond, to be maintained on deposit for futures positions at all times. ***See***: *initial performance bond.*

major bracket the underwriters who consistently subscribe to the largest portion. ***See***: *mezzanine bracket.*

majority holding the ownership in a company by holding more than 50% of its voting stock. ***Also***: controlling interest.

majority shareholder single shareholder who owns more than half of all outstanding shares. ***See***: *interested shareholder.*

majority voting the system under which shareholders vote for each director. ***See***: *cumulative voting.*

Major Market Index (MMI) the price index of 20 component stocks in DJIA without weighting by the number of shares outstanding.

maker the person who operates in a special kind of securities in a particular market.

making a market maintaining firm bids and offers in a security by standing ready to buy or sell round lots at public quoted price. ***Also***: market making.

making a price quoting both the buying and selling prices of a security by the stock broker. ***Also***: price making.

making up day = *continuation day.*

making up price the price at which securities not paid for by a settling day are carried forward to the next settling day.

mambo combo a combination of an in-the-money call and an in-the-money put, both long or short. ***Also***: guts.

managed account = *discretionary account.*

managed bond <UK> a bond obtained by lump-sum payment, running for fixed periods, and regular withdrawal can be made. ***Also***: flexible bond.

managed CDO a CDO, collateralized debt obligation, the collateral of which is actively managed.

managed derivatives fund (MDF) a hedge fund specializing in derivatives instruments.

managed float = *dirty float.*

managed floating rate = *dirty float.*

managed fund a mutual fund managed by an active team of fund managers. ***Also***: actively managed fund.

managed fund costs an array of fees charged by a mutual fund, including sales commissions, management expense, entry fee and exit fee.

managed futures a portfolio of forward or futures contracts managed on a discretionary basis, often using the global futures markets as a medium.

managed futures account the account like a *mutual fund* account, except that positions held in government securities, futures, and options on futures contracts are used to manage the portfolio of assets.

managed static synthetic CDO a synthetic CDO under which the SPV sells a single basket credit default swap to a single CDS counterparty on a diversified portfolio of credit obligations.

managed variable synthetic CDO a synthetic CDO under which the SPV sells a single basket credit default swap or a multiple CDS on a diversified portfolio of credit obligations.

managed synthetic a synthetic asset that is the combination of a customized tranche with the ability of the asset manager.

management buy-in (MBI) the purchase of a controlling interest of a company by an outsider who leaves management unchanged.

management buyout (MBO) purchase of all outstanding shares of a company by the management in an effort to turn it into a private corporation. **See**: *leveraged buyout.*

management fee <1> a fee charged by a bank for managing a bond or other issue. <2> the fee charged by a mutual fund manager for managing the fund.

management share the deferred share intended for the managers of a company as a means of increasing their interest in the success of the company.

manager <1> one who manages a fund. <2> = *managing underwriter.*

managing underwriter the leader and the originator of an underwriting syndicate. ***Also***: lead manager; lead underwriter; manager; originating investment banker; originator; syndicate manager. **See**: *participating underwriter.*

mandarin collar a collar structured with the possibility of an enhanced payout.

mandate of protest = *notice of dishonor.*

mandatory conversion the forced conversion of convertibles under certain circumstances.

mandatory conversion premium dividend preferred stock (MCPDPS) = *participating equity preferred stock.*

mandatory convertible <1> an equity-like instrument that provides a higher yield. <2> a convertible the principal of which is denominated in a stronger currency than the underlying common stock at the time of issuance. <3> = *participating equity preferred stock.*

mandatory par put remarketed security (MOPPRS) = *put-call note.*

manipulation buying or selling to create a false appearance of active trading and thus influence other investors to buy or sell. ***Also***: crossed sale; crossed trade; daisy chain; gunning the market; market manipulation; painting the tape; ramping; stock manipulation. **See**: *chumming*; *wash sale.*

manufactured dividend <1><UK> the payment under for the transfer of shares, usually representing the tax-free dividend as part of the transfer price. <2> = *in lieu of dividend.*

manufactured housing security (MHS) a debt security backed by the mortgage loans on manufactured homes and mobile homes.

mapping decomposition of a portfolio into some time buckets. **See**: *cash flow mapping*; *duration mapping.*

MAPS market auction preferred stock

March cycle *expiration cycle* of options in the following months: March, June, September and December. **See**: *January cycle*; *February cycle*; *MJSD.*

margin <1> the deposit which an investor must put up when trading in futures. <2> = *interest rate spread.*

marginable stock the stock approved for *buying on margin.*

marginal risk the risk that a client may go bankrupt after entering into a forward.

margin buying = *buying on margin.*

margin income = *spread income.*

margin level the margin required based on the value of the position held. ***Also***: level of margin.

margin loan a loan from a broker to a margin account client. **See**: *investor's equity.*

margin of safety <1> the excess of the intrinsic value over the market price. ***Also***: safety margin. <2> the excess of the enterprise value over bonds issued outstanding. <3> = *buffer stock.*

margin of solvency = *net worth.*

margin rate the interest rate charged by a broker on a margin loan.

margin security a security that may be traded in a margin account.

Margrabe option the right to exchange one asset for another. ***Also***: exchange option. **See**: *outperformance option.*

markdown <1> the revaluation of stocks based on a decline in the market price. <2> a reduction in price at which the underwriters offer municipal bonds after the market has shown a lack of interest at the original offer price. <3> the amount subtracted from the selling price when a client sells securities to a dealer in the OTC market. **See**: *mark-up.*

marked-to-market (MTM) <1> to debit or credit on a daily basis in the margin account based on the close of that day's trading session. <2> the treatment of *Section 1256 contracts* held by an investor at year end as if it has been sold on the last business day of the year.

marked-to-market swap a swap the fair value of which must be periodically marked to market. ***Also***: mark-to-market swap.

market <1> the place where buyers and sellers come together to trade. <2> the present or possible future demand for a security or a derivative. ***Also***: tone. <3> = *stock exchange.*

marketability risk = *liquidity risk.*

marketable debt a debt instrument issued in a secondary market.

marketable loan <UK> a long-term loan where the lender's right to the payment of interest and principal might be sold in whole or in part.

marketable security <1> a security that can be easily sold on the market. ***Also***: liquid security. **See**: *non-marketable security.* <2> <UK> a government security traded on the exchange. **See**: *non-marketable security.*

market adjusted debt (MAD) the *mark-to-market* value of an enterprise's debt obligations.

market arbitrage buying and selling the same security at the same time in different markets to take advantage of a price spread between two markets.

market auction preferred stock (MAPS) = *auction rate preferred stock.*

market-based forecast analyzing the future spot rates of exchange on the basis of a market-determined exchange rate.

market basket = *basket.*

market basket trading = *basket trading.*

market capitalization the number of shares outstanding multiplied by the market price of a public company. ***Also***: capitalization; equity base; equity value; gross capitalization; market value; shareholder value; total capitalization.

market capitalization rate = *earnings yield.*

market check the investment banker's investigation to see if a takeover price is fair.

market conversion price = *conversion parity.*

market cycle a period between the two latest highs or lows of the S&P 500.

market day = *business day.*

market discount <1> the amount by which the market price of a bond is below its par or redemption value. **See**: *acquisition discount*; *original issue discount.* <2> the excess of the redemption price of a bond at maturity over the trader's tax basis for it immediately after acquiring it.

market discount bond a bond with market discount, except: <a> short-term bonds having a fixed maturity date of up to one year; <b> the tax-exempt bond bought before May 1, 1993; <c> savings bond; and <d> certain serial bond.

market-driven instrument a credit instrument the exposure of which changes and is determined periodically according to market movements.

market exposure the amount an investor or a mutual fund has invested in the stock market expressed as a percentage.

market gapping = *discontinuity risk.*

market impact cost the result of a bid-ask spread and a dealer's price concession to the cost of an investment. ***Also***: price impact costs.

market index a measure that consists of weighted values of the components that make up a list of companies.

market index deposit (MID) a bank certificate of deposit or deposit note with a return linked to the performance of an index.

market-indexed note (MINE) = *equity-linked note.*

market index target-term security (MITTS) the equity-linked note issued without periodic coupon payments, but with a single payoff at maturity.

marketing premium = *original issue premium.*

market line = *capital market line.*

market-linked CD = *equity-linked CD.*

market maker a bank or dealer prepared to make a two-way price to buy or sell on a continuous basis. ***Also***: price maker.

market maker identifier (MMID) four-letter code assigned by NASD to a market maker, e. g. Merrill Lynch & Co.'s MMID is MOTC.

market maker spread the highest bid and the lowest offer among competing market makers in a security on Nasdaq. ***Also***: inside market; inside quote; inside spread.

market making = *making a market.*

market making bank a bank as a market maker in foreign exchange market.

market manipulation = *manipulation.*

market model the model for describing the relationship between the return on a security and the return on the market and beta.

market neutral of a strategy attempting to profit from the current market direction by taking both long and short positions at the same time.

market neutrality a strategy used to construct a portfolio with a forecasted beta of zero, as compared to a benchmark index.

market option price the price paid in the open market for the option at the time of valuation.

market out clause a clause that allows the underwriters to be released from their commitment if some material adverse developments affect the market such as major law change.

market outperform = *outperform.*

market overhang = *overhang.*

Market Oversight Surveillance System = *Moss.*

market participant <1> <Canada> the firm that trades electricity through the Alberta Electric System Operator. <2> one who trades for the clients and for his own account. ***See***: *broker-dealer; dual trading; participant.*

market participation deposit (MPD) = *equity-linked CD.*

market portfolio a hypothetical portfolio containing every security available to investors in a market in the amounts proportional to their market values.

market price (MP) current price set by buyers and sellers in the market. ***Also***: "and interest" price; free market price; price. ***See***: *quoted price.*

market price of risk of a portfolio, ratio of the extra return, or *risk premium* to the risk.

market rate the bond interest rate in the market that borrowers are willing to pay and buyers are willing to take.

market rate of exchange the exchange rate at which a foreign exchange has just been sold in the market.

market rate of interest the interest rate determined by the demand and supply of funds. ***Also***: natural rate of interest.

market risk <1> a day to day potential for an investor to experience losses from the fluctuations in price. ***Also***: absolute market risk. <2> = *interest rate risk.* <3> = *systematic risk.*

market risk premium the difference between the expected return on a market portfolio and the risk-free rate.

market sentiment measurement of the bullish or bearish attitude of the *crowd.*

market's opinion of volatility = *implied volatility.*

market strength a measure of the general tone of the market by using volume, prices, patterns and other factors that reflect investor confidence in the overall market.

market surveillance investigating and preventing abusive, manipulative, or illegal trading practices on the Nasdaq.

market sweep the second public offering after a tender offer, thus allowing institutional investors to obtain a controlling interest at a price higher than the offer.

market timer an investor who makes excessive short-term trading in futures or securities.

market timing = *market timing 2.*

market timing 1 the mutual fund and other trader's active decision on when to buy different assets. ***Also***: timing the market.

market timing 2 the taking advantage of the information after the market closes to trade mutual fund shares that are valued at 4:00 p.m. and be recorded as being traded before 4:00 p.m. ***Also***: fund scandal; late-day trading; late trading; market timing; mutual fund scandal; NAV arbitrage; net asset value arbitrage; stale price arbitrage; time-zone arbitrage.

market timing cost the costs that arise from the price movement of a stock during a transaction period but attributable to other non-price activity in the stock.

market-to-book ratio = *price to book ratio.*

market tone general state of well-being of a securities market.

market transaction a foreign exchange transaction done between the banks or the bank and other financial institutions.

market transparency characteristic of a bond market where debt management strategies and operation are visible and understood by market participants.

market value <1> of futures, it equals the settlement price × factor × quantity. <2> total number of shares traded multiplied by the closing price. ***Also***: paper value. <3> = *market capitalization.*

market value added (MVA) the difference between the market value of a company (both equity and debt) and the share capital contributed by stockholders. ***See***: *shareholder value added.*

market value CDO a CDO that pays the tranche holders capital gains from the trading of collateral assets.

market value ratio a ratio that relates the market price of the stock to a selected other financial statement item.

market value weighted index = *capitalization weighted index.*

market versus quote (MVQ) comparison between the last traded price and the current bid/ask prices.

market volatility = *implied volatility.*

Market Volatility Index = *CBOE Volatility Index.*

market volatility index a volatility index used for tracking market *volatility* as an independent entity.

marking-to-market = *mark-to-market.*

marking-to-model = *mark-to-model.*

Markov diffusion process = *Brownian motion.*

Markov property in the random walk process and Poisson process, the next step is independent from any of its previous outcomes.

Markowitz efficient frontier = *efficient frontier.*

Markowitz efficient portfolio = *efficient frontier.*

Markowitz portfolio optimization the formula and solution by Markowitz for portfolio optimization for a single period. ***Also***: single-period MVO.

mark-to-market (MTM) <1> valuation of derivative positions on a daily basis. <2> adjustment of the book value of a security to reflect the current market value. ***Also***: marking-to-market.

mark-to-market exposure <1> the credit exposure calculated from the financial instrument's current market value rather than its cost. <2> = *actual exposure.*

mark-to-market selection = *Section 475 (f) selection.*

mark-to-market swap = *marked-to-market swap.*

mark-to-market system a trading system under which investors trading futures are credited with the unrealized gain or loss daily, losses require immediate cash deposit, and gains can be withdrawn.

mark-to-market value = *actual exposure.*

mark-to-model the valuation of a position or a portfolio by a financial model. ***Also***: marking-to-model.

markup amount added to cost price when the client buys securities from a dealer in the OTC market. **See**: *markdown.*

marriage = *merger.*

married put <1> a put held by the owner of the same stock. <2> = *covered put.*

married to a stock of a trader who refuses to sell a stock that has dropped in price.

marrying a put buying a stock and buying a put on the same stock to protect market crash.

martingale a random variable X which satisfies $E^P(X_{n+1} | X_1, \ldots X_n) = X_n$, in other words, the expected value of the next observation is equal to the value of the last observation. **See**: *submartingale.*

martingale approach = *stochastic calculus approach.*

master agreement an agreement spelling out the terms on all swaps between two parties. ***Also***: master swap agreement.

master CDO = *outer CDO.*

master-feeder a hedge fund structure that operates one US based vehicle and one offshore vehicle.

master fund a mutual fund that enables investors to invest money into one or more underlying investments. **See**: *discretionary fund; feeder fund.*

master limited partnership (MLP) the partnership that looks like a corporation and is traded on an exchange like one, but is taxed like a partnership. ***Also***: publicly traded partnership.

Master Swap Agreement an agreement that is maintained by the *International Swaps and Derivatives Association*, that outlines the standard terms and conditions of swap transactions.

master swap agreement = *master agreement.*

master trust <1> the collection of funds pooled together for investment purpose. <2> <Canada> the trust which invests funds from a registered pension plan or a deferred profit sharing plan.

matador bond <Spain> a bond issued by a foreign company and sold in Spain and denominated in pesetas.

matched book <1> the accounts of the securities dealers when their costs of borrowing are equal to interest earned on loans made to clients and other brokers. <2> a situation when the distribution of maturities of a bank's liabilities equal the maturities of its assets.

matched duration = *matched maturities.*

matched hedge the hedge created with the interest rate of the hedged item note equal to the rate of the receivable leg of the hedging swap.

matched maturities a strategy having the maturities of the financial institution's assets and liabilities equal in order to reduce interest rate risk. ***Also***: matched duration. ***See***: *match fund.*

matched sale the action by the Federal Reserve bank to temporarily absorb the reserves by selling securities with an agreement to buy them back in a given period (often 15 days) at a specified price. ***Also***: matched sale purchase transaction; reverse repo; reverse repurchase agreement.

matched sale purchase transaction = *matched sale.*

matched swaps two swaps with identical but mirror image provisions, so that the overhedging-underhedging rate will be zero.

matched transaction the transaction under which two members have both entered identical or corresponding information.

match fund to take a position in assets of the same maturity as the maturity of the liabilities. ***See***: *matched maturities.*

matching strategy a strategy of creating portfolios to meet individual needs of investors through tiered duration.

matilda bond <Australia> the Australian dollar denominated bond that is issued in the Australian market by a foreign entity.

matrix price estimated price for a fixed-income bond based on quoted prices for bonds with similar coupons, ratings, and maturities, rather than on specific bids and offers.

matrix pricing the process of pricing a bond by listing all its characteristics and comparing them to other bonds with the similar characteristics.

matrix trading bond swapping whereby traders seek to take advantage of yield spread differentials between the fixed-income bonds of the same class but with different ratings.

maturity the end of the life of a security.

maturity basis a bond's interest divided by its maturity value.

maturity by maturity (MBM) the bond auction which allows underwriters to submit bids for selected maturities in an issue, rather than for the entire issue on an all-or-none basis.

maturity date <1> the date on which a bill or note, a policy, or bond becomes due for payment or for repayment. ***Also***: date due; date of maturity; day of due date; day of maturity; due date; end date; law day; termination date. <2> = *expiration date.*

maturity factoring an arrangement that provides collection and insurance of the accounts receivable of a business.

maturity gap = *duration gap.*

maturity gap exposure the risk arising from having an asset and liability of the same amount and in the same currency but of different maturity.

maturity interest rate = *discount rate.*

maturity mismatch risk the risk that the value of the offsetting positions will fail to move in concert due to the differences in maturities of the long and the short positions in *cross hedging.*

maturity sector a group of bonds that are categorized based on the maturity dates.

maturity spread the difference between the yield on a bond with one maturity and an otherwise equivalent bond with a different maturity.

maturity swap = *extension swap.*

maturity value <1> the money to be paid when a debt or other financial contract is due. <2> = *accumulated amount.*

maximizing shareholder value management's trying to increase the value of the common stock of a company.

maximum annualized yield to maturity the annualized yield earned on a PERCS or ELKS if the underlying trades above the *lowest call price.*

maximum capital gains mutual fund a fund the objective of which is to produce capital gains for its shareholder.

maximum maturity bond a *collateralized mortgage obligation* that will be retired by minimal required principal payments in a known period of time.

maximum minimum option an option that generates payoff that is equal to the difference between the strike price and the maximum (for call) or the minimum (for put) price.

maximum option a bundle of pure vanilla sold options with a variety of features, e. g. strikes, underliers, but with the same maturity.

maximum payout amount repaid on an accrual option if the asset price trades within a specified range.

maximum rate note = *bull floater.*

maximum return criterion (MRC) the maximum rate of return expected from holding a portfolio. ***See***: *bogey; hurdle rate.*

max-min option = *min-max option.*

max pain the point at which options expire worthless, option holder will lose the premium.

maybe price the bid or ask price not guaranteed to the buyer or seller who has submitted an order to be executed.

MBM maturity by maturity

MBS mortgage-backed security

MCD <1> miscellaneous cash deposit. <2> months of cyclical dominance.

m-commerce the commercial activity that is linked by mobile communication systems and devices.

MCPDPS mandatory conversion premium dividend preferred stock

MDF managed derivatives fund

mean aversion the tendency of an above average return to be followed by another above average return, and a below average return to be followed by another below average return.

mean return average expected return of a given investment or portfolio.

mean reversion <1> a strategy which involves buying an under performing stock, or another type of security, and holding the position until the market rebounds. <2> a process under which variables such as price, rate, index, and volatility tend to return to the mean value after reaching the extremes. ***Also***: Omstein-Uhlenbeck process; red noise.

mean standard error the variance divided by the total number of trials in *variance reduction.*

mean trading price the average of the daily closing price of a security during a 90-day period.

mean-variance efficient portfolio = *efficient frontier.*

mean-variance optimization (MVO) a quantitative tool used in making assets allocation by considering the trade-off between risk and return.

MEC modified endowment contract

mechanical investing buying and selling stocks or bonds based on criteria that meet the predetermined investing screen.

median market cap the middle stock in a fund's portfolio in terms of market capitalization.

medium cap = *mid cap.*

medium grade of investment, implying a degree of risk that most conservative investors may not want to accept. ***Also***: businessman's investment.

medium-term bond a bond with maturity of 2 to 10 years.

medium-term note (MTN) a note or debt instrument with a fixed rate and fixed maturity (typically less than 7 years).

megabite a million-dollar drop in net profit. ***See***: *gigabite.*

mega cap companies having a market capitalization greater than 200 billion.

Mello Roo's the new bonds used for the developments that benefit a particular country or district.

membership stock = *voting stock.*

member short sale ratio the ratio of total shares sold short for the accounts of NYSE members in one week divided by the total short sales for the same week.

mercantile paper = *commercial paper.*

merchandise advance = *produce loan.*

merger combining two or more entities in one. ***Also***: absorption; amalgamation; amalgamation by absorption; business combination; combination; consolidation by merger; gobble; joining; marriage. ***Opp***: *demerger.* ***See***: *takeover.*

merger arbitrage a hedge fund strategy under which the stocks of two merging companies are simultaneously bought and sold to create a riskless profit.

Merrill option volatility expectation (MOVE) Merrill Lynch's measure of the bond market uncertainty based on bond option implied volatilities around Open Market Committee meetings.

Merton model <1> = *asset value model.* <2> = *option theoretic.*

Merton option pricing model a pricing model for European options on stocks or index with a known dividend yield.

method the way the cash flows of the underlying asset are to be handled by the option pricing model.

mezzanine bracket the members of an underwriting group whose participations are of such a size as to place them in the tier second to the largest participants. ***See***: *major bracket.*

mezzanine debt a debt that incorporates equity-based options, such as the stock warrants with a lower-priority debt.

mezzanine financing a preferred stock with a sinking fund to retire the issue in 8 years.

mezzanine level company the company that is in a stage somewhere before IPO.

mezzanine level stage the stage of venture capital financing before IPO. ***See***: *first round.*

mezzanine tranche the class in a synthetic CDO that takes the medium risk, between the *first tranche* and the *equity tranche.*

MFI money flow index

MGE Minneapolis Grain Exchange

MHR modified hedge ratio

MHS manufactured housing security

micro cap capitalization of a company under $250 million. ***See***: *large cap*; *small cap.*

micro hedge a hedge designed to reduce the risk of holding a particular bond or stock. ***See***: *macro hedge.*

micro hedging hedging taken to offset the risk of a particular asset or liability. ***See***: *macro hedging.*

MIDAM Mid-America Commodity Exchange

mid-Atlantic option = *Bermuda option.*

mid cap capitalization of $1 billion to $5 billion. ***Also***: medium cap. ***See***: *large cap*; *micro cap*; *small cap.*

mid-cap SPDR a spider that tracks S&P Mid-Cap 400.

mid-curve option short-term American option on a CME-listed European futures with delivery of 1 or 2 years.

mid-day call demand from the clearing house for an interim margin decreases during the day.

middle rate the average of the buying and selling rate of a foreign exchange. ***Also***: average exchange rate; midpoint rate.

midgets pools of GNMA securities with a 15-year maturity.

midpoint rate = *middle rate.*

mid-price the middle price between the bid and the offer.

MIDS monthly income debt security

MIFE Manila International Futures Exchange

migration change from one credit rating to another rating.

migration risk the risk of loss due to a change in an obligation's credit rating.

milking illegal *asset stripping* before an ownership change or bankruptcy.

milliard 1,000 million.

MINE market-indexed note

mini-manipulation trading on a security underlying an option so as to manipulate the stock price, causing an increase in the value of the option. ***See***: *capping.*

mini-max floater = *collared FRN.*

mini-max option = *collar.*

mini-max strategy = *min-max strategy.*

minimum acceptable rate (MAR) = *hurdle rate.*

minimum attractive rate of return = *hurdle rate.*

minimum cutoff criterion = *hurdle rate.*

minimum fluctuation = *tick.*

minimum option an option like a *maximum option* but only one of them can be exercised at the issuer's favor.

minimum price the price floor set in advance by the seller. ***Also***: lowest price; reserved price.

minimum price contract a forward with a clause that guarantees a minimum price for the delivery of the underlying agricultural commodity.

minimum price fluctuation = *tick.*

minimum rate of return = *target rate of return.*

minimum required rate of return = *hurdle rate.*

minimum reserve legal reserve of a bank.

minimum stock = *buffer stock.*

minimum subscription the minimum shares required to be subscribed if a company intends to raise additional capital to finance the acquisition.

minimum value <1> the intrinsic value which has been adjusted by the time value of money to maturity. <2> fair value of an employee option, calculated by reference to the market call premium and risk-free interest rate.

minimum value method a method used to calculate stock-based compensation cost, calculated as total of the present value of the strike price and present value of the expected dividend times the number of options granted.

minimum variance hedge ratio the ratio of futures contracts to a specific spot position that minimizes the variance of the net gains from the overall hedged position and is invariant to the total cost of the hedge.

minimum-variance portfolio the portfolio with the lowest variance at a specific expected return level.

minimum yield the lesser of yield-to-call and yield-to-maturity.

mini perm short term financing used to pay off commercial or constructional property loans, usually in 4-6 years.

mini-premium option a *contingent premium option* where no initial premium is paid but for which the option buyer agrees to pay some prescribed amounts if the underlying asset moves in-the-money to specific levels over the life of the option.

min-max bond = *collar bond.*

min-max floater a floating-rate note with an embedded collar.

min-max option <1> a collective term for *minimum option* and *maximum option*. ***Also***: max-min option. <2> = *collar.*

min-max strategy a strategy providing both participation and protection while attempting to minimize option premium payment, assuring a minimum and maximum price range. ***Also***: collar; mini-max strategy.

min-max swap = *collared swap.*

minority interest part of the net worth of a subsidiary relating to the shares not owned by the parent company.

minus yield the condition in which a *convertible bond* is selling at a premium higher than the bond's interest yield.

MIP monthly investment plan

MIPS monthly income preferred security

mirror fund mutual fund that enables an investor to access another mutual fund through life insurance policies.

mirror swap <1> an offsetting or contra-swap designed to eliminate the market exposure of an earlier swap. <2> a swap between a derivatives products company and its parent or an affiliate designed to take the market exposure out of the credit enhanced vehicle.

misery index an index which is a combination of the unemployment rate and the inflation rate.

mismatch a discrepancy in the maturities of assets and liabilities.

mismatch bond a floater the interest rate of which is reset at more frequent intervals than the rollover period.

mismatched payment swap the swap in which payment streams will not be exchanged on the same date. ***Also***: mismatched swap.

mismatched swap = *mismatched payment swap.*

mismatch risk market risk created when a hedge does not cover an exposure.

MIT municipal investment trust

MITTS market index target-term security

mixed bag a group of stocks some of which are up, down, and neutral.

mixed distribution model the model of the underlier's value with a mixture of distributions.

mixed fund <UK> the fund consisting of both real estate and personal property.

mixed market the market with no clear price trend.

mixed shares the shares with priority in dividend but with no or less priority in residual assets. ***See:*** *junior stock.*

mixed straddle a straddle of which one position is a regulated futures contract, and each other position is an identified straddle.

MJSD abbreviation of 4 option-maturity months: March, June, September and December. ***See***: *March cycle.*

MKDS = *ARMS index.*

MLC Meat and Livestock Commission

MMID market maker identifier

MMMF money market mutual fund

MMP money market preferred

MMPS money market preferred stock

MOB municipals over bond

MOB spread = *municipal over bond spread.*

mock trading = *paper trading.*

model dependent hedge a hedge based on a model or statistical relationship.

model independent hedge a hedge that will be successful independent of how underlying assets change in value.

model risk the risk of loss that an asset is priced by using a wrong pricing model.

modern portfolio theory (MPT) a strategy seeking to build an optimal portfolio by using the relationship between risk and return, as measured by *alpha, beta and R-squared.* ***Also***: portfolio theory.

modified American option = *Bermuda option.*

modified and combinable REMIC (MA-CR) real estate mortgage investment conduit that lists cash flow combinations letting investors mix and match to create desired instruments without originating a new security.

modified call butterfly a position that is similar to a long call butterfly except that the out-of-the-money calls purchased have a strike price nearer to the average strike price of the calls sold.

modified duration measure of the price sensitivity of a bond to the interest rate movements, it = *Macaulay duration* ÷ (1+ (bond yield ÷ k)), k is the number of compounding periods in one year. ***Also***: adjusted duration. ***See***: *effective duration*; *option adjusted duration.*

modified Dutch auction a Dutch auction in which seller reserves the right to set the final price.

modified endowment contract (MEC) an insurance policy, e. g. a single-premium contract, that fails the 7-pay test.

modified following modifying the reset date in a swap or other agreement.

modified hedge ratio (MHR) the hedge ratio modified by taking into account a change in one particular variable.

modified internal rate of return (MIRR) the internal rate of return adjusted for negative cash flow, by using a safe rate of return.

modified ladder option = *fixed strike ladder option.*

modified mortgage duration a modified mortgage duration to account for the impact on the duration of the mortgage-backed securities resulting from changes in interest rates.

modified pass-through a pass-through guaranteed by the federal government. ***Also***: fully modified pass-through. ***See***: *conventional pass-through.*

modified put butterfly a position that is similar to a long put butterfly except that the in-the-money puts purchased have a strike price nearer to the average strike price of the puts sold.

modified shout option = *fixed strike shout option.*

modified theoretical value (MTV) the theoretical value of option recalculated by taking into account the change in a particular variable.

mogul = *deep pocket.*

momentum fund a fund the managers of which look for stocks with forthcoming earnings releases or price momentum in the short term.

momentum stock a stock with price gain and higher volume.

Monday effect = *weekend effect.*

Monday seasonal = *weekend effect.*

monetary capital = *free capital.*

monetary investment the investment the principal and interest of which are fixed in terms of a given monetary unit.

monetary rate of interest = *explicit interest rate.*

monetization of debt = *monetizing debt.*

monetize <verb> to borrow money to create a cash balance against a purchase without liquidating the position.

monetizing collar a zero-cost equity collar that is combined with the monetizing benefit of a loan.

monetizing debt paying off the national debt by merely printing more paper money. ***Also***: monetization of debt.

monetizing equity collar buying a put to protect a position in stocks from the cash from selling a call, then using the hedged position as collateral to borrow money to invest in another portfolio.

money arbitrage = *interest arbitrage.*

money at call = *call money.*

money at call and short notice = *call money.*

money back certificate the hybrid instrument which promises the investor at least the return of original investment.

money back option a *contingent premium option* that permits only a partial refund of the investment in the event of an adverse move in the underlying.

money exchange = *exchange.*

money flow index (MFI) an index that measures the strength of money in and out of a security, divergence between the MFI and price trend can be interpreted as a possible trend reversal.

money management the principle of managing money. ***Also***: investment management; portfolio management.

money market the financial market for handling the purchase, sale, and transfer of the short-term credit instruments and notes. ***Also***: short-term money market. ***See***: *capital market.*

money market account = *cash management account.*

money market basis = *money market yield.*

money market fund (MMF) an open-end fund which invests in securities that pay the money market rates. ***Also***: money market mutual fund.

money market hedge the hedge that involves borrowing and lending in multiple currencies.

money market instrument a highly liquid guaranteed short-term debt.

money market mutual fund (MMMF) = *money market fund.*

money market preferred (MMP) = *auction rate preferred stock.*

money market preferred stock (MMPs) = *auction rate preferred stock.*

money market yield the bond quotation based on a 360-day year and semi-annual coupons. ***Also***: day count basis; money market basis; yield basis.

money multiplier security a zero-coupon offering by Salomon Brothers, with a choice of maturities. ***Also***: zerals.

moneyness <1> the characteristic of being like cash to be used as a medium of exchange in the settlement of trades. <2> the degree to which the option is in the money and behaving more like a forward contract than an ordinary option.

money pass two traders trading with each other for their own accounts so the profit goes from one account to another.

money rate of interest = *explicit interest rate.*

money-rate stock a stock so likely to pay a regular dividend that it trades on a yield in relation to similar stocks.

money spread = *vertical spread.*

monkey money = *scrip.*

Monte Carlo simulation the computer process that generates asset paths based on user input and random numbers.

Monte Carlo VAR = *simulated VAR.*

month abbreviations the letters used to represent trading months, e. g. in futures trading: F=Jan, G=Feb, H=Mar, J=Apr, K=May, M=Jun, N=Jul, Q=Aug, U= Sep, V=Oct, X=Nov, Z=Dec.

monthly income debt security (MIDS) a 30 to 50 years *security* the monthly interest payments are guaranteed by the issuer's parent company.

monthly income preferred security (MIPS) the *preferred security* that makes monthly payments, issued by subsidiaries formed exclusively to sell the shares and lend the proceeds to the parent. **See**: *quarterly income preferred security.*

monthly investment plan (MIP) = *constant-dollar plan.*

monthly purchase plan = *constant-dollar plan.*

month order a limit order which will be canceled if not executed in one month.

months of cyclical dominance (MCD) the estimate of the months required to identify significant cyclical movements in the market. **See**: *quarters of cyclical dominance.*

Moody's one of the three biggest bond rating agencies in the US. **See**: *FIS; Standard & Poor's.*

MOPPRS mandatory par put remarketed security

MOPS <1> multiple option put securities. <2> municipal option put security.

moral obligation bond the tax-exempt bond issued by a municipality which is backed by the moral obligation of a government to appropriate funds in case of default.

Morningstar risk = *downside risk.*

mortgage-backed certificate = *mortgage bond.*

mortgage-backed security (MBS) the security backed by a *pool* of mortgage loan. ***Also***: mortgage-related security. **See**: *mortgage bond.*

mortgage-backed security arbitrage a strategy that seeks to explore the pricing differentials between various issues of mortgage-backed securities.

mortgage bond a bond that is secured by the issuer's real estates mortgages. ***Also***: mortgage-backed certificate. **See**: *mortgage-backed security.*

mortgage broker a broker functioning as the intermediary between borrowers and lenders in securing loans.

mortgage derivative an instrument that derives its value from a mortgage pool.

mortgage duration the time a mortgage loan will last with a set payment.

mortgage instrument an instrument that is backed by a mortgage.

mortgage pass-through = *pass-through security.*

mortgage pass-through security = *pass-through security.*

mortgage point = *point.*

mortgage pool a pool of mortgages with similar terms for creating a new pass-through security or mortgage backed security.

mortgage prepayment cap the option that protects the holder of the cap from a loss if the prepayment rate in a mortgage pool exceeds the strike expressed relative to a PSA prepayment rate.

mortgage REIT the REIT that invests in mortgages only.

mortgage-related security = *mortgage-backed security.*

mortgage replication swap an indexed principal swap where the fixed-rate side is based on a mortgage-style rate and amortization schedule.

mortgage revenue bond a bond issued by a state or a political subdivision to make or buy mortgage loans on single-family or multifamily residences.

mortgage-subsidy bond a bond, a significant portion of the proceeds of which is used to provide mortgages on owner-occupied residence.

mortgage swap an interest rate swap the cash flows on which are structured to mimic those on portfolios of assets under a mortgage.

Moss an SEC system that combines the monitoring systems of the self-regulatory firms into one single database. ***Also***: Market Oversight Surveillance System.

most active list stocks which have the largest number of shares traded on a day. ***Also***: alpha stock; stocks in the spotlight. **See**: *beta stock.*

most distant futures contract a futures contract that is to be settled last of a pool of contracts.

most distant month = *furthest month.*

movable rate = *flexible exchange rate.*

MOVE Merrill option volatility expectation

moving average the average price of a security over a specified period, often 10, 20, 30, 50, 100 and 200 days.

MSCI World Index the benchmark index that tracks the performance of the stock markets in 22 countries.

M-squared the measure of the investment return of a portfolio of stocks when the risk incurred is considered.

MSRO multi-period strike reset option

MTM marked-to-market

mulligan cap = *flexible cap.*

multi-asset barrier swap a barrier swap on more than one asset.

multi-asset option an option with a pay-out dependent on the performance of more than one underlying asset, e. g. *alternative option*; *outperformance option.*

multi beta pricing derivative pricing with more than one beta of asset return.

multi-European option = *Bermuda option*

multi-factor option <UK> = *alternative option.*

multi-factor pricing derivative pricing with more than one factor of conditional linear combination of price and return.

multi-family revenue bond a bond that is secured by the rental revenue from the multi-family housing projects to be funded by the bond.

multi-index option the *outperformance option* with a payoff determined by the difference in performance of 2 or more selected indexes.

multilateral netting the netting of debt obligations among 3 or more parties.

multi-manager vehicle – *fund of funds.*

multi-nomial model option pricing model with more than two possible outcomes of price at each state.

multiperiod immunization the strategy under which a portfolio is created to satisfy more than one future liability regardless of interest rate changes.

multiperiod MVO the mean-variance optimization (MVO) that covers asset risks and returns in more than one period.

multiperiod option the option the payouts of which are based on the average value of an underlying asset in more than one period.

multi-period strike reset option (MSR-O) = *coupon-indexed note.*

multiple = *price/earnings ratio.*

multiple arbitrage the fund management style that uses more than one arbitrage.

multiple barrier option a barrier option with multiple sets of barrier prices. ***Also***: multiple strike option.

multiple coupon = *graduated rate coupon.*

multiple exchange rates the system under which different exchange rates are used for different transactions. **See**: *single exchange rate.*

multiple-index floater floating rate note the interest rates of which are based on the difference between two indexes, e. g. the *bank prime interest rate, LIBOR.*

multiple index option = *rainbow option.*

multiple-issuer pool under GNMA II, a fund pool formed by the aggregation of individual issuers' loan package.

multiple note a short-term note issued by municipalities in anticipation of a tax receipts or other revenue.

multiple option put securities (MOPS) municipal bonds with 30-year maturities and with 2-, 3- and 5-year puts.

multiple strike option = *multiple barrier option.*

multiple voting share <UK> = *classified stock.*

multiply traded option an option on the same underlying traded on two or more exchanges.

multi-price auction = *English auction.*

multi-rate reset swap a swap in which the reset and payment periods are unusually frequent, often monthly.

multi-strategy fund a hedge fund which uses many investment strategies.

multi-tranche CDO a synthetic CDO with more than one risks. **See**: *single-tranche CDO.*

muni = *municipal bond.*

municipal bond a bond issued by a state or a local municipal entity. ***Also***: muni; tax-exempt bond; tax-exempt security; tax-free bond.

municipal bond fund a mutual fund that invests in municipal bonds.

municipal bond swap the swap of one municipal bond with another.

municipal derivative a derivative designed to accommodate the financing needs of non-sovereign government units and investors in their debt.

municipal floating-rate bond a municipal bond that pays a floating rate of interest that is periodically reset based on an index.

municipal investment trust (MIT) unit investment trust which buys municipal bonds.

municipal note short-term municipal bond issued with a maturity of one year or less.

municipal offering an offering of bonds to another dealer at a fixed price for a limited period.

municipal option a put or call option the underlying asset of which is the municipal bonds.

municipal option put security (MOPS) municipal bond with a detachable put.

municipal over bond spread the yield spread between municipal bonds and Treasury bonds with the same maturity. ***Also***: MOB spread.

municipal revenue bond = *revenue bond.*

municipal security a security issued or guaranteed by a state authority or local government.

municipal strip the zero-coupon bond created by stripping off the coupon payment on a municipal bond.

municipal swap = *tax-exempt swap.*

museum piece quality the security offered by an infrequent issuer who has a high name recognition.

mutilated security a security on which the name of the issue, the issuer or some other details are printed.

mutual capital certificate = *investment certificate.*

mutual fund a fund that collects money from its subscribers and invests for their benefits. **See**: *closed-end fund; open-end fund; unit investment trust.*

mutual fund family = *fund family.*

mutual fund liquidity ratio a ratio that is published monthly by the Investment Company Institute that compares the amount of cash to assets held by mutual funds.

mutual fund scandal = *market timing 2.*

mutual fund share = *share.*

mutual fund trust <Canada> unit trust in which all holdings and transactions comply with regulations.

mutual offset the system which allows trading positions established on one exchange to be offset or transferred on another exchange.

N n

N <1> in newspaper, new issue. <2> the month abbreviation for July in futures and call. <3> Nasdaq descriptor meaning the 3rd class of preferred stock. <4> option strike price for 70.

NAFTA National Association of Futures Trading Advisers

naive hedge = *perfect hedge.*

naked = *uncovered.*

naked bond = *unsecured bond.*

naked call = *uncovered call.*

naked debenture = *floating debenture.*

naked derivative a position in derivative without an underlying asset.

naked index option a position in index option that is not hedged.

naked option = *uncovered option.*

naked option strategy = *uncovered option strategy.*

naked position the position which is not hedged from market risk.

naked put = *uncovered put.*

naked shorting illegal practice of short selling shares which have not been borrowed or do not exist at all.

naked strategy = *uncovered option strategy.*

naked warrant a warrant without a bond.

naked writing = *uncovered writing.*

names <UK> the individuals of Lloyds of London who join together in syndicate to underwrite insurance.

narrow-based index an index based on a group of stocks in the same industry, the gain of which is taxable as short term gain. ***Also***: narrow-based security index. ***See***: *broad-based index.*

narrow-based security index = *narrow-based index.*

narrow basis the condition under which the difference between the spot and futures price is small.

narrow market = *inactive market.*

narrow prices the price fluctuations within a small range, not more than a fraction of a point.

narrow the spread to close the spread between the bid and asked of a security as a result of bidding and offering by market makers and specialists.

NAS bond non-accelerating senior bond

NASD National Association of Securities Dealers

Nasdaq <1> the automated quotation system developed by the NASD for the electronic trading of securities. ***Also***: National Association of Securities Dealers Automatic Quotation System. <2> = *Nasdaq-100 Index.*

Nasdaq-100 Index an index of 100 stocks listed on Nasdaq. ***Also***: Nasdaq.

Nasdaq-100 Index tracking stock = *QQQQ.*

Nasdaq Composite Index the weighted index of all stocks listed on Nasdaq.

Nasdaq descriptor the 5th letter of a Nasdaq stock symbol.

Nasdaq National Market (Nasdaq-NM) created in 1971, the largest electronic equity securities market in the United States.

Nasdaq-NM Nasdaq National Market

National Association of Securities Dealers Automatic Quotation System = *Nasdaq.*

national best bid and offer (NBBO) the highest bid or lowest offer available on a market participating in the *Inter-market Trading System*. (SEC requires that brokers must guarantee customers the *best bid and offer*).

national debt (N.D.) (n.d.) = *government debt.*

national development bond <UK> the bond issued in 1964 to replace defense bonds.

National Market System (NMS) <1> a system of trading OTC stocks under the sponsorship of the NASD and Nasdaq. <2> a national system of trading whereby the prices for stocks and bonds are listed simultaneously on the NYSE and all regional exchanges.

natural = *clean.*

natural currency = *reporting currency.*

natural gas derivative a derivative the underlying asset is natural gas.

natural hedge the condition in which an exposure to a risk factor is offset or partly offset by an opposite exposure to that risk factor.

natural rate of interest = *market rate of interest.*

natural seller the offeror of a security that is currently held in an investment portfolio.

NAV net asset value

NAV arbitrage = *market timing 2.*

NAV per share total net asset value of a mutual fund divided by the number of shares outstanding.

NBBO national best bid and offer

NCL bond non-call life bond

NDF non-deliverable forward

NDO non-deliverable option

NDS non-deliverable swap

nearby delivery month = *nearby month.*

nearby futures contract the futures contract with the closest settlement or expiration date.

nearby month futures contract month or the option delivery month closest to maturity. ***Also***: current delivery month; front month; nearby delivery month; nearest month; near month; spot month. ***See***: *furthest month.*

nearest month = *nearby month.*

near money a debt instrument or option that is near its redemption or maturity.

near month = *nearby month.*

near option that side of a stock spread option position expiring before the other side does.

near perfect floater = *path-dependent floater.*

near term (NT) very soon, within the next few weeks or months.

near-the-money option = *close-to-the-money option.*

need the tick a stock price must move up or down one tick to comply with the SEC regulations.

negative accrued interest <UK> the negative accrued interest when a gilt is quoted ex interest.

negative carry a situation when the cost of money to finance securities is higher than the yield on the securities, implying loss, except if tax advantages may result. ***Also***: benefit of carry; negative cost of carry; negative spread. ***See***: *carry*; *positive carry.*

negative convexity a bond feature under which the price appreciation will be less than the price depreciation for a large change in the yield of a given number of basis points.

negative covenant a bond covenant that limits or prohibits certain actions unless the bondholders agree.

negative cost of carry = *negative carry.*

negative delta the delta of an option that is negative. ***See***: *positive delta.*

negative duration when the price of the mortgage-backed security moves in the same direction as interest rates due to prepayment and unusual structure.

negative duration gap the duration gap in negative figure, meaning cash flow from assets will exceed debt service. ***See***: *positive duration gap.*

negative gamma an option position the delta rate of change is a negative figure. ***See***: *gamma neutral*; *positive gamma.*

negative gearing the strategy in which related costs such as interest exceed income from the asset, thus creating a deduction against other income.

negatively sloping yield curve = *inverted yield curve.*

negative mark-to-market = *paper loss.*

negative net worth = *deficiency.*

negative spread = *negative carry.*

negative yield curve = *inverted yield curve.*

neglected firm effect the phenomenon where the stocks of less widely known companies produce very high returns.

negotiable of an instrument, the title to which can be transferred by delivery.

negotiable CD a large amount, short term CD, payable to bearer.

negotiable offering = *private offering.*

negotiable paper an instrument with an unconditional promise to pay. ***Also***: assignable instrument; open market paper; paper; transferable instrument.

negotiated CD large-denomination CD, over $1 million, that can be transferred but not cashed before maturity.

negotiated offering an offering of new securities the terms are negotiated between the issuer and the underwriters.

negotiation <1> the act by which the negotiable instruments are placed into circulation by being passed from the original holder to another person. <2> the settling of the price and terms by the parties to a deal.

Nellie Mae a company that buys student loans from the lender, and issues them as notes. ***Also***: New England Educational Loan Marketing Corporation.

nested option = *compound option.*

net advantage to merging difference in post- and pre-merger market value minus the cost of the merger.

net assets per share = *book value per share.*

net asset value (NAV) <1> the amount of a firm's assets backing each share of stock or bond it puts out, calculated as (total asset - intangible asset – current liabilities - liquidation value of preferred stock). ***Also***: book value; net book value. <2><mutual fund> = *bid price.*

net asset value arbitrage = *market timing 2.*

net book value = *net asset value.*

net book value per share of common stock = *asset cover.*

net capital total capital in excess of the sum of borrowed capital and deferred capital. ***Also***: pure capital.

net capital ratio an SEC required ratio maintained by every securities firm of aggregate indebtedness to liquid capital of 15:1. ***Also***: net capital rule.

net capital requirement a broker's capital required by SEC to cover its aggregate indebtedness, at least 15 times its liquid capital.

net capital rule = *net capital ratio.*

net change the change in price of a security between the closing price on one day and the closing price on the following day on which the stock is traded.

net commission zero commission in a *net trade.*

net cost of spread excess of premium paid for an option bought and premium received from an option sold in option spreading. ***Also***: spread differential. ***See***: *net premium.*

net credit spread the difference in yield between two securities due to different credit quality. ***Also***: credit spread.

net current asset value per bond the value of current assets applicable to a bond after deduction of prior liabilities.

net debt <1><UK> borrowings of a firm together with related derivatives less cash and liquid assets. <2> the sum of fixed and existing liabilities less sinking fund and other assets that are earmarked for payment of the liabilities. ***Also***: net long-term debt.

net dividend <UK> a dividend excluding the tax credit enjoyed by shareholders.

net earnings = *net income.*

net financing cost = *cost of carry.*

net hedge a hedge against the risk of the difference between the assets and liabilities.

net income (NI) the excess of a company's revenue over all its costs and expenses. ***Also***: income; net earnings.

net income approach an approach under which the value of a firm equals the capitalized net income plus the market value of capital stock minus liabilities.

net income per share of common stock = *earnings per share.*

net investment income per share the investment income of a mutual fund less management fees and administrative expenses, divided by its total number of shares outstanding.

net long position = *long position.*

net long-term debt = *net debt.*

net loss amount by which the expenses exceeds the income produced.

net margin requirement the margin required after the option premium received by the investor is deducted from the stated option margin requirement.

net parity <1> price of an international security, that does not include commissions, fees and other costs. ***See***: *gross parity.* <2> = *clean price.*

net payoff = *profit.*

net position the difference between long and short contracts in a commodity.

net power the excess margin minus the expected risk of loss in open trades.

net premiums the excess of the premium received over the premium paid in option spreading. ***See***: *net cost of spread.*

net-present-value swap = *rollercoaster swap.*

net realized capital gains per share the net capital gains on the securities transactions that a mutual fund realized in its fiscal year divided by the number of outstanding shares on the day the dividend is declared.

net settlement <1> a swap settlement in which only one party makes a payment of the net amount due after subtracting the amount owed by the other party. <2> the net payment from one swap party to the other after their gross obligations to one another are netted. ***See***: *difference check.*

net shares market the European market for US stocks, in which trades are made by banks and brokers as principals rather than agents. ***See***: *net transaction.*

netting <1> reducing fund transfers between affiliates to a net amount. ***Also***: payment netting; payments netting. <2> settling mutual obligations to arrive at the net value of contracts. <3> the offset of payables against receivables to reduce credit exposure. ***Also***: aggregation; right of offset; right of set-off.

netting by novation replacement of all agreements between two parties with a single contract and a single net payment stream. ***See***: *novation.*

net to customer in OTC market, meaning the quote is free of commission.

net to gross ratio (NGR) the ratio of net current market value of open positions between 2 parties to the gross current market value of the positions between them.

net trade a dealer's own trade with no commission. ***See***: *net commission.*

net transaction a securities deal without commissions. ***See***: *net shares market.*

net transaction exposure a risk exposure after offsetting inflows against outflows in a given currency.

net worth (NW) the amount by which total assets exceed total liabilities. ***Also***: capital; capital employed; capital net worth; economic surplus; equity; margin of solvency; owner's equity; proprietorship; stockholders' equity.

net worth to debt ratio = *equity-debt ratio.*

net yield the return from an investment following subtractions for costs or losses incurred in operating an investment.

net yield to redemption the gross yield to redemption on a security after taxes.

neural net the model which mimics the massive parallel processing that occurs in the brain of a human body.

neutral calendar spread = *time spread.*

neutral hedge the hedge that combines positions in various investments to create a risk-free return on the money invested, regardless of the price movement of the underlying securities.

neutral hedge ratio = *delta.*

neutral period the period during which Eurodollars transaction does not start or end on either a Friday or the day before a holiday.

neutral position <1> simultaneously selling out-of-the-money put and call options. <2> = *delta neutrality.*

neutral spread <1> the practice of buying a call option of a stock at a low price, and selling two or more put options of the same stock at a higher price. ***Also***: twofer. <2> = *delta neutrality.*

neutral stock a stock the beta of which is 1.0.

never buy into a lawsuit not to buy the stock of a company which is the defendant in a lawsuit.

New England Educational Loan Marketing Corporation = *Nellie Mae.*

newer issue a *preferred security* such as monthly income debt and trust originated preferred security. ***See***: *traditional preferred security.*

new financial instrument (NFI) a financial instrument that is not a simple debt or equity. ***Also***: innovative financial instrument ***See***: *exotic derivative.*

new for old = *refunding.*

new hybrid product a hybrid security not subject to SEC regulations prior to Nov 12, 1999 the effective date of the Gramm-Leach-Bliley Act.

new issue <1> security sold by a firm for the first time, the distribution of which is covered by the SEC rules. <2> = *initial public offering.*

new issues market = *primary market.*

new issue swap a swap that converts an issuer's lowest relative borrowing cost structure to a structure which fits the issuer's liability management goal.

new money the amount by which cash flow from a replacement issue of bonds exceeds that of the original issue. **See**: *pay-down.*

new money preferred a preferred stock issued after Oct 1 1942, when the tax exemption for the holders was raised from 60% to 85%.

new product risk the risk arising from errors that are made in structuring a new derivative product.

new share off = *ex new.*

New York Stock Exchange (NYSE) the most prestigious securities exchange in the world, opened in 1792, reorganized under its existing name in 1863. ***Also***: Big Board; Exchange.

next-day contract a listed contract that calls for the delivery of securities and payment the next day.

next-day fund an immediate transaction that payments are guaranteed to be available the next business day.

next-day settlement the settlement made on the next day after a trade. **See**: *same day settlement.*

next month in futures trading, meaning the month immediately after the nearby month.

NFI new financial instrument

NGR net to gross ratio

nickel five basis points (0.05%).

NIF note issuance facility

nifty fifty 50 US stocks most favored by institutions. ***Also***: favorite fifty.

Nikkei the leading and most respected index of Japanese stocks traded on the Tokyo Stock Exchange.

Nikkei-linked bond (NLB) an equity index-linked bond with the Nikkei 225 stock average as the underlying index.

nimble dividend rule a state law which allows companies with cumulative loss in the prior periods to pay dividends out of current profit.

nine-bond rule = *9-bond rule.*

NINOW non-interest-bearing negotiable order of withdrawal

NLB Nikkei-linked bond

NO option exchange code for *New York Stock Exchange.* ***Also***: NQ.

no arbitrage hypothesis a notion that holds that there is never a situation when the simultaneous purchase and /or sale of assets can result in a risk-free return.

NOB note over bond spread

no book a situation that arises when there is little or no interest in buying or selling a particular security.

no brainer a market when it is easy to figure out how stocks are performing.

NOB spread note over bond spread

no-cost option = *zero-cost option.*

no-cost option strategy selling options and using the proceeds from premium to buy undervalued options.

no cost risk reversal = *zero premium risk reversal.*

no-dividend shares the shares of the corporation which has never declared dividends for a long time.

noise trader risk market risk associated with the investment decisions based on biased information.

no load <1> of a mutual fund, no charge on sales or purchase of its shares. ***Opp***: *load.* <2> = *at cost.*

no load fund a mutual fund that charges no initial sales fee. **See**: *load fund.*

no-load stock a stock available through a direct purchase program.

nominal the face value of a bond or other financial derivative instrument. ***Also***: nominal amount.

nominal amount = *nominal.*

nominal capital the sum of the face value of all the shares authorized and issued outstanding. ***Also***: dedicated capital; face capital. **See**: *authorized capital.*

nominal cost of capital = *explicit interest rate.*

nominal effective exchange rate the exchange rate not adjusted for inflation. ***Also***: nominal exchange rate. **See**: *real effective exchange rate.*

nominal exchange rate = *nominal effective exchange rate.*

nominal exercise price the strike price of a Ginnie Mae option that is obtained by multiplying the unpaid balance on a certificate by the adjusted strike.

nominal interest rate <1> = *coupon rate of interest.* <2> = *explicit interest rate.*

nominal limit the risk limit based on the notional amount of a derivative.

nominally funded account the asset management account with less capital than being fully funded. ***Also***: notional account. **See**: *fully funded account.*

nominal price <1> the estimated price for a security or a commodity. <2> = *face value.*

nominal quotation = *nominal quote.*

nominal quote bid and offer given by a market maker for valuation purpose not as an invitation to trade. ***Also***: indicative price; nominal quotation; subject quote. **See**: *firm quote.*

nominal rate of interest <1> = *coupon rate of interest.* <2> = *explicit interest rate.*

nominal value = *face value.*

nominal yield the yield from a fixed income security divided by the par value of that security.

nominee the party to whom securities or other assets are transferred in order to facilitate a transaction.

nominee name the name of a company in which the holding of a stock is registered for convenience or concealment.

nonaccelerating senior bond (NAS bond) = *lockout bond.*

nonaccredited investor the individual investor who does not meet the SEC criteria of an *accredited investor.*

nonamortizable bond = *term bond.*

nonamortizing debt a debt in which the full principal is not fully paid off.

nonassented stock the stock held by the shareholders who declined to accept the changes suggested by the issuer company. **See**: *assented stock.*

nonassessable stock a stock whose owner cannot be assessed in the event of insolvency. ***Opp***: *assessable stock.*

nonbase currency = *functional currency.*

nonbearer bond = *registered bond.*

noncallable bond a bond, once issued, is not callable until its maturity.

noncallable bond equivalent yield = *option-adjusted spread.*

noncallable / nonputable convertible bond a convertible bond that is neither callable nor puttable.

noncall life bond (NCL bond) a bond not callable for redemption under any circumstances, and not specifically noted in the indenture.

noncash dividend = *dividend in kind.*

noncompetitive bid the bid to buy US Treasury bills submitted by the smaller investors via one of the Federal Reserve Banks or certain commercial banks. ***Also***: noncompetitive tender.

noncompetitive tender = *noncompetitive bid.*

nonconvertible preferred stock the preferred stock that can not be converted into common stock.

noncumulative = *noncumulative preferred stock.*

noncumulative preferred dividend the dividend on noncumulative stock.

noncumulative preferred stock a class of preferred stock on which the dividend does not accumulate if not paid. ***Also***: noncumulative.

noncyclical stock the stock the market price of which is not directly affected by economic changes, such as food, drug, income, etc. **See**: *cyclical stock.*

nondeliverable forward (NDF) a cash-settled *synthetic forward* on a nonconvertible or thinly traded currency.

nondeliverable option (NDO) an option that extends to the buyer the right to buy via a *call* or sell via a *put* a set amount of foreign currency at a given rate on a predetermined future date.

nondeliverable swap (NDS) the swap like a *non deliverable forward*, but the settlement for both parties is done through a major currency.

nondetachable warrant a warrant that cannot be separated from the host bond and cannot be traded separately. **See**: *detachable warrant.*

nondirectional strategy an option trading strategy that profits from either direction of the market.

nondiscretionary dividend <1> the dividend not based on the operating results of the company. **See**: *discretionary dividend.* <2> = *preferred dividend.*

nondiscretionary proposal proposition on a proxy that requires a quick response from the stockholder which does not fall under the *10-day rule.*

nondividend distribution distribution not treated by tax laws as a dividend but rather as a return of capital if the distributing company lacks earnings. **See**: *liquidating dividend.*

nondollar structure structured security which allows investors to hedge foreign currency risk or to participate in higher overseas interest rates.

nonequity dividend a dividend related to a nonequity share.

nonequity option the option that gives the holder the right to buy or sell an asset other than the common stock, examples include commodities, futures, and indexes. **See**: *equity option.*

nonequity share the share issued by a credit union which represents a debt to the holder. **See**: *equity share.*

nonequity shareholder the holder of a nonequity share.

nonexempt security a security subject to provisions of the Securities Acts of 1933 and 1934.

nonexisting payee = *bearer.*

nonfinancial price risk the risk of unexpected loss not related to the price movement in the market.

nongeneric swap = *exotic swap.*

nonincentive stock option a stock option which does not qualify for the special tax-favored treatment which applies to an *incentive stock option.*

noninterest bearing bond = *zero-coupon bond.*

noninvestment grade bond = *junk bond.*

nonlegals securities that do not conform to the SEC requirements thus not allowed to be sold to mutual funds or institutional investors. ***See***: *approved list.*

nonlinear derivative a derivative the pay-off of which has a nonlinear relationship. ***Opp***: *linear derivative.*

nonmarketable security <1> a security which can not be sold easily in the open market. ***Also***: illiquid security. ***See***: *marketable security.* <2> <UK> government security not traded on the exchange. ***See***: *marketable security; slug.*

nonrenewable resource natural resource that can only be used once, such as natural gas. ***See***: *renewable resource.*

nonparallel shift a shift in the yield curve in which yields will not change by the same amount for every maturity. ***Opp***: *parallel shift.*

nonpar stock = *no-par-value stock.*

nonpar swap a swap with one or both of the equivalent securities underlying the swap payments selling at a discount or a premium to parity. ***See***: *discount swap; par value swap; premium swap.*

nonparticipating preferred stock a stock that entitles its owners only to a fixed or stated dividend. ***See***: *participating preferred stock.*

nonpar value stock = *no-par-value stock.*

nonpath dependent option an option the value of which is not dependent upon the sequence of the market prices of the underlying security. ***Also***: free range option; path-independent option. ***See***: *path dependent option.*

nonpublic information the information that will have a material effect on the stock price when it is released to the public. ***See***: *inside information.*

nonputtable bond a bond not puttable.

nonqualified option an option issued to employees which is not qualified for long term capital gains tax treatment. ***Also***: nonqualifying stock option. ***See***: *qualified option.*

nonqualifying security <Canada> the donated share of a company with which the donor does not deal with at arm's length. ***Also***: prescribed security.

nonqualifying stock option (NSO) = *nonqualified option.*

nonrefundable bond a bond ineligible, in a stated period, for redemption with funds raised through the sale of an issue having a lower interest cost to the issuer.

nonruthless exercise a utility's trading with outside option traders.

nonsecurity-based swap a swap done with a financial instrument other than securities. ***See***: *security-based swap.*

nonspecific capital = *free capital.*

nonstandard derivative = *exotic derivative.*

nonstandard option = *exotic option.*

nonstandard swap = *exotic swap.*

nonstandard warrant = *exotic war-*

rant.

nonstationary time series a time series which appears to have no long term average level, e. g. a stock price series.

nonstatutory option a stock option that creates ordinary income when exercised, to the extent of the difference between the option price and value of the stock. ***Also***: unrestricted option. **See**: *statutory stock option.*

nonsticky jump bond (NSJ bond) the collateralized mortgage obligation the principal paydown of which is changed by the occurrence of one or more triggering events.

nontraded option the option which can only be closed by exercise, declaration or abandonment.

nonuse fee a fee charged by a lender to a prospective borrower for keeping a fixed amount of credit available even if the credit facility is not utilized.

nonvoting stock a stock the holder of which has no right to vote on corporate matters. **See**: *class B stock*; *voting stock.*

no-par stock = *no-par-value stock.*

no-par-value stock (NPV stock) a share of stock without a designated par value. ***Also***: non-par stock; no-par stock; share of no par value; stock without par value. **See**: *par value stock.*

no position of a position in foreign exchange purchased equals the foreign exchange sold. ***Also***: equilibrium position.

no quote no market makers are making an inside market at the moment.

no rebate cash-out option an up-and-out call or a down-and-out put where the seller's obligation is cancelled if the out strike is breached.

no regrets option = *lookback option.*

no-review offering the offering of new securities to the public in 48 to 72 hours, thus without review of the SEC.

normal backwardation the situation in which the futures price is less than the expected spot price at expiration.

normal beta the desired portfolio risk.

normal call premium call premium on a nonconvertible bond.

normal contango the condition in which the futures price is greater than the expected spot price at expiration of a futures contract.

normal difference the price difference between two markets due to shipping and insurance costs.

normal exercise option = *American option.*

normal investment practice investment history of a company used as a benchmark to test the new offering requirement of allocation of a hot issue.

normalized earnings <1> the earnings adjusted for cyclical ups and downs in the economy. <2> on a balance sheet, net earnings adjusted to remove unusual or one-time influence.

normal market size (NMS) the size based on the number of shares outstanding.

normal option = *vanilla option.*

normal portfolio <1> the customized portfolio that includes all the securities from which a fund manager normally chooses. <2> = *benchmark.*

normal price = *average price.*

normal range the level within which the price or volatility falls most of the time.

normal rate of interest = *coupon rate of interest.*

normal trading unit = *round lot.*

normal volatility the volatility level of an option that will return to after an extreme move.

normal yield curve a chart that shows the long-term debt instruments having higher yields than the short-term debt instrument. ***Also***: positive yield curve.

North American terms = *direct quote.*

northbound swap a swap from US dollar to Canadian dollar. ***See***: *southbound swap.*

nostro overdraft the amount that a domestic bank owes a foreign bank due to having sold more bills of exchange than it has bought.

note <1> = *promissory note.* <2> = *short-term debt security.*

note against bond spread = *note over bond spread.*

note discounted a promissory note that has been sold to investors at a discount. ***Also***: discounted note; note on discount.

note for a term = *promissory note.*

note future a futures contract on the US Treasury notes.

note issuance facility (NIF) a syndicate of banks which have agreed to purchase any short to medium term notes that a borrower is unable to sell in the Eurocurrency market.

note of hand = *promissory note.*

note on discount = *note discounted.*

note over bond spread (NOB spread) a spread created by selling the 10-year US Treasury note futures contract and buying the 30-year bond contract. ***Also***: note against bond spread.

note payable to bearer = *bearer note.*

note to bearer = *bearer note.*

notice of dishonor a written notice that payment on or acceptance of a negotiable instrument has been dishonored. ***Also***: mandate of protest; protest jacket; protest note.

notice period the time period preceding the expiration of a futures contract in which the buyer can be called upon to accept delivery.

notional = *notional value.*

notional account = *nominally funded account.*

notional amount <1> = *notional principal.* <2> = *notional value.*

notional bond a standardized bond with hypothetical terms, including coupon and maturity.

notional payment the payment that is applied to the notional amount of a derivative.

notional principal the amount of a swap on which the exchanged payments are based. ***Also***: fictional principal; notional amount.

notional value the value of a futures or options contract, that is the *contracted value* times the contract multiplier. ***Also***: notional; notional amount.

not-optionable stock the stock that does not have options available for trading. ***See***: *optionable stock.*

no-touch option an option that pays a fixed amount if the market never touches the barrier level chosen.

no transaction fee fund (NTF fund) a mutual fund that does not charge for buying and selling its shares.

novation the exchange of new debts or bonds for existing ones. ***See***: *netting by novation.*

NPV stock no-par-value stock.

NPV swap = *rollercoaster swap.*

NQ = *NO.*

NQB not qualified bidders

NR not rated

NRB no real bid

NRO no real offering

NSCC National Securities Clearing Corporation

NSF <1> non-sufficient fund. <2> not sufficient fund.

NSJ bond non-sticky jump bond

NSMIA National Securities Markets Improvement Act

NSO non-qualifying stock option

NSTA National Security Dealers Association

NTF fund no transaction fee fund

NTM near the money

nuclear war two companies compete for the takeover of a target company.

number of shares outstanding the total number of shares issued and held by investors. ***Also***: shares outstanding.

NVI negative volume index

NYBOT New York Board of Trade

NYBT New York Board of Trade

NYCE <1> New York Cash Exchange. <2> New York Coffee Exchange. <3> New York Cotton Exchange.

NYFE (New York Futures Exchange) = *knife*.

NYME New York Mercantile Exchange

NYMEX New York Mercantile Exchange

NYSE New York Stock Exchange

NYSE Common Stock Index = *NYSE Composite Index.*

NYSE Composite Index an index that relates all the NYSE stocks to an aggregate market value as of Dec. 31, 1965, with the base value of $50. ***Also***: NYSE Common Stock Index.

NZFOE New Zealand Futures and Options Exchange

O o

O <1> in options listing of newspaper, meaning old. <2> month abbreviation for August in put options. <3> the Nasdaq descriptor meaning the issue is the 2nd class of preferred stock. <4> the option strike price code for 75.

OAS option-adjusted spread

objective default price the price of a credit derivative when a party defaults.

objective indicator the indicator used to determine when an exchange rate should be changed.

obligation bond a mortgage bond, the face value of which is greater than the value of the underlying property.

obligor <1> a party who is in debt to another. <2> the counterparty which poses the credit risk.

OBS risk off-balance-sheet risk

OCC Options Clearing Corporation

occupation time the time the underlying asset price spent beyond the barrier.

occupation time derivative a derivative the payoff of which depends on the time spent by an index below a given level, such as a hurdle derivative or inside a given range, such as a corridor bond.

October effect the idea that stocks tend to decline in the month of October. ***Also***: fall's fall.

OD down-and-out price

odd date = *broken date.*

odd lot (OL) = *broken lot.*

odd-lot buy/sell ratio the ratio of odd-lot purchasing to odd-lot selling.

odd-lot differential an extra charge, often 1/8 of a point that dealers add to the purchases and subtract from sales in quantities less than the standard quantity. ***Also***: differential.

odd lot interest the total number of shares traded in a period in odd lot amounts.

odd lot of stock = *broken lot.*

odd-lot resale an offer to buy the shares from odd-lot shareholders for resale.

odd-lot selling indicator = *odd-lot short-sale ratio.*

odd-lot short-sale ratio short sales in odd-lot shares divided by total odd-lot sales. ***Also***: odd-lot selling indicator.

odd-lot theory = *Drew's odd-lot theory.*

odd run a forward contract the starting date and ending date of which do not match, such as Jun 22, Oct 25. ***Opp***: *straight-date run.*

odd share = *broken lot.*

OEIC open-ended investment company

OEX the abbreviation for the Standard & Poor's 100 index.

off-balance-sheet derivative = *off-balance-sheet instrument.*

off-balance-sheet instrument derivative instrument, e. g. a swap, an option, which changes a company's risk profile but the notional amount of which will not be shown as an asset or liability. ***Also***: off-balance-sheet derivative.

off-balance-sheet risk (OBS risk) the financial risk imbedded in instruments recognized as assets entailing conditional rights and obligations that expose the company to a loss not disclosed in the financial statements. ***Also***: concentration of credit risk.

off basis = *contango.*

off board market = *over-the-counter market.*

off board price the price of a security traded between individuals or over-the-counter. ***Also***: outside price.

off-board trading = *curb exchange.*

offer <1> in a limit order, the lowest price to sell a security. <2> = *ask.*

offer by tender = *tender offer.*

offered price = *ask.*

offeree <1> a party receiving an offer. <2> = *target company.*

offer for sale <1> = *offering.* <2><UK> = *underwriting.*

offer good until withdrawn by seller an offer to sell a security or other asset that is valid until the seller withdraws. ***Also***: standing offer.

offering the issue of security offered for sale to the public. ***Also***: offer for sale; placing. **See**: *initial public offering; primary offering; secondary offering.*

offering date = *date of issue.*

offering price (OP) <1> price per share at which a new or secondary distribution of securities is offered for sale to the public. ***Also***: public offering price. <2> the transfer price per share of a mutual fund share. <3> = *ask.*

offering scale a price structure at which different maturities of a serial bond are offered to the public by an underwriter.

offering statement a simplified statement required by SEC on debt issues with a maturity of less than 9 months.

offeror <1> the party that makes an offer. <2> = *acquiring company.*

offer price = *ask.*

official debt = *government debt.*

official exchange rate an exchange rate set by the government of a country. **See**: *foreign exchange official rate.*

official support an action taken by a central bank to buy its home currency in the foreign exchange market.

off-market coupon a coupon on a swap that deviates from the currently prevailing market conditions.

off-market coupon swap a swap with a fixed-rate payment materially different from the current coupon rate on bonds or notes of similar terms. ***Also***: adjustment swap; off-market swap. **See**: *at-market swap; high-coupon swap; low-coupon swap.*

off-market forward a forward contract in which the forward price is set so that the value of the contract is not zero.

off-market swap = *off-market coupon swap.*

offset = *offsetting transaction.*

offset stock option a stock option the holder's benefit will be reduced by the in-the-money value of the option.

offsetting swap a swap that exactly offsets the market risk of an existing swap but will not terminate it.

offsetting trade a trade which closes an existing position by an opposite trade. ***Also***: closing trade.

offsetting transaction the transaction to cover a position by counter contracts in the futures or foreign exchange market. ***Also***: offset; unwinding a trade.

offshore finance subsidiary a wholly owned subsidiary incorporated overseas to raise funds by issuing securities in the foreign market.

offshore fund a mutual fund whose shares are sold in the markets outside the USA.

offshore hedge fund a hedge fund set up in another country.

offshore market = *international market.*

off-the-run issue the equity securities not regularly included in pink sheets.

off-the-run Treasury the US Treasury security issued before the most recently issued security of a particular maturity.

O'Hare spread a very large position in a futures market, which will end up either a trip to Hawaii or a fleet out of the US.

OI open interest

OID original issue discount

OIDS original issue discount security

oil-price derivative a financial derivative the underlying of which is an oil index.

OIP official index period

OIS swap <1> *overnight indexed swap.* <2> *overnight index swap.*

OJAJ abbreviation of the four dividend-paying months: October, January, April, and July.

old crop/new crop spread buying new crop futures and simultaneously selling old crop futures.

old money a preferred stock held before Oct. 1, 1942 that was eligible for the $60,000 exempt from taxable dividend income.

omega the rate of change of an option's *gamma.*

omitted dividend the dividend on the common stock scheduled to be declared, but not voted for, by the firm's board of directors. ***Also***: passed dividend. ***See***: *dividend in arrears.*

OMLX Options Market London Exchange

Omstein-Uhlenbeck process = *mean reversion.*

OMX Option Market Index

on account buying = *buying on margin.*

on a clean up words meaning willing to participate in part of a trade if all of the stock available is *spoken for* except for the clean up amount.

on a scale buying or selling equal quantity of stock at prices that are spaced by a constant interval, as the price rises or drops. ***Also***: scale trading; scaling.

on average rising or falling stock prices based on the market average rather than a particular stock.

on balance buying = *buying on margin.*

on-balance sheet product a derivative the fair value of which must be shown on the balance sheet.

on basis = *backwardation.*

on-board security = *listed security.*

on change <1> on the floor of a stock exchange. <2> transacted through an exchange system.

one-decision stock quality stock that is not actively traded, but rather held for growth.

one-instrument collar an option-based collar that combines the put and the call into one instrument.

one man picture the quotation obtained from only one market maker.

one month liquidation = *Section 333 liquidation.*

one-name paper = *promissory note.*

one night stand buying a security with the intention to hold it for a long-term and subsequently panicking, selling it on the following day of trading.

one-sided market = *one-side market.*

one-side market a market in which the trader either buys or sells stock. ***Also***: one-sided market; one-way market.

one-to-one hedge = *perfect hedge.*

one-touch all-or-nothing an all-or-nothing option that pays off if the spot price of the underlying crosses a specified barrier before a specific date. ***Also***: one-touch binary option. **See**: *at-hit option.*

one-touch binary option = *one-touch all-or-nothing.*

one-touch double barrier option a one-touch all-or-nothing option with double barrier feature.

one-touch knock-in option = *double barrier knock-in option.*

one-touch knock-out option = *double barrier knock-out option.*

one-touch option <1> = *binary barrier option*; <2> = *exploding option.*

one-way collared floater = *ratchet floater.*

one way market = *one-side market.*

on stream the investment which is on track to earn its expected return.

on the money (OTM) <1> the current price that is the same price as the *last trade.* <2> = *at-the-money.*

on the run being actively traded.

on-the-run issue the most important issue of government bond in a particular maturity range. ***Also***: bellwether issue; benchmark issue; current-coupon issue; on-the-run Treasury.

on-the-run Treasury = *on-the-run issue.*

on track <1> the commodities delivery for a futures contract deferred and priced according to the seller's location FOB. <2> commodities loaded on railroad cars or trucks ready for delivery.

OP <1> offering price. <2> opening price. <3> opening purchase.

Opals optimized portfolio as listed securities

OPD <1> the opening deal in securities with prices moved more than 2 points on stock selling at $20 or higher. <2> the 1st deal of the day in a stock after delayed opening.

open book = *unmatched book.*

open commitments = *open interest.*

open contract a contract in a commodity or option which has not been exercised, closed out or allowed to expire.

open-ended fund <UK> = *open-end fund.*

open-ended investment company (O-EIC) <UK> an open-end fund which is structured as a limited liability company rather than a trust.

open-end fund a mutual fund without a fixed number of shares. ***Also***: fund open ended; open-ended fund; open-end investment trust; open-end trust. **See**: *closed-end fund.*

open-end investment trust = *open-end fund.*

open-end trust <Australia> = *open-end fund.*

opening bell the bell sound announcing the beginning of a trading session.

opening block the first transaction of a given security after the *opening bell.*

opening in the market a time frame of market opportunity, e. g. a low interest rate period is an opportunity in the market for issuing bonds. ***Also***: window of opportunity.

opening price (OP) <1> the price early in the morning session. **See**: *closing price.* <2> the first offer of a new issue of stock or item under public auction.

opening rate the rate of the first conversion of foreign exchange in a day. **See**: *closing rate.*

opening transaction <1> a buy or sell transaction that establishes a position. ***See***: *closing transaction*. <2> the first transaction of the day in a stock.

open interest (OI) the number of futures contracts currently outstanding in the market. ***Also***: commitment; commitments; open commitments.

open-market operations (OMO) the central bank's buying or selling operation in the money or securities market.

open market paper = *negotiable paper*.

open-market purchase operation a systematic program of repurchasing its own shares in the market by the issuer.

open market rate the interest rate on various debt instruments bought and sold in the market.

open position the dealer's assets and liabilities in a security, option or future. ***Also***: daylight exposure.

open repo a repurchase agreement under which the repurchase date is unspecified, and the agreement can be terminated by either party.

open selling the selling of securities not for the settlement of an account or a trade. ***See***: *fresh buying*.

open tender = *takeover bid*.

operating leverage the high fixed cost can magnify a small percentage change in revenues into large percentage change in net earnings. ***See***: *capital leverage*; *Wall Street leverage*.

operating results = *bottom line*.

operational risk the risk of loss due to an operational failure, not related to market or credit risk. ***See***: *financial risk*.

operator = *speculator*.

OPM <1> options pricing model. <2> other people's money.

opportunistic strategy the strategy that seeks to produce the greatest possible returns by making aggressive investment in the most-efficient products.

opportunity cost <1> the differential between the forward rate and the spot rate. <2> the return that an investor would get if he did not invest in the stock. ***Also***: external return.

opportunity set the possible expected return and standard deviation pairs of all portfolios that can be constructed from a given set of assets.

opportunity value = *volatility value*.

OPTAX Oppenheimer AMT-free Municipal Fund

optimal hedge a hedge that maximizes expected utility. ***Also***: variance-minimizing hedge.

optimal portfolio the efficient portfolio most preferred by an investor because its risk-reward characteristics approximate his utility function.

optimal redemption provision the bond indenture provision that governs the issuer's ability to call the bonds for redemption before scheduled maturity.

optimal stopping a theory of pricing an American option which can be exercised at some rational time.

optimization of a portfolio <1> the process that maximizes the *expected utility* as a function of exposure to the component assets. <2> using a linear or quadratic model to structure the portfolio to maximize yield or to reduce or increase the exposure to some industries, market sectors, or macroeconomic factors. ***Also***: portfolio optimization.

optimized portfolio as listed securities (Opals) the portfolio used to closely track an index without the exposure of buying all securities within that index. ***See***: *exchange traded fund*.

option the right, but not an obligation, to buy or sell a security, commodity or a real property within a stipulated time in accordance with the agreement.

optionable stock the stock with options available. ***See***: *not-optionable stock.*

option account the account kept in a brokerage firm for trading in options.

option-adjusted convexity = *effective convexity.*

option-adjusted duration the modified duration calculation that incorporates the expected duration shortening effect of an issuer's embedded call provision. ***See***: *effective duration*; *modified duration.*

option-adjusted spread (OAS) difference between the *option-adjusted yield* and the US Treasury yield. ***Also***: non-callable bond equivalent yield.

option-adjusted yield the expected *yield to maturity* of a bond or a note after deducting the opportunity loss due to the exercise of a *call provision.* ***Also***: call-adjusted yield.

optional bond = *callable bond.*

optional dividend the dividend where stockholders have the choice of receiving either a stock dividend or cash.

optional payment bond <UK> a bond the holder of which can choose domestic or foreign currency in paying principal and interest.

option arbitrage taking advantage of the discrepancies between the quoted prices of options and the underlying.

option-based collar a collar based on the put and the call options.

option business the trading of options. ***Also***: premium business.

option buyer = *option holder.*

option chain listing of the complete set of options available for a security.

option class the options of the same type in terms of strike, maturity or moneyness. ***Also***: class; class of options; class option; series; series of options.

option contract the agreement between the writers and the buyers for trading in options. ***Also***: options contract.

option currency bond a dual-currency bond with the right to choose which currency for payment.

option cycle = *expiration cycle.*

option-dated forward = *option forward.*

option dealer one who is registered as a dealer in options. ***Also***: options dealer. ***See***: *option trading right holder.*

option dealing buying or selling the right to deal in a security during a fixed period of time at a fixed price.

option-delivery contract a forward contract that allows one party to deliver the asset in whole or in part at any date in the contract period. ***Also***: buyer's option.

optionee = *option holder.*

option elasticity a percentage change in the value of an option given 1% change in the value of the underlying asset. ***Also***: elasticity of option. ***See***: *delta.*

option exchange the physical or virtual marketplace at which *options* are traded. ***Also***: options exchange.

option expiration date = *expiration date.*

option forward the forward contract on foreign exchange having an option with respect to the date of the exchange of currency to be transacted. ***Also***: option dated forward.

option-free bond the bond that is issued without an embedded option.

option/futures spread an option with a futures position, when it is a call, the futures is the opposite side, when it is a put, the futures is the same side.

option grant the right granted to the employee to buy certain shares of the employer's stock at a set price. ***Also***: employee stock option; grant of option; stock option grant.

option grantor = *writer.*

option growth fund a mutual fund that aggressively trades in options for large profits from price fluctuations or changes in volatility.

option hedge <1> price-hedged position created by selling more options than the value of underlying asset held. ***Also***: variable hedge. **See**: *ratio write.* <2> a hedge that uses options as tools for risk management.

option holder one who has bought an option, but has not exercised or sold it. ***Also***: holder; option buyer; optionee; option purchaser. **See**: *writer.*

option income fund a mutual fund that trades in options only.

option issuer = *writer.*

option lifetime = *expiration cycle.*

option loan = *exotic loan.*

Option Market Index (OMX) a stock index of the Swedish equity market.

option-adjusted yield = *option premium.*

option mutual fund the mutual fund that buys or sells options to increase its income and share value.

option not to deliver additional hedge placed in tandem with the forward or substitute sale.

option on a floor = *floortion.*

option on an option = *compound option.*

option on a spread = *spread option.*

option on a swap = *swaption.*

option on CDO tranche = *CDO option.*

option on CDS = *CDS option.*

option on futures = *futures option.*

option on physicals <1> the option to buy a spot commodity on a future date at the specified price. **See**: *futures option.* <2> the interest rate option based on fixed income securities.

option on the best of n-asset an option with a payoff depending on the best performance of a group of assets against a predetermined strike price.

option on the best of n-asset and cash an option with a payoff depending on the best performance of a group of assets and cash against a predetermined strike.

option on the worst of n-asset an option with a payoff depending on the worst performance of a group of assets against a predetermined strike price.

option on the worst of n-asset and cash an option with a payoff depending on the worst performance of a group of assets and cash against a predetermined strike price.

option/option spreads = *straddle.*

option order an order to trade options.

option pool the shares placed at a private company for issuance later.

option premium the price of an option paid by an option buyer to the writer. ***Also***: option money; premium.

option price = *strike price.*

option pricing model a model for valuing options.

option privilege the right to benefit from increases in the value of stock subject to an option.

option purchaser = *option holder.*

option replication <1> a method to create an option-like payoff pattern through a series of transactions in the underlying or in related futures as in *dynamic hedging*. <2> = *synthetic option.*

option rho = *rho.*

Options Clearing Corporation (OCC) an organization for the clearing of derivative instruments in the USA.

options contract = *option contract.*

options contract multiplier the amount (often 100) set by an exchange which when multiplied by the price, gives the dollar value of an option contract.

options dealer = *option dealer.*

option seller = *writer.*

option sensitive the sensitivity measure associated with option pricing, such as *delta, gamma, rho, theta* and *vega*. ***Also***: sensitive.

option series options of the same class with the same strike and maturity.

options exchange = *option exchange.*

option skewing the difference between *implied volatility* and the volatility of the *out-of-the-money* options. **See**: *volatility skewing.*

option specialized broker a broker who specializes in options.

option spread <1> a difference between the strikes of put and call of the same underlying asset. <2> a difference in option premiums resulting from the combination of put and call options of the same class on the same underlying. ***Also***: spread. <3> = *option spreading.*

option spreading simultaneous buying and selling of options of the same class, at the same strike price with different expirations, or at different strike prices with the same or different expiration months. ***Also***: option spread; spreading. **See**: *spread option.*

options table a table showing market information about stock options.

option stock the stock that is acquired through the exercise of an option.

option straddle = *straddle.*

option style the terms of exercise of the option. **See**: *American option*; *Bermuda option*; *European option.*

option tender bond (OTB) the variable rate tax exempt bond with put options that permit the investor to sell bond at par before maturity to the issuer.

option theoretic a method for estimating the probability of default of an obligor. ***Also***: Merton model.

option to double = *double option.*

option to purchase share = *stock option.*

option trading right holder one who has a license to trade options. **See**: *option dealer.*

option transfer program the program offered by JP Morgan Chase which buys underwater options from employees of the issuing company.

option type the class of option based on what the option allows the holder to do, such as buy or sell the underlying asset. **See**: *call option*; *put option.*

option volatility annual percentage of the fluctuation in the price of an option, represented as the standard deviation of the option prices. ***Also***: volatility. **See**: *historical volatility*; *implied volatility*; *relative volatility.*

option with high volatility = *expensive option.*

option with low volatility = *cheap option.*

option writer = *writer.*

option writing the selling of options. ***Also***: writing.

oral stop a stop order placed orally.

ordinary = *common stock.*

ordinary annuity a series of fixed payments made at the end of each period over a specified amount of time. **See**: *annuity due*; *deferred annuity.*

ordinary bond = *term bond.*

ordinary dividend a dividend paid from the ordinary profit of a company. ***Also***: regular dividend.

ordinary income the income from sale or exchange of asset that is neither a capital asset nor a Section 1231 asset.

ordinary share = *common stock.*

organizational risk the risk of loss arising from not having the right people at the right places and the appropriate organizational structure.

organized exchange the market place in which buyers and sellers follow formal rules in trading securities.

original issue discount (OID) amount by which the issue price of a bond is less than its value at redemption. **See**: *acquisition discount*; *market discount.*

original issue discount bond = *zero-coupon bond.*

original issue discount security (OIDS) = *discount security.*

original-issue high-yield bond the high-yield bond without a rating since its issuance.

original issue premium the amount by which the original issue price of a security is above its face value. ***Also***: marketing premium.

original issue stock the stock issued when the corporation is incorporated.

original maturity the interval between the issue date and the maturity date of a bond. **See**: *current maturity.*

original price the price at which an option position was established.

originating investment banker = *managing underwriter.*

originator = *managing underwriter.*

orphan stock = *wallflower.*

OTB option tender bond

OTC over-the-counter

OTC margin stock the stock traded in the OTC market that qualifies as a margin security.

OTC option = *conventional option.*

OTM out-of-the money

OU up-and-out price

"out" barrier = *knockout price.*

"out" clearing checks, bills etc. sent by a bank for clearing at the clearing house. **See**: *"in" clearing.*

outer CDO the basic, underlying portfolio of CDO in a CDO squared. ***Also***: master CDO; underlying CDO. **See**: *inner CDO.*

out-of-cash date the date on which a firm with a high *burn rate* will run out of cash if the current burn rate remains constant. **See**: *internal measure.*

out-of-favor stock = *wallflower.*

out-of-line stock a stock that is too high or too low in price in comparison with the similar quality stocks.

out of the money (OTM) of an option the strike of which is above the market price of the underlying in the case of a call, or below in the case of a put. **See**: *deep out of the money*; *in the money.*

out-of-the-money call a call option with a strike price well above the market price of the underlying asset. ***Also***: upside call. **See**: *in-the-money put*; *underwater option.*

out-of-the-money loan value difference between the futures settlement price and the option strike price multiplied by the factor then by the quantity.

out-of-the-money put a put option with a strike well below the current market price of the underlying. ***Also***: down-side put. ***See***: *in-the-money call.*

out-of-the-money spot an option with no intrinsic value with respect to the current spot rate.

out of the name words meaning no longer having an active position in the stock.

out of the window = *blowout.*

out option = *knock-out option.*

outperform <verb> to have a better return than other similar investments. ***Also***: market outperform. ***Opp***: *underperform.*

outperformance option an option with the payoff based on the amount by which the payoff of one of two underlying assets or indexes outperforms the other. ***Also***: dual option; relative performance option; underperformance option. ***See***: *alternative option*; *differential option*; *Margrabe option*; *multi-index option*; *rainbow option.*

output flag a basis for determining which results will be returned from a particular function.

outright the forward exchange without a corresponding transaction in the spot. ***Also***: outright deal. ***Opp***: *swap*

outright contract = *single option.*

outright deal = *outright.*

outright forward = *forward currency contract.*

outright forward exchange = *pure swap.*

outright forward rate = *outright rate.*

outright method the method of foreign exchange quotation by using numbers. ***Also***: flat outright forward method. ***See***: *point method.*

outright quote a quote in which all the digits of the bid and offer are quoted. ***See***: *points quote.*

outright rate the actual forward rate expressed in dollars per currency unit, or vice versa. ***Also***: outright forward rate.

outside barrier the barrier option under which the asset whose price serves as the trigger price for the price is different from the underlying asset. ***See***: *inside barrier.*

outside debt a debt in the form of a bond. ***Opp***: *inside debt.*

outside market = *over-the-counter market.*

outside price = *off-board price.*

outside quote bid and asked price of an unlisted stock given to a client.

outside the fees an issue of securities that trades outside the fees, thus causing the underwriter to lose money. ***Opp***: *inside the fees.*

outstanding security a security which has not yet been redeemed or bought back by the issuer.

outstanding shares the shares in the hands of stockholders. ***Also***: issued and outstanding; issued capital stock; issued shares; shares outstanding. ***See***: *float.*

outstrike price the *barrier price* the change in which can make the terms of an *exotic option* change. ***Also***: dropout price. ***See***: *instrike price.*

out the window = *blowout.*

out trade a trade which cannot be cleared by the clearing house.

outward arbitrage the conversion of the home currency into the currency of a foreign country whose interest rate is higher. ***See***: *inward arbitrage.*

overall market price coverage the total assets less intangibles divided by the total of the market value of the security issue and the book value of the liabilities and issues having a prior claim.

overallotment an underwriting situation in which more orders for shares of stock exist than there are shares to fill the orders. ***See***: *oversubscribed.*

overallotment provision = *green shoe.*

overall yield = *yield to maturity.*

over-and-away call = *up-and-out call.*

overbooked = *oversubscribed.*

overbought <1> price has risen to an unreasonable high. <2> bought in large scale. <3> = *long position.*

overdue delivery = *delayed delivery.*

overhang a theory which holds that the release of sizable block of securities or commodities would put the prices down. ***Also***: market overhang.

overhanging issue convertible securities that cannot be converted due to a lower market price.

overlap the market to create a crossed market by expressing a willingness to sell on the bid side of the market and buy on the offer side.

overlay program a program designed to reduce the currency risk in a global asset portfolio.

overlay strategy the managed futures portfolio which is added to an existing portfolio to introduce new exposure.

overleveraged when the amount of debt in a firm's capital structure or required debt service is large enough to create potential financial distress and possible business failure.

overnight a transaction from today until the next business day.

overnight buying power two times the equity in a margin account.

overnight delivery risk a risk incurred when the delivery of funds between 2 districts, where there is equation of time, has to be transferred overnight.

overnight financing rate the interest rate at which the investment dealers and other financial market participants lend and borrow funds for a period of one business day. ***See***: *call money rate*; *overnight rate.*

overnight indexed swap (OIS swap) = *overnight index swap.*

overnight index swap (OIS swap) the interest rate swap involving the overnight rate being exchanged for some fixed rate of interest. ***Also***: call-money swap; overnight indexed swap.

overnight limit net long or short position in one or more currencies that can be carried over to the next trading day.

overnight position broker/dealer's long position or short position in a security at the end of a trading day.

overnight price gap the gap between the opening price and the closing price of a previous day.

overnight rate the interest rate at which a bank lends available funds to another bank overnight. ***See***: *call money rate*; *overnight financing rate.*

overnight repo a repo that provides for a secured lending for 24 hours.

overnight swap a foreign exchange swap that involves exchange of overnight rate for a fixed rate.

overnight trade the trade which is not liquidated on the same trading day.

overpriced a situation when the implied volatility is higher than the historical volatility. ***Opp***: *underpriced.*

overreaction hypothesis a supposition that investors overreact to unanticipated news resulting in exaggerated movement in prices followed by corrections.

oversold <1> a market that is believed to have declined to an unreasonable low level and would begin to rise. ***Also***: bottom-out; graveled. ***See***: *grounding*. <2> = *short position*.

oversubscribed the subscriptions from potential buyers to a new issue are more than the planned amount to be issued. ***Also***: overbooked. ***See***: *over-allotment*.

oversubscription privilege in a rights issue, arrangement by which the shareholders are given the right to apply for any shares that are not taken up during the underwriting stage.

over-the-counter (OTC) (o-t-c) <1> = *over-the-counter market*. <2> = *unlisted*.

over-the-counter derivative a derivative traded on the over-the-counter market. ***Also***: customized off-exchange derivative; privately negotiated derivative.

over-the-counter index option an index of the 100 highly capitalized, unlisted securities which will provide profit for investors who correctly gauge short-term, or OTC price movements.

over-the-counter market (OTC mar.) a market that is run by dealers mainly in securities that are unlisted and are not dealt in on the stock exchange. ***Also***: curb; curb exchange; curb market; off-board market; outside market; over-the-counter; unlisted market; unofficial market.

over-the-counter option the option which is traded in the *over-the-counter market* and can be combined into a contract.

over-the-counter security = *unlisted security*.

over-the-counter stock index future an OTC contract in which a client agrees to a delivery date that is based on a stock price index's quoted value.

over-the-counter transaction a financial transaction done other than on an exchange.

overtrading <1> the practice whereby the member of an underwriting syndicate induces a client to buy a portion of a new issue by buying other securities from the client at a *guaranteed spread*. ***Also***: spread swap. <2> = *churning*.

overvalued currency a currency that is traded above what the market believes to be its correct value. ***Opp***: *under-valued currency*.

overvalued stock the stock the current price of which is higher than the value justified by the earnings outlook or the price-earnings ratio. ***See***: *fully valued stock*; *undervalued stock*.

overwriting writing options in excessive quantities assuming to get the premium if they are not exercised.

owner of share = *shareholder*.

owner of stock = *shareholder*.

owner's equity (OE) = *net worth*.

ownership dilution the reduction in a shareholder's ownership percentage that can arise when a firm issues new shares and current stockholders do not buy their proportional share. ***See***: *dilution*.

P p

P <1> in stock listings, meaning paid this year. <2> in options, a put. <3> the month abbreviation for September in put options. <4> Nasdaq descriptor meaning the issue is the 1st class of preferred stock. <5> the option strike price code for 80.

P-1 highest quality commercial paper

P-2 higher quality commercial paper

P-3 high quality commercial paper

PABX private automatic branch exchange

PAC <1> planned amortization class. <2> put and call.

PAC 2 bond PAC bond structured to support another PAC bond.

PAC bond a CMO bond with a sinking fund, and the principal payments are not subordinated to any other bonds. ***Also***: planned amortization class bond.

Pacers preferred adjusted to common equity redeemable stock

PAC IO bond a PAC bond which makes only interest payments.

package <1> an investment vehicle that lets an investor transform a large sum of idle cash for a small, priceless, timeless nugget of a boiler room operator's wisdom. <2> a derivative constructed from a portfolio of plain vanilla options and the underlying asset itself.

package trade = *basket trading.*

packs simultaneous buying or selling an equally weighted, consecutive series of 4 Eurodollar futures.

paid-for offer a firm offer that requires accepting parties to pay option money.

paid-in capital = *contributed capital.*

paid-in dividend = *capital dividend.*

paid-up capital = *contributed capital.*

paid up share = *fully paid share.*

painting the tape = *manipulation.*

paired off matched buy and sell orders.

paired shares the common shares of 2 companies under the same management, sold as one unit. ***Also***: Siamese share; stapled stock.

pairs trade the establishment of a long position in one stock and a short position in another at the same time.

pairs trading the trading of stocks based on the idea that prices of related stocks should be correlated.

panic selling = *unloading.*

panic trading the rapid trading of stocks or bonds in high volume in anticipation of sharply rising or falling prices.

paper <1> = *negotiable paper.* <2> = *security.*

paper EE bond traditional EE bond issued at a discount of 50% of its face value. ***See***: *electronic EE bond.*

paper gain the amount by which the market price is higher than the cost price. ***Also***: unrealized gain.

paper loss amount by which the market price of a security is less than the price it was purchased. ***Also***: negative mark-to-market; unrealized loss.

paper to bearer = *bearer note.*

paper trading making simulated trades with no money. ***Also***: mock trading.

paper value = *market value.*

par <1> = *contract grade.* <2> = *face value.* <3> = *par of exchange.*

parallel bond fixed income bond that is denominated in the respective currencies of the countries where it is sold.

parallel loan an arrangement under which two companies agree to make loans to each other's subsidiaries.

parallel rate of exchanges a situation where there are two exchange rates exist in a market.

parallel shift the movement of each point on a yield curve up or down by the same distance. ***Opp***: *nonparallel shift.*

parametric VAR = *linear VAR.*

par bond a bond sold at par.

parcel = *block.*

par coupon the coupon rate on a *par bond.*

Pareto's law = *80/20 rule.*

par floater bond spread the spread to LIBOR at which the reference entity can issue a floating rate note at the same par of the same maturity.

par forward <1> a facility set up to provide a constant price for gold producers. <2> contract with the same forward rate applying to all forward commitments. ***Also***: flat forward.

Parisian option an option for which the knock-in or knock-out is only triggered after the underlying asset has spent certain time beyond the barrier.

Paris spread = *crush spread.*

parity <1> = *intrinsic value.* <2> = *par of exchange.*

parity bond the bond issued with equal rights to the bond payments and pledged revenues.

parity price the price for a commodity pegged to another price or a composite of prices based on the history price of a prior period.

parity value = *conversion value.*

parking <1> placing the funds in a safe bond while considering alternatives. <2> = *doctoring.*

parking a security <1> placing securities of a target company in a third party in a takeover. <2> buying securities from a party and selling them to the original holder in a short period.

parking violation the illegal holding or financing of stock by a third party, in which the third party's reason for holding is to conceal ownership of a raider.

Parkinson's historical volatility the volatility formula developed by Michael Parkinson in 1980 for estimating the volatility of the expected returns for a random walk using the high and low in any particular period. ***Also***: high low range volatility.

par of exchange the price of money in one national currency exchanged at the official rate in another currency. ***Also***: exchange parity; exchange quotation; par; parity; par value; peg.

PARP price-adjusted rate preferred stock

par swap <1> = *at-market swap.* <2> = *par value swap.*

par swap curve = *swap curve.*

par swap yield curve = *swap curve.*

part contingent knock-in option the *knock-in option* with a low initial premium and an additional premium paid if the knock-in trigger is activated before the expiration date.

partial barrier option an option where barrier exists only in certain time interval. ***Also***: discrete barrier option.

partial double-barrier option a double-barrier option with just the front-end or rear-end barrier.

partial duration applying some of the principles of duration analysis to rate changes that affect only part of the yield curve. ***Also***: reshaping duration.

See: *Macaulay duration; modified duration.*

partial lookback option = *reset option.*

partial lookback warrant = *anti-crash warrant.*

partially participating preferred stock the preferred stock that, in addition to preferred dividends, can participate in receiving common stock dividends on a pro rata basis up to a fixed rate. ***See***: *fully participating preferred stock.*

partially protected equity-linked note an *equity-linked note* with full participation on the upside, but only partial participation on the downside.

partial redemption the corporation's re-acquisition of part of its own stock from a shareholder or shareholders.

partial spinoff a parent company's selling some shares of a subsidiary. ***Also***: carve-out; equity carve-out.

partial strip a bond with a zero-risk property for a given period but behaves like a coupon bond after that period.

partial-term hedging a hedging for only the selected portion of the cash flow of a debt obligation.

participant <1> the partner of a member firm or shareholder of a member company. ***See***: *market participant.* <2> one who uses a clearing agency to clear the transactions in securities or to transfer, hypothecate or pledge securities.

participating buyer <1> the buyer who is willing to buy in line with the market. <2> the buyer who goes along with another buyer in a *percentage order.*

participating cap a partial cap which reduces but does not eliminate exposure to an upward price or rate move.

participating capped floating-rate note the note with features of an ordinary *floating rate note* and a capped floating-rate note. ***Also***: participating note.

participating collar a collar with full participation above a certain level.

participating derivative the derivative that allows the holder to participate in the upside of the instrument either by giving up protection on the downside or by limiting the upside of products that in their vanilla form have unlimited profit potential.

participating equity preferred stock (PEPS) the *convertible preferred stock* with enhanced dividend participation feature. ***Also***: equity redeemable bond; mandatory conversion premium dividend preferred stock; mandatory convertible; preference equity redemption cumulative stock; preferred adjusted to common equity redeemable stock; preferred equity redemption convertible; preferred equity redemption stock; preferred income participation security; premium income common stock.

participating forward a forward contract in which the buyer accepts a rate below the current forward market in return for a fixed-rate participation in a favorable difference between the spot at expiration and the lower rate. ***Also***: profit-sharing forward; ratio forward.

participating mortgage the mortgage with a provision allowing the lender to share in any increase in the value of the underlying asset. ***Also***: shared appreciation mortgage.

participating note = *participating capped floating-rate note.*

participating option the option which changes the rate of participation in a price or rate movement beyond the strike price of the underlying asset. ***Also***: profit sharing option.

participating preferred = *participating preferred stock.*

participating preferred stock a preferred stock that gives the holder the right to participate in the earnings in addition to dividend. ***Also***: participating preferred; preferred ordinary share. **See**: *non-participating preferred stock.*

participating range forward a variant of a range forward with some participation in the movement of the underlying below the lower strike or above the upper strike or both. ***Also***: forward plus.

participating seller <1> the seller who is willing to sell in line with the market. <2> a seller who goes along with another seller in a *percentage order.*

participating swap an interest rate swap with a participating interest rate cap on part of the notional principal modifying the floating-rate payments.

participating swaption the participating option in which the option is a swap on another option.

participating trust = *unit investment trust.*

participating underwriter one who agrees to distribute a fraction of the issue. ***Also***: sub underwriter. **See**: *managing underwriter.*

participation bond the bond with a minimum coupon and an additional payment based on the profitability of the issuing company.

participation certificate (PC) <1> certificate issued by a cooperative evidencing membership. <2> a security issued by a company with a payoff pattern similar to equity-linked note. <3> a security issued to create additional class of shares with a different dividend or reduced restrictions on share transfer. ***Also***: bearer certificate; bearer participation certification. <4> = *pass-through security.*

partly paid share a share the holder of which is required to pay a part of the face value. ***Also***: contributing share. **See**: *called-up capital*; *fully paid share.*

partner's capital = *partner's equity.*

partner's equity the amount by which the asset value of a partnership exceeds its liabilities. ***Also***: capital equity; partner's capital; partnership equity.

partnership equity = *partner's equity.*

par value <1> = *face value.* <2> = *par of exchange.*

par value stock a stock with a par value assigned by the issuing company. ***Also***: stock with a par value. **See**: *no-par-value stock.*

par value swap a standard swap that involves no initial exchange of payment of principal. ***Also***: par swap. **See**: *nonpar swap.*

par yield the coupon rate on a bond necessary for the bond to sell at par.

par yield curve the curve formed by the yields to maturity associated with the bonds currently selling at par.

passed dividend <1> <preferred stock> = *dividend in arrears.* <2> <common stock> = *omitted dividend.*

passive arbitrage the foreign exchange arbitrage without covering long or short position. **Opp**: *active arbitrage.*

passive bond the bond that yields no interest, usually issued for charitable or non-profit purposes.

passive investment management buying a well diversified portfolio of stock to represent a broad-based market index.

passive management an investment strategy which mirrors a market index and does not attempt to beat the market.

passive market-making the process which allows a market maker to be both an underwriter and a buyer of securities in a *secondary offering.*

passive portfolio strategy a strategy that relies on diversification to match the performance of a benchmark index.

passport option an option on an actively managed portfolio or any portfolio with a variable or uncertain composition. ***Also***: preferred trader option.

pass-through = *pass-through security.*

pass-through asset trust security (PATS) = *put-call note.*

pass-through certificate = *pass-through security.*

pass-through coupon rate the interest rate paid on a *pass-through security.*

pass-through security the mortgage-backed security the principal and interest of the underlying mortgages are passed from the mortgagee to the security holders. ***Also***: Ginnie Mae pass-through; mortgage pass-through; mortgage pass-through security; participation certificate; pass-through; pass-through certificate; pay-through security.

past reset rate the rate observed at the rate reset date just before the valuation date.

path-dependent floater the floating-rate note with embedded collars or caps that limit the floating-rate adjustment to, for example, 25 basis points from one reset to the next. ***Also***: near perfect floater.

path-dependent option the option the value of which depends on the sequence of prices of the underlying asset rather than the final price of the asset. ***See***: *nonpath-dependent option.*

path-independent option = *nonpath-dependent option.*

patronage dividend the dividend paid by a cooperative to a person for whom or with whom the cooperative does business, but not necessarily a member.

PATS pass-through asset trust security

pattern gap a gap which usually forms a fixed pattern, like exhaustion gap, run-away gap, breakaway gap, etc.

payable date = *distribution date.*

pay as you go option = *continuation option.*

payback the recovery of the invested capital. ***Also***: return.

payback period <1> period of time which passes before the cash inflow equals cash outflow on an investment project. ***Also***: bailout period; cost recovery period; pay off; period of cost recovery. <2> time needed to pay off the debts.

pay cash = *for cash.*

pay day = *account day.*

pay-down a sum by which the principal amount of bonds maturing exceeds the amount of new bonds being issued to replace them. ***See***: *new money.*

payer default swaption = *protection call.*

payer option a CDS option to buy credit default protection against credit risk. ***See***: *receiver option.*

payer's swaption a swaption giving the holder the right to pay a fixed rate and receive a floating rate in an interest rate swap. ***Also***: buyer's right to pay fixed swaption; call swaption; payer swaption.

payer swaption = *payer's swaption.*

pay-fixed/receive-floating swap a swap that pays fixed interest rate and receive floating interest rate. ***Also***: fixed-floating swap.

pay-floating/receive-fixed swap a swap that pays floating interest rate and receives fixed interest rate. ***Also***: floating-fixed swap.

paying agent the agent, usually a bank paying dividends and bond interests for the issuing company. ***Also***: disbursing agent.

pay-in-kind (PIK) = *payment-in-kind security.*

pay later option (PLO) <1> a *contingent premium option* the buyer of which pays a fixed amount, at expiration, if the option would otherwise have had a positive payoff. <2> = *contingent premium option.*

payment bond a bond for guaranteeing the payment to workers, subcontractors and the material suppliers of a construction project.

payment date = *distribution date.*

payment enhanced capital security (Peacs) = *prescribed right to income and maximum equity.*

payment frequency the frequency of interest payment.

payment-in-kind bond (PIK bond) a bond that gives the issuer an option (during an initial period) either to make coupon payments in cash or to give the bond-holder a similar bond.

payment-in-kind security (PIK security) a bond which pays interest in the form of additional bonds, or preferred stock that pays dividends in the form of additional preferred stock. ***Also***: pay-in-kind.

payment netting = *netting.*

payments netting = *netting.*

payment versus payment (PVP) the simultaneous settlement standard in foreign exchange market, whereby the payment of one currency is made against the payment of another.

payoff <1> the net profit or loss from an option spread. <2> the cash flow realized from a derivative at maturity. <3> = *payback period.* <4> = *rate of return.*

payoff diagram a chart of the profits and losses for a particular options strategy prepared in advance of the execution of the strategy.

payoff table a table with two columns showing the value of underlying and the corresponding payoff by either party.

pay on exercise option = *contingent premium option.*

payout pattern the chart of an option's value at expiration over a range of the prices of the underlying.

payout profile a graph which shows the amount that will be realized from the exercise of an option in relation to the movement in price of the underlying.

payout protected option a put or call option with a strike adjustment feature to compensate for periodic cash payout such as dividends.

payout ratio = *dividend-payout ratio.*

payout return portion of the concurrent spot price that is to be paid out in the remaining life of a derivative.

pay-receive spread = *bid-ask spread.*

pay-through bond a combination of the mortgage-backed bond and pass-through security.

pay-through security = *pass through security.*

pay-to-play the attempts by municipal bond underwriters to gain influence with political officials who decide which underwriters are awarded the business.

pay-up <1> the situation when an investor who wants to buy a stock hesitates and the stock price begins to rise. ***See***: *whipsawed.* <2> a deal when an investor buys shares in a high quality company at what is felt to be a higher price than its fair value.

P/B <1> price/book ratio. <2> price to book ratio.

PBOT Philadelphia Board of Trade

P/C put/call ratio

PCF price/cash flow ratio

P-coast Pacific Stock Exchange

PCPO portfolio currency protection option

P/C ratio put/call ratio

PCS Property Claims Service index

PCS option a CBOT option with the *Property Claims Service index* as the underlying.

PCX Pacific Exchange

PE price/earnings ratio

peace dividend the alternative use of government spending from military to peacetime purposes, such as housing, education, and social projects.

Peacs payment enhanced capital security

pecking-order review the theory which holds the internally generated fund is the most preferred source of capital, followed by the new debt, then debt-equity hybrid, and finally new equity.

P/E effect = *low P/E effect.*

peer group stocks issued by companies engaged in similar business operations.

PEG price/earnings growth

peg = *par-of exchange.*

pegged to the market the price of a new stock offering will be based on the price of the previously issued stocks.

pegging <1> fixing or stabilizing the rate or price. <2> using derivatives to offset a decline in the price of a commodity so that previously written puts will expire worthless, thus protecting the premiums received. <3> = *stabilization.*

pegging the exchange a transaction in foreign exchange with stabilization fund to maintain the exchange rate.

PEG ratio price/earnings growth ratio

PEGY ratio price/earnings to growth and dividend yield ratio

PEN protected equity note

penalty bid syndicate member's bid to stabilize the price of a new issue in the after market.

pence rate <UK> = *direct quote.*

penny stock the stock that sells for less than $1 in initial public offering, which may rise to $10 or above later. ***See***: *cheap stock*; *chop stock*; *drill-bit stock.*

pension obligation bond the municipal bond issued in the hope of earning a return which will exceed the interest cost.

pension parachute a poison pill which provides that in the event of a hostile takeover, any excess pension plan assets can only be used to benefit plan participants.

penultimate coupon date the date on which the penultimate coupon is paid. ***Also***: penultimate coupon payment date.

penultimate coupon payment date = *penultimate coupon date.*

penultimate profit prospect (PPP) the second-lowest-priced of the 10 highest-yielding stocks in the DJIA.

people pill the *poison pill* in which the current management threatens to quit in the event of a *hostile takeover.*

PEP protected equity participation.

PEPS participating equity preferred

stock

PERC preferred equity redemption convertible

percentage of outstanding share traded the number of common shares traded each month divided by the total number of shares outstanding.

percentage premium the premium over the parity of a convertible bond divided by the parity.

percent cap the interest rate cap with a payout that has a percentage relationship to the payout on a normal cap.

percent cash and bonds proportion of a mutual fund's assets represented by cash and government bonds.

percent over/undervalued (% O/U) the percentage difference between the current market price and the theoretical value of an option.

percent-to-double the percentage the underlying has to move for the option to double in price. ***Also***: % double.

PERCS preference equity redemption cumulative stock

perfect asset swap an asset swap one party takes the risk and guarantees the recovery rate of the defaulted asset. ***See***: *clean asset swap.*

perfect capital market a perfect market under which there is no opportunity for arbitrage.

perfect hedge a hedge that equals 100 % of the subject being hedged. ***Also***: naive hedge; one-to-one hedge; risk-free hedge. ***Opp***: *imperfect hedge.*

perfect market view <1> the analysis of a company's capital structure to show the irrelevance of capital structure in a perfect market. <2> the analysis of a dividend policy to show irrelevance of capital structure in a perfect market.

perfect swap = *zero basis risk swap.*

performance bond the funds that must be deposited by a customer with the brokers to ensure the financial integrity of the brokers, clearing houses and exchange.

performance fee the annual fee paid to the hedge fund manager based on his performance. ***Also***: incentive fee.

performance fund = *go-go fund.*

performance index paper (PIP) the commercial paper variation on the currency coupon swap.

performance plus share common share index issued by a financial intermediary which promises buyers the total return from the underlying or index plus an additional return.

performance risk = *credit risk.*

performance stock = *growth stock.*

period-certain annuity = *fixed annuity.*

periodic cap = *step-up cap.*

periodic coupon increase = *jump.*

periodic purchase deferred contract an annuity for which fixed premiums are paid, but does not begin paying out until a time elected by the annuitant.

periodic rate-setting swap = *periodic reset swap.*

periodic redemption plan an investment plan under which a firm systematically redeems small portion of its outstanding stock.

periodic reset swap the swap with the floating-rate based on the average rate on an index rather than the market rate. ***Also***: periodic rate-setting swap.

periodic return a percentage change in the value of an asset, including the reinvestment of income, assuming no contributions or disbursements.

period of cost recovery = *payback period.*

PERLS principal exchange-rate-linked security

permanent capital the sum of *common stock, preferred stock* and *retained earnings*. ***See***: *contributed capital.*

permanent financing long-term financing that uses either debt instrument or equity shares.

permanent interest-bearing share (PI-BS) the share issued by a bank that is redeemable only if the issuing bank is liquidated and last in priority in that event.

Perp perpetual preferred stock

perpendicular spread = *vertical spread.*

per-period return swap a swap with a return that changes in different period.

perpetual American option a perpetual option that can be exercised any time before maturity.

perpetual bond = *annuity bond.*

perpetual floater a floater without fixed maturity.

perpetual option an option without the expiration date. ***Also***: expirationless option.

perpetual preferred stock (Perp) fixed-rate share with no participation in the issuer's earnings and no promise of principal repayment.

perpetual security a security that is never called in for redemption.

perpetual stock = *buffer stock.*

perpetual warrant a stock option which has no expiration date.

PERS preferred equity redemption stock.

petrobond the bond with the principal repayment indexed to oil prices.

petrodollar foreign exchange reserve of oil producing nations from oil sale.

P/FCF price/free cash flow ratio

PFX options = *international options.*

phantom bid placing client's orders to buy certain stocks on the electronic trading systems and later canceling those orders. ***Also***: spoof bid.

phantom option plan a deferred employee compensation plan where employees receive *phantom stock options.*

phantom stock = *shadow stock.*

phantom stock award = *phantom stock option.*

phantom stock option a stock option the holder of which receives a number of units that equate to, but are not, shares in the issuer. ***Also***: phantom stock award.

phantom stock plan the incentive plan that awards managers bonus shares based on the increase in the market price of the company's stock.

phi = *golden ratio.*

phone switching the ability to transfer cash between mutual funds in the same family by a telephone call.

PHQ = *XO.*

physical commodity = *cash commodity.*

physical market = *cash market.*

physical option the right to purchase a *physical commodity*, as opposed to a stock index or commodity contract, at a set price at a later date.

physicals = *cash commodity.*

physical settlement the settlement of a derivative by physically delivering the underlying asset.

PIBS permanent interest-bearing share

pickup the value gained in a bond swap with similar coupon rates and maturities but different basis.

pickup bond a *callable bond* issued with a high coupon and a short call date.

pickup swap a bond swap with the same coupon maturities at a basis which is advantageous to the swapper.

PICS premium income common stock

picture the bid and asked prices and the quantity of a security. ***Also***: run.

pieced-together swap the swap of some small exchange transaction with different parties. **See**: *pure swap*.

piece of action = *active stock*.

PIF pooled income fund

piggyback <1> to buy a stock according to the trades of another person who the buyer thinks will succeed. <2> = *piggy-back offering*.

piggyback offering underwriter's selling of a private stock company's shares in combination with an offering of new shares of other companies to the public. ***Also***: piggyback.

piggyback option the stock option that when converted to a share automatically creates another option.

PIK bond payment-in-kind bond

PIK security payment-in-kind security

PIMS portfolio insurance for municipal securities

PIN portfolio income note

Pine public income note

pink button <UK> a clerk who is not a member in London Stock Exchange. **See**: *blue button*.

pink sheet a quote sheet of stocks dealt over the counter. ***Also***: the sheet.

pink sheet stock inactive OTC stocks not included in Nasdaq's daily listing.

pinning the strike tendency of a stock's price to close near the strike of heavily traded options at the expiration date.

pin risk = *exploding delta*.

PIP performance index paper

pip the smallest price increment in a currency quotation. ***Also***: point; price interest point; tick.

pipeline the process, including registration with SEC, that must be completed before a public offering. ***Also***: 30-day visible supply.

Pipes private investments in public equities

PIPS preferred income participation security

pip value the currency value per pip of a currency pair. $10 for EUR/USD, $8.40 for USD/JPY.

pit = *ring*.

pit broker = *local*.

pivotal stock a listed stock that leads by its movements and price directions of the market.

placed deal = *best effort*.

placement ratio percentage of the past week's new municipal bonds offerings sold by underwriters, compiled weekly, every Thursday by the Daily Bond Buyer.

placing <1> an underwriting in which the underwriter buys the shares and places them to its customers without itself buying the shares. **See**: *private placement*. <2> = *offering*.

placing power the ability of a bank or broker to sell securities to investors.

plain bond = *unsecured bond*.

plain swap a swap with standard terms: the first party pays the fixed rate and the other pays the floating rate. ***Also***: basic swap; conventional swap; generic swap; plain vanilla swap; pure vanilla swap; simple swap; standard swap; vanilla swap. ***See***: *coupon swap.*

plain vanilla without special features.

plain vanilla derivative a derivative that is simple in structure and is priced at current market level and strike price.

plan vanilla fixed-floating swap = *coupon swap.*

plain vanilla option = *vanilla option.*

plain vanilla swap = *plain swap.*

planned amortization bond the CMO bond with minimal prepayment risk.

planned amortization class bond (PAC) = *PAC bond.*

plastic bond the bond collateralized by packaged credit card installment debts, with interest and principal paid from the installment payments.

plateau = *platform.*

platform a short range in which price will not change. ***Also***: plateau.

playing the market = *speculation.*

playing the yield curve <1> funding long-term assets with short-term liabilities with a normal yield curve. <2> = *riding the yield curve.*

PLO pay later option

plowback = *earnings retention.*

plowback ratio = *earnings retention ratio.*

plunge = *dip.*

plus accrued interest = *and interest.*

PND privately negotiated derivative

PO bond a principal only CMO bond that is created by stripping the interest cash flow from the mortgage collateral.

POD account an account payable to one person in his or her lifetime and on death payable to one or more POD payees.

Poisson process a process that changes instantaneously from one value to another at random times.

point <1> unit of the price movement, $1 for a share of stock, 1% of the par value for a bond. ***Also***: base point; basic point. ***See***: *basis point; fluctuation.* <2> fees paid to induce lenders to make mortgage loans at a lower interest rate. ***Also***: buy-down; mortgage point. <3> = *pip.*

point barrier option a barrier option the barrier is only in effect at a single point in time. ***Also***: European barrier option.

point method a method of showing foreign exchange rate movement in points, under which one point equals 0.0004. ***See***: *outright method.*

points quote a quote showing points only. ***See***: *digits deleted; outright quote.*

poison pill *anti-takeover measure* used to make the company less attractive by issuing a new preferred stock that gives the shareholders the right to redeem it at a premium. ***Also***: back-in poison pill.

poison put the covenant allowing the bondholder to demand repayment in the event of a hostile takeover.

policyholder loan bond the bond that is secured by the surrender value of some insurance policies.

Polish dividend = *split down.*

political risk the risk exposure that a country's government will change its policies and rules. ***Also***: country risk; sovereign risk.

pollution future a futures contract that is based on US-based utilities' transferable rights to emit sulphur dioxide.

pool <1> any combination of resources or funds for common benefits. <2>

the combination of persons organized for the purpose of exploiting equity stocks. <3> = *syndicate.*

pooled fund = *commingled fund.*

pooled income fund (PIF) = *commingled fund.*

pooled inventory program the process used to consolidate the financial assets such as residential mortgages into a structure which generates single or multiple payment streams which are then marketed as specific securities.

pooled shares the shares belonging to the owners who have formed a contract whereby those shares will be pooled together for their common benefit.

pooled trust fund = *common trust fund.*

pool operator = *commodity pool operator.*

poop and scoop a group of informed investors trying to push down a stock by spreading false information and rumors on the Internet.

POP public offering price

pop up option a joint and survivor option which allows an employee to be reinstated to the basic pension if the spouse predeceases the retiree.

pork bellies the commodities underlying the majority of futures contracts trading pork livestock.

portfolio the holdings of more than one security, commodity, real estate, cash, or other asset. ***Also***: investment portfolio.

portfolio allocation the proportion of a fund's assets invested in each of stocks, bonds and cash equivalents.

portfolio beta the weighted sum of individual asset betas, according to the proportions of investment in the portfolio.

portfolio credit derivative a credit derivative product with more than one reference entity. **See**: *single name credit derivative.*

portfolio currency protection option (PCPO) = *equity-linked foreign exchange option.*

portfolio delta the weighted sum of the deltas of the securities in a portfolio.

portfolio gamma the weighted sum of the gammas of securities in a portfolio.

portfolio hedging the construction of a portfolio of hedges using derivatives.

portfolio immunization = *immunization.*

portfolio income note (PIN) = *equity-linked note.*

portfolio insurance <1> using a *leveraged portfolio* in the underlying to create a synthetic put to protect the portfolios from a market crash. **See**: *dynamic hedging.* <2> = *dynamic hedging.*

portfolio insurance for municipal securities (PIMS) a portfolio insurance that requires prepayment of premium by the issuing company through the put exercise date, renewable annually thereafter.

portfolio investment = *investment in securities.*

portfolio management = *money management.*

portfolio manager = *investment adviser.*

portfolio mapping the relationship of market value of a portfolio with risk factors.

portfolio of swaps the collection of swaps under one investment. ***Also***: portfolio swaps.

portfolio optimization = *optimization of a portfolio.*

portfolio option a multi-asset option the underlying of which is a portfolio.

portfolio R^2 the number between 0 and 1 which measures the strength of correlation of movement between the portfolio or a stock and the index.

portfolio replicating creating a portfolio which contains the underlying asset that replicates the given payoff.

portfolio restructuring the recomposition of a portfolio's asset mix by selling certain assets and buying desired ones.

portfolio risk = *credit risk.*

portfolio selection the process of selecting assets to obtain optimal balance between risk and reward.

portfolio separation theorem = *fisher's separation theorem.*

portfolio simulation prediction of the future value that a portfolio may have based on changes in the market prices which affect the elements of a portfolio.

portfolio swaps = *portfolio of swaps.*

portfolio theory = *modern portfolio theory.*

portfolio tilting making changes in the industry sector or style weighting in a portfolio in order to improve investment performance.

portfolio trade = *basket trading.*

portfolio transition management = *transition management.*

portfolio turnover the rate of trading activity in a mutual fund's portfolio of investments, it equals the lesser of purchases or sales divided by average total assets in one year.

portfolio variance the weighted sum of the covariance and variances of assets in a portfolio.

position <1> the bank's net balance in a foreign currency. <2> the investor's ownership in a security, either long or short. <3> = *financial position.*

position building the action of buying shares to accumulate long position or selling them to create a short position. ***Also***: taking a position.

position day the first day in the process of making or taking delivery of the actual commodity on a futures contract.

position delta the sum of all positive and negative deltas within a hedged trading position.

position delta neutral zero position delta.

position diagram a diagram showing the possible payoffs from a derivative.

positioning choosing a market niche for a product taking into consideration the price, promotion, distribution, packaging, competition, marketplace, etc.

positioning a swap = *booking a swap.*

position limit <1> the number of contracts that can be purchased in one commodity before a speculator is classified as a large trader subject to oversight by CFTC. ***Also***: trading limit. <2> the maximum number (2000) of the exchange-listed options which can be owned or controlled by the individual holder or by a group of holders acting jointly, in the same underlying asset.

position risk the risk that losses in the value of a position will be incurred as a result of adverse market movements.

position self an investor who is going long or short in anticipation of a stock's movement.

position sizing the dollar value being invested into a particular security.

position squaring eliminating a position by buying back a short position or selling a long position.

position trader <1> commodities trader who takes a long-term position. ***See***: *buy and hold.* <2> = *swing trader.*

position trading = *swing trading.*

positive carry the situation in which the cost of money borrowed to buy securities is lower than the yield of the securities. ***See***: *carry*; *negative carry.*

positive cash flow collar the collar that will result in positive cash flow to end users.

positive covenant the bond covenant that specifies the actions the firm must take. ***Also***: affirmative covenant.

positive convexity a reference to the curvature which is found in the price-yield function on a straight bond.

positive delta the delta of a call or put option, which is a positive figure. ***See***: *negative delta.*

positive duration gap a duration gap in positive figure, meaning that the cash flows from the assets will exceed total debt service. ***See***: *negative duration gap.*

positive gamma an option position the gamma of which is positive. ***See***: *gamma neutral*; *negative gamma.*

positive yield curve = *normal yield curve.*

post date the date on an instrument that is later than the date on which it was drawn. ***Also***: date forward.

post dating setting the date of a financial instrument that is later than the actual date on which it was drawn. ***Also***: dating forward; forward dating.

post-liquidation return an after-tax return for a fund calculated as if the entire position had been liquidated. ***See***: *pre-liquidation return.*

postponed offering the public offering that is held until market conditions improve.

postponement option the option to postpone a project without canceling it.

post-trade benchmark the price after the decision to trade. ***See***: *pre-trade benchmark.*

pot = *institutional pot.*

potential exposure a credit exposure that may develop on an obligation due to possible changes in its market value.

potentially dilutive securities the stock options and convertible securities due to their potential to be exchanged for the common stock and thereby dilute EPS.

potential return the potential return on writing naked calls, it is the premium divided by margin requirement.

pot is clean = *absorption.*

Pound cost averaging <UK> = *constant dollar plan.*

power bond <1> a bond with a coupon bearing an interest rate with exponential relationship to a reference rate. <2> a *bull floater* with the interest rate set to the square value of a benchmark.

power derivative a derivative structure that incorporates leverage that is unusual either on account of its magnitude or non-linearity, e. g. an option with a power of the intrinsic value at maturity. ***See:*** *$LIBOR^2$ swap*

power-law distribution = *excess kurtosis.*

power option an option the payoff of which is based on the price of an asset raised to a power. ***Also***: turbo option.

power swap = *leveraged swap.*

power warrant a stock warrant with the payout determined by the square value of a rate or spread.

PPP <1> penultimate profit prospect. <2> principal protected product. <3> purchasing power parity.

practical merger <1> the merger of a subsidiary into its parent corporation. ***Also***: Section 332 liquidation; short-form merger; upstream merger. <2> = *Type C reorganization.*

pre-announced trading = *sunshine trade.*

pre-arranged trading the fraudulent practice of carrying out risk-free trades at the predetermined prices to acquire tax advantages.

precious metal valuable metal such as gold, platinum and silver.

precision of mean half-width of a 95% confidence interval, calculated as 1.96 multiplied by *mean standard error* used in variance reduction.

predator company = *acquiring company.*

prediction bias the tendency of forward interest rates to forecast higher future spot interest rates than the rates that actually occur. ***Also***: forward rate bias.

pre-emptive right = *stock right.*

preference bond the income bond or adjustment bond with precedence over other bonds of the same issuer. ***Also***: priority bond; prior-lien bond.

preference dependent the approach to valuation in which the value of an asset depends on the investors' particular preferences with respect to risk.

preference equity redemption cumulative stock (PERC) (PERCS) = *participating equity preferred stock.*

preference free an asset valuation method in which the value of an asset is invariant to investors' preferences with respect to risk.

preference option = *as-you-like option.*

preference share = *preferred stock.*

preference stock the stock ranking junior to preferred stock but senior to common stock. **See**: *junior stock.*

preferential rate = *bank prime interest rate.*

preferred adjusted to common equity redeemable stock (Pacers) = *participating equity preferred stock.*

preferred bailout tax avoidance plan whereby the company issues preferred stock tax free, followed by stockholders' sales to outsiders, then the company will buy it back. ***Also***: preferred stock bailout. **See**: *Section 306 stock.*

preferred dividend the dividend paid to stockholders of preferred stock. ***Also***: non-discretionary dividend; preferred stock dividend. **See**: *common dividend.*

preferred dividend coverage income after interests and taxes divided by preferred stock capital.

preferred equity redemption convertible (PERC) = *participating equity preferred stock.*

preferred equity redemption cumulative stock (PERCS) a high yield preferred cumulative stock issued by Morgan Stanley Dean Witter, which can be called any time with a call price at a premium.

preferred equity redemption stock (PERS) = *participating equity preferred stock.*

preferred income participation security (PIPS) = *participating equity preferred stock.*

preferred ordinary shares <UK> = *participating preferred stock.*

preferred preferred = *prior-preferred stock.*

preferred redeemable increased dividend equity security (Prides) = *dividend enhanced convertible stock.*

preferred security a security with fixed payment as bond and dividend preference as preferred stock. **See**: *newer issue; traditional preferred security.*

preferred stock a stock which entities the holder to some preferential rights to dividend. ***Also***: preference share. **See**: *common stock*.

preferred stock bailout = *preferred bail-out*.

preferred stock dividend = *preferred dividend*.

preferred trader option = *passport option*.

PREG price of a stock divided by sales over earnings growth. **See**: *PSSG*.

pre-holiday liquidation heavy selling of stocks on a day before a holiday.

pre-IPO convertible a bond with an initial par value established below the IPO price.

pre-IPO quiet period = *quiet period*.

preliquidation return after-tax return for a fund calculated as if the position was still held at the end of a period leaving unrealized tax consequences. **See**: *post-liquidation return*.

premature distribution = *early distribution*.

premium <1> trade price of an option × factor × quantity. <2> the amount by which the forward rate exceeds spot rate of a foreign currency. ***Also***: agio; cost of hedging; exchange premium; exchange rate differential; forward margin; forward premium. <3> the amount by which one fund exceeds another in buying power. <4> = *agiotage*. <5> = *bond premium*. <6> = *commission*. <7> = *cost of carry*. <8> = *in lieu of dividend*. <9> = *interest*. <10> = *option premium*. <11> = *premium over conversion value*.

premium bond a bond the sales price of which exceeds its par or redemption value.

premium business = *option business*.

premium coupon the bond coupon payment above market rate.

premium currency a currency with a low interest rate. **See**: *discount currency*.

premium disparity the difference in the premiums of two different options on the same underlying. ***Also***: disparity.

premium free option = *zero-cost option*.

premium-gearing ratio the option premium divided by the gearing ratio.

premium income common stock (PICS) = *participating equity preferred stock*.

premium issue an issue of securities at a price above the par or redemption value. **See**: *discount issue*.

premium leg the payment from a credit protection buyer in a credit derivative. **See**: *protection leg*.

premium market the market situation in which the future price is higher than the spot price.

premium neutral option = *zero-cost option*.

premium on bonds = *bond premium*.

premium over bond value the excess of market value of a convertible bond over the price of another bond issued by the same company.

premium over conversion value the market price of a convertible security above its conversion price. ***Also***: premium. **See**: *conversion premium*.

premium over current exercisable value = *extrinsic value*.

premium over theoretical value excess of the market price of a stock warrant over its theoretical value.

premium price the tender offer price higher than the market price of a stock.

premium put convertible a convertible bond with an additional put feature that allows it to be redeemed at a premium sometime during its life.

premium rate the rate of premium on foreign exchange.

premium savings bond <UK> a kind of savings bond first issued in 1956 that carries no interest but a sum of prizes ranging from £25 to £50, to be paid to bonds with the numbers drawn.

premium stock the stock trading with a premium as in the case of short selling.

premium swap *non-par swap* with one or both of the equivalent securities underlying the swap payments being sold above parity. ***See***: *discount swap.*

premium trigger option the contingent premium option, the underlying price that triggers the premium payment of which is above the strike price of a call or below that of a put.

pre-packaged bankruptcy reorganization plan that is negotiated and voted by creditors and shareholders before the company files for bankruptcy.

prepaid forward a variable quantity and price forward agreement created to extract cash from a low-cost equity stock position obtained or to be obtained from the exercise of employee options. ***Also***: variable prepaid forward.

prepaid forward contract the contract that calls for prepayment today and delivery of the asset at a future time.

prepaid forward price current market price of a prepaid forward contract.

prepaid swap <1> a commodity forward contract featuring an upfront payment by the buyer equal to the present value of future deliveries. <2> the annuity-like transaction in which the present value of future payments on one side of swap is paid up front, and other payments are paid on the traditional schedule.

prepaid variable forward a forward contract the investor receives some upfront payment in exchange for a commitment to deliver security in the future.

prepayment <1> the payment for the purchase of a security or other asset before the account day. <2> payment of principal of a loan before it is due.

prepayment protection band a range of prepayment rates between which a PAC bond will redeem principal.

prepayment risk a risk to holders of the mortgage-backed securities that arises from the uncertainty in the rates at which the mortgagors will repay.

prepayment speed the estimated rate at which mortgage loan borrowers pay off their loans early. ***Also***: speed.

pre-refund bond a bond issued by state governments for which, a fund is set up to pay the interest and principal. ***Also***: pre-refunded bond; pre-refunded tax-exempt municipal bond; pre-re's; refunded bond.

pre-refunded bond = *pre-refund bond.*

pre-refunded tax-exempt municipal bond = *pre-refund bond.*

pre-refunding = *advance refunding.*

pre-re's = *pre-refund bond.*

presale order the order to buy part of a new bond issue before announcement of the price or coupon rate.

prescribed right to income and maximum equity (Prime) the income component of an *Americus Trust unit*, that is the equivalent of a five-year covered call writer's position at issuance. ***Also***: payment enhanced capital security.

prescribed security <1> <Canada> the security issued by a company which derives most of its earnings from real estates. <2> = *non-qualifying security.*

present value <1> discounted value of a sum due and payable at a certain date in the future. ***Also***: discounted present value; discounted value; present worth. ***See***: *future value*; *time value of money.* <2> = *capitalized value.*

present value of growth opportunities the net present value of an investment that an investor expects to make before the investment decision.

present value of income pickup the present value of the amount by which the yields on PERCS or ELKS exceed those on the underlying asset.

present value profitability index ratio of present value of future returns to the current value of an investment. ***Also***: cost-benefit ratio; discounted gross benefit-cost ratio; excess present value index; interest rate of return; profitability index; solving rate of return.

present worth (PW) = *present value.*

pre-settlement risk <1> the credit risk of default on a derivative before its settlement. <2> = *fractional exposure.*

presold of bonds that are completely sold out before the price or yield is publicly announced.

presold issue the stock which has been placed with subscribers before an official public offering becomes effective.

pre-spot dates quoted standard periods that fall between the transaction date and the current spot value date.

presumptive underwriter the person, not an underwriter who has bought more than 10% of a public offering and resells it within two years.

pre-syndicate bid a bid entered before the *secondary offering.*

pre-trade benchmark the price before or at the decision to trade. ***See***: *post-trade benchmark.*

prevailing rate of interest = *going rate of interest.*

price = *market price.*

price-adjusted rate preferred stock (PARP) a preferred stock, the dividend rate of which increase if the price of the stock decreases.

price as % liquidating value of an insurance stock, the average price of the year divided by the liquidating value at the year end.

price auction an *auction* technique used in the Treasury bills market in which the buyers are asked to specify the price. ***See***: *yield auction.*

price-based option a credit option the holder of which pays a fixed strike and receives the underlying asset's price in proportional to the strike price.

price basing setting the prices of commercial commodity transactions on the related futures contract prices.

price-book ratio (P/B) = *price to book ratio.*

price/cash flow ratio (PCF) the market value per share divided by cash flow per share of a stock.

price compression the limited price appreciation and depreciation potential for a callable or maturing bond.

price discovery the process of determining market prices through the interactions of buyers and sellers.

price discovery market the market for derivatives without a cash market for the underlying asset.

priced out the condition in which the market has already adjusted the price in light of a specific piece of news.

price/earnings growth ratio (PEG ratio) the P/E ratio obtained by dividing P/E ratio by the current annual growth or forward annual growth estimates.

price-earnings-growth-yield multiple = *price-earnings to growth and dividend yield ratio.*

price/earnings ratio (P/E) current price of a stock divided by its earnings per share. ***Also***: earnings multiple; multiple; price to earnings ratio. ***See***: *price to book ratio.*

price/earnings reciprocal = *earnings yield.*

price/earnings relative a stock's P/E ratio divided by the P/E ratio of a benchmark.

price/earnings to growth and dividend yield ratio (PEGY ratio) the ratio of a company's price/earnings ratio divided by its projected earnings growth rate and dividend yield. ***Also***: price-earnings-growth-yield multiple.

price/free cash flow ratio (P/FCF) the market price per share divided by cash flow per share.

price gap the price of a stock that either jumps or plummets from the previous trading range to a new range. ***Also***: gap.

price give further reduction in price after the quote.

price impact cost = *market impact cost.*

price improvement advantage when an order to buy is executed at a price lower than the best offer, or an order to sell is executed at a price higher than best bid.

price index an index that tracks inflation by measuring price changes.

price interest point = *pip.*

price jump the abrupt change in the price of an asset that prevents anyone from trading it at an intermediate price.

price level risk = *inflation risk.*

price maker <1> a person or a firm that dominates the market. <2> <Australia> = *market maker.*

price making = *making a price.*

price of capital = *interest.*

price of money <1> the daily interest of deferred payment. <2> = *interest.*

price of option = *strike price.*

price of risk = *risk value.*

price on spot = *spot price.*

price participation the extent to which an equity-linked note will benefit from an increase in the price of the stock or index to which it is linked.

price per day spread = *theta spread.*

price range the high and low end of the price fluctuations of a security over a period. ***Also***: range; trading range.

price risk the market value below the cost of a convertible security.

price-sales ratio (P/S) dividing current stock price by revenue per share.

price spread = *vertical spread.*

price swap derivative an obligation made by one company to secure the declining value of another's assets through the commitment of shares.

price taker a party to a deal in which the price was determined by natural forces of market competition.

price to book ratio (P/B) the ratio of market price to the book value per share. ***Also***: market to book ratio; price-book ratio; price to book value ratio; valuation ratio. ***See***: *price/earnings ratio.*

price to book value ratio = *price to book ratio.*

price to cash flow ratio the ratio of a stock's market price to its cash flow per share of the latest fiscal year.

price to earnings ratio = *price-earnings ratio.*

price-to-sales ratio (PSR) current price of a stock divided by sales per share of the company.

price value of a basis point (PVBP) a measure of how a basis point change in yield affects the price of a bond. ***Also***: dollar value of a basis point; PV 01; value of a basis point.

price volatility = *volatility.*

price-weighted index an index the component stocks are weighted by price.

pricey unrealistically low bid or high offer.

pricing by arbitrage the value of a replicable claim is determined by the non-arbitrage constraints.

pricing model a quantitative model for pricing assets, portfolios, options and derivatives.

Prides preferred redeemable increased dividend equity security

primary dealer commercial and investment bank which deals directly with the Federal Reserve in trading government securities.

primary distribution = *primary offering.*

primary earnings per share earnings applied to a share of stock before the dilutive securities. ***Also***: basic earnings per share; basic net income per share. **See**: *fully diluted earnings per share.*

primary instrument the instrument the value of which is determined by the market. ***Also***: cash instrument. **Opp.**: *derivative.*

primary market (PM) an exchange in which the first sale of the security is made. ***Also***: direct market; first market; new issue market. **See**: *secondary market.*

primary mortgage market the lending of mortgage loans to the borrowers. **See**: *secondary mortgage market.*

primary offering the sale of a new issue of security by the issuer. ***Also***: primary distribution. **See**: *initial public offering; secondary offering.*

primary seasoned offering = *follow-on.*

Prime prescribed right to income and maximum equity

prime cap the cap the reference rate of which is tied to the US prime rate.

prime interest rate = *bank prime interest rate.*

prime-LIBOR basis swap a basis swap in which one party pays variable rate based on the prime rate and the other pays variable rate based on LIBOR.

prime rate = *bank prime interest rate.*

prime rate fund a fund that attempts to match the return of the prime rate, by investing in high quality corporate debt instruments.

prime rate of interest = *bank prime interest rate.*

Primex an electronic trading network by four big securities firms: Goldman Sachs, Merrill Lynch, Morgan Stanley Dean Witter, & Solomon Smith Barney.

primitive security = *underlying asset.*

principal <1> the original sum of money, as opposed to the profits or interest made on that money. ***Also***: amount at interest; corpus; fiduciary principal; principal sum; rest. <2> the person for whom a broker executes an order. <3> the major party to a debt, except a guarantor. <4> <of a bond> = *face value.* <5> = *promissory note.*

principal amount the face amount of a debt instrument.

principal and interest = *accumulated amount.*

principal-at-risk security a catastrophe-linked debt with the principal payment subject to an insurer's loss experience. ***See***: *principal-protected security.*

principal currency swap = *foreign exchange swap.*

principal exchange-rate-linked security (PERLS) the US dollar denominated debt instrument the principal repayment of which depends on the exchange rate of US dollar against a foreign currency.

principaling a process whereby a dealer takes a security into position and sells the security as the owner. ***Also***: back-to-backing.

principal of instrument = *face value.*

principal only (PO) <1> of a mortgage-backed security which has the principal as its payoff. ***See***: *interest only.* <2> = *principal only strip.*

principal only strip the tranche of a pass-through security that gives the holder the right to receive a portion of every principal payment but not the interest portion. ***Also***: principal only.

principal protected CD a certificate of deposit the principal value of which is guaranteed by the issuing bank.

principal-protected equity-linked note an equity-linked note the investor is guaranteed the principal in full.

principal protected product (PPP) the structured product that guarantees the principal will be intact during the life of the instrument. ***See***: *guaranteed return structure.*

principal protected security a catastrophe-linked debt security with interest payments subject to an insurer's loss experience and special provisions and/or collateral to protect the principal. ***See***: *principal-at-risk security.*

principal protected structure derivative structure that guarantees to return the investor's initial investment at par.

principal risk the risk of losing some or all of the nominal or face amount or some or all of the purchase cost of an investment.

principals system the system in which members of an exchange deal directly with each other as principals.

principal stockholder a shareholder who has at least 10% of the voting power in the parent company. ***Also***: substantial shareholder.

principal sum = *principal.*

prior deduction method the method of computing bond interest coverage under which the requirements of senior debts are deducted from current earnings, the balance is applied to the issue being considered.

priority bond = *preference bond.*

prior lien-bond = *preference bond.*

prior preferred stock the preferred stock that is ranking ahead of all other issues of preferred stock. ***Also***: preferred preferred.

private activity bond the bond issued by state and local governments for such purposes as educational loans, industrial development, etc.

private annuity the transfer of money or property to an individual or organization in exchange for the transferee's promise to make some lifetime payments to the transferor.

private equity the equity capital invested in a private company. ***See***: *public equity.*

private investments in public equities (Pipes) the purchase of shares in a public company by an investment banker or a private investor at a large discount.

privately negotiated derivative (PND) = *over-the-market derivative.*

private market valuation (PMV) the value of a firm in the merger and acquisition market as opposed to the securities market.

private offering selling bonds or other financial instruments to employees or stockholders. ***Also***: negotiated offering.

private placement selling securities to investing companies instead of selling them in a stock exchange. ***Also***: direct placement; PVT placement. **See**: *placing*; *public offering*.

privileged bond a convertible bond that has attached warrants.

privilege money <UK> facility granted to the British discount houses enabling them to borrow last minute funds from certain banks to balance their books by 3:00 p. m. daily.

probability of loss = *value at risk*.

probability of profit (PP) the chance of an option position to end up profitable.

probability to finish ITM the probability of an option to finish in-the-money.

proceeds sale the over the counter sale of securities where the proceeds are used to buy another one. **See**: *swap*.

produce loan money lent to farmers for certain commodities. ***Also***: merchandise advance.

producer price index (PPI) an index that measures the average change over time in the selling prices received by domestic manufacturers.

production flow commitment the agreement by the loan purchaser to allow a monthly quota to be delivered in batches.

production rate the coupon interest rate at which a pass-through is issued.

profit <1> a gain including both money and increases in the value of property. ***Also***: gain; gravy; net payoff. <2> = *risk value*.

profitability index = *present value profitability index*.

profit and loss statement = *income statement*.

profiteer = *speculator*.

profiteering = *speculation*.

profit generator the strategy designed to achieve high profits.

profit objective = *target profit*.

profit of stock the sum of interest in capital and the entrepreneur profit.

profit on 1000 gamma scalping profit on a + 1000 gamma option using a delta neutral hedge.

profit on stock = *dividend*.

profit pickup the method of making profit after having been hung up in a declining market, e. g. after buying at $18, the price fell, then selling at $17, and when the price dropped to $15, buying it back to make a profit of $2.

profit range the price range in which the position can make a profit.

profit reinvestment = *earnings retention*.

profit sharing the arrangement under which employees share the profit.

profit-sharing forward = *participating forward*.

profit sharing option = *participating option*.

profit taking selling the securities or positions that have increased in value to realize the profit. ***Also***: realization; realizing; ringing the cash register.

profit warning = *earnings warning*.

program trading <1> buying and selling an entire package of stocks traded on the exchange at once. (Program trading is based on the closing price, while *basket trading* can be initiated at any time). <2> = *arbitrage trading program.*

progressive convertible preferred stock a preferred stock which can be converted into common shares on a progressively higher basis of exchange.

Pro-Gro protected growth security

prohibited transaction a transaction that is prohibited by law, such as dealing of which the insider does not disclose the price-sensitive information.

project loan security a security backed by mortgage loans that are insured with the Federal Housing Authority.

project note (PN) the bond issued by a municipality or agency to finance public housing. ***Also***: public housing authority bond.

promised yield = *yield-to-worse.*

promissory note (PN) a written promise to pay a sum of money on demand or by certain time. ***Also***: bill obligatory; bill of debt; bill single; dog; iou; note; note for a term; note of hand; one-name paper; principal; time note.

promoter's share = *founder's share.*

prompt date the date on which a metal has to be delivered to fulfill the terms of contract in a metal exchange.

prompt day = *account day.*

proper stock dividend a dividend paid to stockholders to give them an evidence of specific earnings that have been reinvested for a given period.

property dividend a dividend paid in the form of securities of other companies. ***Also***: asset dividend. ***See***: *cash dividend; dividend in kind.*

property income fund a mutual fund that seeks to invest in real property related securities.

property swap a swap one party pays the LIBOR plus rate for the return of an index of the real estate market.

proportional step option a step option the value of which increases or decreases certain portion of the adjusted balance (original principal plus or minus the change) as the underlying price is beyond a barrier. ***Also:*** exponential step option; geometric step option. ***See***: *simple step option.*

proprietary stock option an employee stock option designed to transfer stock ownership to its holders. ***Opp***: *compensatory stock option.*

proprietorship = *net worth.*

pro rata redemption the redemption of stock in proportion to stockholders share holdings.

pro rata sinking fund the sinking fund that allocates redemption payments on a formula established by the issuing company.

pro rata stock distribution the distribution of stock dividends to shareholders in proportion to their shareholding.

pro rata strip bond (PRS bond) the collateralized mortgage obligation that pays principal in a fixed proportion to the total collateral pay-downs.

prospectus issue = *public offering.*

protected bear = *cover bear.*

protected equity note (PEN) = *equity-linked note.*

protected equity participation (PEP) = *automatically convertible enhanced security.*

protected growth security (Pro-Gro) a callable equity-linked note with principal and upside participation, but with no interest coupon payments until the note matures or is called.

protected price the guaranteed price to a customer to deal at in securities.

protected trader option the option the trader of which can make a large number of synthetic trades in a currency pair by paying a monthly premium.

protection buyer the counterpart that reduces credit risk exposure in a credit derivative. ***See***: *protection seller*.

protection call a third-party protection against the payer's default in a *callable CDS*. ***Also***: payer default swaption.

protection leg payment from a credit protection seller in a credit derivative upon a credit event. ***See***: *premium leg*.

protection put a put option as a protection against the receiver's default in a callable CDS. ***Also***: receiver default swaption.

protection seller the party that takes on credit risk exposure in a credit derivative. ***See***: *protection buyer*.

protective call the call option bought to protect the short position in the underlying stock.

protective put the put purchased for an underlying security that is owned by the holder of the option.

protest jacket = *notice of dishonor*.

protest note = *notice of dishonor*.

provincial Treasury bill <Canada> the short-term promissory note issued by a province.

provisional call feature the feature in a convertible issue enabling the issuer to call the issue if the price hits a level.

provisions for repayments = *sinking fund*.

proxy fight the acquiring company tries to persuade shareholders of the target company, through the proxy votes to gain control of the company. ***Also***: bust up proxy proposal.

proxy hedging the use of a price- or rate-correlated financial instrument to hedge a particular risk when a direct hedge for that risk is not available.

proxy portfolio a basket of stocks that mimics a stock index.

proxy solicitation soliciting shareholders' votes in the annual or special stockholder meetings.

proxy statement a statement required by SEC to be given to potential holders of securities traded on an exchange, supplying minimum description of the stock, timing of proposed sale etc.

PRS price reporting system

PRS bond pro rata strip bond

prudential exercising shrewdness, caution, skills, due diligence and good judgment in portfolio management.

prudent man rule a rule that requires a fiduciary to invest the trust's asset only in a list of securities allowed by a state.

P/S price/sales ratio

PSA Public Securities Association

PSE Pacific Stock Exchange

pseudo-coupon date the date on which a bond with similar terms as a reference bond would pay interest even the reference bond does not pay.

Psi the sensitivity of the option price to the changes in the yield rate.

PSR price-to-sales ratio

PSSG the price of a stock divided by sales over sales growth. ***See***: *PREG*.

pterodactyl a wingspread the inside body options are at least three strikes apart. ***See***: *albatross*.

PTS Proprietary Trading System

public bond the bond issued by public utilities. ***Also***: debenture.

public borrowings = *government debt*.

public company a company which has issued stock through an offering, and now the stock is traded on the stock exchange. ***Also***: public corporation; publicly held company; publicly traded company.

public corporation = *public company.*

public debt = *government debt.*

public debt program <Canada> a program designed to raise funds for the government at stable and low cost.

public equity capital invested in a public company shares. ***See***: *private company.*

public float <Canada> = *float.*

public fund = *government debt.*

public housing authority bond = *project note.*

public income note (Pine) an unsecured unsubordinated debenture issued by a public company, and traded on a stock exchange.

public investor <1> the investor who invests private funds which have been deposited with them. <2> an investor excluding Federal Reserve Banks, who buys US Treasury securities.

public issue = *public offering.*

public liability company (PLC) <UK> the standard legal form for a limited, public company.

publicly floated shares <Canada> = *float.*

publicly held company = *public company.*

publicly traded company = *public company.*

publicly-traded fund = *closed-end fund.*

publicly traded partnership = *master limited partnership.*

publicly traded stock a stock issued by a public company, and is traded in a stock exchange.

public offer = *public offering.*

public offering selling of new securities or previously issued stock to the public. ***Also***: direct offering; distribution; distribution of shares; general cash issue; general cash offer; prospectus issue; public issue; public offer. ***See***: *private offering.*

public offering price (POP) = *offering price.*

public power bond a bond issued to build public power plants.

public purpose bond a municipal bond exempt from federal income tax. ***Also***: essential purpose bond; function bond.

public sale (P/S) = *auction.*

Public Securities Association (PSA) the organization best known for its standardized mortgage-backed securities prepayment rate assumptions.

public shell = *reverse merger.*

public syndicate = *distributing syndicate.*

public trustee <UK> an official appointed as a trustee to deal with trusts where there is a difficulty in finding a trustee. ***Also***: trustee of last resort.

public utility dividend reinvestment plan a plan under which shareholders of the public utilities may elect to receive dividends in the form of common stock in lieu of money.

published price = *quoted price.*

pull to lower a bid, or to raise an offer.

pullback temporary drop in price.

pulling an issue withdrawing an issue of new security after it has been announced.

pulling in their horns the investors' selling off or hedging after a security has gone up sharply.

pull-to-par the tendency for a premium bond to gradually lose its premium and for a discount bond to lose its discount.

pundit the expert on one or more segments of the financial markets.

pup = *laggard.*

purchase acquisition the acquisition of another company by buying its assets or its voting stocks. ***See***: *exchange-of-shares acquisition.*

purchase agreement = *underwriting agreement.*

purchase and sale statement (P&S) a statement prepared by a broker after the settlement of a futures contract that lists price, quantity, commission and profit.

purchased call = *long call.*

purchased debt a past due debt bought by an independent collection firm at a low price.

purchased put = *long put.*

purchase fee = *front-end load.*

purchase fund the cash the issuer of preferred stock must set aside annually with which to redeem the stock.

purchase group = *distributing syndicate.*

purchase group agreement = *agreement among underwriters.*

purchase option the option to buy the leased asset at the end of the lease term.

purchasing power parity (PPP) a theory stating that in the long run the exchange rate between two currencies will adjust to the relative purchasing power.

purchasing power risk the risk that an investment may lose its purchasing power after being liquidated.

pure arbitrage = *academic arbitrage.*

pure capital = *net capital.*

pure discount bond = *discount bond.*

pure expectation theory a theory that states that forward rates represent purely the expected future rates. ***Also***: biased expectations theory.

pure index fund a portfolio managed so as to perfectly match the performance of the overall market.

pure interest the interest that does not include risk and inflation factors. ***Also***: true interest.

pure no-load fund a mutual fund which does not impose sales load or 12b-1 fee.

pure play a company devoted to one line of business, or a company whose stock price is correlated with the fortunes of a specific investing strategy.

pure security = *arrow-debreu security.*

pure stock fund a mutual fund that invests in only one stock. ***Opp***: *balanced fund.* ***See***: *common stock fund.*

pure swap a swap where the purchase and sale are done with the same party. ***Also***: outright forward exchange. ***See***: *pieced-together swap.*

pure vanilla swap = *plain swap.*

pure yield pickup swap a transaction in which bonds with lower yields move to higher yield-bonds.

purgatory and hell bond a bond with a cap on the redemption proceeds.

purpose credit the bank credit for the purpose of financing the trading subject to Regulation T.

push-up the corporate reorganization under which the acquiring company transfers acquired assets to its parent company.

put <1> = *put option.* <2> = *redemption privilege.*

put and call broker a broker who trades options contracts and who is not allowed to operate on the exchange floor.

put and call option = *double option.*

put an option = *exercise.*

put bear spread = *bear put spread.*

put bond a bond the holder of which has the right to redeem at face value based on the schedule set forth at the time of issuance. ***Also***: bullet bond; puttable bond. ***See***: *callable bond.*

put bull spread = *bull put spread.*

put calendar a position created by buying long expiration puts and selling short expiration puts with the same strike.

put-call arbitrage the arbitrage profiting from the put-call parity opportunities.

put-call note a note consisting of a plain vanilla medium-term note sold to fixed-income investors and a put-call option sold to a derivatives dealer. ***Also***: mandatory par put remarketed security; pass-through asset trust security; reset put security.

put/call parity the option pricing principle that says, given a stock's price, a put and call of the same class must have a static price relationship because arbitrage will always reestablishes such a relationship.

put/call ratio (P/C)(P/C ratio) put volume divided by call volume for a given period. ***Also***: put/call volume ratio.

put/call volume ratio = *put/call ratio.*

put credit spread = *bull put spread.*

put date the date on which the holder can redeem the security.

put debit spread = *bear put spread.*

put diagonal a position created by buying long expiration puts and selling shorter expiration puts with a higher strike price.

put IV implied volatility for put options.

put LEAPS the LEAPS to sell. ***See***: *call LEAPS.*

put-of-more option the right to sell the same commodities to the former buyer. ***Also***: seller's option to double.

put on a call a *put option* with an option to buy another *call option.*

put on a put a put option with an option to buy another *put option.*

put on a spread to buy or sell financial instruments to comprise a spread.

put option the option buyer's right to sell the securities to the writer at an agreed price in the future. ***Also***: put. ***See***: *call option.*

put OTM premium added to the value of an out-of-the-money put to increase its value to what is implied by a smile.

put price the price paid by the issuer of a puttable bond if the holder elects to put it back to the issuer.

put provision a provision that gives the holder of a floating-rate bond the right to redeem it at par on the coupon date.

put ratio backspread a strategy where-by an investor combines long and short puts to create a spread with little risk of loss but a limited profit potential. ***See***: *call ratio backspread.*

put spread a spread created by selling a put and buying a put on the same underlying, with different expiration dates or different strike prices.

put swaption = *receiver's swaption.*

puttable bond = *put bond.*

puttable floater the note with a variable coupon rate based on an index.

puttable stock a unit which consists of common stock and a put giving the buyer of the unit the right to put the stock back to the issuer.

puttable swap the swap the fixed-rate receiver has the right to terminate. ***See***: *callable swap*; *extendable swap*.

puttable warrant a warrant with a cash redemption value as an alternative to exercise. ***Also***: redeemable warrant.

put-through deal a large deal between a buyer and a seller through a jobber at an agreed price below the market price.

put to seller to exercise a put option and buy the underlying asset.

put warrant a stock warrant sold by a company to investors giving them the right to sell shares back to the company at a specified price.

PV 01 = *price value of a basis point.*

PVT placement = *private placement.*

pyramiding <1> the financial advantage that it needs to own only 51% the voting stock in all subsidiaries to control them. <2> reducing the buying volume of securities when their prices are increasing. ***Opp***: *downscale buying.* <3> treating the customers' profit as new margin for their futures transaction. <4> = *averaging up.*

Q q

Q <1> in bond listings of newspapers, meaning in receivership or bankruptcy proceedings. <2> month abbreviation for August in futures and call options. <3> Nasdaq descriptor that means it is in the bankruptcy proceedings. <4> the option strike price code for 85.

Q bond the inverse floating-rate *collateralized mortgage obligation.*

QCD quarters of cyclical dominance

QIB <1> qualified institutional buyer. <2> qualified investment buyer.

QQQQ exchange trading fund that allows investors to essentially invest in all of the stocks that make up the Nasdaq 100 index. ***Also***: Nasdaq-100 Index tracking stock; Q's; Qubes.

Q ratio the ratio named after Laureate J. Tobin of Yale University, who hypothesized that the combined market value of all the companies on the stock market should be equal to their replacement costs. ***Also***: Tobin's Q ratio.

Q's = *QQQQ.*

QT <1> questioned. <2> quotation taker.

quadratic approximation method the method for calculating the value of an early exercise option, adding it to the value calculated by the Black-Scholes-Merton model to obtain the value of an American option.

quadratic portfolio the portfolio whose mapping function is a quadratic polynomial.

quadrix the stock valuation system that uses over 100 variables in 7 major categories to determine the value of a stock.

qualified covered call a covered call the writer of which can be exempt from the tax straddle rule if he avoids very short-term and most in-the-money calls.

qualified dividend a mutual fund dividend from shares held for more than 60 days, qualified for the 15% tax rate.

qualified farm indebtedness a debt incurred directly in connection with the taxpayer's farm business if at least 50% of the total gross receipts for the 3 years preceding the tax year is attributable to farming.

qualified funding asset an annuity with payment periods corresponding to those of the liability, which the assignee purchased in 60 days before or after the date of the assignment, and uses to satisfy that liability.

qualified independent underwriter (QIU) the party that assures investors that a security's offered price is fair relative to other publicly traded securities and the market conditions.

qualified institutional buyer (QIB) the institution which manages at least $100 million of assets.

qualified investment buyer (QIB) the investor permitted to buy securities not offered to the public, with emphasis on instruments offered under Regulation 144a.

qualified investor <1> = *accredited investor.* <2> = *qualified purchaser.*

qualified option the stock option the income from which is capital gains to the holder. ***See***: *non-qualified option.*

qualified purchaser the person who can buy exempt securities. ***Also***: qualified investor.

qualified security = *covered security.*

qualified stock the stock held by non-corporate holders if they actually hold at least 10% of the outstanding stock of the distributing company.

qualified stock purchase the purchase of at least 80% of the shares of a firm in order to obtain tax savings.

qualifying annuity an annuity which a qualified plan is allowed to invest.

qualifying dividend the dividend that qualifies for the 100% dividends received deduction available to affiliated companies which do not file consolidated returns. ***See***: *eligible dividend.*

qualifying employer securities employer securities on which a leveraged ESOP may invest.

qualifying share <1> the common stock held in order to qualify as a director of the issuing firm. <2> <Canada> the share issued by a company after May 22, 1985 and before 1987.

qualifying stock option an option that is granted by a company to its employees to buy its shares at a discount.

qualitative credit restriction a Treasury directive which aims at restricting bank credit to purposes regarded as being in the national interest.

quality basis the difference between 2 prices caused by the difference in quality of two commodities.

quality option seller's choice of deliverables in the form of Treasury futures contracts. ***Also***: substitution option; switching option. ***See***: *timing option; wild card option.*

quality spread <1> the spread between Treasury securities and non-Treasury securities identical in all respects except for rating. <2> the difference between the borrowing cost of a poor credit firm and that of a good credit firm.

quality spread differential difference between *quality spread* in a fixed-rate market and that in a floating-rate market.

quality spread option = *credit risk option.*

quality stock (QS) = *blue chip.*

quality swap a bond swap that aims to upgrade from a low-credit to a higher-credit rating.

quant the mathematician who observes the price of a derivative or other asset in practice and tries to figure out what it is in theory.

quantile option = *alpha quantile option.*

quantitative analyst a person who applies a high level of knowledge in statistical, mathematical, and econometric modeling techniques to investment.

quantitative arbitrage using mathematical techniques to spot and profit from the tiny differences in the value of assets.

quantitative variable a variable that is measurable by real numbers.

quantity adjusting option (quanto) = *quanto option.*

quantity risk the risk that occurs when the quantity of an asset to be hedged is not certain.

quantize <verb> to give a derivative the quanto features.

quanto quantity adjusting option

quantoed option = *quanto option.*

quantoed swap = *cross-rate swap.*

quanto forward the forward contract under which the buyer will receive a random number of units of the underlying asset.

quanto option <1> an option in one currency, but pays out in another. ***Also***: cross-currency derivative; currency protected option; currency quantity adjusting option; currency quanto; currency-translated option; fixed exchange rate foreign equity option; guaranteed exchange rate option; quantity adjusting option; quantoed option. <2> = *fixed exchange rate foreign equity option.*

quanto swap = *cross-rate swap.*

quant shop the money management company that uses statistically and mathematically trained persons to direct the commitment of funds based on models.

quantum finance a field that seeks to resolve problems that are experienced with the Standard Model.

quarter day <UK> one of the four days in one year on which quarterly payments become due: Lady Day (Mar 25), Mid-summer (Jun 24), Michaelmas (Sep 29), and Christmas (Dec 25). ***Also***: term day.

quarterly income debt security (QUID) a 30 to 50 years *debt instrument* the quarterly interest is guaranteed by the parent company of the issuer.

quarterly income preferred security (QUIP) the *preferred security* with quarterly payments, issued by subsidiary formed exclusively to sell the shares and lend the proceeds to the parent. **See**: *monthly income preferred security; trust originated preferred security.*

quarters of cyclical dominance (QCD) an estimate of the quarters required to identify significant cyclical movements in the price of a security. **See**: *months of cyclical dominance.*

quarter stock the stock with a par value of $25 for each share.

quasi-American option = *Bermuda option.*

quasi-arbitrage the replacement of one asset or position with another with the equivalent risk and a higher expected return.

quasi-public company private company with government backing, such as Fannie Mae, Sallie Mae.

quasi-reorganization the reorganization that occurs when a company in financial difficulty modifies the capital structure without filing for bankruptcy.

Qubes = *QQQQ.*

query questioning a company about its shares or its performance.

QUID quarterly income debt security

quiet filing an IPO filing in which some important details are intentionally excluded.

quiet period time period an issuer is "in registration" with SEC. ***Also***: blacked-out quiet period; pre-IPO quiet period. **See**: *cooling period.*

QUIPs quarterly income preferred securities

quittance a cancellation of debt.

quotation taker (QT) the person who requests quotation of a security.

quote <1> <verb> to tell the counterpart the bid or offer. <2> the bid or offer.

quoted company = *listed company.*

quoted currency a currency that has a stated exchange rate.

quoted price (QP) stated price at which the last sale and purchase of a particular security or commodity took place. ***Also***: published price. **See**: *market price.*

quoted rate of interest = *coupon rate of interest.*

quoted security = *listed security.*

quoted share the stock permitted to be traded on an exchange and is granted a quotation. ***Also***: listed stock.

quote size the number of shares that are being offered for purchase at the bid price. ***Also***: bid size. **See**: *ask size.*

R r

R <1> month abbreviation for October in puts. <2> the Nasdaq descriptor meaning with stock right. <3> option strike price code for 90. <4> the rate of interest.

r. <1> declared or paid in the past 12 months plus stock dividend. <2> the option not traded today (in newspaper listing.)

R^2 = *R-square.*

raging bull strategy the option trading strategy profiting from a major price movement to a higher level. ***Also***: doomsdayer strategy.

raid <1><verb> to buy the stock of another company for controlling purpose. <2> an attempt by professional traders to depress the price of a stock.

raider = *acquiring company.*

raider company = *acquiring company.*

rainbow a blended index of equity returns for indexing the reference rate on an equity swap.

rainbow option the option with a payoff linked to the performance of 2 or more instruments or indexes. ***Also***: multiple index option. ***See***: *alternative option*; *maximum option*; *minimum option*; *outperformance option.*

rake off = *commission.*

ramping <UK> = *manipulation.*

ramp up increase in trading volume.

RAN revenue anticipation note

random walk process the steps in a random direction and with a step-length that has some characteristic value. ***Also***: fractional Brownian motion.

range = *price range.*

range accrual note = *accrual note.*

range accrual option = *accrual option.*

range accrual swap = *accrual swap.*

range accumulation note = *accrual note.*

range accumulation option = *accrual option.*

range binary option an option that pays off a fixed amount at expiration if the underlying price remains in the range for the option's entire life.

range box an accrual note with payout if the reference price or rate stays within a range until maturity and a knock-out feature if the reference price touches the edge of the range.

range derivative = *hurdle derivative.*

range floater = *accrual note.*

range floater note = *accrual note.*

range forward a contract that places upper and lower limits on the future cost of the foreign exchange. ***Also***: cylinder; forward rate bracket; risk reversal; tunnel. ***See***: *equity risk reversal*; *interest rate collar.*

range note <1> = *accrual note.* <2> = *corridor note.*

range option = *range security.*

range security the security the interest of which depends on the number of days the designated index falls within the range. ***Also***: range option.

range straddle the combination of a lookback call and a lookback put with the same trade date and expiration.

range warrant <UK> the warrant that allocates a fixed return on the premium pool collected to range tranches on the basis of the underlying price at maturity.

rapid-payoff mortgage = *growing equity mortgage.*

ratchet a variety of derivative structures in which key variables such as strike price are resettable, usually in an asymmetrical manner.

ratchet bond the non-callable, puttable bond with a long nominal life.

ratchet cap a cap whose strike is reset to the current rate for each caplet.

ratchet floater a floater with a resettable floor and a periodic cap. ***Also***: one-way collared floater; sticky floater.

ratchet floor a floor whose strike is reset to the current rate for each floorlet.

ratchet option = *cliquet option.*

ratchet swap a swap under which the fixed payment stream can be reset to a number of levels should the market rates of interest breach the designated levels.

rate <1> = *interest rate.* <2> = *rate of return.*

rate anticipation swap the swap in the bond market done in anticipation of a change in the overall level of the bond interest rate.

rate cap = *cap.*

rate-capped swap = *capped swap.*

rate differential swap = *diff swap.*

rate earned on common stockholders' equity = *rate of return on common stockholders' equity.*

rate fixing date the date on which a swap payment rate is fixed, usually a business day prior to the first date the new rates become effective. ***Also***: fixing date; reset date; roll date. ***See***: *coupon roll-over date.*

rate in foreign money = *indirect quote.*

rate of conversion = *conversion ratio.*

rate of discount = *discount rate.*

rate of exchange (RE)(RoE) = *exchange rate.*

rate of foreign exchange = *exchange rate.*

rate of interest = *interest rate.*

rate of redemption = *call price.*

rate of return (ROR) the earnings as a percentage of the investment. ***Also***: payback; rate; pay off; return on investment; return ratio. ***See***: *yield.*

rate of return on common stockholders' equity the after-tax earnings and preferred dividends divided by the common stockholders' equity. ***Also***: rate earned on common stockholders' equity.

rate of time-value decay = *theta.*

rating sensitive note = *credit linked note.*

rating transition a change in the bond credit rating from one value to another.

ratio = *yield curve ratio.*

ratio backspread a backspread involving the purchase of out-of-the money options in a ratio of 3:2 or 2:1 to the in-the-money options sold.

ratio bull spread a spread composed of one long call and two short calls in the same underlying asset with the same expiration, the long-expiration call has a lower strike. ***Also***: ratio call option.

ratio calendar spread option strategy using either puts or calls, whereby one sells more near term options than buying longer term options.

ratio call option = *ratio bull spread.*

ratio call spread a call option spread in which there is not a one-to-one ratio between the numbers of long and short call options.

ratio call writing selling calls against more shares than the seller owns. ***See***: *covered call writing.*

ratioed strangle swap a strangle swap

in which the options bought are not the same amount of the options sold.

ratio forward = *participating forward.*

ratio hedge the number of options compared to the number of futures to establish a risk-neutral hedge.

ratio of capital to liabilities = *equity-debt ratio.*

ratio of debt to capital = *debt-equity ratio.*

ratio of liabilities to net worth = *debt-equity ratio.*

ratio put spread a put spread in which there is not a one-to-one ratio between the numbers of long and short puts, but rather a one to two or more.

ratio spread a spread created by the purchase of one call and the sale of 2 calls with a higher strike price. ***Also***: tailed spread. **See**: *backspread.*

ratio strategy holding an unequal number of short options and long options or long stock.

ratio swap = *leveraged swap.*

ratio vertical spread = *backspread.*

ratio write selling multiple options per 100 shares of the underlying stock owned. ***Also***: variable write. **See**: *option hedge*; *variable ratio write.*

raw basis the spot rate of a bond minus the futures rate multiplied by the conversion factor.

RC <1> registered check. <2> reserve currency. <3> risk capital.

RCH recognized clearing house

RCN reverse convertible note

RCR registered commodity representative

RE <1> rate of exchange. <2> retained earnings.

reacquired stock = *treasury stock.*

reaction = *dip.*

ready market a market in which dealers' spreads are quite narrow. **See**: *active market.*

ready, willing and able buyer = *able buyer.*

real body on a candlestick line, the broad part consisting of the difference between opening and closing prices.

real capital = *capital stock.*

real effective exchange rate an effective exchange rate which has been adjusted for inflation. **See**: *nominal effective exchange rate.*

real estate investment trust (REIT) the trust which uses the pooled capital of many investors to buy and manage income properties and mortgage loans.

real estate mortgage investment conduit (REMIC) an entity which holds a fixed pool of mortgages secured by the interests in real estates.

real estate swap the swap involving the exchange of the returns from a pre-agreed property index, such as the US Russell NCREIF Property Index.

real interest rate the interest rate minus the inflation rate. ***Also***: real rate of interest. **See**: *effective interest rate.*

realization = *profit taking.*

realized compound yield = *total return.*

realized volatility <1> the statistical measure of variation in prices. ***Also***: integrated volatility. <2> = *historical volatility.*

realized volatility contract a forward contract on realized volatility whose delivery price is the implied volatility.

realized volatility swap a swap the payoff of which is equal to the difference between the realized volatility and implied volatility.

realized yield the bond yield that is actually generated in the holding period.

realizing = *profit taking.*

reallowance that maximum portion of the selling concession that an underwriter may give up or re-allow to another NASD member who needs not be a syndicate member.

real option an option or the option-like feature embedded in capital budgeting that gives investors the right, not the obligation to make capital investment decision.

real rate of interest = *real interest rate.*

real return bond (RRB) <Canada> = *Treasury inflation-protected security.*

REALS real yield security

real stock a stock held for a long term.

real-time current, as with quotes or news. ***Opp***: *delayed.* **See**: *level 1 quotes.*

real-time gross settlement (RTGS) the continuous settlement of payments on an individual order basis without netting the debits with credits across the books of a central bank.

real-time quote = *current price.*

real-time trade reporting the requirement that *market makers* report each *trade* in a Nasdaq security to *Nasdaq* within 90 seconds of execution.

real yield security (REALS) = *inflation derivative.*

rebate <1> the unearned interest which may be returned to a borrower if the loan is prepaid before maturity. ***Also***: interest rebate. <2> a reduction from payment. <3> the amount repaid to option buyers if a knock-in option is not activated or a knock-out option is terminated because the underlying asset hits the *outstrike.*

rebate barrier option a *barrier option* which offers a predetermined rebate payable to the holder should the option be knocked-out.

rebate option an option that pays $ 1 each time the price of the underlying reaches a barrier.

rebate range binary a structured note or other financial instrument in which the premium is rebated if a given price range is breached.

rebate strangle option a pair of knock-out options with unusual rebate and pay-out features.

recast earnings the recalculation of the earnings of a *target company* and the *acquiring company* based on the assumption that certain cost could be eliminated after the merger.

receiver default swaption = *protection put.*

receiver option a CDS option to sell credit default protection. **See**: *payer option.*

receiver's swaption a swaption giving the holder the right to receive fixed rate and pay a floating rate. ***Also***: put swaption; receiver swaption.

receiver swaption = *receiver's swaption.*

receive versus payment (RVP) = *delivery versus payment.*

receiving quote = *indirect quote.*

reclaration the right of the party to a transaction to recover losses caused by bad delivery.

reclassification the adjustment in the number of shares to reflect changes in par value, authorized shares or other changes.

recommended list a list of securities that are recommended for purchase by the securities analysts.

reconversion = *reverse conversion.*

record date = *date of record.*

recovery sudden rising of market price which has been declining for a while.

recovery forward contract the double barrier option with a rebate provision embedded in a currency forward.

recovery note an *equity-linked note* the principal of which is guaranteed if the market falls. ***See***: *guaranteed bond.*

recovery rate <1> in the event of a default, the fraction of the outstanding obligation expected to be recovered. <2> the rate paid to the swap party when negative credit event occurs.

recovery value par value received by the holder of credit derivative when default.

recuperate of price, to become higher.

red chip <1> a stock the price of which jumped up at IPO and later significantly dropped. <2> a company which is incorporated and listed in Hong Kong with controlling Chinese shareholders.

redeemable bond = *callable bond.*

redeemable loan = *call money.*

redeemable preference share <UK> = *redeemable stock.*

redeemable security = *callable security.*

redeemable stock the preferred stock that can be redeemed by the issuer. ***Also***: redeemable preference share.

redeemable trust certificate = *unit.*

redeemable warrant = *puttable warrant.*

redemption <1> the process of redeeming or paying off a loan. <2> the right of a mortgagor to recover mortgaged property on repayment of the loan and interest due. <3> = *bond redemption.* <4> = *stock* redemption.

redemption charge = *back-end load.*

redemption date = *call date.*

redemption fee = *back-end load.*

redemption premium = *call premium.*

redemption price <1> <mutual fund> = *bid price.* <2> = *call price.*

redemption privilege the bondholder's right to sell the bond back to the issuer before maturity. ***Also***: put. ***See***: *call provision.*

redemption provision = *call provision.*

redemption value amount that must be paid for the return of one share of preferred stock.

redemption yield = *yield to maturity.*

rediscount <verb>to discount a short term negotiable note after being discounted with a bank.

red months the futures contract trading months that are at least one year distant and trade concurrently with identical near term trading months.

red noise = *mean reversion.*

reduced cost option an option with a reduced premium as a result of the implicit or explicit sale of another option, acceptance of a less favorable strike or participation rate, or introduction of a barrier provision.

reducible-rate bond the bond for which the issuer has the right to lower the interest rate as well as its call premium.

reengineered asset = *synthetic asset.*

reference asset the asset designated in a total return swap as the reference for the floating rate.

reference credit the credit quality of the reference asset or reference entity in a credit swap.

reference currency the currency used in making payments to the holders of Euro-bonds.

reference entity an entity the credit of which is used in a credit derivative.

reference index rate = *reference rate.*

reference obligation a debt instrument used to determine the payout in a credit derivative.

reference rate <1> the interest rate for determining the floating rate of an interest rate swap or other derivatives. ***Also***: reference index rate. ***See***: *swap coupon*. <2> = *equilibrium rate.*

reference security a security to which the subject security of an offering may be converted or exchanged.

reference swap a swap that is chosen by a dynamic credit swap to be the reference.

refinancing = *refunding.*

refund date the date on which old bonds can be redeemed from the proceeds of a new bond.

refunded bond = *pre-refund bond.*

refunding the issuing of new bonds to redeem the mature bonds. ***Also***: new for old; refinancing; rollover. ***See***: bond swap; *extension swap.*

refunding restriction the clause in a callable bond that prohibits the retirement by call if the funds for retirement are from the issuance of a new bond.

refundment bond = *bid bond.*

registered bond a bond entered on the books of the issuing firm in the name of the owner. ***Also***: nonbearer bond. ***See***: *coupon bond.*

registered broker a broker registered with SEC under Section 15 of the Securities Exchange Act, 1934.

registered capital = *authorized capital.*

registered competitive trader = *floor trader.*

registered coupon bond a bond that registers for the principal only, the interest is payable to anyone holding a coupon on the payment date.

registered exchange the exchange doing inter-state business and securities traded are registered with the SEC.

registered options principal (ROP) the employee of a brokerage firm who observes and regulates options exposure and other activity in client accounts.

registered retirement income fund (RRIF) <Canada> the fund established with a carrier and registered with the Canada Customs and Revenue Agency.

registered secondary offering a secondary offering by a holder of a large amount of shares acquired in a previous primary offering.

registered security the security where-by ownership is registered with the issuer or the agent.

registered stock = *inscribed stock.*

registered trader = *floor trader.*

registration-required obligation a debt issue that must be registered with SEC.

Registration Statement a document filed with SEC before an initial public offering is effective. ***Also***: Form S-1; initial filing; S-1.

regular chooser option = *as-you-like option.*

regular delivery the delivery of government security made on the business day following its purchase (the 5th day for bonds). ***Also***: regular way delivery.

regular dividend = *ordinary dividend.*

regular settlement = *settlement.*

regular voting a form of voting whereby each shareholder is entitled to one vote per share. ***Also***: statutory voting.

regular way delivery = *regular delivery.*

regular way trade sale of security that must be delivered on the fifth business day following the trade. ***See***: *cash sale.*

regulated futures contract (RFC) the futures contract traded, which is deemed to be sold at the end of year in order to be treated as a 60% long-term capital gain or loss and 40% short-term capital gain or loss. ***See***: *Section 1256 contract.*

regulated investment company (RIC) REIT or mutual fund eligible to pass the taxes on capital gains, dividend, or interest onto the individual investors.

regulatory arbitrage an arbitrage trying to exploit the differences in regulatory régimes.

regulatory risk the risk from changes in the regulatory environment pertaining to derivatives and financial contracts.

regulatory spread the difference in yields as a result of the difference in fees and registration requirements that borrower encounters in the traditional market relative to the Eurobond yield.

rehedge a hedge done in addition to an existing hedge.

reimmunization the adjustment to the positions held to bring a formerly immunized assets and liabilities back to immunization.

reinvestment rate the yield rate on reinvestment of bond interests. ***See***: *earnings retention ratio.*

REIT real estate investment trust

rejected option trade notice (ROTN) the form and procedure used to return a listed option trade that cannot be compared to the broker who reported it.

rejection refusal of a buyer to accept the instrument presented for delivery.

relapse of market prices, to slip back to return to a former low level.

related company = *affiliated company.*

relationship trade = *basis trading.*

relationship trading = *basis trading.*

relative P/E the P/E ratio obtained by dividing by the market price to earnings ratio.

relative performance derivatives the derivatives e. g. spread, *outperformance option, share ratio contract.*

relative performance option (RPO) = *outperformance option.*

relative purchasing power parity (RP-PP) an idea that the rate of change in the price level in one country relative to that in another country determines the rate of change of the exchange rate between their currencies.

relative strength index (RSI) the index that shows the stock price changes in two weeks, calculated as 100 - [100 ÷ (1 + up/down)]. (When the RSI is higher than 70, the market is overbought and lower than 30, oversold.)

relative value the value measured in terms of risk, liquidity, and return of one instrument relative to another, or, for an asset of one maturity relative to another.

relative value arbitrage = *relative-value strategy.*

relative-value strategy a strategy which seeks to identify investments whose relative values are attractive. ***Also***: relative value arbitrage.

relative volatility <1> the volatility used to compare the exposure levels of different portfolios, it is the standard deviation of a portfolio's return divided by the standard deviation of a benchmark. ***See***: *actual volatility; forecast volatility; historical volatility; implied volatility.* <2> = *volatility coefficient.*

relative yield spread of bonds, the ratio of the *yield spread* to the yield level.

release = *abandonment.*

relevant discounted security <UK> the security the issue price of which is less than the redemption amount by more than 0.5% of the issue price times the number of years between issuance and redemption. ***Also***: discounted security.

relinking entering into an interest rate swap to offset exposure to a floating-rate note or reverse floating-rate note that has begun to move against an investor.

reload option the stock option granted upon the exercise of an existing option using shares in the employee's possession. ***Also***: restoration option.

reload stock option a stock option that is automatically granted if an outstanding stock option is exercised in a *window period.*

remaining maturity = *duration.*

remapping an approximation of a risk vector with some other risk vectors.

remarketed preferred stock = *auction rate preferred stock.*

rematerialization the transfer of securities in electronic form back to physical certificates. **See**: *dematerialization.*

Rembrandt bond the bond sold in the Netherlands to Dutch investors by non-Dutch issuers.

REMIC real estate mortgage investment conduit

Rendelman-Bartter model the model that uses a binomial approach to approximate options with the rate of interest as the random variable.

renewable resource natural resource that can be used more than once, such as timber, solar energy. **See**: *non-renewable resource.*

renewal note the promissory note the maturity of which has been extended.

rent periodic payment under an *annuity.*

reoffered yield the yield offered by a bond at the time its original investor bought it.

reoffering the reselling of securities to the public by an underwriter after buying them in an IPO.

reoffering yield the *yield to maturity* at which an underwriter offers to sell new bonds to investors.

reorganization bond a bond issued to the creditors by the company which is in reorganization proceedings. **See**: *adjustment bond.*

reorganization exchange = *exchange-of-shares acquisition.*

repack trade a derivative under which a bank issues small securities that are backed by a large notional instrument.

repairing spread the spread created to protect a current position for further loss.

reparations the compensation paid to a wronged party in a future or an option contract.

repayment risk = *credit risk.*

replacement cost <1> = *actual exposure.* <2> = *swap replacement cost.*

replacement risk the consequence of the *Herstatt risk.*

replacement share a share that is bought back by the investor in less than 30 days after selling a similar share.

replacement swap a comparable instrument used to replace a defaulted or a canceled in-the-money option. ***Also***: swap replacement.

replicating portfolio strategy a portfolio investment strategy that uses *replication.*

replication the creation of new derivative position to hedge against an existing derivative position.

repo repurchase agreement

repo rate the interest rate specified in the repurchase agreement.

reported factor a *pool factor* as reported by The Bond Buyer for a specified period of time.

reporting currency the currency used by an organization in preparing its financial statements. ***Also***: base currency; natural currency. ***Opp***: *functional currency*.

repricing lowering the price of a stock option by the issuing company to allow its employees to exercise the options after a significant drop in the price of its stock.

REPS reset put security

repurchase agreement (repo) (r.p.) the agreement by a borrower where he sells securities with a commitment to buy them back at the same price plus interest in the future. ***Also***: squeeze agreement.

repurchase of stock a public company's buying back its shares from shareholders in cash.

required rate of interest = *hurdle rate*.

required rate of return = *hurdle rate*.

required yield the bond yield required by the marketplace to match available expected returns for financial instruments with comparable risk and reward structure.

reserve = *retained earnings*.

reserved price = *minimum price*.

reset bond a bond that allows the initial interest rate to be adjusted on specific dates to maintain a stable price. ***Also***: cram-down bond.

reset date = *rate fixing date*.

reset frequency the frequency at which the rate of a floating rate note will be reset.

reset option an equity index option the strike price of which may be reset to a lower strike price (for call), or a higher strike price (for put), at some point during the life of it if the option is out of the money on a reset date. ***Also***: partial lookback option; strike reset option.

reset put security (REPS) = *put-call note*.

reset risk the exposure to a mismatch between the frequency of investor coupon resets and the frequency of rate resets on the underlying collateral in an asset backed security.

reset swap = *arrears swap*.

resettable cap the reset option, usually providing for a reset of a forward cap rate downward if a prior actual rate was below a trigger rate.

resettable note = *exchangeable note*.

reshaping duration = *partial duration*.

residual dividends approach a method under which a company pays dividends if and only if any acceptable investment opportunities for the funds are currently unavailable.

residual interest bond (RIB) municipal reverse floater that is paired with select auction variable-rate securities.

residual interest tax-exempt security (RITES) synthetic tax-exempt municipal reverse floating-rate note.

residual return the return of an asset that is independent of the benchmark, calculated as *excess return* minus *beta* times *benchmark return*.

residual risk the risk (annualized standard deviation) of the *residual return*.

residual security = *dilutive security*.

residual unhedged risk the basis risk or other unmatched risk that exists after the implementation of a hedging position.

resource accretion = *asset accretion.*

resource recovery revenue bond a bond that is issued to build waste recovery facilities.

rest <1> the time at which one period ends and the next begins in calculating the interest on loans payable quarterly, annually or half-yearly. <2> = *principal.*

restoration option = *reload option.*

restricted list a list of securities which a firm cannot hold or sell short because of its involvement with the company in a merger or underwriting.

restricted security the security issued under Regulation D of the 1933 Act, meeting strict requirements before selling.

restricted stock the stock granted to the employee that can not be sold for a given period. ***Also***: 144 stock; restricted stock grant. ***See***: *blackout.*

restricted stock grant = *restricted stock.*

restricted stock option the stock option granted to an employee with restrictions.

resumption reopening the following day of specific futures and options markets that trade in the evening session.

resumption of dividends stockholder's acquisition of the company's surplus or assets after receiving dividends.

reswap to reverse a swap of bonds to gain the advantage of a yield spread or tax loss and restore a portfolio to its position before the original swap. ***Also***: reverse a swap.

retail investor = *individual investor.*

retail price index swap = *inflation swap.*

retail repurchase agreement a method by which a bank borrows from investors using government securities to secure the loan agreeing to repurchase them later.

retained earnings (RE) the excess of net current earnings over the dividend declared to be paid. ***Also***: earned surplus; earnings retained; internal reserve; reserve; revenue capital; seed capital; surplus capital; surplus reserve; undistributed profit. ***See***: *accumulated earnings.*

retention the percentage or amount of a syndicate member's underwriting participation that is retained for his own retail sales.

retirement of debt = *early extinguishment.*

retirement of securities <1> cancellation of stocks or bonds because the issuer has bought them back. <2> the removal of the asset from securities markets because of maturity.

retraceable note a promissory note with an embedded option giving the issuer the right to call it at selected dates.

retraceable swap the swap with an embedded option giving one party, usually the fixed-rate payer, the right to cancel the swap under certain conditions.

retractable bond the bond with both an embedded call, held by the issuer, and an embedded put, held by the investor, with the same expiration date and strike price.

retrospective yield the average annual yield of a stock including dividends and market appreciation.

return <1> the change in value and the gain or loss of an investment in a given period. <2> = *payback.*

return if called the return that a covered writer would achieve if the underlying is called away.

return multiplier in representing rate of return, a number indicating how much the value is after a period, such as for a return of 14%, the return multiplier is 1.14. ***Also***: return relative.

return of capital the return of capital to the shareholders, not dividend. ***Also***: capital distribution.

return on investment (ROI) = *rate of return.*

return on risk-adjusted asset (RORA) the ratio of a bank's net income after tax to its total risk-weighted assets.

return ratio = *rate of return.*

return relative = *return multiplier.*

return to hedged portfolio (RHP) = *implied repo rate.*

revenue anticipation note (RAN) the short-term bond issued by a municipal entity, to be repaid out of the anticipated revenues such as sales tax.

revenue bond a municipal bond that is supported by a pledge of revenue from a specified income generating facility such as a toll bridge, a power plant. ***Also***: municipal revenue bond. **See**: *authority bond.*

revenue capital = *retained earnings.*

revenue hunter merger the corporate merger in which the acquiring company simply wants to generate more revenue.

reversal <1> a change in direction of the market. ***Also***: trend reversal. **See**: *back up*; *inflection point.* <2> the restoration of a bond portfolio to its former position after a swap transaction. <3> = *forward reversal.* <4> = *short conversion.*

reversal arbitrage = *short conversion.*

reverse acquisition = *reverse merger.*

reverse a swap = *reswap.*

reverse butterfly = *sandwich spread.*

reverse calendar spread = *reverse diagonal spread.*

reverse calendar strangle buying a wide strangle in a nearby month and selling the same strangle in a deferred month. ***Also***: dual reverse calendar spreads; strangle swap.

reverse contingent premium option an option that requires payment of premium if it is out of the money at maturity, and no premium if it is not.

reverse conversion <1> the exchange of a synthetic call option for a put option. ***Also***: reconversion; reverse crush spread. <2> = *forward reversal.* <3> = *short conversion.*

reverse convertible note (RCN) the *synthetic instrument* that behaves like both bonds and stocks, providing high coupon payments with final payoffs dependant upon the stock market.

reverse crush spread <1> selling soybeans futures and buying soybeans oil and soybeans meal. **See**: *crush spread.* <2> = *reverse conversion.*

reverse diagonal calendar spread = *reverse diagonal spread.*

reverse diagonal spread a spread under which the option bought has a shorter expiration date than that of the one sold. ***Also***: diagonal reverse spread; reverse calendar spread; reverse diagonal calendar spread.

reverse digital cap the clause of a fixed versus floating interest rate swap that specifies the fixed-rate payment below market rates as long as the floating rate stays below a set cap rate.

reverse dollar roll the holder of the high coupon GNMA bonds sells them during a period of lower rates with the expressed agreement to recapture them in about one month or so.

reverse equity risk reversal a combi nation of a short out-of-the-money put, a long out-of-the-money call, and a short futures or cash market position. ***Also***: reverse forward rate bracket; reverse range forward. **See**: *floored put.*

reverse floating-rate note = *bull floater.*

reverse floating-rate swap a swap that is structured with a reverse floating-rate payment from one counterpart. ***Also***: inverse floating rate swap.

reverse forward rate bracket = *reverse equity risk reversal.*

reverse hedge the hedge that is opposite to the hedge made in the previous period. ***Also***: Chinese arbitrage. **See**: *Chinese hedge.*

reverse horizontal spread the spread in which the option bought has a shorter expiration date than the one sold. ***Also***: horizontal reverse spread.

reverse index principal swap a swap with the notional amount that increases as through prescribed barrier levels, thus the payments will increase over time as the principal decreases. **See**: *accreting swap; index principal swap.*

reverse interest rate collar the combination of an interest rate collar and a reverse floating-rate note, that provides an interest cost or yield that decreases as market rates rise, increases as the market rates fall in a range.

reverse leveraged buyout bringing back into publicly traded status a company that had been privitized by way of a *leveraged buyout.*

reverse merger the acquisition of a public company by a private company. ***Also***: public shell; reverse acquisition; reverse takeover; shell merger. **See**: *demerger.*

reverse option hedge = *bull straddle.*

reverse pyramiding the action of selling more shares or other assets as the price goes higher.

reverse range forward = *reverse equity risk reversal.*

reverse ratio spread a spread created by selling a call at one strike price, and buying several calls at a higher strike price.

reverse repo = *matched sale.*

reverse repurchase agreement = *matched sale.*

reverse split = *split down.*

reverse stock split = *split down.*

reverse swap <1> a swap that restores a bond portfolio to its former position following a recent yield swap. **See**: *swap reversal.* <2> = *back-to-back swap.*

reverse takeover = *reverse merger.*

reverse triangular merger a merger in which an outside acquiring company A acquires the assets of a target company B, which is a subsidiary of its parent company C, in exchange for the voting shares of C. **See**: *forward triangular merger.*

reverse yield gap a situation in which fixed interest securities yield more than industrial shares.

reverse zero coupon swap a swap contract under which the zero coupon payment is made upfront, and interest rate and principal payments are to be paid by the counterpart over time. **See**: *dual coupon swap; zero coupon swap.*

reversible swap the combination of an interest rate swap and a swaption on twice the notional amount of that interest rate swap.

reversing trade entering the opposite side of a currently held futures position to close it out.

reversion to the mean the characteristic of option volatility which after reaching an extreme high or low, will return to a more "normal", average level.

reward-to-volatility ratio a ratio of excess return to portfolio standard deviation. ***Also***: Treynor ratio.

RFC <1> registered floor clerk. <2> regulated futures contract.

RFP <1> request for procurement. <2> request for proposal.

RFQ request for quotation

rho a measure of how much the option price will change if the risk-free interest rate changed by a small amount, e. g. 0.1%. ***Also***: option rho.

RHP return to hedged portfolio

RIB residual interest bond

riding the yield curve trading in interest rate futures according to the expectations of change in the yield curve. ***Also***: playing the yield curve; rolling down the yield curve.

rigged market the manipulation of prices in a market to attract new buyers and sellers.

rigging the market = *tampering with the market.*

right = *stock right.*

right-hand side the price of currency that a bank is willing to buy. ***See***: *bid*; *left-hand side*

right of offset = *netting.*

right of preemption = stock right.

right of set-of = *netting.*

right on = *cum rights.*

rights issue the issue of common stock to the existing stockholders who hold rights that entitle them to buy newly issued shares at a discount from the price at which shares will later be offered. ***Also***: rights offering. ***See***: *bonus share.*

rights letter <UK> = *stock warrant.*

rights of accumulation the way for a shareholder to qualify for a reduced sales charge by adding the value of the shares owned to the amount of a new purchase.

rights offering = *rights issue.*

rights on of shares trading with rights attached to them. ***See***: *cum rights.*

rigidly fixed rate system = *fixed rate system.*

ring location on the floor of an exchange where trades are executed. ***Also***: pit.

ringing out the commission merchant's settling of existing futures.

ringing the cash register = *profit taking.*

rip up the option market's counterpart of the torn up, worthless betting receipts that litter the floors of the exchange.

rising market = *bull market.*

rising star a bond the rating of which has been increased by a rating agency as a result of the improvement in the credit quality of the issuer. ***See***: *fallen angel.*

risk the chance of loss, expressed as the standard deviation. ***Also***: uncertainty.

risk-adjusted probability the probability that has been adjusted by risk.

risk-adjusted rating (RAR) a risk-return rating calculation used by the Morningstar mutual fund service.

risk adjusted return the measure of how much an investment returned in relation to the amount of risk it took on.

risk appetite the amount that a trader is willing to lose.

risk arbitrage buy the stock of a company being acquired and sell the shares of the raider on the speculation that the raider's shares will rise. ***Also***: takeover arbitrage.

risk assessment the mental process of evaluation of risk.

risk averse wanting to avoid risk. ***See***: *risk neutral*; *risk seeking*.

risk/award ratio the relationship between the probability of loss and profit.

risk capital <1> investment in common stock issued by a new company. ***Also***: venture capital. <2> the long-term loans or capital invested in high risk business. ***See***: *security capital.*

risk-controlled arbitrage a self-hedged trade that uses mortgage-backed security as the primary assets.

risk equivalent the number of units of an instrument with exactly the same amount of a certain risk as another.

risk factor a random variable whose value will affect the market value of a portfolio.

risk-free asset <1> = *riskless asset.* <2> = *zero-beta portfolio.*

risk-free hedge = *perfect hedge.*

risk-free rate = *riskless rate.*

risk-free return <1> = *basic yield.* <2> = *benchmark return.*

risk-free security a bond or stock that is nearly risk-free. ***Also***: fine paper.

risk indifferent = *riskless neutral.*

riskless arbitrage locking in or profiting from the difference in the prices of two securities or commodities that are traded in two different exchanges.

riskless asset an asset the future return of which is known today with certainty, such as short-term obligations of Treasury. ***Also***: risk-free asset.

riskless principal two transactions that occur at the same price that are recorded only once as an agency trade excluding all fees, markups or markdowns.

riskless rate the rate of return on a *riskless asset.* ***Also***: risk-free rate.

riskless return = *benchmark return.*

riskless transaction the deal in which a security has high marketability and the dealer takes no risk in completing the deal, e. g. a simultaneous transaction.

risk lover an investor who is willing to take on additional risk for an additional return on investment.

risk measure the procedure used to calculate the risk metrics.

risk metric the interpretation of risk, such as beta, theta, volatility etc.

risk neutral insensitive to risk. ***Also***: risk indifferent. ***See***: *risk averse*; *risk seeking.*

risk neutral approach = *stochastic calculus approach.*

risk position the exposure to fluctuations in exchange rates, index, or interest rates.

risk premium a return in excess of the risk-free rate.

risk/return trade-off the relation between risk and return in which one must be willing to accept greater risk if one wants to pursue a greater return. ***Also***: risk/reward trade-off.

risk reversal <1> = *cylinder.* <2> = *range forward.*

risk/reward trade-off = *risk/return trade-off.*

risk seeking of an investor, accepting low return for high risk but uncertain higher return. ***See***: *risk averse*; *risk neutral.*

risk value extra return for taking a risk. ***Also***: compensation for risk; price of risk; profit.

risk vector the random vector of a risk factor or risk factors.

risk-weighted asset credit risk equivalent multiplied by some risk-weighting factor.

RITES residual interest tax-exempt security

RLO restricted life option

roach motel a trade which is easy to get into, but not easy to get out of, just like a graveyard. ***See***: *graveyard market.*

rocket scientist = *financial engineer.*

roll <1> selling an option in one expiration month and buying another option in another expiration month. <2> difference between the near term and next futures contract.

roll back to replace an old option with a new one with an earlier expiration and the same strike. ***Also***: backward induction; roll backward. ***See***: *roll forward.*

roll backward = *roll back.*

roll date = *rate fixing date.*

roll down <verb> to move from one option position to another with a lower strike price, assuming that the position with the higher strike price is closed out. ***See***: *roll up.*

roll-down and forward any change to a new option position which involves a lower strike price and a later *expiration date.*

roll-down call a call option sold with a special provision providing for reset of the strike price to a lower level if the underlying asset falls far enough to hit the trigger price.

rollercoaster swap an interest rate swap with a notional principal amount that fluctuates periodically or in response to a change initiated by a counterparty. ***Also***: accordion swap; concertina swap; net-present-value swap; NPV swap; seasonal swap.

roll forward <verb> to move from one option position to another with a later expiration date. ***Also***: rolling over. ***See***: *roll back.*

Roll-Geske-Whaley model an application of Geske's option pricing model which yields an exact formula for the value of an American call on a discrete dividend-paying asset.

roll in <verb> to substitute a call or put option of the same class and same strike price, but with earlier expiration date. ***See***: *roll out.*

rolling call a call feature available to the issuer. ***See***: *stepped call.*

rolling down the hedge using relatively high liquidity in the exchange-traded futures and options to maintain a continuous (relatively short-term) risk-offsetting position by closing out some contracts as they approach maturity and opening more distant positions.

rolling down the yield curve = *riding the yield curve.*

rolling EPS the *earnings per share* calculated by using the previous two quarters and adding them to the following 2 quarter's estimated EPS.

rolling foreign exchange hedge <Australia> a hedge which reduces the exposure to the foreign exchange rate changes and is periodically renewed.

rolling hedge = *stack hedge.*

rolling of futures selling a futures contract before maturity or buying a new one.

rolling over = *roll forward.*

rolling reset swap a swap where one party pays the lower of the arranged swap rate or the prevailing market rate on the roll date for the same tenor.

rolling settlement securities settlement process that occurs a specified number of days after a trade is completed.

rolling strip hedge a hedge under which new futures are bought continuously to replace those just matured.

roll-lock swap a swap agreement set up to hedge rollover risk. ***Also***: rollover lock.

roll order = *dividend capture.*

roll out <verb> to substitute a call or put of the same class and same strike price, but with later expiration date. ***Also***: roll-out forward. **See**: *roll in.*

roll-out forward = *roll out..*

rollover = *refunding.*

rollover CD CD with a maturity divided into a series of six-month periods for which the CDs are issued when the previous six-month CD matures. ***Also***: roly poly CD.

rollover hedge = *stack hedge.*

rollover lock = *roll-lock swap.*

rollover option the option given to the investors in a closed-end mutual fund to reinvest the amount.

rollover replication the method of replicating or hedging a long-term option position with a series of shorter-term option positions.

rollover risk the exposure to actual or opportunity loss from mis-pricing of an option or futures contract at the time an old position must be closed and a new one opened. ***Also***: roll risk.

rollover swap a swap in which the first trade is for delivery the next business day, and the simultaneous sell, or buy is for delivery on the day after the next day. ***Also***: tomorrow-next swap.

roll risk = *rollover risk.*

roll up to move from one option position to another with a higher strike. **See**: *roll down.*

roll-up and forward the change to a new position that involves a higher strike price and a later *expiration date.*

roll-up fund foreign currency investment fund that pays no dividends.

roll-up put a put with a special clause that provides for reset of the strike to a higher level if the price of the underlying rises enough to hit the trigger price, the same as the reset strike.

roly poly CD = *rollover CD.*

ROP registered options principal

rotation a process where all option series in a particular underlying are opened in turn using a call auction procedure.

ROTN rejected option trade notice

round lot a unit, 100 shares for stock, 5 units or $5,000 par value for bonds, 10 shares for inactive shares, or $1 million for CDs. ***Also***: board lot; even lot; full lot; normal trading unit. **See**: *broken lot.*

round lot cash buy/sell ratio the cash account selling of round lots divided into the cash account buying of round lots.

round lot margin buy/sell ratio margin accounts selling of round lots divided into those buying of round lots.

round lot short-cover ratio the total round lot shares covered divided into the total round lot shares shorted by the investor.

round trip <1> buying and selling a futures or options contract. <2> the trading of options between two utilities within the same city.

round trip cost total commission, taxes and fees of buying and later selling the security. ***Also***: in-and-out cost.

round trip trade = *in and out.*

round-trip transaction cost the cost to complete a transaction, including commission, *market impact cost* and taxes.

round turn the buying and selling of a futures contract and the offsetting sale or purchase of futures of the same quantity and delivery month for full commission.

round turn trade = *in and out.*

round up <verb> to buy a specific amount of securities through the fixed dollar amount system of investing while leaving a debit in the account,

royalty bond = *Bowie.*

r.p. repurchase agreement

RPO relative performance option

RPPP relative purchasing power equity

RRB real return bond

RRIF registered retirement income fund

R-square a measurement of how closely a portfolio's performance correlates with the performance of a benchmark index, such as S&P 500. ***Also***: R^2.

RTGS real-time gross settlement

rubbers the shares of stock issued by companies in the business of making finished rubber or rubberized synthetic products.

Rubinstein-Dupir-Derman model = *Dupir-Derman-Rubinstein model.*

RUF revolving underwriting facilities

Rule 504 exemption the exempt issuance of securities up to 1 million dollars sold in 12-month period to unlimited number of investors. ***Also***: seed capital exemption.

Rule 505 exemption an exemption of up to $5 million in 12-month period sales of securities to 35 unaccredited investors and unlimited number of ac credited investors.

Rule 506 exemption an exempt private placement of securities of an unlimited amount up to 35 unaccredited investors must be sophisticated.

rumortrage the stock trading based on a rumor of a takeover. ***See***: *garbatrage.*

rump a group of investors who refuses to tender their shares in a merger or corporate acquisition.

run = *picture.*

rung = *value lock level.*

running in the shorts buying a number of securities that are sold short in an effort to push the market price up, but doing so encourages the sellers to buy back the securities, that will push the prices up even further.

running margin = *carry income and loss.*

running yield = *current yield.*

run rate the average annual dilution from company stock option grants over the most recent three year period recorded in the annual report.

run up a security's rapid appreciation in market value.

Rupee-cost averaging = *constant-dollar plan.*

Russell 2000 an index that measures the performance of the 2,000 stocks of the smallest companies in the Russell 3000 Index. ***Also***: RUT.

Russian option a *lookback option* without an expiration date.

RUT = *Russell 2000.*

S s

S <1> in newspapers, meaning split or stock dividend, or no option offered. <2> month abbreviation for November in put options. <3> Nasdaq descriptor meaning it is a beneficial interest. <4> the option strike price code for 95.

S&M abbreviation of the two dividend-paying months: September and March.

S&P Standard and Poor's

S&P 500 <1> = *spider* . <2> = *Standard & Poor's 500 Stock Average.*

S&P ASX 200 = *ASX 200.*

S&P Mid-Cap 400 an index comprising of 400 stocks of small companies.

S&P phenomenon the tendency for a stock that is newly added to the S&P index to temporarily increases in price after being included in the S&P index.

S-1 = *Registration Statement.*

safety cushion the difference between the initial available immunization level and the *safety-net return.* ***See***: *contingent immunization.*

safety inventory = *buffer stock.*

safety margin = *margin of safety.*

safety-net return the minimum available return that will trigger an immunization strategy under the *contingent immunization* strategy.

SAILS stock appreciation income-linked securities

sale against the box = *against the box.*

sale by auction = *auction.*

sales charge fee paid for buying shares in a mutual fund that charges fees. ***Also***: sales load.

sales fee = *commission.*

sales load = *sales charge.*

Sallie Mae a company that buys student loans and resells them as short-term and medium-term notes. ***Also***: Student Loan Marketing Association.

salt-down stock a stock held for a long time, even it shows large paper profits.

salvage value the value of a default credit derivative, usually the LIBOR flat.

SAM shared appreciation mortgage

same = *unchanged.*

same-day fund a transaction the payments of which are guaranteed to be available the same day.

same day securities settlement (SDSS) = *same day settlement.*

same day settlement (SDS) settlement of transaction the same day. ***Also***: cash settlement; same day securities settlement. ***See***: *next day settlement.*

same day substitution the offsetting of changes in a margin account in a day resulting in neither a margin call nor a credit to the miscellaneous account.

same day transaction = *cash transaction.*

Sammie bees Small Business Administration's pooled loans which are securitized as a unit trust certificate.

sample grade = *contract grade.*

Samurai bond yen-denominated bond issued in Tokyo by a foreign company.

samurai market <Japanese> = *foreign market.*

samurai warrant a European style capped call option that is convertible into non-voting equity.

sandbag the strategy used by the target company to delay or discourage a hostile takeover.

sandwich bond a CMO bond structured so that principal cash flows are first directed to reduce the bond's principal for the given payment date to the maximum balance.

sandwich spread <1> selling 2 options with high and low prices, and buying 2 options with middle prices. ***Also***: reverse butterfly. ***Opp***: *butterfly spread.*

sans warrant = *ex warrant.*

Santa Claus rally the rise in stock price that occurs in the week after Christmas. ***See***: *January effect.*

SAR stock appreciation right

Sarbanes-Oxley Act (SOx) a law enacted in 2002 to improve transparency and the quality in financial reporting, public audits and accounting services.

satellite = *sector fund.*

Saturday night special a sudden attempt by one company to take over another by making a tender offer announced over the weekends. ***Also***: creeping tender; creeping tender offer.

savings bond government bond issued at a discount and redeemed at face value ranging from $50 to $10,000.

saw-toothed convergence using numerical methods to price options under which the approximation to the analytical value improves with some periods, gets worse, then improves, then worsens.

SBIC stock small business investment company stock

SCA subsequent coupon attached

scale the coupon rates on the different maturities of a serial bond.

scale trading = *on a scale.*

scaling = *on a scale.*

scaling in = *scaling into.*

scaling into entering a small position, and increasing the position if the stock begins to move up. ***Also***: scaling in.

scaling up = *selling on the good news.*

scalper <1> a speculator who constantly sells his shares at small gains or at one or two points unreasonable earnings per share. ***Also***: flipper; in-and-out trader. <2> market maker who charges excessive commissions. <3> the investment adviser who buys stocks before recommending them, then sells out after the prices have risen.

scalping <1> trading for small gains in very short period. <2> buying up good IPOs. <3> trading the underlying asset to adjust the delta of an option.

scenario analysis the use of the horizon analysis to project total returns under different reinvestment rates and yields.

scheme of arrangement a reorganization plan of a firm.

scholarship funding bond government bond issued to fund some scholarship for college students.

scientific method = *yield method.*

SCOOP small cost option

scorched-earth policy a method used by the target company to make itself unattractive to the acquirer by selling off the most attractive portion of its business or by scheduling all debts to become due after the merger.

Score Special Claim on Residual Equity

Scottish dividend = *split-down.*

SCOUT shared currency option under tender

screen stocks to analyze various stocks in search of stocks that meet some pre-determined criteria.

scrip <1> a temporary note for payment of dividends deferred. ***Also***: dividend scrip; dividend stock scrip; stock scrip. <2> a temporary note entitling the holder to receive stock in a company. ***Also***: interim certificate; monkey money. <3> = *stock certificate.*

scrip dividend the dividend entitling the shareholder to receive cash, securities or other assets at some future date. ***Also***: dividend in scrip; liability dividend.

scripophily the collection of old stock and bond certificate for scarcity value.

S/D settlement day

SDMJ abbreviation of the four dividend-paying months: September, December, March, and June.

SDR savings deposit rate.

SDS same day settlement

SDSS same day securities settlement

seagull <1> a long at- or near-the-money call financed by the sale of an out-of-the-money call and put. <2> = *albatross.*

search cost the expense associated with locating a counterpart for a trade.

seasonal stock the stock of a company the sales of which vary due to seasonal effects, such as weather, business cycle and holidays.

seasonal swap = *rollercoaster swap.*

seasoned dating = *dating.*

seasoned issue securities issued by some well established companies. ***Also***: seasoned security; secondary issue. **See**: *unseasoned security.*

seasoned pool a pool of mortgages that are aged at least 12 months.

seasoned public offering = *follow-on.*

seasoned security = *seasoned issue.*

SEC EDGAR = *EDGAR.*

secondary currency option the option with a payoff in a different currency than the underlying's trading currency.

secondary issue = *seasoned issue.*

secondary market (SM) the market for transactions in existing securities after IPO when their prices have established. ***Also***: after market; second market. **See**: *primary market.*

secondary mortgage market a market for buying and selling mortgage loans, designed to provide additional liquidity for the lenders. **See**: *primary mortgage market.*

secondary offering a registered *offering* of a large block of the previously-issued security to the public by a shareholder. ***Also***: secondary public offering. **See**: *follow-on*; *primary offering.*

secondary public offering = *secondary offering.*

secondary reserve the assets retained by banks other than *primary reserve.*

secondary seasoned offering an offering of stocks to the public by the founders or the venture capitalists.

secondary stock the stock with smaller market capitalization, less quality and more risk than *blue chip* issues. **See**: *blue chip.*

secondary warrant a stock warrant with another warrant as the underlying.

second fixing the fixing of gold price at 3:00 p.m. by 5 representatives of the London Gold Market.

second generation duration the measure of duration in which relevant cash flows are discounted not by the yield to maturity of the instrument in question, but rather by those yields associated with zero-coupon bonds that mature simultaneously with each cash flow.

second generation option = *exotic option.*

second generation structured assets the bonds and notes incorporating design complexity in addition to the simple embedded options.

second hand option = *special option.*

second market = *secondary market.*

second pass regression cross-section regression of portfolio returns on beta.

second-preferred stock preferred stock which ranks below the first preferred stock in terms of priority of claim on dividend. ***See***: *first preferred stock.*

second-tier penalty the penalty for violation of the Securities Exchange Act 1933 that shall not exceed the greater of (1) $50,000 for any natural person or $250,000 for other person, or (2) the gain as a result of the violation.

second-to-default a derivative feature that stops and the investor no longer bears the credit risk after two or more credit events.

Section 306 stock the stock issued as a stock dividend, which when redeemed or sold, will result in ordinary income to the shareholder. ***Also***: tainted stock. ***See***: *preferred bailout.*

Section 332 liquidation = *practical merger.*

Section 333 liquidation the liquidation which may result in a substantial gain realized from the transfer of an asset. ***Also***: one-month liquidation.

Section 338 acquisition the acquisition where the acquirer after acquiring 80% of a firm, may elect in 75 days, to treat the firm as a new company.

Section 351 transactions = *Type C reorganization.*

Section 475(f) election the election to treat gain and loss from stock trading as ordinary gain and loss for income tax purpose. ***Also***: mark-to-market selection.

Section 988 hedging a hedging entered into primarily to reduce the risk due to foreign exchange fluctuation.

Section 1244 stock a stock the gain from which is a capital gain, but loss is ordinary loss. ***Also***: 1244 stock; small business corporation stock; small business investment company stock; small business-related security; small business stock.

Section 1256 contract the *regulated futures contract*, foreign exchange contract, non-equity option, dealer security future or the dealer equity option. ***Also***: 60/40 contract.

sector fund a fund that concentrates on a narrow market sector. ***Also***: satellite. ***See***: *broad index fund.*

sector option a basket option consisting of a group of securities drawn from a particular industry sector.

sector spread = *intermarket spread.*

sector warrant any warrant, similar to a sector option, but with longer duration.

secured bond a bond that is made safe or backed by some collateral. ***Also***: backed bond. ***See***: *unsecured bond.*

secured debenture <UK> = *fixed debenture.*

secured equity-linked loan (SELL) = *convertible adjustable rate bond.*

secured loan trust (SLT) = *asset-linked trust securities.*

Securities and Exchange Commission (SEC) a Federal agency responsible for ensuring that newly issued securities comply with requirements and for the proper administering of the securities industry. ***Also***: Commission.

securities arbitrage the simultaneous buying and selling of the same security in different exchanges to yield profit from pricing discrepancy.

securities exchange = *stock exchange.*

securities investment = *investment in securities.*

securities laws the *Securities Exchange Act 1933, Securities Exchange Act 1934, Sarbanes-Oxley Act, Public Utility Holding Company Act, Trust Indenture Act, Investment Company Act, Investment Advisers Act and Securities Investor Protection Act.*

securities lending loaning portfolio position to custodians, dealers, and short sellers who must make delivery of fungible positions. ***Also***: stock lending.

securities loan <1> = *lending stock.* <2> = *loan on securities.*

securities market line (SML) = *capital market line.*

securities rand = *financial rand.*

securities transaction the buying and selling of marketable securities. ***Also***: deal.

securitization transferring receivables, IOUs, loans, insurance policies etc. into debt securities that can be traded in the market. **See**: *commoditization.*

securitized option the packaged option that is combined with another security.

securitized receivables the accounts receivable that have been transferred into debt securities.

securitized structure a structured asset designed and sold to individual investors.

security the stock or bond placed by a debtor with a creditor with authority to sell for the creditor's account if a debt is not paid. ***Also***: instrument; paper.

security-based swap a swap done with securities. **See**: *nonsecurity-based swap.*

security capital the capital invested in government bonds, housing mortgage, etc. with a lower risk exposure. **See**: *risk capital.*

security dollar = *investment currency.*

security future a futures contract with a security or a narrow-based index as the underlying asset.

security market line (SML) = *capital market line.*

security underwriter = *underwriter.*

SEC yield a yield calculation by *SEC* that allows for fairer comparisons among bond mutual funds. ***Also***: standardized yield.

seed capital = *retained earnings.*

seed capital exemption = *Rule 504 exemption.*

segmentation theory the theory of the term structure of interest rates which explains the shape of the yield curve by the existence of some distinct markets for debt issues of different maturities. ***Also***: segmented market theory.

segmented market theory = *segmentation theory.*

segregated account the special account used to hold and separate customers' assets from those of the broker or firm. **See**: *investor control rule.*

segregated fund the amount of money, securities and asset due to commodity futures or options customers held in *segregated accounts.*

select 10 portfolio the mutual fund that buys and holds for 1 year the 10 stocks in DJIA with highest dividend yields. ***Also***: select ten portfolio.

selected dealer agreement the set of rules that govern the selling group in an underwriting.

selective disclosure the disclosure of financial information of a public firm to a selected group of investors.

selective hedge the partial hedge which occurs when hedgers have made determinations on a price rise or fall in a coming period.

select ten portfolio = *select 10 portfolio.*

self-adjusting forward a forward contract where the party can adjust the points.

self-regulatory organization (SRO) the organization that enforces fair, ethical and efficient practices in the securities, options and futures industry.

self-supporting bond the bond sold to finance a particular project, revenues of which will be used to pay off the interest and principal. **See**: *revenue bond.*

self tender an offer by the issuing firm to repurchase a specific number of its own shares outstanding.

SELL secured equity-linked loan

sell <1> a rating that recommends others to sell. ***Also***: sell rating. <2> = *cash in.*

sell active a situation in index arbitrage program trading when the difference of the future minus the spot index declines, causing more sell programs.

sell-at-the-high option = *lookback option.*

sell-at-the-max option = *lookback option.*

sell-down an issue that was purchased by a participant outside the syndicate.

seller <1> a person who sells securities or commodities. ***Also***: vendor. **See**: *buyer.* <2> = *writer.*

seller of the swap = *swap seller.*

seller's 7 sale an agreed upon delay of 7 days for the delivery of a security.

seller's call the agreement between a buyer and a seller whereby a commodity purchase occurs at a specific price above the contract price for a specific grade and quantity. ***Also***: call purchase.

seller's ... days a transaction whereby the seller agrees to deliver securities in some days, from 2 to 60 days.

seller's market a market with more buyers than sellers. **See**: *depressed market.*

seller's option (SO) <1> the right of a seller to select within the terms of the contract certain quantity of securities. <2> a transaction on an exchange the seller who holds the option can deliver the securities at any time within a specified period, from 6 to 60 days.

seller's option to double = *put-of-more option.*

sell hedge = *short hedge.*

selling against the box = *against the box.*

selling a butterfly = *short butterfly.*

selling concession the reduction in the price of a new offering of securities offered to a selling group, being the profit of the group. ***Also***: concession; take-down; take-down concession.

selling consolidated group a group of companies that, in the taxable year one of its members acquired 80% or more of the voting power of another member.

selling dividends inducing investors to buy mutual fund shares in order to get a dividend soon due, but the dividend is already part of the share price.

selling flat <1> = *at cost.* <2> = *ex interest.*

selling group = *distributing syndicate.*

selling hedge = *short hedge.*

selling off = *unloading.*

selling offer = *ask.*

selling on the good news selling the stocks after good news is released. ***Also***: scaling up; selling the bulge.

selling short (SS) selling an asset the seller does not own, but a borrowed asset is used to effect delivery. ***Also***: for short account; going short; short account; short selling.

selling short against the box = *against the box.*

selling syndicate = *distributing syndicate.*

selling the bulge = *selling on the good news.*

selling the crown jewels = *crown jewel defense.*

selling the spread = *credit spread.*

selloff sudden drop in price as a result of widespread selling.

sell-out <1> when a buyer fails to pay for the delivery the seller sells out the securities and charges the buyer with costs involved. <2> = *absorption.* <3> = *liquidation.*

sell program the simultaneous (short) sale of all stocks in the index and the purchase of the index futures contract.

sell rating = *sell.*

sell-side analyst the *analyst* working for a broker and whose recommendation is passed to the clients. ***Also***: Wall Street analyst.

sell signal the technical measurements of the previous movements indicate that this is time to sell. ***Also***: signal to sell. ***See***: *buy signal.*

sell threshold in program trading, the spread between futures price and the spot index at which sell programs would commence. ***See***: *SIR maximum.*

semi-American option = *Bermuda option.*

semi-annual rate the interest rate that is paid in 2 semi-annual installments.

semi-fixed swap the fixed-for-floating interest rate swap with the "fixed" rate for each period set above or below the market rare dependent on the level of a designated index on the reset date.

semi-government security the security issued by a government that operates like an enterprise.

semi-strong-form efficiency the form of pricing efficiency that holds the price of a security reflects all public information. ***See***: *strong-form efficiency; weak-form efficiency.*

semi-volatility the upside or downside volatility that is higher than the normal volatility. ***See***: *downside volatility; full volatility; upside volatility.*

sender net debit cap a cap on the net debit balance or open position.

senior mortgage bond a mortgage bond that will be redeemed before other bonds.

senior security a security having claim prior to a junior security or an equity share, e. g. bond, debenture, debt, note etc. ***Also***: unsubordinated debt.

senior swap = *long-term swap.*

senior tranche <UK> = *first tranche.*

Sensex = *Bombay Stock Exchange Sensitive Index.*

sensitive = *option sensitive.*

sentiment indicator the sum of all bullish and bearish outlook among all market participants about a security, a futures contract, an option or an index.

separate account the account maintained by an insurance company for investment.

separately managed account (SMA) a portfolio of securities guided by a professional money manager who makes decisions according to a given investment objective.

separately traded registered interest and principal securities (STRIPS) zero-coupon securities created by trading the coupon and principal payments stripped from Treasury securities. ***Also***: certificate of accrual on Treasury securities; certificate of government receipts; Treasury receipts; Treasury STRIPS. ***See***: *American corporate accrual receipts*; *Lion*.

separation property a portfolio asset that can be divided into different groups by the degree of risk aversion.

Sepon stock exchange pool nominees

SEQ bond sequential pay bond

sequential pay bond (SEQ bond) a CMO, collateralized mortgage obligation which starts to pay back the principal when the classes with an earlier priority reduce to zero.

serial bond a bond issue consisting of a number of bonds issued at the same time with different maturities. ***Also***: installment bond. ***See***: *drawn bond*.

serial option the option which permits trading in specified months other than the existing 4 delivery months: March, June, September and December.

serial redemption the redemption of a *serial bond*.

series = *option class*.

series A the preferred stock offered in the early stages of a startup to the venture capitalist, convertible into common stock if the company goes public or is sold. ***See***: *class A stock*.

series B the preferred stock issued after *series A*.

series bond the bond issued at different times but under the same indenture.

series E bonds savings bonds issued by the US Government from 1941 to 1979, replaced by series EE bonds and series HH bonds.

series EE bonds savings bonds issued by the US Government at a deep discount, and which permits holders to realize discount now or at maturity.

series HH bonds savings bonds issued by the US Government, the interest income of which must be reported semi-annually, and into which series EE bonds can be converted.

Series I bond = *I-bond*.

series of option = *option class*.

session = *trading session*.

set aside the percentage of a municipal or corporate bond underwriting that is allocated for handling by minority-owned broker/dealer firm.

set bill a bill of exchange with copies.

setoff <UK> = *termination payment*.

set price = *strike price*.

settlement <1> the conclusion of a transaction by delivery and payment on the fifth day following the transaction. ***Also***: regular settlement. <2> the clearing of a foreign exchange transaction. <3> the five-day period for the settlement of transactions. ***See***: *account period*.

settlement date <1> the date on which securities are to be delivered and paid. <2> the date on which payment is to be made. <3> the date on which interest on bonds is figured and stopped.

settlement day = *account day*.

settlement price the official price set by a futures exchange at the close of each day, used to set strike price and determine the out-of-the-money or in-the-money status. ***Also***: settling price.

settlement risk <1> = *delivery risk*. <2> = *Herstatt risk*.

settling day = *account day.*

settling price = *settlement price.*

setup <1> the arbitrage of being long the convertible and short the underlying. ***See***: *Chinese hedge.* <2> close price or a series of previous close prices.

setup swap an interest rate swap whose fixed-rate payments will rise over time according to a schedule determined at the outset of the swap. ***Also***: escalating rate swap.

seven-day put bond = *7-day put bond.*

several and joint agreement = *jointly and severally.*

severally but not jointly an underwriting in which members agree to buy a certain portion of an issue but do not agree to the joint liability for shares that are not sold by other members of the underwriting syndicate. ***Also***: divided account. ***See***: *jointly and severally.*

shade a rate <verb> to narrow the spread between the bid and ask on a currency, and possibly alter one side of the quote in favor of a good client.

shadow calendar the issue which has no effective registration date available due to SEC backlog, or a volatile market.

shadow rating <1> bond rating performed on an issuer by a credited institution, without public announcement. <2> the rating given by S&P to Israel Bonds not permitted to be traded on the secondary market.

shadow security = *shadow stock.*

shadow stock shares that do not exists, on which executives receive dividends or bonus. ***Also***: phantom stock; shadow security.

share <1> the holding interest of a shareholder in the company measured by a share of capital stock. ***See***: *stock.* <2> unit of ownership in a mutual fund. ***Also***: mutual fund share. <3> the ownership interest represented by the share in a general or limited partnership.

share bonus = *stock dividend.*

share buyback = *stock redemption.*

share consolidation = *split down.*

shared appreciation mortgage (SAM) = *participating mortgage.*

shared currency option under tender (SCOUT) = *contingent currency risk.*

share dividend = *stock dividend.*

shareholder one who holds the shares of a company or mutual fund. ***Also***: equity holder; owner of share; owner of stock; shareowner; stockholder.

shareholder's fund <UK> called-up share capital plus reserves minus minority interest.

shareholder value <1> the value that a shareholder is able to obtain from a company, including capital gains, dividends, buyback and other payout. <2> = *market capitalization.*

shareholder value added (SVA) the measure of a company's worth to the shareholders, usually the net profit after tax in excess of the cost of capital. ***See***: *market value added.*

shareholder value transfer (SVT) the amount of shareholders' equity flowing out of a corporation to its executives through exercised stock options.

share of capital stock = *share.*

share of common = *common stock.*

share of no par value = *no-par-value stock.*

share option = *stock option.*

shareowner = *shareholder.*

share-price index futures contract (SPI) a futures contract the underlying asset of which is a stock price index.

share pushing <UK> selling shares at a much higher price with glowing but unsubstantiated news of the company.

share quotation = *stock quotation.*

share ratio contract <Australia> a contract the payoff of which is based on the difference between a stock's performance and that of a market index.

shares authorized = *authorized shares.*

shares outstanding <1> = *number of shares outstanding.* <2>= *outstanding shares.*

share split-up = *stock split.*

share warrant = *stock warrant.*

shark repellent *golden parachute, safe harbor, poison pill,* and *scorched-earth policy* etc. used to protect a company against a *takeover.* ***See***: *lock-up option; shark watcher.*

Sharpe index = *Sharpe ratio.*

Sharpe ratio a ratio of the annualized *excess return* to the *total risk.* ***Also***: Sharpe index. ***See***: *Sortino ratio.*

shell merger = *reverse merger.*

SHIELD synthetic high-income equity-linked debenture

shock absorber a temporary restriction placed on the trading of index futures due to a sudden intraday decrease in the index. ***See***: *circuit breaker.*

shogun security dollar denominated security issued by US companies sold in Japan only. ***Also***: geisha security.

short the state of selling a security, option or futures contract not own. ***Opp***: *long.* ***See***: *bear.*

short account = *selling short.*

short against the box = *against the box.*

short backspread a spread created by buying one *near-the-money option* and selling two or more out-of-the-money options with the same expiration on the same underlying asset. ***Also***: short ratio vertical spread. ***See***: *long backspread.*

short-biased of an investment that holds more short positions than long.

short bond a bond for less than 5 years. ***Also***: floating bond; short-term bond.

short butterfly a butterfly created by selling a low strike option and buying two middle strike options, and selling one higher strike option. ***Also***: selling a butterfly.

short calendar iron butterfly spread a spread that is comprised of one long calendar spread and one long butterfly spread and one short box spread.

short calendar iron condor spread a spread that is comprised of one long calendar spread and two long butterfly spreads and one short box spread.

short call a call the seller of which hopes the price of the underlying asset to fall. ***Also***: written call.

short call butterfly a position created by selling one low strike call, buying two middle strike calls with the same strike, and buying a higher strike call.

short call condor selling a low strike call option, buying two middle strike call options with different strike price, and buying a higher strike call option.

short call strategy an option trading strategy that involves a short position in call options.

short call synthetic straddle a straddle created by selling two at-the-money calls for every 100 shares owned.

short combination = *bear combination.*

short combo = *bear combination.*

short condor a condor with a short strangle and long a farther out-of-the-money call and put.

short conversion selling put, buying call and then selling the underlying asset. ***Also***: reversal; reversal arbitrage; reverse conversion.

short cost-of-carry the cost of carry received for the short positions.

short coupon the bond interest payment covering a period less than six months.

short covered call a short call the writer of which has bought the underlying asset.

short covered put a short put the writer of which has bought the underlying asset.

short-dated security a security having a period of not more than five years.

short-dated swap the *foreign exchange swap* for less than one week.

short delta a situation in which the option holder will gain if the market price of the underlying asset falls.

short exchange the foreign exchange that must be settled in eight or ten days.

short exempt a special situation where a short sale is allowed on a minus-tick.

shortfall risk the risk that the return will fall below some target level.

short-form merger = *practical merger*.

short forward the party to a forward contract who has an obligation to sell the underlying. ***See***: *long forward*.

short gut = *bear gut*.

short hedge the sale of futures to hedge against the possible drop in price of a commodity planned to be sold in the future. ***Also***: sell hedge; selling hedge. ***See***: *long hedge*.

shorting against the box = *against the box*.

short interest <1> the total of the short sales outstanding in a security or commodity or on an exchange. <2> the securities sold short and not covered on a particular date. <3> the interest earned on a loan in a short period of time. <4> the balance of borrowed stock.

short-interest ratio = *days to cover*.

short interest rebate (SIR) the percentage of interest earned on the short sale proceeds in a sell program that is rebated to the arbitrageur.

short interest theory the theory which holds that a large short interest is the predecessor of a rise in the price.

short iron butterfly a position created by combining a bull call spread with a bear put spread.

short leg the part of a spread indicating a commitment to sell the underlying asset.

short leverage selling metal to a leverage firm at a given price hoping that the prices will fall and the contract can be closed out at a profit.

short-life option the option with a few weeks until expiration.

short market value the total value of all securities shorted in an account in a brokerage firm.

short on a bounce down to sell the stock short once it has risen to the resistance at the indicated price and then dropped below.

short option an option held by someone who hopes the price of the underlying asset to fall. ***See***: *long option*.

short option hedge = *time hedge*.

short option value the fair market value of the call option embedded in PERCS or ELKS.

short position (SP) the position of one who has sold more securities than the quantity he or she has in possession to cover the sales. ***Also***: bear position; oversold. ***Opp***: *long position*.

short proceeds the cash received from the short sale of a security or other derivative instruments.

short-put the put option sold by the investor who wants the price to fall. ***Also***: written put.

short put butterfly a position created by selling a low strike price put, buying two middle strike puts with the same strike, and selling a higher strike put.

short put condor a position created by selling one lower-strike put, buying two middle-strike puts with different strike prices, and selling one higher-strike put.

short put strategy the strategy that builds short position in options by selling puts.

short put synthetic straddle a straddle that involves selling two at-the-money puts for every 100 shares sold.

short rate the exchange rate for checks, bills of exchange payable on demand or at sight or with eight or fewer days until maturity. ***Also***: cable rate; check rate; demand rate; sight rate.

short ratio vertical spread = *short back-spread.*

short rebate the rate of return paid on the collateral when shares are borrowed to cover short sales.

short sale (SS) the sale by the seller who does not own what he sold. ***Also***: bear sale; box short sale; type 5.

short-sale account a brokerage account for short selling customers only. ***Also***: type 5 account.

short seller one who tries to profit by selling short. ***See***: *bear raider.*

short selling = *selling short.*

short squeeze buying all shares outstanding to push up prices and make the short sellers have to borrow shares or to pay an inflated price. ***Also***: cornering; corners squeeze. ***Opp***: *long squeeze.* ***See***: *bear squeeze*; *squeeze.*

short straddle = *bear straddle.*

short strangle = *bear strangle.*

short strip a strip under which two puts and one call of which are held short. ***See***: *long strip.*

short swing trading = *insider trading.*

short synthetic future a position created by selling calls and buying the same amount of puts with the same strike price and expiration date.

short tender <1> = *leveraged buyout.* <2> = *short tendering.*

short tendering the sale of borrowed securities to the acquiring company that is making a takeover bid. ***Also***: short tender.

short-term auction rate (STAR) = *auction rate preferred stock.*

short-term bond = *short bond.*

short-term debt = *unfunded debt.*

short-term debt security a debt security with a maturity of less than five years. ***Also***: note.

short-term equity participation units a synthetic *participating equity preferred stock* using a portfolio or index rather than one stock as the reference. ***Also***: STEP units.

short-term interest rate contract (STIR) the short-term interest rate futures or options contract.

short-term investment the investment which can be converted into cash in one year or less. ***Also***: temporary investment.

short-term money market (STMM) = *money market.*

short-term note (S.T. note) a promissory note issued for less than one year in maturity. ***Also***: current note; current paper; debit paper.

short-term preferred share <Canada> a preferred share issued by a private firm after Dec 15 , 1987.

short-term swap a swap contract the early termination date is within one year. ***Also***: junior swap.

short-term tax exempt the short-term security issued by a state, municipality, and quasi-government entity.

short-term trading index = *ARMS index.*

short the basis the situation under which the dealer who is short in the cash market and is long hedged by a futures position. **See**: *long the basis.*

short vega a situation when the volatility is extremely high, causing investors to sell options. **See**: *long vega.*

short volatility the volatility which will benefit the investors who are holding short positions.

shout <verb> to reset the strike price of a shout option.

shout call option a European call with the features of a shout option.

shout option an exotic option that allows the investor to lock into a defined profit while maintaining the right to continue participating in gains.

show-stopper the strategy to thwart the takeover attempt of an unwelcome raider by closing down the businesses.

SIA swap in arrears.

Siamese shares = *paired shares.*

side = *leg.*

side of the market = *size.*

sight exchange = *spot exchange.*

sight rate = *short rate.*

sigma the standard deviation (volatility of the price) of the option underlying asset.

SIGN stock index growth security

signaling approach <1> a notion that the choice of capital structure by insiders can signal information to the outsiders. ***Also***: asymmetric information approach. <2> a theory which holds that dividend changes are important signals about future earnings.

signal to buy = *buy signal.*

signal to sell = *sell signal.*

silver parachute a severance paid to employees of a company should it be acquired. **See**: *golden parachute.*

similar bond a bond with the same yield, maturity or credit rating as the one sold.

simple arbitrage the arbitrage between two parties or between two currencies. ***Also***: bilateral arbitrage; bitrage; direct arbitrage; single arbitrage; vanilla arbitrage. **See**: *compound arbitrage.*

simple bond = *unsecured bond.*

simple return today's price change divided by previous day's price. ***Also:*** arithmetic return.

simple step option a step option the value of which increases or decreases by a simple percentage on the original principal or investment. ***Also***: arithmetic step option. **See**: *proportional step option.*

simple swap = *plain swap.*

simulated VAR value at risk calculated by using simulation method. ***Also***: Monte Carlo VAR.

simulation = *financial simulation.*

sinful stock a stock issued by companies associated with activities which are considered to be unethical or immoral. ***Also***: sin stock.

Singapore dollar CD a certificate of deposit denominated in Singapore dollar.

single arbitrage = *simple arbitrage.*

single barrier option a barrier option with one barrier set above or below the strike.

single commodity hedge a hedge that is for one single commodity only.

single currency swap a swap on *foreign exchange* involving one foreign currency only. ***See***: *covered interest arbitrage.*

single exchange rate an exchange rate applicable to both trade and non-trade items. ***Also***: unitary rate. ***See***: *multiple exchange rates.*

single family mortgage revenue bond a bond secured by mortgage loan repayments on single family home mortgages.

single issue option <UK> the low strike option traded in Finland to provide the investors with most features of stock ownership when actual ownership of the registered shares can't be transferred.

single layer CDO = *single-tranche CDO.*

single maturity bond = *term bond.*

single name credit derivative a credit derivative with one reference entity only. ***See***: *portfolio credit derivative.*

single option a single put or a call option rather than a straddle or spread. ***Also***: outright contract.

single-payment bond a bond which makes one payment of principal and interest only, usually at maturity.

single-period MVO <1> mean-variance optimization that covers asset return and risk for a period only. <2> = *Markowitz portfolio optimization.*

single-rate system a system under which there is only one exchange rate.

single-state municipal bond fund the mutual fund that invests in government obligations in a single state only.

single stock futures (SSF) one single trade that is equivalent to the simultaneous sale of a put and purchase of a call.

single-tranche CDO a CDO representing a specific portion of risk. ***Also***: Bespoke tranche; customized CDO; single layer CDO; single-tranche synthetic CDO. ***See***: *multi-tranche CDO.*

single-tranche synthetic CDO = *single- tranche CDO.*

single transaction a transaction which includes all purchases or sales for one account of a single security.

sinker = *sinking fund bond.*

sinking fund (SF) the fund created by borrowers for redeeming a bond. ***Also***: continual redemption sinking fund; extinguishment fund; long-term debt offsets; provisions for repayments.

sinking fund bond a bond with a sinking fund established for the payment of principal and interest. ***Also***: sinker.

sin stock = *sinful stock.*

SIR short interest rebate

SIR maximum a level that determines the *sell threshold* in program trading.

SIR minimum a level that determines a *sell active* when the difference of the future minus the spot index declines.

SIRS stock index return security

sitting on a gain of an investor, holding a stock that has been appreciated in value.

sixty-day 6% method = *6% 60 days method.*

size <1> in quotation, the total number of shares available at a given price. <2> the actual number of shares represented in the bid or offering in a quotation. ***Also***: side of the market; size of market. <3> = *contract size.*

size of market = *size.*

skew = *volatility smile.*

skewing = *volatility skewing.*

skip-day settlement the settlement of a trade one business day later.

sleeper stock of a *sleeping beauty.*

sleeping beauty a company with some attractive features, such as undervalued assets, hidden mineral reserves, etc.

sliding parity = *crawling peg.*

slippage <1> the difference between the estimated cost and the actual transaction costs. <2> cost to an investor that results from buying at the asked price and selling at the bid. <3> the difference between the theoretical value and the market price of an option.

slug non-marketable US Treasury security sold to state and local governments only. ***See***: *nonmarketable security.*

small business corporation stock = *Section 1244 stock.*

small business investment company stock (SBIC stock) = *Section 1244 stock.*

small business-related security = *Section 1244 stock.*

small business stock = *Section 1244 stock.*

small cap a company with $250 million to $1 billion capitalization. ***See***: *large cap*; *micro cap*; *mid cap.*

small cap stock a stock the total market capitalization is from $250 million to $1 billion. ***Also***: ankle biter.

small cap stock fund a mutual fund that invests in small cap stocks.

Small Corporate Offering Registration (SCOR) the OTC sale of securities that allows for up to $1 million to be raised while avoiding the costs and formalities of an IPO.

small cost option (SCOOP) an embedded digital range option.

small firm effect the tendency of small firms to outperform the general stock market.

small investor an investor who trades in small size. ***Also***: *individual investor.*

small issue the issue of securities $15 million or less in value.

small issue exemption <1> an issue of industrial development bond the interest of which is exempt from tax if the proceeds are used in buying land, or depreciable properties. <2> an issues of securities of $1 million or less.

small piece a bond in denomination of less than $1,000.

small savings certificate the certificate of deposit which represents small amount time deposits.

small stock dividend a stock dividend that is 25% or less in value of a firm's total outstanding shares.

smart trading the trading that takes into account the tax. ***Also***: tax smart trading.

SMBS stripped mortgage-backed security

smidge small amount of price, 1/8 or ¼.

SML <1> securities market line. <2> security market line.

snowballing the process by which the activation of stop orders in a declining or advancing market will cause further upward or downward pressure on the prices thus triggering more stop orders and more price pressure and so on.

soaring price = *inflated price.*

SOB warrant stock-over-bond warrant

soccer mom indicator the concept which holds that what parents are talking about at their children's soccer game, the popularity of the topic, such as the Internet stock, will be ending.

socially conscious investing = *green investing.*

socially conscious mutual fund = *ethical fund.*

socially responsible investing = *green investing.*

SOE short of exchange

SOFFEX Swiss Options and Financial Futures Exchange

soft arbitrage an arbitrage between the public sector stock and the private sector stock.

soft call protection the feature added to the convertible fixed-income and debt securities, which dictates that a premium will be paid by the issuer if early redemption occurs.

soft commodity the commodity which is grown rather than mined, such as coffee. ***See***: *hard commodity.*

soft currency the currency of a country expected to drop in value relative to other currencies. ***See***: *hard currency.*

soft dollar the amount invested in the development or purchase of real estate, such as prepaid fee. ***See***: *hard dollar.*

soft market = *depressed market.*

soft spot a rapid decline in one kind of securities while the market as a whole remains firm.

sold away having sold stock to another OTC dealer before the present offering.

sold last a trade that occurs in sequence but is reported at a later time.

sold-out market the unavailability of a futures in a particular commodity or date of maturity.

sold sale the trade that is reported at a later time than it occurred.

solicitation fee a charge to a company by the stock exchange for requesting stock tenders through its members.

solicitors' fund the fixed-interest fund available by solicitors from investment funds supplied by clients.

solvency either the ability to pay debts when due or having more assets over debts. ***Also***: debt-paying ability; debt-servicing capacity; financial solvency.

solvency ratio <1> = *equity-debt ratio.* <2> = *equity-to-assets ratio.*

solving rate of return = *present value profitability index.*

Sonnie Mae a note issued by the New York Mortgage Agency. ***Also***: Sony Mae.

Sony Mae = *Sonnie Mae.*

SOR stockholder of record

Sortino ratio the same as Sharpe ratio, except it uses downside deviation for the denominator, not the standard deviation. ***Also***: upside potential ratio.

source of funds seller the seller of a stock for the purpose of raising cash for other purchases.

source spread = *crush spread.*

sour crude the barrels of crude oil that do not meet content requirements, such as low levels of sulfur and hydrogen. ***See***: *sweet crude.*

southbound swap the trade to swap the investments from Canadian dollar to US dollar. ***See***: *north-bound swap.*

sovereign risk = *political risk.*

space arbitrage = *arbitrage in space.*

SPAN <1> spread-adjusted note. <2> Standardized Portfolio Analysis.

spark spread the difference between the market price of electricity and its cost of production (natural gas price).

spark spread option an option on the spark spread, with both the power price and the natural gas price as the underlying assets.

spatial arbitrage = *arbitrage in space.*

SPDR = *spider.*

special arbitrage account a special margin account reserved for the transactions in which the risk is hedged by an offsetting trade or position.

special assessment bond the municipal bond with interest paid by the taxes of the community benefiting from bond-funded projects.

special bid = *exchange acquisition.*

special bonus dividend = *extra dividend.*

special bracket a group of banks other than the managing underwriter.

special call price the price at which bond trustees call bonds for redemption.

special claim on residual equity (SCORE) the certificate which entitles the holder to the appreciation of an underlying, not to the dividend or interest.

special dating = *dating.*

special dividend = *extra dividend.*

special expiration price option = *barrier option.*

specialist block purchase the purchase by a specialist for his own account of a large block of stock outside the regular market on an exchange.

specialist block sale the sale by the specialist of a block of stock outside the regular market on the exchange.

specialist's short-sale ratio the ratio of the amount of short sales by specialists on the floor of an exchange, e. g. NYSE to total short sales.

specialized mutual fund the mutual fund that limits its investments to a particular industry.

special offering the offering of a stock with announcement that all costs and commissions are paid by the seller.

special option a conventional OTC put or call with some remaining life time offered for resale by a broker-dealer or a client in secondary market dealing. ***Also***: second-hand option.

special purpose entity (SPE) an entity that at least 3% of the capital has been invested from independent investors.

special purpose vehicle (SPV) an entity created to participate in derivative or *securitization.* **See**: *bankruptcy remote entity; derivatives product company.*

special security a security with a special demand in the repo market.

special situation stock <1> a stock that should soon rise in value due to a forth-coming favorable event, such as a new product. <2> the stock that fluctuates widely due to some news, e. g. merger.

specialty option <1> = *alternative option.* <2> = *exotic option.*

specie = *hard currency.*

specific issue market the market for a specific security the price of which is expected to fall.

specific risk <1> the risk that is unique to an asset. <2> = *unsystematic risk.*

speculating in differences = *dealing in differences.*

speculation trading based on conjectures about the price changes and profiting from price fluctuations. ***Also***: playing the market; profiteering; speculative business; venture.

speculation index a ratio comparing the volume of trades on the American Stock Exchange and the NYSE.

speculation in stocks the practice of selling forward with the hope of buying back at a lower price. ***Also***: agiotage.

speculative business = *speculation.*

speculative buy an advice to buy a stock but the price may drop.

speculative capital structure capital structure with only a small portion of capitalization in common stock.

speculative-grade bond <1> a bond that is rated Ba or lower by Moody's, or BB or lower by S&P, or any unrated bond. <2> = *junk bond.*

speculative hold an advice recommending others to hold a stock but the price may drop.

speculative limit maximum position in one commodity future (or option) or in all futures (or options) of one commodity combined that may be held by an investor. ***Also***: speculative position limit.

speculative motive desire to hold cash to speculate in attractive investments. **See**: *transaction motive.*

speculative position limit = *speculative limit.*

speculative sell an advice to sell a stock but the price may go up.

speculative stock a very risky stock the issuing company may default.

speculator the person who is willing to assume a large risk in the hope of large gain. ***Also***: gunslinger; operator; profiteer. **See**: *investor.*

speed = *prepayment speed.*

SPI share-price index futures contract

spider an unmanaged unit investment trust of the S&P 500 that trades on the Amex like a stock. Symbol: SPY. ***Also***: genus; habitat; S&P 500; SPDR; spyder; Standard & Poor's Depositary Receipt; the Amex.

spinning an illegal practice of brokerage houses exchanging IPO shares with top executives of the issuing company for reciprocating business from their companies.

spin-off a company sets up and funds a new subsidiary and gives the shares of this new subsidiary to the old company's shareholders on a pro rata basis. **See**: *diverstiture*; *split-off*; *split-up.*

spin-off share <Canada> the share in other company, received on the eligible distribution in respect of the original share.

split = *stock split.*

split-back = *split down.*

split capital the capital structure of a mutual fund by which the capital consists of two kinds of shares: income shares and capital shares.

split close the market which closes with price discrepancies in a series of final daily futures-contract transactions.

split coupon bond = *zero coupon bond.*

split down to increase the face value of shares by issuing a new share to replace two or more outstanding shares. ***Also***: consolidation of capital; consolidation of shares; Irish dividend; Polish dividend; reverse split; reverse stock-split; Scottish dividend; share consolidation; split-back; stock split-down.

split-fee option the *compound option*, the buyer first pays an initial fee, then a second fee to extend the option to a further maturity date.

split investment company = *dual purpose fund.*

split-off occurs when a company sets up and funds a new company and gives the shares of this new company to the stockholders of the old company in exchange for their shares in the old company. ***See***: *spin-off*; *split-up*.

split-offering a new municipal bond, part of which is represented by the serial bonds and part by fixed maturity bonds.

split opening occurs on an exchange when there are different opening prices for the same security because 2 groups of traders have stated simultaneously.

split rating 2 different rating agencies, such as Standard & Poor's and Moody's, assign a different rating to a security.

split share a share that is being or has been split or divided into a number of new shares. ***Also***: split stock.

split spread <UK> a spread over LIBOR that has different figures in different periods of the credit.

split stock <1> purchase or sale of stock shared with others. <2> = *split share*.

split up occurs when a company divides into 2 or more new companies, gives its old shareholders the shares of the new companies, and goes out of business. ***See***: *spin-off*; *split-off*; *stock split*.

spoiling the market causing the market price of a security to rise or fall suddenly by buying or selling a very large quantity at one time.

spoken for the opposite demand or supply that the investor has in efforts to cross the stock.

spoof bid = *phantom bid*.

spot-against-forward buying a spot currency or commodity against a forward commitment.

spot commodity = *cash commodity*.

spot-cross-currency arbitrage an arbitrage that involves three currencies in the spot market.

spot curve = *zero-coupon curve*.

spot date two days after a transaction.

spot deferred contract a contract giving the seller the option to roll the contract forward rather than making delivery on a specific date. ***Also***: undated forward.

spot exchange the foreign exchange that must be delivered two days after the transaction has been made. ***Also***: sight exchange. ***See***: *forward exchange*.

spot exchange contract a contract that provides for prompt delivery of foreign exchange.

spot exchange rate the exchange rate used in the spot exchange transaction. ***Also***: spot rate.

spot-forward arbitrage an arbitrage that involves the spot and forward prices.

spot futures parity theory a theory that describes the theoretically relationship between the spot and futures prices, violation of the relationship gives rise to arbitrage opportunities.

spot hedge the hedge that uses the spot exchange rates. ***Also***: borrower arbitrage. ***See***: *forward hedge*.

spot interest rate = *spot rate*.

spot loan a loan that commences now.

spot market = *cash market*.

spot month = *nearby month*.

spot/next an extra charge on a purchase of a foreign currency today that is to be settled on the next business day rather than being settled today.

spot position the difference between the spot exchange bought and the spot exchange sold.

spot price (SP) the price of a security or the spot commodity sold for immediate delivery and payment. ***Also***:

cash price; price on spot. **See**: *forward price.*

spot rate <1> interest rate fixed today on a loan made today. ***Also***: spot interest rate. **See**: *forward rate.* <2> the yield on zero-coupon bond. ***Also***: zero coupon rate. <3> = *spot exchange rate.*

spot rate curve a curve showing the relationship between the spot rates and different maturities.

spot secondary the *secondary offering* which may not require a *Registration Statement* with the SEC, and may be released soon.

spot-to-futures arbitrage = *swap.*

spot trading cash trading for immediate delivery.

spot versus forward delta hedge the adjustment in the size of the hedging position to allow for the effect of cost of carry on the forward price.

spot volatility the volatility used to price a multi-period option, when each option employs a different volatility.

spot yield rate the curve that plots spot rates against term to maturity.

spraddle a straddle the put strike price is above, but the call strike price is below the market price of the underlying at the time the spread is created.

spread <1> the difference between the prices of 2 stocks of the same kind. <2> the difference between a stock index and a future based on that index. <3> the difference between the high and low price of a security over a given period. <4> two concurrent and opposite positions exist in the futures market. <5> in futures trading, the difference between the delivery months in the same or different markets. <6> difference between the redemption price and the book value of a stock. <7> = *bid-ask spread.* <8> = *gross spread.* <9> = *option spread.* <10> = *TED spread.* <11> = *yield spread.*

spread-adjusted note (SPAN) a note with a base rate fixed or linked to a benchmark and supplemental spread linked to credit spreads prevailing in the market at designated reset dates.

spread-based option a credit option the holder of which pays a strike spread and receives the difference between the underlying spread and the strike spread.

spread betting an OTC derivative with a payout determined by a spread between two or more financial indexes. ***Also***: financial spread betting.

spread conversion = *collar.*

spread differential = *net cost of spread.*

spreader a person who is long or short on positions of equal amounts.

spread hedge a hedge in a commodity complex.

spread income the difference between interest income from loans and the cost of funds. ***Also***: margin income.

spreading = *option spreading.*

spread lock <1> the clause allowing the bond issuer to lock in a fixed interest with the underwriter. <2> = *deferred rate-setting swap.*

spread-lock option <1> an option to enter into a spread-lock agreement on a yield spread. <2> an option to roll one or a sequence of futures contracts forward to more distant months at a fixed spread or a spread relative to the fair value basis.

spread-lock swap = *deferred rate setting swap.*

spread option <1> an option the underlying of which is an interest rate spread or other type of spread. ***Also***: international spread option; option on a spread. **See**: *option spreading.* <2> = *difference option.*

spread order an order which designates the securities of listed options the client wishes to trade with the price difference between the two contracts.

spread position the status of a trading account after an option *spread order* is executed.

spread premium extra spread in a credit derivative to cover additional risk.

spread product the corporate bond and mortgage-backed bond which provide higher yields than the Treasury bonds.

spread put bond a bond puttable to the issuer or to an underwriter at a spread measured in basis points over the yield of a comparable maturity Treasury issue.

spread risk the exposure to the changing spreads between two yields.

spread sheet a sheet indicating the offer price of the gross spread dividend or interest etc. of a new issue.

spread strike = *credit spread strike.*

spread swap = *overtrading.*

spreadtion = *spread option.*

spread to LIBOR = *LIBOR spread.*

spread trade the trade designed to profit from movements in the spread between two or more underlying indices or a trade involving the simultaneous purchase and sale of different options on the same underlying asset to profit from the spread.

spread trading the trading of spreads in futures.

spread warrant the instrument with a return pattern linked to the cross-border interest rate spreads. ***Also***: international spread warrant.

springing warrant an option attached to a deep discount bond the holder of which can exercise when a triggering event like a hostile takeover occurs. **See**: *debt with springing warrants.*

spurt a sudden quick jump upwards in the market price. ***Also***: bulge; intermediate rally.

SPV special purpose vehicle

spyder = *spider.*

square a position in a currency, security or commodity which is balanced. ***Also***: square off.

square off = *square.*

squeeze <1> the period of tight money policy when interest rates are high and borrowing is difficult. <2> accumulating a position in forward trading larger than the underlying spot market supply. **See**: *short squeeze.*

squeeze agreement = *repurchase agreement.*

SRD social rate of discount

SRO <1> self-regulatory organization. <2> standing room only.

SSF single stock futures

S_t the price of the underlying asset in the option pricing model

stabilization underwriter's intervention to keep the market price from falling below the public offering price, often by placing order to buy. ***Also***: pegging.

stabilized bond = *indexed bond.*

stabilizing bid a bid submitted in order to stabilize the price of a security. **See**: *penalty bid.*

stable rate of exchange = *fixed exchange rate.*

stack and roll a *stack hedge* periodically rolled into the next delivery month.

stacked view option quote display format with calls listed first, then puts. ***See***: *straddled view*.

stack hedge a hedge in which a long-term commitment is hedged with a rolling sequence of offsetting contracts expiring on dates appropriate to the risk hedged. ***Also***: rolling hedge; roll-over hedge.

stag a speculator who applies for a stock allotment in a new offering with the intention to make it oversubscribed so the price will be higher than the original issue price, then sells the shares for a profit. ***Also***: dolphin.

staged drawdown swap = *accreting swap*.

stagflation slowing growth in economy accompanied by a general rise in the market prices. ***Also***: stagnation.

staggered maturities = *staggering maturities*.

staggering maturities buying the short-, medium-, and long-term bonds to avoid the risk of interest rate fluctuation. ***Also***: staggered maturities; staggering the market. ***See***: *laddered maturity strategy*.

staggering the market = *staggering maturities*.

stagnation = *stagflation*.

STAIRS stepped tax-exempt appreciation on income realization security

stair step option strategy the position created with options and the underlying that has a profit-loss profile similar to two stair-steps when profit and loss is graphed against the price of the underlying.

stair-step promoting offering new stock in a series of separate categories, each priced slightly above the other to give the impression of a rising demand.

stakeholder <1> a party with an interest in a firm, such as stockholder, creditor, employee, supplier. <2> <UK> a person holding a sum of money paid as a deposit on a contract for the purchase of a real property.

stale closing price the most recent price of a mutual fund share at 4:00 p. m. ***Also***: stale price.

stale price = *stale closing price*.

stale price arbitrage = *market timing 2*.

stalking horse the potential buyer, in a situation where several raiders exist for one target firm, who has agreed to make a tender offer in order to elicit offers from others.

stalking horse bid the strategy used by bankrupt companies whereby they obtain an initial bid on their assets from an interested buyer of their choice.

stand-alone risk the risk of loss on a single loan or other contract, ignoring portfolio effects.

Standard & Poor's (S&P) one of the three best known bond rating agencies in the USA. ***See***: *FIS*; *Moody's*.

Standard & Poor's 500 Stock Average an index composed of 425 industrials, 50 utilities, and 25 railroads, supplied by S&P. ***Also***: S&P 500.

Standard & Poor's Depositary Receipt = *spider*.

standard amount in foreign exchange market, $1 million or the multiple of it.

standard date typical date for a foreign exchange forward contract, e. g. in 1, 2, 3, 6 and 12 months. ***See***: *broken date*.

standard deviation <1> the daily volatility converted into the trading units of asset. <2> measure of the dispersion of a set of data from its mean.

standard futures month the month abbreviations in futures trading: F=Jan, G=Feb, H=Mar, J=Apr, K=May, M=Jun, N=Jul, Q=Aug, U=Sep,

V=Oct, X=Nov, Z=Dec. ***Also***: futures month abbreviations.

standardized yield = *SEC yield.*

standard maturity in foreign exchange, 1, 3, 6 or 12 months, and some currencies, 1, 2, 3, 4, 5, 6, 9 or 12 months in other currencies.

standard option the option with standard features and terms, such as a *vanilla option.* **See**: *exotic option.*

standard swap = *plain swap.*

standby fee the fee paid to an underwriter who agrees to buy all stock not purchased by public investors in a rights offering.

standby offering the offering of a rights issue by a company in which an under-writer offers to standby to buy the rights the corporation is unable to sell for a standby fee.

standing offer = *offer good until withdrawn by seller.*

standing order the *banker's order* for regular intervals.

standstill yield to maturity the yield to maturity on a PERCS, ELKS or DECS when the underlying's price is unchanged at maturity. **See**: *static return.*

stapled stock = *paired shares.*

STAR short-term auction rate

state bond a bond issued by the state government or its agency, the income from which is free of federal tax.

state contingent claim = *arrow-debreu security.*

stated capital total capital calculated by its stated value. ***Also***: declared capital; legal capital.

stated conversion price the price that is fixed when a *convertible security* is issued, calculated as the par value of security divided by the conversion ratio.

stated interest rate = *coupon rate of interest.*

stated maturity the date the last payment would occur at zero *constant prepayment rate.*

stated rate of interest = *coupon rate of interest.*

stated value the issue price of a no par value stock as stated in the articles of association.

statement in lieu of prospectus <UK> a document similar to but instead of, the prospectus sent to the Registrar of Companies by a public firm that intends to make new issue of shares.

statement of assets and liabilities = *balance sheet.*

statement of the sources and composition of company capital = *balance sheet.*

state price the price at time zero of a state-contingent derivative that pays one unit in a certain future state.

state price deflator a deflator with which the property that the deflated price process is a martingale.

static hedge a hedge that does not have to be changed once it is in place.

static hedging the hedging that employs static positions in vanilla options.

static replication the *portfolio replicating* that requires a buy-and-hold strategy on several other instruments. **See**: *dynamic replication.*

static return option return that realizes on a particular position if the underlying were unchanged at the expiration.

static spread a measure of the risk premium on a corporate bond relative to US Treasury bonds.

static statement = *balance sheet.*

stationary time series a time series

that appears to have a long term average level.

statistical arbitrage (statarb) an attempt to profit from the pricing inefficiencies identified through the use of mathematical models. ***See***: *pairs trade.*

statistical volatility = *historical volatility.*

statutory consolidation = *consolidation.*

statutory stock option the stock option with tax benefits made available to the taxpayer under the tax laws. ***See***: *non-statutory option.*

statutory voting = *regular voting.*

steenth = *teeny.*

s'teenth one sixteenth of $1 or 1%, a common profit margin on a trade in a liquid stock, such as IBM. ***See***: *teeny.*

steepening of the yield curve a change in the yield curve where the spread between the long- and short-term Treasury has increased.

STEER structured enhanced return trust

stem the tide to stop a prevailing trend. ***Also***: stop the bleeding.

step barrier option an option the principal of which is gradually amortized (knocked out option) or increased (knocked in option) based on the time the underlying asset price is beyond the barrier. ***Also***: step option.

step-down bond a bond in which the rate of interest is high at first and, then it will step down to a lower rate in later periods.

step-down floater a security designed to provide a spread over the benchmark index during the initial years, but offer a decreasing yield over time.

step-down note the floating-rate note the interest rate of which declines after a specified period of time.

step-down option = *anti-crash warrant.*

step-down preferred stock = *fast-pay preferred stock.*

step-down spread interest rate spread that falls in later periods of a loan.

step-down swap <1> an interest rate swap with a decrease in the fixed payment rate over the life of the swap. <2> variety of amortizing swap with a small number of reductions in the notional principal amount.

step-down warrant = *anti-crash warrant.*

step-lock option = *ladder option.*

step option = *step barrier option.*

step-out trading the broker's execution of an order but giving other firms credit and commission for the trade.

step payment option = *strike step option.*

stepped call a call feature that allows a bond to be called on coupon dates only. ***See***: *rolling call.*

stepped-coupon bond the bond in which all coupons have the same interest rate, which is set to rise periodically.

stepped tax-exempt appreciation on income realization security (STAIRS) a zero-coupon bond that is converted to an interest-bearing security at a some time after issuance.

step premium option a contingent premium option with the feature that the buyer pays no upfront premium.

STEP units = *short-term equity participation units.*

step-up bond a bond that pays a coupon rate for an initial period followed by a higher coupon rate.

step-up cap a cap structure that limits an interest coupon increase to a certain amount at each reset date. ***Also***: periodic cap. **See**: *jump*.

step-up coupon note = *callable step-up note.*

step-up coupon swap a swap the coupon payments of which increase on schedule.

step-up floater the floating rate note that provides for an increase in the spread to the index if the note is not called after a certain period.

step-up inverse floater the floating rate note whereby the fixed rate from which the index is subtracted increases if the note is not called after a certain period.

step-up option the call option with one or more scheduled increases in the strike price.

step-up price the conversion price of a convertible security that gets higher as time passes. ***Also***: accumulation price.

step-up recovery floater (SURF) the variation on a floating-rate note which typically pays one-half of the constant maturity Treasury rate plus a spread and is subject to a floor.

step-up security a callable security if not called, the interest rate will be higher.

step-up strike price an option the strike price of which increases based on the preset schedule.

step-up swap = *accreting swap.*

step-up warrant a call warrant with one or more increases in the strike price on specified dates.

sterling Eurobond <UK> sterling bond treated as a foreign currency bond for exchange control and tax purposes.

sterling ratio <UK> the ratio which determines the advisors who have the highest returns with the least volatility, calculated as: the compounded annual return ÷ (average drawdown - 10%).

sterling security <UK> the security of which both capital and interest are payable in sterling or in another currency in the sterling area.

sticks <slang> the financial areas away from New York.

stick-to-strike = *sticky strike.*

sticky-by-strike = *sticky strike.*

sticky deal = *underbooked.*

sticky delta = *sticky moneyness.*

sticky floater = *ratchet floater.*

sticky moneyness the implied volatility of an option with a given moneyness does not change when the underlying asset price changes. ***Also***: sticky delta.

sticky prices the commodity prices that react more slowly than the asset prices to monetary shocks.

sticky strike the implied volatility of a particular strike price of an option does not change when the underlying asset price changes. ***Also***: stick-to-strike; sticky-by-strike.

STIF short-term investment fund

stimulating conversion stimulating the holder of convertibles to convert the holdings by setting a higher conversion price. **See**: *forcing conversion.*

STIR short-term interest rate contract

STMM short-term money market

stochastic calculus approach the derivative pricing approach that uses stochastic calculus combined with risk neutral assumption. ***Also***: martingale approach; risk neutral approach.

stochastic process the process whose behavior is non-deterministic in that the next state is partially, but not fully determined by the previous state.

stochastic volatility serial correlation in squared stock price changes. ***Also***: conditional heteroskedasticity.

stochastic volatility model the model whereby both the underlying asset's value and its volatility are stochastic processes.

stock <1> the legal capital of a company divided into shares. (In UK, stock can be transferred in any value, while shares can be transferred in units of face value). ***Also***: concern; corporation's stock; equity. <2> a security representing the right in a loan. <3> = *stock certificate.*

stock acquisition = *acquisition of shares.*

stock appreciation income-linked securities (SAILS) = *dividend enhanced convertible stock.*

stock appreciation right (SAR) the privilege under which employees can elect to exercise the option or take the value of the stock's appreciation.

stock average the arithmetic mean of the prices of a stock, or a group of option prices of the same stock. **See**: *average.*

stock basket = *basket.*

stock bonus = *stock dividend.*

stock certificate (SC) the evidence of ownership of a company that issues shares. ***Also***: capital stock certificate; certificate; certificate of capital stock; certificate of stock; scrip; stock; stock trust certificate.

stock discount the amount a stock's par value in excess of its paid-in capital amount.

stock dividend the dividend paid out by a company in its own shares or shares of another company held by the company. ***Also***: share bonus; share dividend; stock bonus. **See**: *bonus share.*

stock/equity ratio the ratio of the market price of the junior stock issues to the total face amount of total capital of the issuing company.

stock exchange an organization that provides a market place for the trading of security. ***Also***: bourse; exchange market; house; market; securities exchange.

stock exchange account = *account period.*

stock exchange index an index number indicating the proportional change of the market value of some selected shares over that of a base day.

stock exchange pool nominee (Sepon) an account into which the seller of a stock transfers title which then will be passed to the buyer.

stock-for-stock exchange = *exchange-of-shares acquisition.*

stock-for-stock swap = *exchange-of-shares acquisition.*

stock fund a mutual fund which invests primary in stocks.

stock grant stock given to the employee of the issuer free. **See**: *bonus share.*

stockholder (SH) = *shareholder.*

stockholder's capital = *capital stock.*

stockholders' equity = *net worth.*

stockholders' meeting = *annual meeting.*

stock index the measure of the value changes in a selected group of stocks.

stock index arbitrage an arbitrage made between the S&P 500 index and a futures contract based on that index.

stock index contingent option option on a stock index that has value only if it is in-the-money and if an additional condition, an interest rate, is satisfied.

stock index future <1> the combination of futures trading with securities trading by using a composite index. <2> a cash settled futures contract with a stock index as the underlying.

stock index futures arbitrage = *index*

arbitrage.

stock index growth note (SIGN) = *equity-linked note.*

stock index option = *index option.*

stock index return security (SIRS) = *equity-linked note.*

stock index swap a swap that involves a stock index. as the reference **See**: *index swap.*

stock insurance company the insurance company owned by a group of shareholders.

stock interest = *dividend.*

stock in trade the quantity of securities held by an investor.

stock jobber = *jobber.*

stock jobbing irresponsible or dishonest manipulation of the prices of a stock.

stock lending = *securities lending.*

stock-linked note = *equity-linked note.*

stock loan = *lending stock.*

stock manipulation = *manipulation.*

stock market buying and selling of corporate stocks. ***Also***: equity market.

stock market crash = *crash.*

stock note a note given on the sale of stock which the bank had purchased or taken in the payment of doubtful debts.

stock option <1> the option issued by a company to its employees giving them the right to buy the company's stock at a favorable price. ***Also***: option to purchase share; share option; term stock right. <2> = *equity option.*

stock option grant = *option grant.*

stock option warrant = *stock warrant.*

stock-over-bond warrant (SOB warrant) outperformance warrant with the payoff based on the performance of a benchmark index less the return on a bond index.

stock power a power of attorney giving ownership of a security to another person, brokerage firm, bank, or lender after it has been sold or pledged to that party.

stock purchase warrant = *stock warrant.*

stock quotation the current market price of a stock. ***Also***: share quotation.

stock rating the evaluation by a rating agency of the expected performance or the inherent risk of stocks.

stock reacquisition expense amount paid or incurred by a company in buying back its own stock.

stock redemption the mutual fund buys back its shares or a company acquires its own shares in order to hold, cancel, or retire them. ***Also***: redemption; share buyback.

stock replacement strategy a strategy used when the futures price is expensive, involving a swap between the futures, US Treasury bill portfolio and securities.

stock right the right of common shareholders to have the first opportunity to buy additional shares of common stock issued by the company. ***Also***: preemptive right; right; right of preemption; subscription privilege; subscription right.

stock scrip = *scrip.*

stocks in buying stocks in an investment portfolio.

stocks-in, bonds-out selling bonds and using the proceeds to buy stocks.

stocks in the spotlight = *most active list.*

stocks out selling stocks in an investment portfolio.

stocks-out, bonds-in selling stocks and using the proceeds to buy bonds.

stock split the division of a company's outstanding shares into larger number without reducing the total value of its capital stock. ***Also***: bifurcation; share split-up; split; stock split-up; subdivision of shares. **See**: *split-up.*

stock split down = *split down.*

stock split-up = *stock split.*

stock swap = *exchange-of-shares acquisition.*

stock symbol the letters used to identify listed companies on the exchanges, i. e. KO for Coca Cola. ***Also***: ticker symbol; trading symbol. **See**: *cusip code.*

stock trust certificate = *stock certificate.*

stock upside note security (SUNS) an annual reset or cliquet-type note with the coupon linked to the annual appreciation percentage of a designated instrument or index less a fixed percentage to pay for the option component of the return.

stock warrant a document the bearer of which has the right to buy certain stock at a given price. ***Also***: letter of rights; rights letter; share warrant; stock option warrant; stock purchase warrant; subscription warrant; warrant.

stock watcher a system that monitors all trading activities and the price movement in the stocks listed on the NYSE.

stock without par value = *no-par-value stock.*

stock with par value = *par value stock.*

stop = *suspended trading.*

stop and reverse the *stop price* which, when hit, is a signal to close the current position and open an opposite position.

stop basis entering OTC trades without reporting.

stop down = *limit down.*

stop-out bid the highest accepted competitive bid in terms of yield on a competitive auction of debt securities.

stop-out price <1> the lowest acceptable price for the Treasury bills at the regular weekly auction. <2> in a single price auction, the uniform price paid by the bidders. <3> = *clearing price.*

stop-out rate the difference between a currency's spot rate and its contract rate in futures trading.

stopped out the situation when a position is offset by the execution of a stop order.

stopped stock the stock executed at the stop price.

stopping curve the curve showing the refunding rates for different times at which the expected value of refunding immediately equals the expected value of waiting for the refund.

stopping curve refunding rate the refunding rate that falls on a *stopping curve.*

stopping time the expected length of time until the first breaching of a barrier on a barrier option.

stop the bleeding = *stem the tide.*

stop up = *limit up.*

story stock the stock of a company that has a compelling scenario, e. g. a new management, unique product or service.

straddle <1> a combination of a put and a call option on the same security, at different or same strike price for the same expiration date. ***Also***: option-option spreads; option straddle; strike arbitrage. **See**: *combination option.* <2> trading in futures of one month against another.

straddle arbitrage the arbitrage between the spot market and derivative market.

straddled view the option quote display format with calls and puts on both sides. ***See***: *stacked view.*

straddle option an option to buy or sell 100 shares of a stock at a price for a given period. ***See***: *as-you-like option.*

straddler one who buys a spot commodity and enters into a future contract.

straddle rule IRS rule under which any loss realized from one leg of a straddle is deferred to the extent that there is an unrealized gain on the open leg, but the gain must be recognized immediately.

straddle sale the sale of assets at a loss by a company before liquidation, followed by the sale of asset at a gain, so the loss can offset the ordinary income and gains.

straight bond = *term bond.*

straight-date run a forward contract the starting date and ending date match, e. g. Jun 22, Oct 22. ***Opp***: *odd run.*

straight paper an unsecured note, bill of exchange and bank acceptance.

straight run Euro the interest rate of the Eurodollar in the *neutral run.*

straight value = *investment value.*

strangle buying or selling of out-of-the-money options close to expiration at a low premium. ***See***: *gut.*

strangle swap = *reverse calendar strangle.*

strap a combination of 1 put and 2 calls, which is a straddle plus an additional call option to protect against the down side. ***Also***: triple option.

stratified equity indexing building an investment portfolio by classifying the stocks in an index into strata representing each in the portfolio.

stratified sampling approach indexing method that divides an index into cells, each cell will represent a different characteristic of the index, such as duration.

stray of a situation not a meaningful indication of the customer's desire to take a position or be involved in a derivative instrument.

street certificate = *bearer stock.*

street loan = *call money.*

stress testing a test of the risk management methods to evaluate their reactions to the changes in the market condition.

strike arbitrage <1> = *straddle.* <2> = *strike option arbitrage.*

strike bonus option the value added to a standard option by a lookback or a strike reset feature.

strike index the price at which the buyer of an index option can buy or sell the underlying stock index.

strike level of a swaption the nominal fixed-rate debt obligation underlying the subject swap contract.

strike option arbitrage option arbitrage that involves the buying and selling of options with different strike prices. ***Also***: strike arbitrage.

strike premium the premium paid for the second option in a compound option.

strike price <1> the settling price of the underlying when the option is exercised. ***Also***: exercise price; option price; price of option; set price; striking price. <2> the predetermined price at which an underlying future or actual commodity may be established upon the exercise of the option. <3> the cost of the stock when a convertible bond is being converted into that stock.

strike price fraction = *fractional strike.*

strike reset option = *reset option.*

strike security a security that combines a *fixed-rate security* and a *bull floater.*

strike sensitivity the sensitivity of an option price to changes in the strike.

strike slope a measure of the amount that implied volatility changes for every 10 point increase in the call delta in the intra-month skew.

strike spread <1> the difference in strike price between 2 options. <2> = *vertical spread.*

strike-step option a barrier option with a change in the strike price when a barrier or a trigger price or rate is touched or breached. ***Also***: step payment option.

striking price = *strike price.*

strip <1> an option which consists of a straddle plus one put option. <2> the portion of the bond that represents the principal or the interest.

strip and stack hedging a combination of *strip hedge* and *stack hedge.*

strip bond <Canada> = *zero-coupon bond.*

strip hedge a risk-offsetting position that uses a strip of risk management forward or options expiring on dates appropriate to the specific risk being hedged. **See**: *stack hedge.*

strippability characteristics of a bond that makes it suitable for coupon stripping.

strip PC an instrument which represents interest in a mortgage purchased by Freddie Mac from a single seller.

stripped bond the bond which can be subdivided into a series of zero-coupon bonds.

stripped mortgage-backed security (SMBS) <1> a specialized instrument decomposed from a collateralized mortgage obligation. <2> a segment of the mortgage payment stream which is the underlying asset of a collateralized mortgage obligation or a real estate mortgage investment conduit that has been divided into tranches.

stripped municipal a municipal bond that can be separated into the principal and interest portions.

stripped preferred stock a preferred stock without participating privilege, but with a fixed redemption price.

stripped spread the difference between the US long bond rate and the yield on the Brady bonds.

stripped yield the return on the debt portion of a bond/warrant unit after subtracting the face value of the issued warrant segment.

stripping = *dividend stripping.*

STRIPS separately traded registered interest and principal securities

strips = *futures strips.*

STRIP yield the schedule of yields that are associated with the STRIPS market.

strong backwardation a backwardation when the futures basis is negative. **See**: *weak backwardation.*

strong basis a relatively small difference between cash and futures prices.

strong dollar the appreciated dollar with respect to other currencies. **See**: *weak dollar.*

strong-form efficiency a form of pricing efficiency which holds that the price of a security reflects all information, whether or not it is known. **See**: *semi-strong form efficiency*; *weak-form efficiency.*

strong hands the intention of the holders of futures contracts to receive delivery of commodities.

structured arbitrage transaction any self-funding, self-hedged transaction that uses mortgage-backed securities as the primary assets.

structured asset = *synthetic asset.*

structured debt a derivative which will change in value with the movements of an underlying index.

structured enhanced return trust (STEER) a special purpose trust developed by Merrill Lynch to facilitate the asset swap transactions.

structured finance CDO a CDO that is backed primarily by asset-backed securities and mortgaged backed securities.

structured note <1> an investment that changes in value with the movements of an underlying index. ***See***: *equity-linked note*; *recovery note.* <2> a note the issuer of which can alter the required cash flows by swap arrangements.

structured portfolio strategy a strategy in which a portfolio is designed to match or exceed the performance of some specific liabilities which will need to be paid out in the future.

structured security a security bundled with additional feature and rights such as risk management. ***See***: *callable security*; *collateralized mortgage obligation*; *step-up security.*

structured settlement an agreement in settling a lawsuit that involves specific payments made over a period of time.

structuring the creation of a wide variety of financial derivatives by customizing terms based on the participant's need.

stub a stamped stock certificate indicating that the issuing company is now being liquidated.

stub period the period which is shorter than the *rest.*

Student Loan Marketing Association (SLMA) = *Sallie Mae.*

style allocation = *asset allocation.*

subdivision of shares <UK> = *stock split.*

subindex a group of stocks that are part of a major index, but tracked as an index of their own.

subject market a quote in which prices are subject to confirmation. ***See***: *fast market.*

subject quote = *nominal quote.*

sub-LIBOR financing the ability of a firm to obtain loans at a rate below LIBOR.

sub-major bracket the underwriters listed behind the *mezzanine bracket.*

submartingale a random variable X that satisfies $E^P(X_{n+1} | X_1, \ldots X_n) \geq X_n$, i. e. the expected value of the next observation is equal to or larger than the last observed value. ***See***: *martingale.*

subordinated debt a debt with a claim on the corporation's assets only after the claims of the holders of senior debt are satisfied. ***Also***: junior debt; subordinate debt.

subordinate debt = *subordinated debt.*

subordinate PAC bond a PAC bond that is paired with a super PAC bond to make most of the prepayment risk.

subordination clause a clause in a bond indenture that restricts the issuer's future borrowing by subordinating the future lenders' claims to existing bondholders.

subpar = *below water.*

subparticipation a method of lending in which a bank makes a loan to a borrower and then arranges for other banks to take on part of it.

sub-period return portfolio return over a period that is shorter than the evaluation period.

subscription privilege = *stock right.*

subscription ratio the number of stock rights needed to buy a share of a new issue.

subscription right = *stock right.*

subscription warrant = *stock warrant.*

subsequent coupon attached (SCA) the words meaning the unredeemed interest coupon is attached to a bond, especially a bond in default.

subsequent offering = *follow-on.*

subshare = *dividend warrant.*

subsidiary a company all or part of the voting stock of which is held by a parent company in the consolidated statements. ***Also***: affiliated company; child company; subsidiary corporation. ***See***: *controlled company.*

subsidiary corporation = *subsidiary.*

substantial shareholder one who owns more than 40% of the stock value. ***Also***: principal stockholder.

substitute sale hedge against the price risk by using debt market instruments, such as the interest rate futures, or by selling borrowed securities as primary assets.

substitution <1> substitution of another security of equal value for a security acting as the collateral for a margin account. <2> a *bond swap* established to improve some characteristics of the original bond.

substitution option <1> an option under which one party buys the right to substitute one asset for another at a given time or upon a credit event. <2> = *quality option.*

substitution swap the swap in which the money manager exchanges one bond for another which is similar in terms of coupon, maturity, and credit quality, but that offers a higher yield.

sub-underwriter <UK> = *participating underwriter.*

successive volatility = *forward-forward volatility.*

successor company = *acquiring company.*

sudden huge profit = *exorbitant profit.*

suicide pill an extreme version of *poison pill* in which a target company engages in an activity that might destroy the company to avoid a *hostile takeover.*

suitability rule the NASD enforced rule that brokers must ensure that investors have the financial means to assume risk that they wish to undertake.

sum certain the predetermined settlement price for a contract or other negotiable instrument.

summer crack spread buying or selling futures in gasoline, and a spread with the crude oil. ***See***: *winter crack spread.*

sundry income = *windfall profit.*

SUNS stock upside note security

sunshine laws the state and federal laws requiring most regulatory meetings and decisions to be made available to the public. ***See***: *blue sky laws.*

sunshine trade a high volume transaction prematurely revealed to the street before the order is even entered. ***Also***: pre-announced trading.

superannuation bond a bond like a *life insurance bond* but with a different tax structure subject to *superannuation* rule and regulations.

Super Bowl indicator a theory that if a team from the old American Football League pre-1970 wins the Super Bowl, the stock market will decline, if a team from the old pre-1990 National Football League wins the Super Bowl, stock prices will go up.

super-efficient portfolio the portfolio incorporating into the *efficient fron-*

tier analysis of an asset which pays a risk-free rate, created by James Tobin in 1958.

superfloater swap fixed-for-floating-rate swap with a reverse risk reversal on the floating-rate payment.

supermajority amendment in a company's charter requiring a large majority (from 67% to 90%) of the shareholders to approve important changes, such as a merger. ***Also***: control share acquisition law.

supernormal growth stock a stock that experiences a continued long period of growth rate above the economy as a whole.

supershare option = *arrow-debreu security*.

super sinker bond a bond with long-term coupons but with short maturity, e. g. housing bond.

supervisory analyst an NYSE analyst who is qualified to approve publicly distributed research report.

support bond <1> the bond which takes most of the prepayment risks in a PAC CMO. <2> = *companion bond*.

support point the exchange rate at which a central bank will intervene to support its currency.

SURF step-up recovery floater

surplus capital = *retained earnings*.

surplus equity = *excess margin*.

surplus reserve = *retained earnings*.

surveillance department the department that monitors trading activity on the stock exchange.

surviving company the new company that continues to operate after a merger.

survivorship annuity an annuity payable for the life of an annuitant and then to a survivor.

survivorship bias the tendency for failed companies to be excluded from the performance studies due to the fact that they no longer exist. ***See***: *look-ahead bias*.

survivor's option = *death put*.

sushi bond the Eurobond issued by a Japanese company.

suspended trading a decision to cease trading that results from an unusual occurrence, such as a jump in buy or sell orders on all or several securities. ***Also***: stop; trade halt; trading halt; trading stopped.

suspense account the account used to temporarily store short-term funds or securities until a permanent decision is made about the allocation.

suspension the decision made by a stock exchange prohibiting a securities firm or a broker-dealer from conducting business for a period.

sustainable growth rate (SGR) the maximum growth rate that a firm can sustain without having to increase its financial leverage, calculated as ROE × (1 – dividend-payout ratio).

swap <1> the contract under which two parties exchange payments based on the price changes and distributions of a security and the cost of carrying that security. <2> the purchase or sale of a spot currency combined with a simultaneous sale or purchase of a forward currency. ***Also***: change over; spot-to-futures arbitrage; swapping. ***Opp***: *outright*. <3> the sale of one security for the purchase of another. ***See***: *bond swap*; *proceeds sale*. <4> = *bed and breakfasting*.

swap arrangement the bilateral stand-by credit agreement made among a number of central banks under which temporary payments of the imbalances of a country may be financed by swaps in foreign exchanges. ***Also***: swap line.

swap assignment = *swap sale.*

swap book a bank's portfolio of swaps, arranged by currency and maturity.

swap broker a broker who helps finding parties in a swap transaction. ***Also***: swap intermediary.

swap buyback the purchase or sale of an interest rate swap to effectively end the swap.

swap buyer the party to an interest rate swap the payment of which is based on a swap rate, the coupon of a long-term fixed-income bond, or set at the same level in each payment interval. ***Also***: buyer of the swap; fixed rate payer.

swap buyout the reversal of an existing swap, with the difference in the market value paid out, thus eliminating credit exposure and continuing the contractual obligation.

swap cost = *discount.*

swap coupon the fixed interest rate in an interest rate swap. **See**: *reference rate.*

swap curve the curve of the payoff on a swap against their maturities, it is above Treasury curve. ***Also***: par swap curve; par swap yield curve; swap yield curve.

swap dealer = *swap market maker.*

swap-driven issue a bond or note that is issued simultaneously with an agreement to a swap.

swap format a derivative contract format that requires no front payment. ***Also***: unfunded format. **See**: *credit linked note format.*

swap fund a fund that allows investors to transfer appreciated securities to a newly formed investment company on a tax free basis. ***Also***: exchange fund.

swap guarantee the guarantee of the payments under a swap agreement by a third party.

swap in arrears (SIA) = *arrears swap.*

swap intermediary = *swap broker.*

swap line = *swap arrangement.*

swap market maker the financial intermediary who runs an unmatched swap book and quotes terms for a variety of swaps. ***Also***: swap dealer.

swap novation = *swap sale.*

swap option = *swaption.*

swap participant <1> an entity that, at any time before the filing of the petition, has an outstanding swap with the debtor. **See**: *eligible swap participant.* <2> an investor with three million in minimum investment and 10 million in gross asset. **See**: *accredited investor.*

swapper the participant in a swap.

swapping = *swap.*

swap pricing the pricing of a swap.

swap rate <1> the market interest rate paid by the party responsible for the fixed payments in an *interest rate swap.* <2> the difference between the forward rate and the spot rate for a currency.

swap rate differential the difference between the yield of a bond or a note and the swap rate of an interest rate swap for the same expiration date. ***Also***: differential.

swap rate lock an agreement that sets the absolute swap rate level for a swap with a future start date.

swap replacement = *replacement swap.*

swap replacement cost <1> the cost to replace a defaulted or canceled in-the-money swap with a comparable swap. ***Also***: cost of default; replacement cost. <2> = *actual exposure.*

swap reversal a swap to end a counterpart's role in another interest rate swap, accomplished by counterbalancing the original swap in maturity, the *reference rate* or the notional amount. ***See***: *reverse swap*; *swap sale.*

swap sale the transaction that ends one party's role in an interest rate swap by substituting a new party whose credit standing is acceptable to the original counterparty. ***Also***: swap assignment; swap novation. ***See***: *swap reversal.*

swap seller an investor who is required to make the variable interest payments determined by the reference index rate in the swap contract. ***Also***: floating-rate payer; seller of the swap.

swap spread <1> the difference between the negotiated rate with the dealer and the fixed rate under a swap contract. <2> the difference between the swap rate and the lending rate offered through other investment vehicles.

swap spreadlock = *deferred rate setting swap.*

swap tenor the lifetime of a swap. ***Also***: swap term; tenor.

swap term = *swap tenor.*

swaption an option to enter into a swap. ***Also***: option on a swap; swap option. ***See***: *interest rate swap.*

swap type = *leg type.*

swap with timing mismatches a swap in which one party is paying on a more frequent interval than the other, so that the opportunities for offsetting or netting flows are limited.

swap yield curve = *swap curve.*

sweat equity <1> an equity share acquired by a company's executives on favorable terms. <2> the equity in a company as a direct result of hard work by the owner.

sweep-out dividend the dividend that an investment company may deduct for a tax year, provided that it is declared in that year or paid soon after the close of the tax year.

sweet crude the barrels of crude oil that meet certain content requirements, e. g. low levels of sulfur and hydrogen. ***See***: *sour crude.*

sweetener = *kicker.*

swing <1> a dramatic reversal in either the market or a trader's profit/loss. <2> mid-term, as in swing trading.

swing option a strip of options with caps on the payout of each of the component options and on the strip as a whole.

Swings sterling warrants into gilt-edged securities

swing trader one who engages in swing trading. ***Also***: position trader.

swing trading the strategy which tries to profit by holding positions in stocks that have been moving, for relatively short periods, e. g. one day to one week. ***Also***: position trading. ***See***: *day trading*; *in and out.*

switchback option a financial instrument combining a capped call and an up-and-in put or a floored put and a down-and-in call.

switch derivative = *hurdle derivative.*

switching <1> selling short-dated stocks and using the proceeds to purchase the medium-dated stock or long dated stock. ***Also***: going longer. <2> the swap done between two similar issues based upon an anticipated change in their relative prices. ***Also***: arbitrage. <3> the moving of assets from a mutual fund to another. ***Also***: twisting.

switching option <1> an option the exercise of which creates one or more additional options. <2> = *quality option.*

switch trading the trade finance used where restrictions exist on the availability of foreign currency.

swoop a significant drop of the market price. ***See***: *crash.*

SWP systematic withdrawal plan

Sycom Sydney Computerised Overnight Market

Sydney Futures Exchange (SFE) one of the largest futures exchange in the world located in Sydney, Australia.

symbol book special illiquid, inactively traded stock in a not familiar market.

symmetric cash matching the extension of *cash flow matching* that allows for the short-term borrowing to satisfy a liability prior to its due date, reducing the cost of funding liabilities.

sympathetic buying the purchase of stock because good news has developed about another company in the same or related industry.

syndicate <1> the association of 2 or more companies to carry out a business. ***Also***: pool. <2> a group of bankers involved in a Eurobond issue. <3> = *distributing syndicate.*

syndicate bid a bid that can be entered in the Nasdaq System to stabilize the price of a security before the secondary offering of the same security is effective.

syndicate contract = *agreement among underwriters.*

syndicate covering the syndicate's purchases after an offering in order to cover a short position.

synthetic financing the financing that involves derivatives.

syndicate invitation the offer from the managing underwriter to join the underwriting group of a security offering.

syndicate manager = *managing underwriter.*

syndicate real estate investing the investment in the stocks issued by companies in the business of buying, renting and selling real estate.

synthesizing = *dynamic hedging.*

synthetic asset an asset created by a swap or a combination of swaps. ***Also***: reengineered asset; structured asset.

synthetic bond a bond created by the combination of the feature of a series of bonds.

synthetic call = *synthetic long call.*

synthetic CDO a CDO created from synthetic assets, such as credit default swap, without owning cash positions in the assets. ***See***: *cash CDO.*

synthetic CDO squared a portfolio of credit default swap (CDS) with a two-layer structure of risk. ***See***: *cash CDO squared.*

synthetic CLO a note or bond or tranches of notes or bonds that a lender issues, plus related credit swaps, designed to reduce the lender's credit exposure and raise money.

synthetic convertible a combination of usable bonds and warrants (that expire on or after the bonds' maturity) which resembles convertible bond.

synthetic equity the derivative with the essential risk/reward characteristics of a direct investment in a stock, a specific basket of stocks, or a weighted basket of stocks equivalent to an index.

synthetic fixed rate asset the asset created by exchanging a floating rate asset by a swap or a series of swaps.

synthetic fixed rate debt a debt that is created by issuing floating rate debt and swapping cash flows into fixed rate debt or fixed income securities.

synthetic floating rate asset an asset that is created by exchanging a fixed rate asset into floating cash flow by a swap or a series of swaps.

synthetic floating rate debt a debt created by issuing fixed rate debt and swapping cash flows into floaters.

synthetic forward the forward which is constructed through the borrowing in one currency, lending in another currency, and offsetting transactions in the spot exchange market.

synthetic futures contract a position created by combining calls and puts for mimicking the payout schedule and the characteristics of a futures contract.

synthetic high income equity-linked debenture (SHIELD) = *convertible money market units.*

synthetic instrument customized hybrid instrument created by blending the underlying price on a cash instrument with the price of a derivative.

synthetic long call the purchase of a stock and a put option on that stock, with the strike price and expiration date of the call that would have been purchased. ***Also***: synthetic call.

synthetic long put selling short a stock or currency and buying a long call on that stock or currency. ***Also***: converted put; synthetic put.

synthetic long stock a stock artificially created by the combination of a long call option and a short put option.

synthetic option a long-term option created out of a sequence of short-term options. ***Also***: option replication.

synthetic put <1> OTC put option issued by a broker-dealer to accommodate a customer's request for a put option. <2> = *synthetic long put.*

synthetic short call selling short a stock, and selling a put with the same strike price and expiration date as in the call which would have been sold.

synthetic short put buying a stock, and selling a call with the same expiration date and strike price as in the put that would have been sold.

synthetic short stock the artificially created stock by the combination of a long put option and a short call option on the same underlying stock.

synthetic spread the option spread position created by buying a call, selling a put and buying the underlying asset. ***Also***: synthetic spread arbitrage. **See**: *conversion arbitrage.*

synthetic spread arbitrage = *synthetic spread.*

synthetic stock the artificially created stock using the combination of other assets, e. g., a long call option and a short put option.

synthetic straddle buying 100 shares of stock and buying two calls or puts. ***Also***: long synthetic straddle.

synthetic warrant = *covered warrant.*

synthetic zero-coupon convertible bond a combination of a zero coupon note and a detachable warrant with the same date of maturity.

systematic investment plan a method involving regular investments to take advantage of dollar-cost averaging.

systematic risk the risk that can not be avoided by diversification. ***Also***: beta risk; market risk; unavoidable risk; undiversifiable risk. **See**: *unsystematic risk.*

systematic risk-free asset = *zero-beta portfolio.*

systematic risk principle the principle under which only the systematic portion of risk matters well diversified portfolio.

systematic withdrawal plan (SWP) the option that allows mutual fund investors to withdraw a fixed sum of money on a regular basis.

T t

T <1> December in put options. <2> the Nasdaq descriptor meaning the stock has warrant or rights. <3> option strike price code for 100. <4> theoretical value. <5> option expiration date.

T+5 trade date plus five days.

table top a combination that consists of a bullish call spread with a short call at a higher strike, or a bearish put spread with an additional put at a lower strike. ***Also***: Christmas tree; ladder trade.

TAC bond target amortization bond

tack the time remaining before a stockholder can sell a restricted stock.

tag alongside rights a procedure under which if a majority shareholder sells his stake, the minority shareholders have the right to sell their minority stake. ***Also***: co-sale rights.

tail <1> the difference between the average issuing price and the *stop-out price* of the Treasury bill. <2> the decimal places following the dollar amount of the bid by a potential underwriter.

tailed spread = *ratio spread.*

tailgating a broker, after clients place an order to buy or sell, places an order for the same security for his own account.

tail hedging the adjustment of the number of futures contracts in a hedge so that the present market exposure of the hedge will offset the risk exposure. ***Also***: dollar equivalency hedging; tailing a hedge.

tailing a hedge = *tail hedging.*

tailored swap a changing notional swap designed to meet the financing or the currency needs of a firm with seasonal interest rate or currency risk management requirements.

tainted stock = *Section 306 stock.*

take-back recapture of securities by the syndicate manager of a new issue that have been allotted for the retention of the selling group or underwriter.

take-down <1> the number of shares or bonds allotted to the underwriters or members of the selling group of a new issue. <2> = *selling concession.*

take-down concession = *selling concession.*

take in to charge backwardation to the short sellers.

take-out <1> the bid for the remainder of a seller's holdings that he has been selling piece meal. <2> the bid a Ginnie Mae dealer offers to finance a mortgage banker's loans offered at a GNMA auction. ***Also***: back-up bid. <3> the increase in cash flow resulting from the sale of one block of bonds and the purchase of another block at a lower cost. <4> the withdrawal of cash from a brokerage account.

takeover acquiring the control of a target company by purchase or exchange of shares. ***Also***: highjacking. ***See***: *merger.*

takeover arbitrage = *risk arbitrage.*

takeover bid (TOB) an offer to buy all the shares in a company at a price higher than the market with a time limit for acceptance. ***Also***: buying tender; open tender; tender for cash.

takeover target = *target company.*

take under a takeover where the target firm is offered a price per share that is less than its current market value.

take-up fee a fee paid to an underwriter for an underwritten rights offering or an underwritten forced conversion.

taking a flier = *flier.*

taking a position = *position building.*

taking a view <UK> forming an opinion as to where market prices are headed.

taking off a leg = *lifting a leg.*

talon a printed slip that is attached to a bearer bond, which allows the bondholder to exchange for a new sheet of coupons.

tampering with the market operations by dealers to affect the course of market prices, profiting from the swings. ***Also***: rigging the market.

tandem option the sequence of options of the same type (call or put) that covers non-overlapping time periods and often with variable strikes.

tandem spread the combination of the calendar or ratio spreads on two different commodities or instruments.

tandem stock option stock right issued together such that the exercise of one affects the right to exercise the other.

tap <UK> the supply of Government stock available for sale through the Government brokers at a stated price, without using the money market or the exchange. ***Also***: tap issue; tap offering.

tap CD a CD issued by a bank on an as-required basis with a minimum denomination of $25,000 or £50,000 and for a minimum of one month in dollars, three months in sterling up to a maximum of five years.

tape dancing the practice whereby the trader who buys from institutional sellers, pays 1/8 or ¼ above the last sale and charges a larger-than-usual fee.

tap issue = *tap.*

tap offering = *tap.*

tap stock a stock that is always on tap (available at a known price).

target amortization bond (TAC bond) the bond that offers one-sided protection against the prepayment risk but does not protect against low prepayment risk.

target company a company chosen as the target for takeover by the *acquiring company*. ***Also***: acquisition target; offeree; takeover target; target firm.

targeted registered offerings the security issues sold to targeted foreign financial institution according to SEC guidelines.

target exit point the price level set by an investor at which a position in derivatives will be closed.

target firm = *target company.*

target price the price of the underlying asset at which the options held will be profitable.

target profit earnings to be made from an investment or a portfolio. ***Also***: profit objective.

target rate of return the minimum return on an investment set by the investors. ***Also***: minimum rate of return.

target stock = *tracking stock.*

tau = *vega.*

taxable equivalent yield = *tax-equivalent yield.*

taxable municipal bond a bond issued by a state to finance some prohibited project such as sports stadium, a toll etc., the interest income is taxable to the investor.

taxable preferred share <Canada> a preferred share that was issued after Jun 18, 1987 or a *short-term preferred share.*

taxable stock dividend a stock dividend that is taxable if the employee has the option to take cash instead of the stock.

tax anticipation bill (TAB) the special bill that the US Treasury occasionally issues which matures on corporate quarterly income tax dates and can be used at face value by the corporations to pay their tax liability.

tax anticipation note (TAN) a short-term note issued by a state in anticipation of future tax collections.

tax arbitrage a trading that takes advantage of the difference in tax rates or tax systems as the basis for profit.

tax-driven swap asset-based swap used to alter the tax character of a cash flow stream.

tax efficiency characteristic of a financial instrument that permits a dealer or an end user to establish or modify a position in a way that requires lower tax payments to the transactions than an alternate similar instrument.

tax-equivalent yield the pre-tax yield required from a taxable bond to match the tax-free yield of a municipal bond. ***Also***: taxable equivalent yield.

tax-exempt bond = *municipal bond.*

tax exempt income fund a mutual fund that seeks investment income which is exempt from federal, state and local income taxes.

tax-exempt money market fund money market fund that invests in short-term tax-exempt municipal securities.

tax-exempt sector the municipal bond market where state and federal governments raise funds.

tax-exempt security = *municipal bond.*

tax-exempt swap an interest rate swap with one or both payments based on tax exempt municipal securities yields. ***Also***: municipal swap.

tax-free bond = *municipal bond.*

tax-free bond fund a tax-free mutual fund which invests in municipal bonds.

tax-free covenant bond the bond with a clause that the issuer will pay the holder's tax on income from the bond.

tax-free yield the yield on tax-exempt bonds.

tax hedging the hedging created to reduce tax liability.

tax-managed fund a mutual fund that is designed specifically to minimize tax consequences for its investors.

tax rate swap a swap under which one counterpart pays the tax rate of the other. ***See***: *tax swap.*

tax selling the sale of securities near year end to obtain tax gains or losses.

tax smart trading = *smart trading.*

tax spread a yield or interest rate spread structured to take some tax advantage.

tax straddle a straddle in which investors simultaneously enter into a contract to deliver a commodity at a future date and a sale of a contract for delivery of the same item in a different month, so that they can close out the losing leg.

tax swap a bond swap created in order to create tax deductible loss. ***See***: *tax rate swap.*

tax switch selling securities that have declined in value to deduct tax loss for the current year, and using the proceeds to buy another depressed stock.

tax-timing option the option to sell an asset and claim a loss for tax purposes or not sell the asset and defer the gains.

TB Treasury bill

T-bill Treasury bill

technical analysis evaluating the mar-

market by relying on the assumption that market data, such as charts of price, volume, and open interest, can help predict future market trends.

TED T-bond /Eurodollar

TED spread the difference between the price of a Treasury bill and the price of the Eurodollar. ***Also***: spread.

teenie = *teeny.*

teeny 1/16 or 0.0625 of one full point in price. ***Also***: steenth; teenie; teenyo. **See**: *s'teenth.*

teenyo = *teeny.*

temperature swap = *degree-day swap.*

temporal arbitrage = *arbitrage in time.*

temporary asset hedge the hedge under which a bank borrows long term money and then sells futures against rate risk.

temporary investment = *short-term investment.*

temporary liability hedge a hedge under which a bank makes a long term loan and sells futures to lock rates in.

tenbagger a stock that grows in value 10-fold.

ten-day rule = *10-day rule.*

tender <1> <verb> to offer to supply or to buy securities. <2> <verb> to give a notice to the clearing house with the intention of delivery of the commodity under a futures contract. <3> <verb> an *auction* with bids sought for the purchase of a commodity, a bond or a security. <4> = *Treasury bill.*

tenderable grade = *contract grade.*

tender for cash = *takeover bid.*

tender issue <UK> the weekly issue of Treasury bills by the Bank of England.

tender offer the offering of shares to the public by inviting tenders to bid, and selling to the highest bidder. ***Also***: offer by tender. **See**: *auction.*

tender offer premium the premium above the market price in a tender offer.

tender option put security (TOPS) = *adjustable tender security.*

tender to contract cover <UK> an insurance to bridge the gap between an exchange rate when an exporter makes a tender and the contract rate.

tenor <1> the entire life of a contract. **See**: *duration.* <2> = *swap tenor.*

tenor to early exercise = *time to early exercise.*

term the length of time a security or a financial instrument is outstanding.

term bond a bond that comes due at the fixed period of time. ***Also***: fixed bond; non-amortizable bond; ordinary bond; single maturity bond; straight bond.

term CD a CD with a long-term maturity, 1 to 10 years. ***Also***: term certificate.

term certain annuity = *annuity certain.*

term certificate = *term CD.*

term currency a currency used as a reference in pricing a *commodity currency.* ***Also***: terms currency.

term day = *quarter day.*

termed money risk = *interest rate risk.*

terminal market <UK> = *futures market.*

terminal reserve a *self-insurance fund* balance at year end. ***Also***: investment reserve. **See**: *initial reserve.*

terminal value = *accumulated amount.*

termination amount = *accumulated amount.*

termination date = *maturity date.*

termination payment the payment to terminate a counterpart's contractual liability under a swap contract. ***Also***: setoff. ***See***: *difference check.*

term of discount = *discount period.*

term preferred share <Canada> the share issued or acquired after Jun 28, 1982.

term repo a repo with a long term.

terms currency = *term currency.*

term stock right = *stock option.*

term structure derivative a derivative featured by the term structure of interest rates.

term structure of interest rates the relationship between the interest rates on different maturities on a yield curve.

term structure of volatility = *volatility term structure.*

term to maturity = *duration.*

term volatility the volatility measured over a specified period of time. ***Also***: inter-temporal volatility; time-series volatility.

Texas hedge two or more related positions the risk of which is increasing rather than offsetting.

the Amex = *spider.*

the crowd = *crowd.*

theoretical Dow the DJIA that assumes all index components hit their high or low at the same time during the day.

theoretical futures price = *fair price.*

theoretical price = *theoretical value.*

theoretical value the value of an option calculated by the pricing model. ***Also***: fair value; theoretical price.

the sheet = *pink sheet.*

The Street = *Wall Street.*

theta a daily change in an option's price to the decrease in the time before expiration. ***Also***: daily time decay; decay; rate of time-value decay; time decay; time decay factor. ***See***: *delta*; *gamma.*

theta 7 theta multiplied by 7.

theta spread the spread created on the theta. ***Also***: price per day spread.

thinly traded of a security that is traded infrequently.

thin market = *inactive market.*

third generation option = *exotic option.*

third market trading of large blocks over the counter by non-members.

third-tier penalty a penalty for violation of the Securities Exchange Act, 1933 which shall not exceed the greater of (1) $ 100,000 for an individual or $500,000 for an entity, or (2) the gain as a result of the violation.

thirty-day wash sale rule = *wash sale rule.*

three steps and a stumble rule the rule predicting that stock and bond prices will fall following three increases in the discount rate by the Federal Reserve.

threshold a price level in ladder option.

threshold level = *value lock level.*

tick <1> the minimum price change that is allowed by a given futures contract. ***Also***: minimum fluctuation; minimum price fluctuation. <2> = *pip.*

ticker symbol = *stock symbol.*

tick-test rule an SEC-imposed rule on when a short sale may be executed when the market price is falling under Rule 10a-1.

tidal wave purchase a cash rich firm's open purchase of the stock in a target company.

tier a class or a group of securities, futures, or options.

tie up to secure an option to buy or sell a stock or commodity at a given price for a specified period.

Tiger federal backed zero-coupon bonds issued by Merrill Lynch, Pierce, Fenner and Smith. ***Also***: Treasury Investment Growth Receipts; Treasury Investors Growth Receipt. **See**: *Lion.*

tight market a market in which volume is high, trading is active, and consequently the spreads between bid and ask prices are narrow.

TIGR Treasury Investment Growth Receipt

tilted portfolio an indexing strategy that is linked to the active management through the emphasis of a particular industry sector.

time = *basic time.*

time-adjusted rate of return (TA RoR) = *internal rate of return.*

time arbitrage = *arbitrage in time.*

time bargain = *account dealing.*

time basis a portion of the difference between the spot price of a commodity and the futures price of that commodity attributable to the cost of carry.

time box offsetting synthetic positions with options with different expirations and strikes.

time decay <1> nonlinear loss of the value of options over time when all other factors are constant. ***Also***: time value decay; time value erosion. <2> = *theta.*

time decay factor = *theta.*

time dependent barrier a barrier price that is changing as time goes by.

time discount option the contingent premium option with no premium paid until expiration.

time hedge a short option hedge in the hope that position will improve with time if the underlying security is not volatile. ***Also***: short option hedge.

time note = *promissory note.*

time-series volatility = *term volatility.*

time spread a spread created through the purchase or sale of options with identical strike but different expiration dates. ***Also***: calendar spread; inter-month spread; neutral calendar spread. **See**: *diagonal spread; horizontal spread.*

time spread using calls a time spread created by buying calls and selling calls with a shorter expiration date.

time spread using puts the time spread created by buying puts and selling puts with a shorter expiration date.

time-to-decay risk = *fractional exposure.*

time to early exercise the time from the present, or value date, until the time at which the option can be exercised, for *American option*, it is 0, for *Bermuda option*, time until the *early exercise date*, for European option, it is the *basic time.* ***Also***: tenor to early exercise.

time to expiration elapsed time from the current date to the expiration date of an option. **See**: *duration.*

time to maturity = *duration.*

time until maturity = *duration.*

time value <1> the excess of the price at which the company is merged over its price before the merger. <2> = *extrinsic value.* <3> = *time value of money.*

time value decay = *time decay.*

time value erosion = *time decay.*

time value of money the value money can produce in a given period, which equals *future value* in excess of *present value*. ***Also***: time value.

time value of option = *extrinsic value.*

time-varying variance = *conditional variance.*

time-weighted rate of return compound rate of growth of the initial portfolio value by using the geometric total and mean. ***Also***: geometric mean return.

time-weighted value of money the value of money taking into account the rate of return it will earn and the length of time for which it will be used.

time-zone arbitrage = *market timing 2.*

timing and exercise risk the risk that an option holder may set or unwind the hedges due to foreign holidays and the time-zone differences.

timing option seller's choice of which day in the delivery month to deliver. **See**: *quality option*; *wild card option.*

timing the market = *market timing 1.*

TIMS theoretical indicative margin system

Tinkertoy approach the approach which uses the combination of futures and options to gain more yield.

TIPS Treasury inflation-protected security

tips = *inside information.*

Titanic stock a stock the price of which is going to crash. ***Opp***: *Good-Ship-Lollipop stock.*

T-note Treasury note

to-arrive contract a contract providing for subsequent delivery on a future date of a specific grade of a commodity.

tobaccos the stock issued by companies in the business of processing tobacco for consumer smoking products.

Tobin's Q ratio = *Q ratio.*

toehold purchase a purchase of less than 5% of the shares of a target company. **See**: *Chinese water-torture tactic.*

toll revenue bond municipal bond that is repaid with revenues from tolls that are paid by users of the public project built with the bond revenue.

tombstone advertisement listing of the underwriters of a stock offering. ***Also***: tombstone advertisement.

tombstone advertisement = *tombstone.*

tom/next meaning from tomorrow to the next business day.

tomorrow-next swap = *rollover swap.*

tone = *market.*

tontine an annuity in which investors own shares and rights in a fund.

top-down approach the method of investing under which investors first look at the trends in the economy, the industry, then look at specific companies in that particular industry. ***Also***: top-down investing. **See**: *bottom-up approach.*

top-down equity management the investment style which begins with the assessment of the overall economic and makes a general asset allocation decision regarding various sectors of the financial markets and industries. **See**: *bottom-up equity management.*

top-down investing = *top-down approach.*

Topic teletex output of price information computer

Topix Tokyo Stock Price Index

TOPS <1> tender option put security. <2> triple-option preferred stock. <3> trust originated preferred security.

Toronto Stock Exchange (TSE) <Canada> a major exchange in Canada.

torpedo stock a declining stock which will most likely continue to decline.

total assets to equity ratio = *asset-equity ratio.*

total asset turnover = *asset turnover.*

total business return (TBR) the weighted total shareholder return of a private company.

total capital = *capitalization.*

total capitalization = *market capitalization.*

total dollar return the dollar return on a non-dollar investment, including the sum of dividend/interest income, capital gain or loss, and currency gains or losses.

total enterprise value (TEV) the value of an enterprise calculated as: *market capitalization + interest bearing debt + preferred stock* - excess cash.

total market fund a fund set up to track the broad stock market in a country.

total market volatility = *total volatility.*

total rate of return swap (TRORS) (T-RR swap) = *total return swap.*

total return <1> return on investment including income from dividends and interest, as well as appreciation in the price of the securities. ***Also***: absolute return. <2> for bonds held to maturity, the discount rate at which the initial investment in the bond will grow to the total value available at maturity with the interim cash flow invested at an assumed rate of return. ***Also***: horizon return; realized compound yield.

total return index the index that calculates the performance of a group of stock assuming that all dividends and distributions are reinvested.

total return option a put option on debt with credit risk.

total return swap (TR swap) the swap in which the non-floating rate side is based on the total return of an equity or fixed income instrument with a longer life. ***Also***: total rate of return swap.

total return volatility the combined volatility of spread return and asset value.

total risk the sum of *systematic risk* and *unsystematic risk.* ***Also***: absolute risk; total volatility.

total shareholder return (TSR) <1> the total return of a stock to an investor (capital gain plus dividends). <2> the internal rate of return of cash flows in the holding period of an investment.

total volatility <1> the squared returns of the market. ***Also***: absolute volatility; total market volatility. <2> = *total risk.*

to the buck the offer side of a quotation when the bid side is closed to the offer and the offer is a round point.

touch down option the binary option with a fixed payout at expiration if the underlying drops below the spot price.

touch option the barrier option which becomes in, out, or explodes at an early exercise trigger when the in-strike, out-strike, or early exercise price is touched once, twice, or more times, or when the underlying asset trades at or through the barrier. ***See***: *baseball option.*

touch up option the binary option with a fixed payout at expiration if the underlying touches a level above the spot.

toxic convertible the convertible bond that is convertible into as many shares of the common stock as the market price drops. ***Also***: death spiral; death spiral convertible; floorless convertible.

TP trigger price

TR trust receipt

tracker fund = *index fund.*

tracking error = *active risk.*

tracking stock the shares issued by a company the dividend of which is to be determined by its future earnings. ***Also***: alphabet stock; designer stock; lettered stock; letter stock; target stock.

tradeable asset <UK> an asset that can be sold easily on the market.

trade by appointment a stock which is difficult to trade because of illiquidity or low volume.

trade-clearing interest rate = *equilibrium rate of interest.*

trade date the day on which a security or a commodity futures trade actually takes place. **See**: *business day.*

traded option an option that can be sold to someone else of the same security, month and strike price.

trade flat for convertible securities, being traded without accrued interest. **See**: *flat.*

trade halt = *suspended trading.*

trade note = *commercial paper.*

trade option the off-exchange option that is offered to a manufacturer or user of a commodity.

trade paper = *commercial paper.*

trade-through rule the SEC rule under which all market participants can not trade at a price inferior to that displayed by another market.

trade-weighted dollar foreign currency price of US dollar or the export value of US dollar. ***Also***: trade-weighted index.

trade-weighted exchange rate = *effective exchange rate.*

trade-weighted index = *trade-weighted dollar.*

trading advisor = *commodity trading advisor.*

trading ahead of the client = *front running.*

trading at the edge buying at the current bid or selling at the current offer, so the positions can be reversed with little or no adversity.

trading below cash the company's total capital is less than its cash minus debts.

trading cost the cost of buying and selling securities or derivatives. **See**: *transaction cost.*

trading curb a temporary restriction in trading in a particular security, usually to reduce dramatic price movements, e. g. a tick test. **See**: *curb.*

trading day the day in which a market or an exchange is open for trading. ***Also***: dealing day.

trading desk a department at an international bank responsible for trading foreign exchange. ***Also***: dealing desk.

trading dividends buying and selling of stocks issued by other corporations in order to maximize dividends income.

trading down selling portfolio securities and buying of securities with higher risk or lower ratings. **See**: *trading up.*

trading floor = *floor.*

trading halt = *suspended trading.*

trading index = *ARMS index.*

trading limit = *position limit.*

trading loss <UK> the expenses in a trade exceed the gross receipts from the trade.

trading on the curb = *curb exchange.*

trading paper the CD purchased that is likely to be resold to another investor.

trading price the price at which a security is currently selling.

trading privilege the authorization to transact orders on an exchange.

trading range = *range.*

trading securities the securities not classified as *available-for-sale securities* or *held-to-maturity securities.*

trading session the period of trading from the time a market opens until it closes. ***Also***: session.

trading stock a very popular stock that fluctuates continually in price.

trading stopped = *suspended trading.*

trading symbol = *stock symbol.*

trading the market = *crowd.*

trading unit a number of securities that is generally accepted for ordinary trading purpose on the exchange, such as round lot, odd lot, etc. ***Also***: unit; unit of trading. ***See***: *unit of trade.*

trading up selling portfolio securities and buying those with lower risk or higher rating. ***See***: *trading down.*

trading variation an increment to which securities price is rounded up or down.

trading volatility the price fluctuations on which trades are actually transacted.

trading volume the dollar amount or the number of shares, bonds or futures contract traded during a given period. ***Also***: volume; volume of trade.

traditional preferred security *preferred security* such as adjustable rate preferred stock, American depository share and convertible security. ***See***: *newer issue*; *preferred security.*

traditional view the argument that the investors prefer higher dividends.

traditional swap a swap the notional amount of which is fixed. ***See***: *accreting swap*; *amortizing swap.*

trailer commission = *trailer fee.*

trailer fee the fee that a mutual fund manager pays to the salesperson who sold the fund. ***Also***: trailer commission.

trailing commission the fee paid to stock brokers in addition to any front-end fees.

trailing EPS the sum of the *earnings per share* for the previous four quarters.

trailing floors the put options the strike prices of which are adjusted upward when the price of cash position rises.

trailing P/E the P/E ratio based on the reported earnings from the latest year.

tranche <1> a financial structure, a segment of the entire value represented by a different security and time period. <2> <UK> two or more debt offerings by one foreign issuer. <3> <French> = *bond.* <4> <French> = *foreign bond.*

tranched credit risk credit risk that has multi-layer structure.

tranche delta the rate of change in the tranche value divided by the rate of change in the index value.

transaction as principal to principal = *direct transaction.*

transaction cost the cost of buying or selling a financial instrument, such as commission. ***See***: *trading cost.*

transaction exposure the risk that the currency exchange rates will change after some obligations are entered into.

transaction fee a charge by an intermediary, such as a bank, for assisting in the sale or purchase of a security.

transaction motive the desire to hold the cash to conduct cash-based transactions. ***See***: *speculative motive.*

transaction risk the exchange rate risk associated with the time delay between entering into a contract and settling it.

transaction tax a tax that applies to transactions in international equities.

trans-Atlantic arbitrage an arbitrage that seeks to profit from the shipment of crude oil across the Atlantic ocean.

transfer <1> the delivery of the stock certificate from the seller's broker to the buyer's broker. <2> <verb> to record the change of ownership on the books of the company by the transfer agent.

transferable contract = *transferable option.*

transferable instrument = *negotiable paper.*

transferable option an option that permits the position to be offset by a transaction on the opposite side in the same contract. ***Also***: assignable contract; transferable contract.

transferable shares the shares that can be transferred from one to another.

transfer agent the party who keeps a record of the name of each registered shareowner, the address, the number of shares owned, etc.

transfer of share conveyance of share to another.

transfer pricing rate (TRP) the cost to a particular department in a bank for intra-bank borrowing of funds. ***Also***: cost of carry.

transfer trades <1> the transfer of existing trades between the accounts in the books of a *futures commission merchant* where no change of ownership is involved. <2> = *exchange of spot.*

transition management service offered by brokerage firms and consultants to assist portfolio managers and fiduciaries in the process of transitioning from one set of portfolios to another set. ***Also***: portfolio transition management.

transitory income = *windfall profit.*

translation exposure the risk that a company's equity, assets, or earnings will change as a result of the exchange rate changes in the foreign exchange market. ***Also***: accounting exposure.

translation risk the exchange rate risk associated with companies that deal in foreign currencies or list foreign assets upon their balance sheets.

transparency the extent to which some important information and prices are visible to all investors.

transparent market the market in which current trade and quote information is readily available to the public.

transportation the stocks issued by firms that provide truck, railroad and other transportation and logistics services.

traunch the influx of cash that is part of a single round of investment.

Treasury adjustable-rate bond <Australia> the floating-rate note issued by the commonwealth of Australia.

Treasury auction = *auction.*

Treasury-backed zero the zero-coupon bond created by separating the interest and principal of a Treasury bond.

Treasury bill (TB) (T bill) <1> the US government short-term security sold to the public each week, maturing in 91 to 182 days. ***Also***: deliverable bill;

tender; US Treasury bill. <2> <UK> the short-term bond issued by the government. ***Also***: exchequer bill.

Treasury bill rate the short-term rate of interest of the US Treasury bill, less than one year.

Treasury bond the US government long-term security having a maturity longer than 5 years. ***Also***: long-term loan; US Treasury bond.

treasury bond a bond reacquired by its original issuer.

Treasury bond future the futures contract on Treasury bonds.

Treasury bond option an option to buy or sell a Treasury bond.

Treasury bonds investment series = *investment bond.*

Treasury coupon the Treasury security bearing a coupon.

Treasury index an index that is used to determine the interest rate changes for certain adjustable rate mortgages or other debt obligations.

Treasury inflation-indexed security = *Treasury inflation-protected security.*

Treasury inflation-protected security (TIPS) a special type of Treasury note or Treasury bond the principal of which increases annually with inflation. ***Also***: indexed security; real-return bond; Treasury inflation-indexed security.

Treasury Investment Growth Receipt (TIGR) = *Tiger*

Treasury Investors Growth Receipt = *Tiger.*

Treasury lock the customized derivative security used by investors to lock in the yield or price of a Treasury security.

Treasury note (T-note) US Government medium term security having a maturity of one year. ***Also***: US Treasury note.

Treasury note future a futures contract written on Treasury notes.

treasury offering issuance of additional shares which have been existing in a firm's treasury.

Treasury rate the interest rate on the US treasury security.

Treasury rate based swap a swap the interest rate of which is based on the US Treasury rate.

Treasury receipts (TRs) = *separately traded registered interest and principal securities.*

Treasury security Treasury bond or note.

treasury stock a previously issued stock that has been reacquired by the issuing corporation. ***Also***: reacquired stock.

Treasury stocks <UK> gilt-edged securities by the UK Government, e. g. 8.5% 1984 to 86, 5% 1986 to 89, 9%, 1994, etc.

Treasury STRIPS = *separately traded registered interest and principal securities.*

Treasury swingline the structure established for the transactions in two or more Treasury products which permits caps to be reallocated by the parties in the transaction.

tree model = *Cox-Ross-Rubenstein model.*

trend option an average rate option where pre-expiration price behavior is time-weighted according to a formula agreed upon by the parties prior to trade.

trend reversal = *reversal.*

Treynor Index named after Jack Treynor, a measure of a portfolio's excess return per unit of risk, calculated as the rate of return minus the risk-free rate of return, divided by the portfolio's beta.

Treynor ratio = *reward-to-volatility ratio.*

triangular arbitrage = *3-point arbitrage.*

triangular investing buying less shares as the price goes higher.

trigger <1> an event under which an investor will make a specific trade. <2> the event that causes an option to change.

trigger forward = *break forward.*

trigger option <1> an option that can be terminated early with the settlement at its maximum value if the underlying index is priced at or through the cap or outstrike price. ***Also***: early exercise price trigger. <2> = *knock-in option.*

trigger price (TP) minimum price below which imported steel can not be sold in the USA.

trilateral arbitrage = *3-point arbitrage.*

TRIN = *ARMS index.*

trinomial model a model the underlying asset price of which can move to three different levels before another trade is possible.

triple A the highest credit rating of bonds as rated by Standard & Poor's, Moody's and FIS. ***Also***: AAA.

triple bypass a lending facility with the option of pricing funds relative to the prime rate, banker's acceptance rate or the Eurodollar rate.

triple option = *strap.*

triple-option preferred stock (TOPS) a preferred stock that permits the holder to tender the stock back to the issuer and to receive common stock, bond, or cash. ***See***: *back-end right.*

triple tax exempt security the municipal bond, the interest from which is exempt from federal, state and local taxation. ***Also***: fully tax-exempt security.

triple witching day the third Friday of each month, when the options expire.

triple witching hour 3:00 to 4:00 p.m. on a *triple witching day.* ***Also***: witching hour. ***See***: *double witching hour.*

TRORS total rate of return swap

TR payer one who pays the total return under a total return swap.

TR receiver one who receives the total return under a total return swap.

TRR swap total rate of return swap

TR swap total return swap

true delta a delta of an option calculated taking into account *volatility variance.*

true gamma the gamma of an option calculated when *volatility variance* is taken into account.

true interest = *pure interest.*

true interest cost coupon rate required to provide an identical return assuming a coupon-bearing instrument of like maturity that pays interest in arrears.

true interest rate = *annual percentage rate.*

true range a measure of volatility which is the greatest of the following: (a) current high less the current low. (b) absolute value of the current high less previous close. (c) the absolute value of the current low less the previous close.

true rate of return = *internal rate of return.*

truncated risk the ability of an option investment to resist additional loss due to uncertainty.

trust (TR) <1> the arrangement under which one person holds the property for the benefit of a named party. <2> = *close combination.*

trust deed = *deed of trust.*

trustee of last resort = *public trustee.*

trust originated preferred security (TOPS) the preferred security issued by a trust that exits only for issuing securities and lending the proceeds to the parent company. ***Also***: cumulative trust preferred security. **See**: *quarterly income preferred security.*

trust-preferred security a security with characteristics of both equity and debt.

trust receipt (TR) a receipt given by the borrower to a bank requesting the bank to release documents of title to goods that have been pledged as collateral.

tuck-in acquisition the acquisition of a company with the purpose and intent of merging it into a division of the acquirer.

tunnel = *range forward.*

tunnel option a set of collars with constant strikes which cover the non-overlapping periods from the trade date.

turbo option <1> a combination of two calls on the same side of the market with different strikes. <2> = *power option.*

turbo swap = *LIBOR² swap.*

turbo warrant a stock option with low vega and sensitive to implied volatility.

turn the difference between the cost and selling price of a *parcel* of securities.

turnaround <1> a sharp, positive reversal in the performance of a company or the overall stock market. <2> <verb> to become profitable.

turning point = *inflection point.*

turn of the market = *jobber's turn.*

turnover the volume of business in a security or the entire market.

turnover rate the rate at which a mutual fund buys and sells funds, a higher rate means more expenses to the investors.

turnover ratio (TRO) the number or volume traded divided by the number or volume of shares listed in a stock exchange.

TV stock = *active stock.*

twin-in barrier option = *knock-in option.*

twin-out barrier option = *knock-out option.*

twin security the security traded in the market with the same risk characteristic as those of the investment under consideration.

twin stocks two stocks issued by the same company but are traded in two markets.

twisting <1> the use of misrepresentation to get someone to lapse a life insurance policy and buy another policy. <2> = *churning.* <3> = *switching.*

twist risk the risk as a consequence of a change in the shape of the yield curve.

two-asset correlation option an option linked to two underliers, and pays off like a *vanilla option* on one underlier if the expiration value of the other is in a range.

two-dimensional diversification the diversification strategy consisting of buying both call and put options.

twofer = *neutral spread.*

two-fund separation theorem a theory which holds that the investors will hold a combination of the risk-free asset and the market portfolio.

two-handed deal a stock underwriting in which 2 underwriters or broker-dealers are co-managing the forthcoming issue of shares.

two-layer CDO = *CDO squared.*

two-named paper the short-term paper with two people guaranteeing payment. ***Also***: double-named paper; two way out.

two-name exposure the credit exposure which the protection buyer bears to the seller, contingent on the reference credit.

two-tier market an exchange rate system which insulates a country from the balance of payments effects of capital flows while in the free market.

two-tier offer = *2-tier offer*.

two-way market ***See***: 2-way market.

two-way out = *two-named paper*.

two-way price = *two-way quotation*.

two-way quotation the quotation of rate of exchange or interest in both the buying and selling or both the bid and offered rates. ***Also***: double barreled quotation; two-way price.

two-way trade buying and selling stocks so that the funds are not left idle.

tycoon = *deep pocket*.

type 5 = *short sale*.

type 5 account = *short-sale account*.

Type B reorganization = *exchange-of-shares acquisition*.

Type C reorganization the acquisition in exchange for its shares of all assets of the target company. ***Also***: practical merger; Section 351 transactions.

U u

U <1> the month abbreviation for September in futures and call options. <2> the option strike price code for 7 1/2.

U/A underwriting account

UIT unit investment trust

UKI upper barrier knock-in

UKO upper barrier knock-out

UKO 2 upper barrier knock-out 2

ultimatum a final offer.

ultra badla/backwardation the process of carrying forward a sell position to the next settlement (forward date) by paying carry forward charges.

ultradot the software which stores, and sends baskets of stock through SEAQ to either NYSE or the Curb.

ultra-short-term bond fund the mutual fund that invests in bonds with short maturity periods, one year or less.

umbrella fund the highest level fund in a fund-of-funds structure.

unacceptable accounts the people for whom brokerage firms can not transact orders, e. g. minors or incompetents.

unamortized bond discount difference between the par value of a bond and the proceeds received by the issuing firm, which will be written off to interest expenses periodically.

unamortized bond premium difference between the par value of a bond and the price paid by the investor.

unapproved share option <UK> the option from an unapproved share option scheme.

unauthorized exchange rate = *black exchange rate.*

unavoidable risk = *systematic risk.*

unborrowed policy cash value = *inside buildup.*

unbundled stock unit (USU) a division of the return on common stock into three components: a 3-year bond with a yield equal to the stock's current dividend, a preferred issue that would pay dividends equal to the increase in the dividend, and a 3-year option on common stock.

unbundling <1> the separation of a multi-national company's transfers of funds into discrete flows for specific purposes. <2> combining of several securities into one portfolio. ***See***: *bundling.*

uncalled capital <UK> *unpaid capital* not required to be paid. ***See***: *called-up capital.*

uncapped risk a risk that is not limited.

uncertainty = *risk.*

uncertificated share the mutual fund share maintained on a transfer agent's books, no stock certificate is issued. ***Also***: book share. ***See***: *book entry security.*

unchanged (UNCH) of the price of a stock or average price that closed at the same figure as it did at the close of the previous trading session. ***Also***: same.

unclassified shares <UK> = *unissued stock.*

unconditional call money funds lent for an initial period of 2 days and may be called for repayment upon notice.

uncovered of a short option, sold without holding the underlying asset. ***Also***: naked.

uncovered arbitrage the arbitrage the foreign exchange risk of which is not covered. ***See***: *covered arbitrage.*

uncovered bond = *unsecured bond.*

uncovered call a call option the *writer* of which does not own the underlying asset. ***Also***: naked call. ***See***: *covered call.*

uncovered option the option sold by the *writer* who does not own the underlying asset. ***Also***: naked option. ***See***: *covered option*; *dressed option.*

uncovered option strategy a strategy of writing options without holding the underlying asset. ***Also***: naked option strategy; naked strategy. ***See***: *covered option strategy.*

uncovered put a put the *writer* of which does not own the underlying asset. ***Also***: naked put. ***See***: *covered put.*

uncovered put sale the selling of an uncovered put.

uncovered short sales the number of shares borrowed and sold short.

uncovered short straddle a straddle created by the simultaneous selling of equal number of puts and calls of the same underlying asset, same strike price and expiration month without owning the underlying asset.

uncovered writer a call option writer who does not own, or a put option writer who is not short the underlying asset.

uncovered writing the writing of uncovered options. ***Also***: naked writing.

undated forward = *spot deferred contract.*

undated stock = *annuity bond.*

underbanked of a new issue, when the leading bank finds it difficult to find the other banks to joint the underwriting syndicate.

underbooked of a new issue, when the brokers find it difficult to find buyers. ***Also***: sticky deal; under-subscribed.

undercutting an offering = *dumping.*

underlier = *underlying asset.*

underlyer = *underlying asset*

underlying <1> = *underlying asset.* <2> = *underlying stock.*

underlying asset a stock, future, index, currency, bond etc. on which an option or future is subject to delivery. ***Also***: asset; primitive security; underlier; underlyer; underlying; underlying security.

underlying bond a bond which takes priority over others in satisfying claims of the creditors.

underlying CDO = *outer CDO.*

underlying equity = *underlying stock.*

underlying future the futures contract received upon the exercise of an option. ***Also***: underlying futures contract.

underlying futures contract = *underlying future.*

underlying security = *underlying asset.*

underlying stock a stock that underlies an option, if the option is exercised, delivery would be made in the underlying stock. ***Also***: actual stock; underlying; underlying equity.

underperform to generate a return lower than other similar investments. ***Opp***: *outperform.*

underperformance option = *outperformance option.*

under pressure a situation when heavy offerings of securities cause depressed price.

underpriced the situation when implied volatility is lower than the historical volatility. ***Opp***: *overpriced.*

underpricing issuing securities at less than their fair market value as determined by the analyst.

under reference a deal which can not be finalized until it is confirmed.

undersubscribed = *underbooked.*

under the belt = *long position.*

under the rule the exchange's official selling or buying to complete a deal that is entered into by a delinquent member of the exchange who is charged with any difference in price that occurs.

undervalued currency a currency that is traded below what is perceived to be its market value. ***Opp***: *overvalued currency.*

undervalued stock a stock the current price is below its liquidation value. **See**: *fully valued stock; overvalued stock.*

underwater = *deep out of the money.*

underwater option an employee stock option the strike price of which is higher than the current market price, so no one will exercise it.

underwater roll the rollover of a position with a mark-to-market loss deferred.

underwriter one who, when an issue of securities is being made, agrees with the issuer to buy or find buyers for the securities not taken up by the public. ***Also***: investment adviser; investment banker; security underwriter.

underwriter's discount gross spread less management fee, and selling concession. ***Also***: dealer's discount.

underwriter's warrant the stock warrant granted to an underwriter.

underwriting the underwriter's buying the whole issue of securities and reselling them to the public. ***Also***: offer for sale; underwritten offering.

underwriting agreement the agreement between the issuer and the managing underwriter. ***Also***: purchase agreement. **See**: *agreement among underwriters.*

underwriting commission = *underwriting fee.*

underwriting discount = *underwriting fee.*

underwriting fee the fee payable to the members of the underwriting syndicate of a security issue. ***Also***: underwriting commission; underwriting discount.

underwriting group = *distributing syndicate.*

underwriting recapture the broker and underwriter trying to sell part of the underwriting to an institution that they manage.

underwriting risk uncertainty as to the ultimate loss under a new security underwriting contract.

underwriting spread = *gross spread.*

underwritten offering = *underwriting.*

undigested securities any securities that are issued beyond the need for or ability of the public to absorb them.

undistributed profit = *retained earnings.*

undiversifiable risk = *systematic risk.*

undue retention the excess of retained earnings over the present and future investment needs. ***Also***: excess cash accumulation.

unearned dividend a declared dividend that impairs the capital of a company.

unemployed capital = *idle money.*

unexpected loss the loss due to some unexpected event or extreme change in market volatility.

unfranked dividend <Australia> the dividend paid out of corporate earnings which have not been subject to tax.

unfriendly takeover = *hostile takeover.*

unfunded debt a debt maturing within a year. ***Also***: short-term debt. **See**: *funded debt.*

unfunded format = *swap format.*

unified bond a bond issued for consolidating several other bond issues.

Uniform Practice Code the NASD codes which prescribe the procedures for OTC trades.

uniform volatility the volatility assumed to be constant with different strike and maturity. ***Also***: constant volatility. **See**: *forward / forward volatility.*

unique risk = *unsystematic risk.*

unissued stock that part of authorized capital stock that is not issued or outstanding. ***Also***: unclassified shares. **See**: *outstanding shares.*

unit <1><UK> the share in a unit trust. ***Also***: redeemable trust certificate. <2> = *trading unit.*

unitary rate = *single exchange rate.*

United States security the security issued by a US corporation.

unitholder a person or company that owns shares in a unit investment trust or an investment club.

unit investment trust (UIT) the SEC-registered investment company which purchases a fixed, unmanaged portfolio of income-producing securities and then sells shares in the trust to investors. (A mutual fund is actively managed, while a UIT is not managed). ***Also***: authorized unit trust; fixed investment trust; participating trust.

unitized risk = *coefficient of variation.*

unit of account bond the bond that is denominated in artificial unit, e. g. EEC, designed to provide a consistent reference value against varying exchange rates.

unit of trade a single, indivisible unit in a transaction, a share, an options contract, etc. **See**: *trading unit.*

unit of trading = *trading unit.*

unit share investment trust (USIT) a unit investment trust that comprises one unit of PRIME and one unit of SCORE.

unit trust (UT) <UK> a fund that operates like an *open-end mutual fund.* ***Also***: unit trust fund.

unit trust fund <UK> = *unit trust.*

universal bond a bond issued both in the US and European markets.

universal hedge the theory by Fischer Black who argues that some currency hedging is appropriate and one universal hedging ratio applies to all traders.

universal volatility model a model that combines the elements of local volatility, jump-diffusion and stochastic volatility models.

universe of securities a group of stocks with a common feature.

unleveraged beta the beta of an unleveraged required return.

unlimited risk the risk in buying futures contract for having to put up money in the event of an adverse move. **See**: *limited risk.*

unlimited tax bond the municipal bond backed by a full faith and credit commitment to tax at whatever rate and or whatever duration is necessary to fulfill the obligation.

unlisted of the stock of a company, not traded on an exchange. ***Also***: over-the-counter.

unlisted CIV <Australia> the collective investment vehicle not listed on a stock exchange.

unlisted company a company the stock of which is not listed in a stock exchange. ***Also***: unquoted company; unquoted trading company.

unlisted market = *over-the-counter market.*

unlisted security a security not listed on the exchange. ***Also***: bid and asked; over-the-counter security.

unlisted stock a stock not listed on the exchange. ***Also***: unquoted stock.

unlisted trading the trading of securities not listed on the exchange but traded on that exchange as an accommodation to its members.

unlisted trading privileges the status of a company when its stock is admitted for trading on a stock exchange without the requirement of financial reporting.

unloading the sale of stocks to avoid a loss during a period of a falling market. ***Also***: capitulation; heavy selling; panic selling; selling off.

unmargined spread an option spread in which the short option is margined as a naked option rather than as part of a spread.

unmatched book the average maturity of a bank's liabilities is shorter than that of its assets. ***Also***: open book.

unmatched swap a swap agreement not linked to a specific asset or liability of either party.

unofficial market = *over-the-counter market.*

unpaid capital the amount of capital not paid by the shareholder, usually the total capital authorized exceeds the *contributed capital.*

unpaid dividend = *accumulated dividend.*

unquoted company <UK> = *unlisted company.*

unquoted stock <UK> = *unlisted stock.*

unquoted trading company <UK> = *unlisted company.*

unrated securities the fixed income securities that have not been rated for credit worthiness and repayment risk by the independent rating services such as S&P.

unrealized gain <1> appreciation in the market value of asset that has not yet been realized. ***See***: *appreciated financial position.* <2> = *paper gain.*

unrealized loss <1> a decrease in stockholder's equity resulting from decline in the market value of the equity shares held in the noncurrent investment portfolio. ***Also***: embedded loss. <2> = *paper loss.*

unregistered stock = *letter stock.*

unrestricted option = *nonstatutory option.*

unseasoned issue = *unseasoned security.*

unseasoned security <1> a security that is new to the market. ***Also***: unseasoned issue. <2> a security that has not been registered. ***See***: *seasoned security.*

unsecured bond a bond not secured on any of the borrower's property. ***Also***: debenture; funny money; naked bond; plain bond; simple bond; uncovered bond. ***See***: *secured bond.*

unsecured note a short term note with higher interest rates, and no security.

unstated interest = *imputed interest*

unsubordinated debt = *senior security.*

unsystematic risk the risk which can be avoided by diversification. ***Also***: alpha risk; avoidable risk; company-specific risk; diversifiable risk; firm-specific risk; idiosyncratic risk; specific risk; unique risk. ***See***: *systematic risk.*

unwinding reversing a position.

unwinding a trade = *offsetting transaction.*

up <1> with higher strike price. <2> the total price increase of the futures contract of a commodity in 10 days. ***See***: *down.*

up-and-away option <1> the collar under which the short option expires, and the long option pays off at maximum value when the underlying trades through the outstrike price. ***Also***: automatic cash-out option; exploding option. <2> = *up-and-out call.*

up-and-in option a *knock-in option* that becomes effective when the price of its underlying rises above a given level.

up-and-in price (IU) a *knock-in price* set above the barrier when the contract was initiated. ***See***: *down-and-in price.*

up-and-out call a call that expires if an outstrike is breached. ***Also***: automatic cash-out call; call option with rebate; cash-out call option with rebate; exploding call; over-and-away call; up-and-away option.

up-and-out option the *knock-out option* which becomes worthless if the market price of the underlying rises above a level. ***See***: *down-and-out option.*

up-and-out price (OU) the *knock-out price* set below the barrier price when the contract was initiated. ***See***: *down-and-out price.*

up-and-out put a put option which expires if the market price of the underlying rises above a specific level.

upfront fee = *front-end load.*

upfront payment a payment on a contract or a swap to cover a fee or a dealer's spread or the current value of the right to pay or receive the fixed rate called for in the swap.

upfront sales charge = *front-end load.*

upgrade positive change in ratings for a security, from a lower rating to a higher rating. ***See***: *downgrade.*

upper barrier the higher barrier price set in a double barrier option. ***Also***: higher barrier. ***See***: *lower barrier.*

upper barrier knock-in (UKI) a double barrier option, if the upper barrier is breached before the lower barrier is breached, the holder receives a call or put option.

upper barrier knock-out (UKO) a double barrier option, if the upper barrier is breached before the lower barrier, the option is terminated; if the lower is breached before the upper, the option has payoff.

upper barrier knock-out 2 (UKO 2) a double barrier option, if the upper barrier is breached before the lower barrier, the option is terminated; if the lower is breached before the upper, the option has payoff; if neither of the barrier is breached, the holder gets nothing.

upper break-even point the strike price of an option plus the total amount paid for the straddle. ***See***: *lower break-even point.*

upset price the minimum price at which a seller of property will accept a bid at an auction.

upside the gain in price or volume, or the potential for gain.

upside call = *out-of-the-money call.*

upside capture a fraction of the risky asset's terminal value that is captured by the overall portfolio insurance strategy. ***See***: *insured portfolio.*

upside contingency a situation under which the stock price is higher than a level so the holder of a *contingent* *convertible* can convert to the stock.

upside/downside ratio total number of shares traded which increased to those decreased in a given period.

upside potential the amount by which a derivative may rise in value.

upside potential ratio = *Sortino ratio.*

upside volatility market volatility that is measured when prices are going up.

upstairs trade a trade in a stock that is listed on an exchange, but the trade is not executed through the exchange system. ***Opp***: *downstairs trade.*

upstream merger = *practical merger.*

uptick rule the SEC rule that selling short is allowed only on an up tick.

uptick trade a trade that takes place at a higher price than the preceding trade involving the same security.

uptrend an upward price movement. ***See***: *downtrend.*

up volume the trading volume of a stock that closes in positive territory of a day.

upward sloping yield curve the curve that shows the yields for short bonds are lower than the yields on long-term bonds. ***Also***: ascending yield curve.

usable bond a bond issued as a unit with a detachable warrant.

usable preferred stock a preferred stock that may be valued at par and used as a substitute for cash in the exercise of a warrant.

USIT unit share investment trust

US Treasury the US Department of the Treasury. ***Also***: back door.

US Treasury bill = *Treasury bill.*

US Treasury bond = *Treasury bond.*

US Treasury note = *Treasury note.*

USU unbundled stock unit

UT unit trust.

utility the subjective value of an outcome.

utility revenue bond a municipal bond issued to finance the construction of public utility services.

utility value the value a given investor assigns to an investment with a particular expected return and risk.

utilization fee the fee charged on Euro-credits in lieu of a commitment fee.

UTP unlisted-trading privilege

V v

V <1> abbreviation for November in futures and call options. <2> the Nasdaq descriptor meaning when issued or when distributed. <3> the option strike price code for 12 1/2.

valuable document = *valuable security.*

valuable security a document generally accepted as a security for debt. ***Also***: valuable document; value paper.

valuation ratio = *price-to-book ratio.*

value added the enhancement a company gives its products before offering them to the customers.

value added monthly index (VAMI) an index that tracks the monthly performance of $1,000 investment, calculated as previous VAMI × (1 + current rate of return).

value additivity principle the principle which holds that the value of an investment portfolio should equal the sum of the values of individual assets in that portfolio.

value at risk (VAR) using the statistical analysis of historical market trends and volatilities data to estimate the likelihood that a portfolio's losses will exceed a level. ***Also***: probability of loss.

value averaging the strategy designed to reduce volatility in which securities are bought at regular intervals in amounts which increase when the market drops and decrease when the market rises.

value currency a reference currency that specified whether the returned values are expressed in units of the pay leg or the receive leg currency.

value date <1> the time frame considered to be the present time when valuing a stock, usually the current date. ***See***: *date of value.* <2> the date of actual payment in a spot exchange deal. <3> = *effective date.*

value fund a mutual fund that invests in companies which it determines to be underpriced by the fundamental measure. ***See***: *growth fund.*

value investing an investment that favors good stocks at great prices over great stocks at good prices, by using valuation measures as PE and yield.

Valueline index an index that contains 1,700 companies from NYSE, Amex, Nasdaq, and over-the-counter market.

value lock level the minimum payout on a ladder option. ***Also***: rung; threshold level.

value manager an investment manager who seeks to buy the undervalued stocks.

value of a basis point = *price value of a basis point.*

value on default (VOD) a risk of loss due to a sudden credit default.

value paper = *valuable security.*

value recovery right an option embedded in some *Brady bonds* which increase investor returns when oil prices rise.

value stock a stock that is considered to be a good stock at a great price, based on its fundamental analysis.

value stock fund a fund that invests in stocks of companies with great growth opportunities.

value today = *cash transaction.*

value trap a stock that has experienced a large price drop and is mistaken to be a value stock.

value weighting = *capitalization weighting.*

VAMA volume adjusted moving average

VAMI value added monthly index

vanilla arbitrage = *simple arbitrage.*

vanilla derivative a derivative that contains one elementary instrument only. ***Opp***: *exotic derivative.*

vanilla fixed-for-floating interest rate swap = *coupon swap.*

vanilla issue security issue that has no unusual features.

vanilla option a *standard option* with no special features. ***Also***: normal option; plain vanilla option. ***See***: *exotic option.*

vanilla swap = *plain swap.*

vanilla transaction the transaction in which the company either sells pieces of itself as shares or issues debt securities to borrow money for 30 years.

vanishing option the down-and-out call, up-and-out put, or any option with an expiration price.

Vanna the sensitivity of vega to change in the underlying asset's price. ***Also***: volga; vomma.

vapor paper asset backed debt securities issued with non existent collateral.

VAR value at risk

variability a change in return.

variable annuity an annuity the rents of which vary in amount according to the value of the investments made by the funds.

variable common right (VCR) a limited term average price call option issued to the current shareholders of an acquired company.

variable convertible preferred stock = *convertible adjustable preferred stock.*

variable exchange rate = *floating exchange rate.*

variable forward contract the contract to sell a security in the future with the number of shares to be delivered at maturity varying with the underlying share price.

variable hedge = *option hedge.*

variable interest rate = *floating rate.*

variable maturity option an option that matures sooner than its normal final expiration date if the underlying asset has moved significantly.

variable maturity swap the swap whose maturity is uncertain but whose range is predefined.

variable prepaid forward = *prepaid forward.*

variable price security a bond or stock sold at the market-determined price.

variable principal redemption security a security that is subject to redemption at a different percentage of the principal based upon the level of an index rate.

variable principal swap a swap contract the notional principal of which is not fixed. ***See***: *accreting swap; amortizing swap.*

variable rate = *floating rate.*

variable rate CD = *floating rate CD.*

variable-rate debt = *floating-rate debt.*

variable-rate demand bond (VRDB) the floating-rate bond that can be periodically redeemed by the issuing firm as scheduled on the date of issue.

variable-rate gilt <UK> gilt-edged security on which the interest rate payable varies in contrast to the rate on the Treasury bonds.

variable-rate note = *floating rate note.*

variable-rate renewable note the floating rate note with a coupon rate set monthly at a fixed spread over the one-month commercial paper rate.

variable ratio formula a *formula investing* plan whereby the ratio of stock in a portfolio is adjusted to maximize purchases at low prices and minimize the acquisition at high prices. ***See***: *constant-dollar plan*; *constant-ratio formula*.

variable ratio write selling of multiple option contracts per 100 shares of stock owned, with varying strike prices. ***See***: *ratio write*.

variable redemption bond a bond with fixed and variable components of principal redemption.

variable spread simultaneous purchase and sale of options on the same underlying where the number of contracts sold varies from the number of contracts purchased.

variable volatility = *forward / forward volatility*.

variable write = *ratio write*.

variance-covariance VAR = *linear VAR*.

variance gamma a process obtained by subjecting the Brownian motion to a random time change obeying a gamma process with parameter $\mu = 1$.

variance-minimizing hedge = *optimal hedge*.

variance reduction the technique for reducing the variance of some stochastic estimators.

variance swap a *volatility swap* where the payout is linear to the variance between the implied and the realized volatilities.

VAR measure an algorithm with which the value at risk of a portfolio's is calculated.

VAR metric interpretation of the output of the VAR measure.

VAR model a model which motivates a VAR measure.

Vasicek model a term structure model developed by Vasicek in 1977 for interest rate modeling.

vault receipt a document evidencing the ownership of the precious metals stored in a bank, a public warehouse or the treasury. ***Also***: warrant for metal. ***See***: *warehouse receipt*.

VBT volatility-based trading

VCT venture capital trust

vega the change in the price of an option that results from 1% change in volatility. ***Also***: foreign rho; kappa; lambda; tau. ***Opp***: *constant elasticity of volatility*.

vega hedging = *volatility hedging*.

vega neutral of a portfolio which has been hedged against the vega.

vega trade a trade that is based on the changes in volatility.

vendor = *seller*.

venture = *speculation*.

venture capital (VC) <1> funds available from the issue of the new stock. ***Also***: risk capital. <2> new money reinvested in the company by its stockholders. <3> the fund invested in the businesses which do not have access to the conventional sources of capital.

venture capital company = *venture capital fund*.

venture capital fund a fund which manages money for investors seeking private equity stakes in the small and medium-size firms with strong growth potential. ***Also***: venture capital company.

venture capital partnership a partnership between a start-up company and a venture capitalist that provides capital to the business.

venture capital trust (VCT) <UK> an investment trust with both equity and loan features introduced in 1993.

versus cash = *exchange of spot.*

vertical acquisition taking over a firm in the same industry.

vertical bear spread = *bear vertical spread.*

vertical bull spread = *bull vertical spread.*

vertical cap <1> upper cap on a corridor interest rate cap agreement. <2> the entire corridor structure.

vertical credit spread a vertical spread with the premium received higher than the premium paid, such as *bear call spread* and *bull put spread.*

vertical debit spread a vertical spread with the premium received lower than the premium paid, e. g. *bear put spread* and *bull call spread.*

vertical line charting the technical tool which charts the high, low and close of a given security each day, in an attempt to spot patterns that might help predict the future price movement.

vertical market a focused market capable of meeting the need of one industry.

vertical spread the simultaneous purchase and sale of options of the same class at different strikes but with the same date of maturity. ***Also***: money spread; perpendicular spread; price spread; strike spread. **See**: *diagonal spread; horizontal spread.*

vest charge = *hurdle rate.*

vested capital = *contributed capital.*

veto stock a stock that entitles the holder to cast a vote on some corporate business but not on electing the board.

viatical settlement = *death future.*

victim company = *acquired company.*

virtual currency option the option that is introduced by the PHLX in 1994 which is settled in US dollars rather than in the underlying currency. ***Also***: 3-Ds; dollar-denominated delivery.

virtual global stock market the global securities market linked by the Internet.

visible supply the new muni bond issue scheduled to come to market in 30 days.

VIX = *CBOE Volatility Index.*

VOD value on default

vol = *volatility unit.*

volatile stock a stock that rises or falls sharply in price in a short-term period.

volatility <1> a measure of the fluctuation in price, it is the relative rate at which the price moves up and down. ***Also***: absolute volatility; price volatility. **See**: *implied volatility; statistical volatility.* <2> = *option volatility.*

volatility arbitrage an arbitrage based on the volatility of options.

volatility-based trading (VBT) = *volatility trading.*

volatility clustering the tendency of a volatility measure to cluster at one or more common values over time. ***Also***: GARCH effect.

volatility coefficient the ratio of implied volatility for the next n days to historical volatility. ***Also***: relative volatility.

volatility cone a technique for calculating the implied volatility that uses a range of historical volatility data for each option's maturity form depending on the maturities of instruments currently available.

volatility effect a reference to the fact that a higher volatility reduces the sensitivity of delta to the differences in maturity.

volatility elasticity = *constant elasticity of volatility.*

volatility event an occurrence such as a news or earnings report that causes a temporary change in volatility.

volatility game trying to profit from the changes in the implied volatility of an option.

volatility hedging the hedging of the effect of a change in implied volatility on an option. ***Also***: vega hedging.

volatility matrix the table depicting the implied volatilities for a particular class of options on the particular underlying asset.

volatility option a proposed option with a payoff linked to the level of volatility.

volatility point 1% of the annualized standard deviation used in analyzing the volatility of some over-the-counter options.

volatility puzzle = *excess volatility puzzle.*

volatility quote trading the method of quoting option contracts whereby bids and asks are quoted according to the implied volatilities rather than prices.

volatility risk the risk that the holder of an option is exposed to, based on the potential for the volatility of the underlying security or the market's perception of that volatility to change in the future.

volatility skew <1> the condition in which implied volatility varies by strike. ***Also***: volatility strike skew. <2> = *volatility smile.*

volatility skewing <1> the tendency of volatility of an underlying stock or index to be inversely correlated with the stock price. ***Also***: skewing. <2> the tendency of interest rate volatility to be inversely correlated with the level of interest rate. **See**: *option skewing.*

volatility skewness = *volatility smile.*

volatility smile the relationship between the strike price and implied volatility of a group of options with the same expiration date. ***Also***: skew; volatility skew; volatility skewness.

volatility smile puzzle the phenomena that implied volatilities generated by the Black-Scholes model vary systematically across different strike prices.

volatility smirk the shape of the volatility smile for options on shares or an index.

volatility spillover the situation in which any change of volatility in one market causes the volatility to change in another market.

volatility spread the difference between the price an option can be sold for and the price at which a hedge can be purchased to offset the risk.

volatility strike skew = *volatility skew.*

volatility structure the volatility implied by a pricing model at a given price. It is divided into two parts: volatility smile and volatility term structure.

volatility surface the three-dimensional graph indicating the implied volatility by both strike price and expiration.

volatility swap a forward contract the underlying of which is the volatility of a given product. **See**: *variance swap.*

volatility swap cap the cap on the payment one or both parties to a volatility swap must make.

volatility term structure the curve which describes the relationship between the implied volatilities and time to maturity for a given strike price level. ***Also***: term structure of volatility.

volatility time skew where options with the same strike but with different number of days remaining until expiration have different volatility.

volatility trader one who buys options with low volatility and sells those with high volatility. ***Also***: V-trader.

volatility trading trading options based on the volatility level. ***Also***: volatility-based trading; V-trading. ***See***: *trading volatility.*

volatility unit the standard deviation of the annual percentage change continuously compounded over a given period. ***Also***: vol.

volatility value the value of an out-of-the money option over the intrinsic value of an in-the-money option. ***Also***: opportunity value.

volatility variance the variance of stock volatility.

volga = *vanna.*

volume = *trading volume.*

volume adjusted moving average (VAMA) the moving average which uses a number of volume units instead of the day numbers.

volume of trade = *trading volume.*

volume price trend indicator (VPT) the technical indicator which consists of a cumulative volume line that adds or subtracts a multiple of percentage change in share price trend and current volume, dependent on their upward or downward movements.

volume-weighted average price (VWAP) an indicator calculated by adding up the dollars traded for every transaction and then dividing by the total shares traded in the same day.

voluntary accumulation plan a plan that allows shareholders of a mutual fund to buy shares over a period of time on a regular basis.

vol-vol the volatility of a volatility.

vomma = *vanna.*

von Neumann-Morgenstern utility = *expected utility.*

voting certificate a nonvoting certificate issued by a voting trust to shareholders in exchange for their voting stock.

voting right <1> the right to vote when preferred dividends are in default for a given period. <2> the common stockholder's right of voting in the annual meeting of stockholders.

voting stock a stock the holder of which has the right to vote on corporate matters. ***Also***: membership stock. ***See***: *class A stock; non-voting stock.*

VPT volume price trend indicator

V-rating the grading of the collateralized mortgage obligations according to their volatility.

VRDB variable-rate demand bond

VTC voting trust certificate

V-trader = *volatility trader.*

V-trading = *volatility trading.*

vulnerable Black-Scholes option pricing model a variation of the Black-Scholes option pricing model incorporating default risk into the pricing equation.

vulnerable market = *vulnerable prices.*

vulnerable option a call or put option that is subject to writer default risk.

vulnerable prices securities prices that have been forced up by the erratic, low-volume buying in spite of unfavorable news, and may go down suddenly. ***Also***: vulnerable market.

vulture capitalist <1> *venture capitalist* who deprives an inventor of control over their own innovations and most of the money they should have made from the invention. <2> = *bottom fisher.*

vulture fund a fund that buys securities in distressed investments, such as high-yield bonds in default or equities that are in bankruptcy.

VWAP volume-weighted average price

VXN CBOE Nasdaq Volatility Index

W w

W <1> Nasdaq descriptor meaning it is a particular stock or a warrant. <2> the option strike price code for 17 1/2.

WAC weighted average coupon

WAI wealth added index

waiting period = *cooling period.*

waiver of dividend majority shareholder's disclaimer of his or her right to receive dividends, while other shareholders continue to receive dividends.

wallflower a bond or a stock that is no longer attractive to investors, because of low price/earnings ratio. ***Also***: big ugly; orphan stock; out-of-flavor stock. **See**: *in-favor stock.*

wall of worry bullish market trend in the face of expected negative uncertainties.

wallpaper = *worthless security.*

Wall $treet = *Wall Street.*

Wall Street <1> the street in New York around which is concentrated the US financial community. ***Also***: The Street; Wall $treet. <2> investment professionals. **See**: *Main Street.*

Wall Street analyst = *sell-side analyst.*

Wall Streeter a person with a profession in finance, investment and trading.

Wall Street leverage a profit increase will cause the stock of a public company to rise and thus increase its value. **See**: *capital leverage; operating leverage.*

Wall Street rule a rule that says selling a company's stock is better than trying to change its policies.

Walrasian market = *call market.*

Walter's formula the formula for determining a corporation's optimal dividend-payout ratio for maximizing stock prices. P = [D + r × (E - D) /p] ÷ p, where P is the market price, D the dividend, E the EPS , r the rate of return, p the capitalization rate. (Changing D can obtain the highest P).

wanted for cash = *deliver versus payment.*

war babies <slang> the securities of the corporations in the defense industry.

war bond a debt issued by a government that uses the proceeds to finance military operations during times of war.

warehouse receipt the document which guarantees the existence and availability of a given quantity and quality of a commodity in the public storage. **See**: *vault receipt.*

warehouse securities the securities that have been accumulated or will be accumulated by a fund or trust in order to issue depository receipts.

warehousing the accumulation of the shareholdings in the name of nominees with the intention of mounting a subsequent takeover bid.

warrant <1> <UK> the document of title to metal stored in a warehouse of London Metal Exchange. <2> <UK> the stock option or index option with expiration longer than one year. **See**: *LEAPS.* <3> = *stock warrant.*

warrant coverage the agreement between a company and its shareholders whereby the company issues warrants equal to a percentage of the amount of the shareholder's equity.

warrant dilution the dilution of earnings per shares by a stock warrant.

warrant-driven swap the swap with an attached warrant allowing a counterpart affected by a bond warrant exercised to increase the size of the swap.

warrant for metal = *vault receipt.*

warrant hedging buying a stock warrant and hedging it by a short position in the underlying stock.

wart a warrant that gives its holders the right to buy the Treasury securities issued by the US government.

wash purchase the purchase of asset either simultaneously or in less than 30 days after the sale of the asset.

wash sale purchase or sale of a security either simultaneously or in less than 30 days to profit from the price changes. ***Also***: 30-day wash sale. **See**: *manipulation.*

wash sale rule an IRS rule prohibiting a taxpayer from claiming a loss that is realized on the sale of an investment or asset if that investment or asset was purchased within 30 days before or after the sale date. ***Also***: 30-day wash rule; thirty-day wash sale rule.

wash trading entering into transactions to give the appearance that trading is still active, without resulting in any change in the trader's market position.

wash transaction selling the securities and buying the same securities back in 30 days or less.

watch list a list of securities being closely to spot irregularities that may be caused by rule violations.

watered stock a stock that is put out as if fully paid for but is not because some or all of the shares were sold (or given out) for less than full price.

water revenue bond a bond issued for the construction of new water treatment plants.

weak backwardation the backwardation when futures price is less than fair, but more than the spot price. **See**: *strong backwardation.*

weak basis a condition in which spot is significantly below forward indicating lower demand. ***Also***: wide basis.

weak dollar depreciated dollar with respect to other currencies. **See**: *strong dollar.*

weak-form efficiency a theory which holds that the price of a security reflects past price and trading history, implying that security prices follow a random walk. **See**: *semi-strong-form efficiency*; *strong-form efficiency.*

weak hands the intention of futures-contract holders not to receive delivery of the underlying.

weak market a market with few buyers and many sellers and declining prices.

weak sister the worst performing stock in a portfolio.

wealth added index (WAI) an index that measures wealth intuitively as returns exceeding shareholder's cost of capital.

weather derivative a derivative product the value of which depends on the risky weather variables.

weather risk the risk of loss because of weather related phenomena.

WEBS world equity benchmark series

wedding band swap <1> the swap variation with a relatively low floating-rate payment if an index rate stays within a preset range over a period of time. <2> a corridor swap that is outside the designated range at a settlement date.

wedding warrant = *harmless warrant.*

weekend effect the tendency of stocks to exhibit large returns on Friday compared to those on Mondays. ***Also***: day-of-week effect; Monday effect; Monday seasonal.

weekly auction = *auction.*

weekly swap a swap contract to be settled weekly.

weekly tender <UK> = *auction.*

weighted alpha an alpha recalculated by putting more weight on recent activity and less weight on earlier trade.

weighted average coupon (WAC) the coupon of each position in a mortgage pool weighted by the size of the position to compute an average coupon for the pool.

weighted-average market capitalization the stock market index weighted by the value of all shares outstanding for each stock.

weighted-average maturity weighted average of the remaining duration of the mortgage underlying the collateral pool. ***Also***: weighted-average remaining maturity.

weighted-average portfolio yield the weighted average of the yield of all the bonds in a portfolio.

weighted-average remaining maturity = *weighted-average maturity.*

weighted collar a collar with an imbalance between the quantities covered by the cap and the floor.

weighted hedge the hedge against a cash position with the futures contracts of different securities, e. g. by selling 90-day CD futures up to 1/3 of the amount of the cash position built on a 30-day CD.

well-diversified portfolio the portfolio including a variety of securities so that the weight of a security is small enough.

wet delivery the procedure allowing the long to post cash or Treasury bills in the amount of the futures contract and to receive immediate delivery upon payment to seller rather than receiving a receipt for subsequent presentation before receiving delivery.

We the People shares of the Merrill Lynch & Co.

when, as, and if issued = *when issued.*

when distributed (WD) the transactions that are conditional on the secondary distribution of shares issued and outstanding but closely held as those of a wholly owned subsidiary.

when-in-the-money option = *contingent premium option.*

when issued (WI) refers to a transaction made conditionally because a security, although authorized, has not yet been issued. ***Also***: when, as, and if issued; with ice.

when-issued contract the contract of buying and selling securities and commodities that is not yet issued, and will not be considered complete until such securities are delivered.

when issued option the option on the next Treasury bond or note to be issued with a specific maturity.

whip reversal of position due to technical happenings, such as misleading signals, causing losses on both transactions.

whipsaw a sudden move in price rapidly followed by an equally sudden reversal.

whipsawed a trader is whipsawed if he buys just before prices fall and sells just before prices rise. ***See***: *pay up.*

whisper estimate = *whisper number.*

whisper number the rumored earnings about to be reported by public company. ***Also***: forecast; whisper estimate.

whisper stock a stock rumored to be the target of a takeover, drawing speculators who hope to make a profit after the takeover is completed.

white chip a stock representing a valid speculation in a company in developing new products through heavy borrowing.

white knight a person or a company who saves a target company from an unfriendly takeover by in turn taking over the raider. ***See***: *black knight.*

whitemail the sale of a large amount of stock by a target company to a friendly party at below-market prices, so that the raider is forced to buy more of the high-priced shares to accomplish the takeover.

white squire a risky anti-takeover tactic calling for a *target company* to place a large block of its stock with a friendly investor to insulate itself from a hostile attack.

White's rating a rating of municipal securities using market factors instead of credit scores.

wholesale market = *inside market.*

wholesale price index the measure of price changes in the wholesale market.

WI when issued

wide basis = *weak basis.*

wide spread the *bid-ask spread* that is considered large.

wide strangle a strangle with a wide range between the strike price of the call option and the strike price of the put option.

widget the synthetic basket instrument issued by an investment bank or other financial institutions and listed on an exchange to permit investors to avoid dividend withholding taxes.

widow-and-orphan stock the stock that pays high dividends and is very safe, e. g. AT&T, IBM etc.

Wiener process the continuous-time Gaussian stochastic process, created by Wiener, with independent increments used in modeling Brownian motion and some random phenomena.

wild card option the right of the seller of a US Treasury bond future to give notice of intent to deliver at or before 8:00 a.m. after the closing of a trading day when the settlement prices have been fixed. ***See***: *quality option*; *timing option.*

wild card play having the right to deliver on a futures contract at the last closing price, even though the contract is no longer trading.

Williams %R the momentum indicator which measures the overbought and the oversold levels, if it is over 80%, the stock is oversold, and if it is below 20%, it is overbought.

Wilshire 5000 Equity index market-value weighted index which includes all NYSE, Amex and some active OTC stocks. ***Also***: Wilshire 5000 Stock index; Wilshire index.

Wilshire 5000 Stock index = *Wilshire 5000 Equity index.*

Wilshire index = *Wilshire 5000 Equity index.*

windfall = *windfall profit.*

windfall profit the income that requires no investment or effort. ***Also***: sundry income; transitory income; windfall.

winding-up risk the risk of not being able to close out a position quickly or at lower cost.

window <1> the discount window of a Federal Reserve Bank. <2> the amount of time the underlying price spent beyond the barrier. <3> = *window period.*

windows barrier warrant the stock option the barrier feature applies to a given window (period) only.

window contract a guaranteed investment contract purchased with deposits over the window period.

window dressing <1> the practice in which recent weak stocks are sold and strong stocks are bought, to give the appearance that a mutual fund has been holding good stocks. ***Also***: dressing up. <2> = *doctoring.*

window of opportunity = *opening in the market.*

window open the interest rates are at a particular level indicating it is attractive to borrow or lend, or enter into a swap or other transaction.

window option an exotic option where the predetermined parameters are valid only for an agreed period of time.

window Parisian option a Parisian option with a changing window for the price of the underlying.

window period the period after an option holder first becomes vested in the right to exercise the stock option under a stock option plan. ***Also***: window.

window warrant the warrant that can be exercised only during limited intervals in the life of a host bond.

wing the lower strike option or the higher strike option in a butterfly or condor. **See:** *body.*

wing out = *deep out-of-the-money.*

wingspread a spread, such as butterfly, with wings.

wing strike the strike price of the wing of a wingspread.

winner's curse the idea that the highest bidder in competitive bidding will be one of the people who overestimate the value.

winning bid the highest bid in a competitive offering. **See**: *cover bid.*

winter crack spread a spread created by buying and selling the heating oil futures contracts spread with the crude oil. **See**: *summer crack spread.*

wire house <1> a brokerage firm which has a branch office network. <2> the company that links all branches by a network for sharing financial information and other data.

witching day a day on which 2 or more classes of options and futures expire.

witching hour <1> = *double witching hour.* <2> = *triple witching hour.*

with dividend = *cum dividend.*

withdrawal plan = *automatic withdrawal.*

with ice = *when issued.*

with interest = *cum interest.*

with no interest = *ex interest.*

without dividend = *ex dividend.*

without interest = *ex interest.*

without rights = *ex rights.*

without stock (XS) of the bonds issued pursuant to some plan of reorganization, issued without the right to purchase a specified amount of stock. **See**: *with stock.*

without warrant = *ex warrants.*

with rights (WR) = *cum rights.*

with stock (WS) of bonds issued pursuant to some plan of reorganization, issued with the right of certain amount of stock. **See**: *without stock.*

with warrant (WW) = *cum warrant.*

wi wi Treasury bills traded before they are auctioned.

wood duck a party in a trade who is likely to unwittingly provide higher-than-anticipated profits for the operator.

working ratio a ratio calculated by taking the company's total annual expenses (after deducting depreciation and debt-related expenses), dividing the result by the annual gross income.

work-out period the period in which temporary yield discrepancies between fixed income securities are adjusted.

work-out quotation the estimate of a quotation on a security subject to the brokerage firm finding the stock to buy or sold. ***Also***: work-out quotc.

work-out quote = *work-out quotation.*

world equity benchmark series

(WEBS) the securities, like SPDRs, traded on Amex that track the *MSCI World Index.*

world fund = *global fund.*

worse-of option a bundle of forward contracts with the same expiration dates but different underliers, only one will be settled at the issuer's favor. **See**: *better-of option.*

worse-of-two-assets option = *worst-of-two option.*

worst-case credit loss potential credit loss represented by some point multiple standard deviation from the mean of the credit loss distribution.

worst-case exposure credit exposure based on an extreme market movement.

worst-of structure a structured note that pays a high rate if the price of the worst stock in the portfolio is above the barrier.

worst-of-two option an *alternative option* the payoff of which is equal to the minimum of two option payoffs. ***Also***: worse-of-two assets option. **See**: *best-of-two option.*

worthless collar = *cashless collar.*

worthless security a security treated as if it had been sold or exchanged, which has no capital value to holders. ***Also***: blue-skying stock; wallpaper. **See**: *junk bond.*

WQ = *CO.*

WR with rights

wrangle an option spread which is long (short) both a ratio call spread and a ratio put spread.

wrap around annuity an investment that allows the annuitant the choice of the underlying investments tax-deferred.

wrap around coverage the combined excess of loss and Difference-in-Conditions placement where the insured is seeking to develop capacity and breadth of cover.

wrinkle a new and unusual feature or security which makes an investment more attractive to a potential buyer.

writer one who sells options and receives premium. ***Also***: grantor; option grantor; option issuer; option seller; option writer; seller. **See**: *option holder.*

writer extendible option an option that extends automatically if some conditions are met, e. g. out-of-the-money.

writing = *option writing.*

writing calls to sell stock bulls writing a call exercisable at a price they think they will sell the stock, if the stock rises, and option exercised, they will sell the stock at the strike and earn the premium.

writing cash-secured put the option writer's writing of put options by depositing cash equal to the exercise price, rather than by using a margin account.

writing puts to acquire stock the bear's writing a put exercisable at a price they think they will buy the stock, if the stock falls, and option exercised, they will buy the stock at the strike and earn premium.

written call = *short call.*

written loan commitment a signed loan commitment which promises to lend certain amount of money to the borrower in the future at a fixed interest rate. ***Also***: loan commitment.

written notice of allocation the notice from a cooperative by which the recipient can receive certain amount of distributions.

written put = *short put.*

written straddle the simultaneous sale of a call and a put with the same strike price and maturity.

X x

X <1> exchange. <2> Nasdaq descriptor that means it is a mutual fund. <3> the option strike price code for 22 1/2. <4> = *XD*.

x ex interest (in bond listings)

x.a. ex all

XAC bond index allocated principal bond

x.b. ex bonus

X.C. ex coupon

x.c. ex capitalization

X-cap exchangeable capital security

X change exchange

X c/p ex coupon

X-CRIBS cross-currency cross-index basis swap

XD ex dividend (in stock listings of newspapers). ***Also***: X.

X-dis. ex distribution (in stock listings of newspapers).

X div. ex dividend

xenocurrency currency that trades outside of its own borders.

X int. ex interest

X new ex new

XO option exchange code for Philadelphia Stock Exchange. ***Also***: PHQ; XQ.

XQ = *XO*.

XR ex rights

x.r. ex rights (in stock listings of newspapers).

X-rated option an option with particularly obscene provisions, making it highly likely that the buyer will wake up the morning after with either clear evidence or a strong supposition that he has been raped.

XS without stock

x.s. ex. scrip

XW ex warrants (in bond and stock listings of newspapers).

Y y

Y Nasdaq descriptor meaning it is an ADR.

Yankee bond a bond issue made in the US by a foreign borrower payable in US dollars and registered with SEC. ***See***: *bulldog bond; foreign bond.*

Yankee CD the CD issued in the US market by a branch of a foreign bank.

Yankee market foreign market in the United States.

yard <slang> one billion currency units.

Yates adjusted Black-Scholes model = *Yates model.*

Yates model a refined version of *Black-Scholes formula* developed by Mr. Len Yates that takes into account dividends and early exercise. ***Also***: Yates adjusted Black-Scholes model.

year-end dividend a dividend declared by the board of directors at the end of a fiscal year.

year-end rally a rise in the stock prices in the last few trading days of a calendar year.

yearling <UK> the stock issued by local authorities for a period of a year or more and quoted either on the stock exchange or the discount market.

yellow color theory a theory that holds when color yellow is on the rise in clothing, product packaging, and home decoration, the stock market is on the rise, when yellow falls out of popularity, the stock market will fall. ***See***: *hemline theory.*

yellow knight a situation where a company making a takeover attempt ends up merging with the target company.

Yen bond the bond that is denominated in Japanese Yen.

Yen carry trade borrowing low-interest Yen and converting it to US dollars and investing the proceeds in the US bonds.

yield the income received from a security expressed as a percentage of the money invested or of the current price of the security. ***Also***: efficiency; yield-to-work-out. ***See***: *rate of return.*

yield advantage the extra amount of earnings an investor earns if he buys a convertible security instead of the common stock of the same company.

yield auction an *auction* technique that is used in the Treasury notes and bond market in which buyers are asked to specify the yield they are prepared to lend out. ***See***: *price auction.*

yield basis = *money market yield.*

yield burning illegal practice in which an underwriter places excessive mark-ups on bonds used to complete some types of municipal bond offerings. ***Also***: burning the yield.

yield curb the difference in current yield between the convertible and the underlying stock.

yield curve a curve which shows the relationship between the yields on different types of bonds.

yield curve arbitrage buying or selling of Treasury securities of one maturity while taking the opposite position on futures or options with longer or shorter maturities, in the hope that the yield curve will deepen or flatten.

yield curve arbitrage swap a swap in which the floating rate payments are calculated by reference to a formula and the yield curve.

ield curve basket option an option

with more than one underlying assets based on the spread between two rates at different maturities on a yield curve.

yield curve fitting the process of fitting the interest rate model to the yields on different bonds.

yield curve note = *bull floater.*

yield curve option the option based on the spread between two rates at different maturities on a yield curve.

yield curve option pricing model option pricing model which can incorporate different volatility assumptions along the yield curve. ***Also***: arbitrage-free model.

yield curve ratio the ratio of long term yield to short term yield. If it is greater than 1.15, bullish, if it is smaller than 1, bearish. ***Also***: ratio.

yield curve risk the risk that there will be a shift in the yield curve or a change in the slope of the yield curve.

yield curve security the security which allows investors to implement a given yield curve view.

yield curve strategy the strategy which positions a portfolio to capitalize on the expected changes in the shape of the Treasury yield curve.

yield curve swap <1> a swap with interest payments reflecting floating rates at two different points on the yield curve. ***Also***: arbitrage swap; CMT swap; constant maturity Treasury swap. ***See***: *frogs.* <2> a basis swap with one or two of the floating rate is a long term floating rate.

yield curve twist an interest rate shift characterized by a change in the spread between two interest rates at different maturity points along the yield curve.

yield decrease warrant an interest rate warrant that increases in value as long bond yields decline.

yield difference = *yield spread.*

yield differential the graph showing the term structure of interest rates by plotting the yield of all bonds of the same quality with maturities ranging from the shortest to the longest available. ***Also***: yield pickup.

yield differential warrant the contract in which the payoff is a function of the yield differential in two markets. ***Also***: yield spread option.

yield elbow a point on the yield curve at which the interest rate is the highest.

yield enhanced stock (YES) = *dividend enhanced convertible stock.*

yield enhancement the creation of a synthetic security with the same characteristics but with a higher yield.

yield enhancement swap a swap done to achieve yield enhancement by switching from longer duration to shorter duration.

yield equivalence = *equivalent taxable yield.*

yield gap <1> the difference between the average yield on stocks constituting the F.T. Industrial Ordinary and on 2.15 % consols. <2> the difference between the yield on equity and corresponding yield on long dated fixed income bonds.

yield maintenance <1> the adjustment upon delivery of the price of a GNMA or other mortgage security bought under a futures contract. <2> a standby commitment to provide the same yield to the buyer who was specified in the contract.

yield method the method of amortizing bond premium by the annual yield. ***Also***: scientific method.

yield on Dow Jones Averages the annual yield on the stocks included in the Dow Jones Averages.

yield on shares = *earnings yield.*

yield pickup = *yield differential.*

yield rate the continuously compounded rate that describes the cash flows of the underlying asset of an option during the option's life.

yield ratio the quotient of the yields of two bonds.

yield running the investment banker's act of buying the Treasury securities in the ordinary markets and selling them at the inflated prices and depressed yields to some sleepy state and local government agencies.

yield spread the difference between the yields on securities of the same quality but different maturities, or of the same maturity but different quality. ***Also***: spread; yield difference.

yield spread option = *yield differential warrant.*

yield spread strategy a bond investment strategy which positions a portfolio to capitalize on expected changes in the yield spreads between sectors of the bond market.

yield swap the bond swap which aims to improve the yield.

yield to adjusted minimum maturity <UK> the measure designed to give the yield to the shortest possible life of a bond. ***Also***: yield to crash; yield to worst.

yield to average life the yield derived when the average maturity of the bond is substituted for the final maturity date of the issue.

yield to call (YTC) a yield calculated on the assumption that the bond is called on the first permissible date, and is redeemed at the price laid down in the indenture for the first call.

yield to crash = *yield to adjusted minimum maturity.*

yield to maturity (YTM) the bond yield calculated when the bond is retained until maturity. ***Also***: overall yield; redemption yield.

yield to put the return a bond earns assuming that it is held until a certain date and put to the issuing company at a specific price.

yield to warrant call the effective yield of the usable or synthetic convertible bonds determined against the first date at which the warrants can be called.

yield to warrant expiration the effective yield of usable convertible bonds determined by the expiration date of the applicable warrants.

yield-to-workout = *yield.*

yield to worst <1> the lowest of the yield to maturity. ***Also***: promised yield. <2> = *yield to adjusted minimum maturity.*

yield trading = *basis trading.*

yield value of a price change the difference in a yield measure that is consistent with the specific price change in a bond or note.

you choose option = *as-you-like option.*

you choose warrant <UK> = *as-you-like option.*

your discretion an order authorizing the trader who is handling the inquiry to use this own judgment as to when and how he will consummate the trade.

yo-yo option a stock appreciation feature of a company's option plans, under which the option price is lowered $1 each time the company's stock price goes up $1.

yo-yo stock (YYS) the high-priced stock that fluctuates in price greatly. ***Also***: high flier.

yo-yo trade the purchase (or sale) which quickly reverses a sale (or purchase).

Y share = *institutional share.*

Z z

Z <1> month abbreviation for December in futures and calls. <2> Nasdaq descriptor meaning it is the 5th class of preferred stock, a stub, a limited partnership ownership certificate, foreign preferred stock when issued or the 2nd class of warrants.

zaitech <1> an investor who violates the securities anti-fraud laws. <2> Japanese company which was highly profitable in the late 1980s.

Z-bond = *zero-coupon bond.*

Z-certificate <UK> a certificate issued by the Bank of England to the discount houses in lieu of shares to facilitate their transactions in the short-dated gilt-edged securities.

zebra basis risk swap = *zero basis risk swap.*

zebra swap = *zero basis risk swap.*

ZEBRS zero basis risk swap

zeitgeist any industry emerging in the Internet age.

zerials = *money multiplier security.*

zero basis risk swap (ZEBRS) the swap agreement between a municipality and a financial intermediary. ***Also***: actual rate swap; perfect swap; zebra basis risk swap; zebra swap.

zero-beta portfolio a portfolio the beta risk of which is zero. ***Also***: risk-free asset; systematic risk-free asset.

zero-cost collar = *cashless collar.*

zero-cost hedge = *equity risk reversal.*

zero-cost option the position created by selling one option with the premium received equals the cost to buy another option. ***Also***: no-cost option; premium free option; premium neutral option; zero premium option. ***See***: *cashless collar.*

zero-cost structure = *zero premium structure.*

zero-coupon accrual note a range accumulation note with an initial price set below par.

zero-coupon bond <1> a bond sold at a discount and pays no periodic interest, the par value of which is paid in one sum at maturity. <2> a bond used in some CMOs the interest is never paid but rather is used to pay down the principal on the earlier bonds. ***Also***: accrual bond; accrual tranche; in-competition compound interest bond; non-interest bearing bond; original issue discount bond; split-coupon bond; strip bond; Z-bond; zero-interest bond. ***See***: *discount bond.*

zero-coupon convertible <1> the *zero-coupon bond* convertible into the common stock of the issuer after the stock reaches a certain price, using an embedded put option. <2> a *zero-coupon bond* which is convertible into an interest bearing bond at a certain time before maturity.

zero-coupon currency swap a long-term currency forward exchange agreement in the form of a swap agreement with a single cash exchange at maturity.

zero-coupon curve the curve of spot rates as a function of maturity. ***Also***: spot curve.

zero coupon-for-fixed swap a variant of a fixed-for-floating interest rate swap in which the floating rate payer does not pay the periodically observed reference rate but continues to receive fixed rate.

zero coupon-for-floating swap variant of the fixed-for-floating interest rate swap in which the fixed rate payer does not pay the periodically observed reference rate but pays all coupon interest at maturity of the swap.

zero-coupon inflation swap the swap under which one participant pays fixed inflation rate while the other pays the variable inflation rate at maturity, no periodic payments are exchanged.

zero-coupon note a note that is sold at a discount and pays no periodic interest, the par is paid in one sum at maturity.

zero-coupon rate = *spot rate.*

zero-coupon split bond a zero-coupon bond issued by a municipality that can be convertible into interest-bearing bonds under certain circumstances.

zero coupon swap an interest rate swap with the fixed-rate leg based on a zero-coupon bond. ***Also***: accrual swap. **See**: *dual coupon swap*; *reverse coupon swap.*

zero-coupon yield curve a graph of the term structure of the default-free zero-coupon rates.

zero curve a curve used to discount and project cash flows for a pay leg or receive leg of a swap.

zero downtick = *zero-minus tick.*

zero exercise price option (ZEPO) = *zero strike price option.*

zero-gain collar a *cashless collar* that consists of a short at-the-money call and long at-the-money put.

zero-interest bond = *zero-coupon bond.*

zero-investment portfolio a portfolio of zero net value established by buying and shorting component securities, usually in the context of an arbitrage.

zero-minus tick sale that takes place at the price of the previous sale, but that price must be lower than the last different price. ***Also***: zero downtick.

zero premium option = *zero-cost option.*

zero premium risk reversal the collar the premium taken from the sale of the call (cap) is designed to exactly match the cost of the put (floor) purchased. ***Also***: no cost risk reversal.

zero premium structure a combination of options bought and sold so that the net premium payable is zero. ***Also***: zero cost structure.

zero-rate preference share <UK> the share without dividend payments but will be redeemed on a payment higher than the issue price.

zero strike price option the exchange traded option with an exercise price of zero or close to zero. ***Also***: zero exercise price option.

zero sum a situation where the gain of one person is the loss of another person.

zeta the percentage change in an option price per 1% change in implied volatility. ***Also***: zetz.

zetz = *zeta.*

zigzag in a bull market, an Elliott three-wave pattern that subdivides into 5-3-5 pattern with the top of wave B noticeably lower than the start of wave A. (In a bear market, this pattern will be inverted).

zombie a bankrupt or insolvent company which continues to operate while it is waiting for a closure or a merger. ***Also***: zombie company.

zombie company = *zombie.*

ZR in bond listings of newspaper, meaning zero-coupon issue.

Z share the mutual fund shares of a class available to employees of the fund.